Contents at a Glance

MrExcel
LIBRARY

Pivot Table
Data Crunching
Microsoft® Excel® 2010

Bill Jelen

Michael Alexander

800 East 96th Street,
Indianapolis, Indiana 46240
USA

Pivot Table Data Crunching

Copyright © 2011 by Pearson Education, Inc.

ISBN-10: 0-7897-4313-2

ISBN-13: 978-0-7897-4313-8

Printed in the United States of America

First Printing: September 2010

Trademarks

Warning and Disclaimer

Bulk Sales

Que Publishing offers excellent discounts on this book when ordered in quantity for bulk purchases or special sales. For more information, please contact

U.S. Corporate and Government Sales
1-800-382-3419
corpsales@pearsontechgroup.com

For sales outside of the United States, please contact

International Sales
1-317-428-3341
international@pearsontechgroup.com

Executive Editor
Greg Wiegand

Acquistions Editor
Loretta Yates

Development Editor
Sondra Scott

Technical Editor
Bob Umlas

Managing Editor
Sandra Schroeder

Project Editor
Seth Kerney

Copy Editor
Jovana San Nicolas-Shirley

Indexer
Tim Wright

Production
Jake McFarland

Cover Designer
Anne Jones

Book Designer
Anne Jones

Contents

Dedication

To Josh Jelen
—Bill Jelen

To Josh Jelen, too. Hey, this is the third edition...why not?
—Mike Alexander

Acknowledgments

Mike Alexander is one of the two funniest guys doing live Excel seminars. I appreciate him as a coauthor on all three editions of this book, which has earned the #1 spot on the Amazon Computer Book bestseller list (for 54 minutes one day in January). Rob Collie from Microsoft had the unlikely happenstance of transferring to Cleveland. Our regular lunches drove most of my understanding for the PowerPivot chapter. Thanks to Pito Salas, who invented the pivot table concept back at Lotus in the 1980s. Thanks to Allan Foltang and all the pivot table team at Microsoft for continuing to improve pivot tables. Donald Farmer, Amir Netz, and the rest of the PowerPivot team should win a Nobel prize in science for bringing the PowerPivot add-in to 500 million people using Excel. At MrExcel. com, thanks to Schar Oswald, Tracy Syrstad, Wei Jiang, Scott Pearson, and an entire community of people passionate about Excel. Not to be forgotten: My sons Josh and Zeke are picking up a few hours after school each day keeping the podcasts edited and posted. Thanks to VoG and Richard Schollar for teaching me about the UNION function in Excel VBA. You saved the VBA chapter for me. Loretta Yates at Pearson Education is the best editor ever. Finally, thanks to my wife Mary Ellen for her support during the writing process.

—Bill Jelen

Thanks to Bill Jelen for deciding to coauthor this book with me many editions ago. His knowledge of Excel still blows me away to this day. My deepest thanks to Loretta Yates, for all the hours of work put into bringing this book to life. Thanks also to Bob Umlas for making sure Bill and I don't embarrass ourselves with technical errors. Bob suggested numerous improvements to the examples and text in this book. Finally, a special thank you goes to the wife and kids for putting up with all the time spent locked away on this project.

—Mike Alexander

About the Authors

Bill Jelen is Mr. Excel! He is the principal behind the leading Excel website, MrExcel.com. He developed his pivot table wizardry during his 12-year tenure as a financial analyst for a fast-growing public computer firm. He has written 30 books on Excel and produced more than 1,200 podcast episodes. His website hosts more than 20 million page views annually.

Mike Alexander is a Microsoft Certified Application Developer (MCAD) and author of several books on advanced business analysis with Microsoft Access and Excel. He has more than 15 years of experience consulting and developing Office solutions. Mike has been named a Microsoft MVP for his ongoing contributions to the Excel community. In his spare time, he runs a free tutorial site, www.datapigtechnologies.com, where he shares basic Access and Excel tips to the Office community.

We Want to Hear from You!

As the reader of this book, you are our most important critic and commentator. We value your opinion and want to know what we're doing right, what we could do better, what areas you'd like to see us publish in, and any other words of wisdom you're willing to pass our way.

As an associate publisher for Que Publishing, I welcome your comments. You can email or write me directly to let me know what you did or didn't like about this book—as well as what we can do to make our books better.

Please note that I cannot help you with technical problems related to the topic of this book. We do have a User Services group, however, where I will forward specific technical questions related to the book.

When you write, please be sure to include this book's title and author as well as your name, email address, and phone number. I will carefully review your comments and share them with the author and editors who worked on the book.

Email: feedback@quepublishing.com

Mail: Greg Wiegand
           Associate Publisher
           Que Publishing
           800 East 96th Street
           Indianapolis, IN 46240 USA

For more information about this book or another Que Publishing title, visit our website at www.quepublishing.com. Type the ISBN (excluding hyphens) or the title of a book in the Search field to find the page you're looking for.

Introduction

Pivot tables are the single most powerful command in all of Excel. They came along during the 1990s when Microsoft and Lotus were locked in a bitter battle for dominance of the spreadsheet market. The race to continually add enhanced features to their respective products during the mid-1990s led to many incredible features, but none as powerful as the pivot table.

With a pivot table, you can take 1 million rows of transactional data and transform it into a summary report in seconds. If you can drag a mouse, you can create a pivot table. In addition to quickly summarizing and calculating data, pivot tables allow you to change your analysis on the fly by simply moving fields from one area of a report to another.

No other tool in Excel gives you the flexibility and analytical power of pivot tables.

What You Will Learn from This Book

It is widely agreed that close to 50 percent of Excel users leave 80 percent of Excel untouched. That is, most users do not tap into the full potential of Excel's built-in utilities. Of these utilities, the most prolific by far is the pivot table. Despite the fact that pivot tables have been a cornerstone of Excel for more than 15 years, they remain one of the most underutilized tools in the entire Microsoft Office Suite. Having picked up this book, you are savvy enough to have heard of pivot tables or even have used them on occasion. You have a sense that pivot tables have a power that you are not using, and you want to learn how to leverage that power to increase your productivity quickly.

Within the first two chapters, you will be able to create basic pivot tables, increase your productivity, and produce reports in minutes instead of hours. Within the first seven chapters, you will be able to output complex pivot reports with drill-down capabilities accompanying charts. By the end of the book, you will be able to build a dynamic pivot table reporting system.

What Is New in Excel 2010's Pivot Tables

Excel 2010 introduces three new features designed to solve common problems with pivot tables. Combined with the two items added to Excel 2007, you have five great improvements to pivot tables.

- Beginning in Excel 2007, multiple items could be selected from the filter drop-down. However, this feature left behind a confusing report because the filters section left the ambiguous words "(Multiple Items)" to explain which items are included in the filter. As shown in Figure I.1, the new Excel 2010 Slicers feature provides a graphical view of which items are selected for the pivot table. Read more about Slicers in Chapter 4, "Grouping, Sorting, and Filtering Pivot Data."

Figure I.1
Slicers visually show which items are included in a filter.

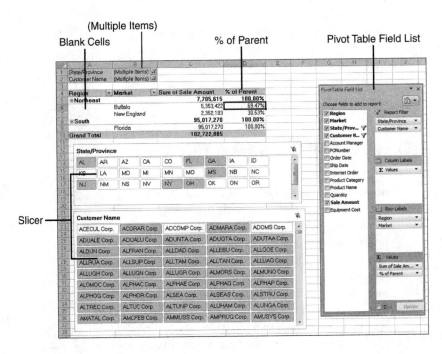

- In legacy versions of Excel, one of the many calculation options available in pivot tables has been "Percentage of Column." This feature was fine when you had only one field along the left side of the pivot table. However, if you had two or more fields, you might want to show the percentage of the next subtotal. In Excel 2010, Microsoft added new calculation options including % of Parent and Rank. Calculation options are discussed in Chapter 3, "Customizing a Pivot Table."

■ A constant annoyance is the blank cells included in the outermost column fields. For an example, see A6:A7 in Figure I.1. At last, Excel 2010 offers the Design, Report Layout, Repeat All Item Labels to fill in those blank cells.

■ PowerPivot is a free add-in from Microsoft that allows you to create pivot tables from external data or from separate sheets.

■ If you skipped Excel 2007, you notice that the Pivot Table Field List has been expanded. Rather than dragging fields to drop zones on the pivot table itself, beginning with Excel 2007, you drag the fields to the drop zones in the pivot table field list. Excel 2007 also added filtering options.

Skills Required to Use This Book

We have created a reference that is comprehensive enough for hard-core analysts yet relevant to casual users of Excel. The bulk of the book covers how to use pivot tables in the Excel user interface. The final chapter describes how to create pivot tables in Excel's powerful VBA macro language. This means that any user who has a firm grasp of basics, such as preparing data, copying, pasting, and entering simple formulas, should not have a problem understanding the concepts in this book.

CASE STUDY   LIFE BEFORE PIVOT TABLES

Imagine that it is 1992 and you are using Lotus 1-2-3 or Excel 4. You have thousands of rows of transactional data. Your manager asks you to prepare a summary report showing revenue by region and product. The following case study walks you through how this report would have been prepared in 1992.

In 1992, preparing this report was a daunting task. It required superhuman spreadsheet skills that few could master. Here are the steps you needed to take to prepare a summary report showing revenue by region and product:

1. You need to get a list of the unique regions in the data set. Use the Advanced Filter command with Unique Records Only to extract a list of the unique regions (see Figure I.2).

Figure I.2
Even today, the Advanced Filter command is not a lot of fun to use.

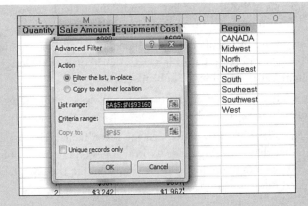

2. You also need to get a list of the unique products in the data set. Use the Advanced Filter command with Unique Records Only a second time to extract a list of the unique products.

3. Turn the list of regions sideways so that it runs across the columns. Copy the list of unique regions. Then select Edit, Paste Special, Transpose to arrange the regions as headings going across the report. You now have a skeleton of the report, as shown in Figure I.3.

Figure I.3
After using a second Advanced Filter command and selecting Edit, Paste Special, Transpose, you have this skeleton of the final report. You still have a long way to go.

	R	S	T	U	V	W	X	Y	Z
4									
5		CANADA	Midwest	North	Northeast	South	Southeast	Southwest	West
6	Pizza Humidified Merchandiser								
7	Cotton Candy Maker Stainless Steel Whirlwind								
8	Gas Griddle 3 Burners								
9	Open Top Fryer 15 Lb								
10	4 Qt. Cap. Batch Bow								

4. Next, you need to build a DSUM formula to get total Sales for one product and region. DSUM requires that you build a criteria range as shown in R1:S2 in Figure I.4.

5. In the corner cell of the report, build the formula to get total sales for the selected product and region: **=DSUM($A$5:$N$93160,$M$5,$R$1:$S$2)**. This is a formula to test whether the region column is Canada and if the product is a Pizza Merchandiser.

Figure I.4
Use the ancient DSUM function with a four-cell criteria range.

Extract	▾		*fx*	=DSUM($A$5:$N$93160,$M$5,$R$1:$S$2)		

	R	S	T	U
1	Product Name	Region		
2	Pizza Humidified Merchandiser	CANADA		
3				
4				
5	57673	CANADA	Midwest	North
6	Pizza Humidified Merchandiser			
7	Cotton Candy Maker Stainless Steel Whirlwind			
8	Gas Griddle 3 Burners			
9	Open Top Fryer 15 Lb			
10	4 Qt. Cap. Batch Bow			
11	Built-In Warming Display 1270W			

6. You are a long-time, hard-core data analyst if you remember pressing the keystrokes for /Data Table 2 in Lotus 1-2-3. Figure I.5 shows the equivalent function in Excel. In Excel 2010, this command is found in Data, Data Tools, What If Analysis, Data Table.

Figure I.5

The Data Table command replicates the formula in the top-left corner of the table, but replaces two references in the formula with the headings at the top and left of the report.

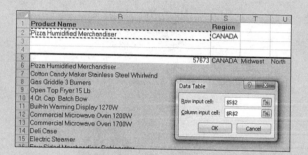

7. Finally, after using two advanced filters and a Paste Tranpose command, writing an obscure DSUM formula, and then using the Data Table command, you have the result your manager is looking for, as shown in Figure I.6. If you could pull off this analysis in 10 minutes, you were doing an amazing job.

Figure I.6

After displaying knowledge of obscure spreadsheet commands in 10 minutes, you have produced the needed report.

	57673	CANADA	Midwest	North	Northeast
6 Pizza Humidified Merchandiser	57673		44345	73108	43267
7 Cotton Candy Maker Stainless Steel Whirlwind	23525.2	41364.8		62212	41735.6
8 Gas Griddle 3 Burners	56192.4	40299.6	97343.4		74450.2
9 Open Top Fryer 15 Lb	43214.1	31667.7	60830.85		42959.4
10 4 Qt. Cap. Batch Bow	6704	39075.7	33057.1		26816
11 Built-In Warming Display 1270W	4956	43736.7	43365		39235
12 Commercial Microwave Oven 1200W	18947.8	34983.8	67435.6		47601.6

Now, if your manager looks at the report and asks you to add Market to the analysis, you are nearly back at square one because it will take an additional 10 minutes to produce the new report.

Invention of the Pivot Table

The concept that led to today's pivot table came from the halls of the Lotus Development Corporation with a revolutionary spreadsheet program called Lotus Improv. Improv was envisioned in 1986 by Pito Salas of the Advanced Technology Group at Lotus (see Figure I.7). Realizing that spreadsheets often have patterns of data, Salas concluded that if a user could build a tool that could recognize these patterns, then he could build enhanced data models. Lotus ran with the concept and started developing the next-generation spreadsheet.

Figure I.7
Salas, inventor of the
pivot table concept,
is always working on
cutting-edge products at
www.salas.com.

Throughout 1987, Lotus demonstrated its new program to a few companies. In 1988, Steve Jobs saw the program and immediately wanted it developed for his upcoming NeXT computer platform. The program, finally named Lotus Improv, was eventually shipped in 1991 for the NeXT platform. A version for Windows was introduced in 1993.

The core concept behind Improv was that data, data views, and formulas should be encapsulated as separate entities and treated as different animals. For the first time in a spreadsheet program, a data set was given a name that could be grouped into larger categories. This naming and grouping capability paved the way for the most powerful feature in Improv: rearranging data. With Improv, a user could define and store a set of categories and then change the view by simply dragging the category names with the mouse. The user could also create totals and group summaries.

Microsoft eventually incorporated this concept in its pivot table functionality in Excel 5. Years later, with the release of Excel 97, Microsoft offered users an enhanced pivot table wizard and key improvements to pivot table functionality such as the capability to add calculated fields. Excel 97 also opened the pivot cache to developers, fundamentally changing the way pivot tables are created and managed. Microsoft introduced the pivot chart with Excel 2000, providing users a way to represent pivot tables graphically. Excel 2002 added the GetPivotData function. Excel 2007 added new filters such as selecting dates in the "last quarter" or "this year." Excel 2010 continues improving pivot tables with new features described previously.

CASE STUDY LIFE AFTER PIVOT TABLES

Say you have 100,000 rows of transactional data, as discussed in the previous case study. Your manager asks you to pre-pare a summary report showing revenue by Region and Product. Fortunately, you have pivot tables at your disposal. Here are the steps you would follow today using Excel 2010:

1. Select a single cell in your data set. Select PivotTable from the Insert tab. Click OK. You are given a blank pivot table, as shown in Figure I.8.

Figure I.8
After three mouse clicks, you have a blank pivot table report. Three more mouse clicks to go.

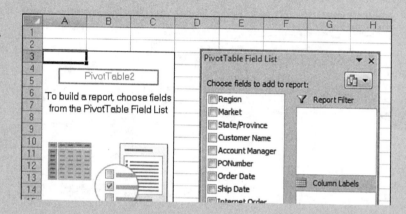

2. From the Pivot Table Field List, select the Product Name check box. Excel adds a unique list of products to the left side of the pivot table. Select the Sale Amount check box. Excel adds total sales by product to the report. Click the Region field in the Field List and drag it to the Column Labels drop zone. After six mouse clicks, you have the required report, as shown in Figure I.9.

Figure I.9
Add three fields to the report.

If you are racing, you can actually create the report shown in Figure I.9 in exactly 10 seconds. This is an amazing accomplishment. Realistically, it would take you about 50 seconds at normal speed to create the report. If you are a spreadsheet wizard following the steps in the previous case study, the nonpivot table solution would take you at least 12 times longer.

To see the creation of a pivot table, search for Pivot Table Data Crunching Intro at YouTube.

In addition, when your manager comes back with the request to add Market to the analysis, you need just seconds to drag the Market field to the Column Labels drop zone in the PivotTable Field List to add it to the report, as shown in Figure I.10.

Figure I.10
To create a new report with the Market field, simply drag the field to a drop zone.

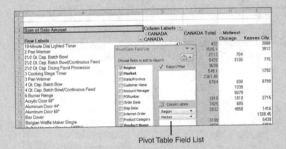

Pivot Table Field List

Sample Files Used in This Book

All data files used throughout this book are available for download from www.mrexcel.com/pivotbookdata2010.html.

Conventions Used in This Book

This book follows certain conventions:

■ Monospace—Text messages you see onscreen or code that appears in a monospace font.

■ **Bold Monospace**—Text you type appears in a **bold, monospace** font.

■ *Italic*—New and important terms appear in *italics*.

■ Initial Caps—Tab names, dialog box names, and dialog box elements are presented with initial capital letters so you can identify them easily.

Referring to Versions

From 1997 through 2003, Microsoft released similar versions of Excel known as Excel 97, Excel 2000, Excel 2002/XP, and Excel 2003. This book will refer to those versions as "legacy versions" of Excel.

Referring to Ribbon Commands

Office 2007 introduced a new interface called the Ribbon. The Ribbon is composed of several tabs labeled Home, Insert, Page Layout, and so on. When you click on the Page Layout tab, you see the icons available on the Page Layout tab.

When the active cell is inside a pivot table, two new tabs appear on the Ribbon. In the help files, Microsoft calls these tabs "PivotTable Tools, Options" and "PivotTable Tools, Design." For convenience, this book refers to these elements as the Options tab and the Design tab, respectively. The new Slicer feature introduces a new Ribbon tab that Microsoft calls "Slicer Tools, Options." This book refers to this as the Slicer tab.

In some cases, the Ribbon icon leads to a drop-down with additional choices. In these cases, the book lists the hierarchy of Ribbon, Icon, Menu Choice, and Submenu Choice. For example, in Figure I.11, the shorthand specifies "Select Design, Report Layout, Repeat All Item Labels.".

Figure I.11
For shorthand, instructions might say Select Design, Report Layout, Repear All Item Labels.

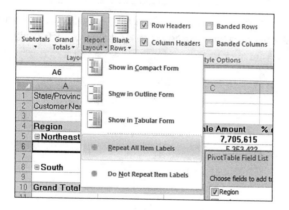

Special Elements

This book contains the following special elements:

 Some topics will be demonstrated in a short video cast at YouTube.

CASE STUDY

Case studies provide a real-world look at topics previously introduced in the chapter.

NOTE
Notes provide additional information outside the main thread of the chapter discussion that might be useful for you to know.

TIP
Tips provide you with quick workarounds and time-saving techniques to help you do your work more efficiently.

CAUTION
Cautions warn you about potential pitfalls you might encounter. Pay attention to Cautions because they alert you to problems that otherwise could cause you hours of frustration.

Pivot Table Fundamentals

What Is a Pivot Table?

Imagine that Excel is a large toolbox that contains different tools at your disposal. The pivot table is essentially one tool in your Excel toolbox. If a pivot table were indeed a physical tool that you could hold in your hand, a kaleidoscope would most accurately represent it.

When you look through a kaleidoscope at an object, you see that object in a different way. You can turn the kaleidoscope to move around the details of the object. The object itself does not change, and it is not connected to the kaleidoscope. The kaleidoscope is simply a tool that you use to create a unique perspective on an ordinary object.

Think of a pivot table as a kaleidoscope that is pointed at your data set. When you look at your data set through a pivot table, you have the opportunity to see details in the data you might not have noticed before. Furthermore, you can turn your pivot table to see your data from different perspectives. The data set itself does not change, and it is not connected to the pivot table. The pivot table is simply a tool you are using to create a unique perspective on your data.

A pivot table allows you to create an interactive view of your data set. We call this view a *pivot table report*. With a pivot table report, you can quickly and easily categorize your data into groups, summarize large amounts of data into meaningful information, and perform a wide variety of calculations in a fraction of the time it takes by hand. But the real power of a pivot table report is that you can interactively drag and drop fields within your report, dynamically changing your perspective and recalculating totals to fit your current view.

Why Should You Use a Pivot Table?

As a rule, your dealings in Excel can be split into two categories: calculating data and shaping or formatting, data. Although many built-in tools and formulas facilitate both of these tasks, the pivot table is often the fastest and most efficient way to calculate and shape data.

Let's look at one simple scenario that illustrates this point. Say you have just given your manager some revenue information by month, and he has predictably asked for more information. He adds a note to the worksheet and emails it back to you. As you can see in Figure 1.1, your manager wants you to add a line that shows credits by month.

Figure 1.1

Your manager predictably changes his request after you provide the first pass of a report.

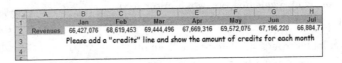

	A	B	C	D	E	F	G	H
1		Jan	Feb	Mar	Apr	May	Jun	Jul
2	Revenues	66,427,076	68,619,453	69,444,496	67,669,316	69,572,075	67,196,220	66,884,7
3		Please add a "credits" line and show the amount of credits for each month
4								

To meet this new requirement, you run a query from your legacy system that provides the needed data. As usual, the data is formatted specifically to make you suffer. Instead of data by month, the legacy system provides detailed transactional data by day, as shown in Figure 1.2.

Figure 1.2

The data from the legacy system is by day instead of by month.

	A	B	C
1	Document Number	In Balance Date	Credit Amount
2	D29210	01/03/03	(34.54)
3	D15775	01/03/03	(313.64)
4	D46035	01/03/03	(389.04)
5	D45826	01/03/03	(111.56)
6	D69172	01/03/03	(1,630.25)
7	D25388	01/03/03	(3,146.22)
8	D49302	01/03/03	(1,217.37)
9	D91669	01/03/03	(197.44)
10	D14289	01/03/03	(33.75)
11	D38471	01/03/03	(6,759.20)
12	D18645	01/03/03	(214.54)

Your challenge is to calculate the total dollar amount of credits by month and shape the results into an extract that fits the format of the original report. The final extract should look like the data shown in Figure 1.3.

Figure 1.3

Your goal is to produce a summary by month and transpose the data to a horizontal format.

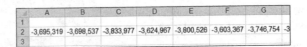

	A	B	C	D	E	F	G
1							
2	-3,695,319	-3,698,537	-3,833,977	-3,624,967	-3,800,526	-3,603,367	-3,746,754	-3
3							

Creating this extract manually takes 18 mouse clicks and three keystrokes:

- Format dates to month: three clicks
- Create subtotals: four clicks
- Extract subtotals: six clicks, three keystrokes
- Transpose vertical to horizontal: five clicks

By contrast, creating this extract with a pivot table takes nine mouse clicks:

- Create the pivot table report: five clicks
- Group dates into months: three clicks
- Transpose vertical to horizontal: one click

Both methods produce the same extract, which can be pasted into your final report, as shown in Figure 1.4.

Figure 1.4
After adding credits to the report, you can calculate net revenue.

	A	B	C	D	E	F	G	H
1		Jan	Feb	Mar	Apr	May	Jun	Jul
2	Revenues	66,427,076	68,619,453	69,444,496	67,669,316	69,572,075	67,196,220	66,884,771
3	Credits	-3,695,319	-3,698,537	-3,833,977	-3,624,967	-3,800,526	-3,603,367	-3,746,754
4	Adjusted Revenues	62,731,757	64,920,916	65,610,519	64,044,349	65,771,549	63,592,853	63,138,017

However, using a pivot table to accomplish this task not only cuts down the number of actions by more than half, but also reduces the possibility of human error. Above that, using a pivot table enables for quick and easy shaping and formatting of the data.

What this example shows is that using a pivot table is not just about calculating and summarizing your data. Instead, pivot tables can often help you do a number of tasks faster and better than using conventional functions and formulas. For example, you can use pivot tables to instantly transpose large groups of data vertically or horizontally. You can use pivot tables to quickly find and count the unique values in your data. You can also use pivot tables to prepare your data to be used in charts.

The bottom line is that pivot tables can help you dramatically increase your efficiency and decrease errors on a number of tasks you may have to accomplish with Excel. Even though pivot tables cannot do everything for you, understanding how to use just the basics of pivot table functionality can take your data analysis and productivity to a new level.

When Should You Use a Pivot Table?

Large data sets, ever-changing impromptu data requests, and multilayered reporting are absolute productivity killers if you have to tackle them by hand. Doing hand-to-hand combat with one of these tasks is not only time consuming, but it also opens the possibility of an untold number of errors in your analysis. So how do you recognize when to use a pivot table before it is too late?

Generally, a pivot table serves you well in any of the following situations:

- You need to find relationships and groupings within your data.
- You need to find a list of unique values for one field in your data.
- You need to find data trends using various time periods.
- You anticipate frequent requests for changes to your data analysis.
- You need to create subtotals that frequently include new additions.
- You need to organize your data into a format that is easy to chart.

Anatomy of a Pivot Table

Because the anatomy of a pivot table is what provides its flexibility and, ultimately, its functionality, truly understanding pivot tables is difficult without understanding their basic structure.

A pivot table is composed of the following four areas:

- Values area
- Row area
- Column area
- Filter area

The data you place in these areas defines both the utility and appearance of the pivot table. Keeping in mind that you will go through the process of creating a pivot table in the next chapter, let's prepare by taking a closer look at the four areas and the functionality around them in the following sections.

Values Area

The *values area* is shown in Figure 1.5. It is a large rectangular area below and to the right of the headings. In this figure, you can see that the values area contains a sum of the revenue field.

Figure 1.5
The heart of the pivot table is the values area. This area typically includes a total of one or more numeric fields.

	A	B	C	D	E	F
1	REGION	(All)				
2						
3	Sum of REVENUE	MONTH				
4	MODEL	January	February	March	April	May
5	2500P	$33,073	$29,104	$25,612	$22,538	$19,834
6	3002C	$36,880	$31,574	$27,785	$24,451	$21,517
7	3002P	$90,258	$79,427	$69,896	$61,508	$54,127
8	4055T	$13,250	$11,660	$10,261	$9,030	$7,946
9	4500C	$100,197	$98,173	$77,593	$68,281	$60,088
10						

The values area is the area that calculates. The values area is required to have at least one field and one calculation of that field within this area. The data fields that you drop into the values area are those that you want to measure or calculate. The values area might include Sum of Revenue, Count of Units, and Average of Price.

It is also possible to have the same field dropped in the values area twice, but with different calculations. For example, a marketing manager might want to see Minimum of Price, Average Price, and Maximum of Price.

Row Area

The *row area* is shown in Figure 1.6. This area is composed of the headings that go down the left side of the pivot table.

Figure 1.6
The headings down the left side of the pivot table make up the row area of the pivot table.

	A	B	C	D	E	F
1	REGION	(All)				
2						
3	REVENUE	MONTH				
4	MODEL	January	February	March	April	May
5	2500P	$33,073	$29,104	$25,612	$22,538	$19,834
6	3002C	$35,880	$31,574	$27,785	$24,451	$21,517
7	3002P	$90,258	$79,427	$69,896	$61,508	$54,127
8	4055T	$13,250	$11,660	$10,261	$9,030	$7,946
9	4500C	$100,197	$88,173	$77,593	$68,281	$60,088

Dropping a field into the row area displays the unique values from that field down the rows of the left side of the pivot table. The row area typically has at least one field, although it is possible to have no fields. Recall the example presented earlier in this chapter, in which you needed to produce a one-line report of credits. This report is an example of when there are no row fields in the row area.

The types of data fields that you drop into the row area include those that you want to group and categorize such as Products, Names, and Locations.

Column Area

The *column area* is composed of headings that stretch across the top of columns in the pivot table. For example, in the pivot table in Figure 1.7, the month field is in the column area.

Figure 1.7
The column area stretches across the top of the columns. In this example, it contains the unique list of months in your data set.

	A	B	C	D	E	F
1	REGION	(All)				
2						
3	Sum of REVENUE	MONTH				
4	MODEL	January	February	March	April	May
5	2500P	$33,073	$29,104	$25,612	$22,538	$19,834
6	3002C	$35,880	$31,574	$27,785	$24,451	$21,517
7	3002P	$90,258	$79,427	$69,896	$61,508	$54,127
8	4055T	$13,250	$11,660	$10,261	$9,030	$7,946
9	4500C	$100,197	$88,173	$77,593	$68,281	$60,088

Dropping fields into the column area displays your items in column-oriented perspective. The column area is ideal to show trending over time. The types of data fields that you drop into the column area include those you want to trend or show side by side such as Months, Periods, and Years.

Report Filter Area

The *Report Filter area* is an optional set of one or more drop-downs located at the top of the pivot table. In Figure 1.8, the filter area contains the Region field. In this case, the pivot table is set to show all regions.

Figure 1.8
Filter fields are great for quickly filtering a report. The Region drop-down in Cell B1 allows you to print this report for one particular region manager.

	A	B	C	D	E	F
1	REGION	(All)				
2						
3	Sum of REVENUE	MONTH				
4	MODEL	January	February	March	April	May
5	2500P	$33,073	$29,104	$25,612	$22,538	$19,834
6	3002C	$35,880	$31,574	$27,785	$24,451	$21,517
7	3002P	$90,258	$79,427	$69,896	$61,508	$54,127
8	4055T	$13,250	$11,660	$10,261	$9,030	$7,946
9	4500C	$100,197	$88,173	$77,593	$68,281	$60,088

Dropping fields into the filter area allows you to filter the data items in your fields. Even though the filter area is optional, it comes in handy when you need to filter results dynamically. The types of data fields that you drop into the filter area include those that you want to isolate and focus on such as Regions, Line of Business, and Employees.

Pivot Tables Behind the Scenes

It is important to understand that pivot tables come with a few file space and memory implications for your system. To get a better idea of what this means, let's look at what happens behind the scenes when you create a pivot table.

When you initiate the creation of a pivot table report, Excel takes a snapshot of your data set and stores it in a *pivot cache*. A pivot cache is nothing more than a special memory subsystem in which your data source is duplicated for quick access. Although the pivot cache is not a physical object that you can see, you can think of it as a container that stores the snapshot of the data source.

CAUTION

Any changes you make to your data source are not picked up by your pivot table report until you take another snapshot of the data source or "refresh" the pivot cache. Refreshing is easy; you simply right-click the pivot table and then click Refresh Data. You can also select the large Refresh button on the Options tab.

Each pivot table report you create from a separate data source creates its own pivot cache, which increases your memory usage and file size. The increase in memory usage and file size depends on the size of the original data source that is being duplicated to create the pivot cache.

Your pivot table report is essentially a view that gets its data solely from the pivot cache. This means that your pivot table report and your data source are disconnected.

The benefit of working against the pivot cache and not your original data source is optimization. Any changes you make to the pivot table report, such as rearranging fields, adding new fields, or hiding items, are made rapidly and with minimal overhead.

Limitations of Pivot Table Reports

Before discussing the limitations of pivot table reports, it is important to note that beginning with Excel 2007, Microsoft introduced a dramatic increase in the number of rows and columns allowed in one worksheet. However, increasing limits had a ripple effect on several of the tools and functions in Excel, which forced limitation increases in many areas including pivot tables.

Table 1.1 highlights the changes in pivot table limits from Excel 2000 to Excel 2010. Whereas some of these limitations remain constant, others are highly dependent on available system memory.

Table 1.1   Pivot Table Limitations

Category	Excel 2000	Excel 2002/2003	Excel 2007/2010
Number of Row Fields	Limited by available memory	Limited by available memory	1,048,576 (Might be limited by available memory)
Number of Column Fields	256	256	16,384
Number of Page Fields	256	256	16,384
Number of Data Fields	256	256	16,384
Number of Unique Items in a Single Pivot Field	8,000	32,500	1,048,576 (Might be limited by available memory)
Number of Calculated Items	Limited by available memory	Limited by available memory	Limited by available memory
Number of Pivot Table Reports on One Worksheet	Limited by available memory	Limited by available memory	Limited by available memory

A Word About Compatibility

If you are working in an environment where legacy versions of Excel are still being used, you should be aware of the compatibility issues between legacy versions of Excel and Excel 2010. As you can imagine, the extraordinary increases in pivot table limitations lead to some serious compatibility questions. For instance, what if you create a pivot table that contains more than 256 column fields and more than 32,500 unique data items? How are users with legacy versions of Excel affected? Fortunately, Excel comes with some precautionary measures that can help you avoid compatibility issues.

The first precautionary measure is *Compatibility mode*, which is a state that Excel automatically enters when opening an .xls file. When Excel is in Compatibility mode, it artificially takes on the limitations of legacy versions of Excel. For example, while you are working with an .xls file, you cannot exceed any of the Excel 2003 pivot table limitations shown in Table 1.1. This effectively prevents you from unwittingly creating a pivot table that is not compatible with legacy versions of Excel. If you want to get out of Compatibility mode, you have to save the .xls file as one of Excel's new file formats, which are .xlsx or .xlsm.

> **CAUTION**
>
> Beware of the Convert option found under Info section of the File menu. Although this command is designed to convert a file from Excel 2003 to Excel 2010, it actually deletes the Excel 2003 copy of the file.

The second precautionary measure is Excel's Compatibility Checker. The Compatibility Checker is a built-in tool that checks for any compatibility issues when you try to save an Excel workbook as an .xls file. For example, if your pivot table exceeds the bounds of Excel 2003 limitations, the Compatibility Checker alerts you with a dialog box similar to the one shown in Figure 1.9.

Figure 1.9
The Compatibility Checker alerts you of any compatibility issues before you save to a legacy version of Excel.

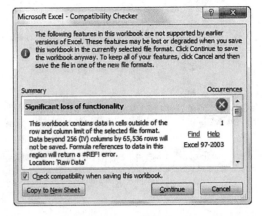

With this dialog box, Excel gives you the option to save your pivot data as hard values in the new .xls file. If you choose to do so, the data from your pivot table is saved as hard values, but the pivot table object and the pivot cache are lost.

> **NOTE** For information on Excel's compatibility tools, pick up Que Publishing's *Excel 2010 In Depth* (ISBN 978-0789743084) by Bill Jelen.

Next Steps

In the next chapter, you learn how to prepare your data to be used by a pivot table. Chapter 2, "Creating a Basic Pivot Table," also walks through creating your first pivot table report using the Pivot Table Wizard.

Creating a Basic Pivot Table

2

Preparing Data for Pivot Table Reporting

When you have a family portrait taken, the photographer takes time to make sure that the lighting is right, the poses are natural, and everyone smiles his or her best smile. This preparation ensures that the resulting photo is effective in its purpose

When you create a pivot table report, you are the photographer taking a snapshot of your data. Taking time to make sure your data looks its best ensures that your pivot table report is effective in accomplishing the task at hand.

One of the benefits of working in a spreadsheet is that you have the flexibility of laying out your data to suit your needs. Indeed, the layout you choose depends heavily on the task at hand. However, many of the data layouts used for presentations are not appropriate when used as the source data for a pivot table report.

As you read the next section that discusses how to prepare your data, keep in mind that pivot tables have only one hard rule as it pertains to your data source: Your data source must have column headings that are labels in the first row of your data describing the information in each column. If this is not the case, your pivot table report cannot be created.

However, just because your pivot table report is created successfully does not mean that it is effective. A host of things can go wrong as a result of bad data preparation—from inaccurate reporting to problems with grouping and sorting.

Let's look at a few of the steps you can take to ensure you end up with a viable pivot table report.

Ensure Data Is in a Tabular Layout

A perfect layout for the source data in a pivot table is a *tabular layout*. In tabular layout, there are no blank rows or columns. Every column has a heading. Every field has a value in every row. Columns do not contain repeating groups of data.

Figure 2.1 shows an example of data structured properly for a pivot table. There are headings for each column. Even though the values in D2:D6 are all the same model, the model number appears in each cell. Month data is organized down the page instead of across the columns.

Figure 2.1
This data is structured properly for use as a pivot table source.

	A	B	C	D	E	F
1	REGION	MARKET	STORE	MODEL	MONTH	REVENUE
2	North	Great Lakes	65061011	4055T	April	$2,354
3	North	Great Lakes	65061011	4055T	February	$3,040
4	North	Great Lakes	65061011	4055T	January	$3,454
5	North	Great Lakes	65061011	4055T	March	$2,675
6	North	Great Lakes	65061011	4055T	May	$2,071
7	North	New England	2105015	2500P	April	$11,851
8	North	New England	2105015	2500P	February	$15,304
9	North	New England	2105015	2500P	January	$17,391
10	North	New England	2105015	2500P	March	$13,468
11	North	New England	2105015	2500P	May	$10,429
12	North	New England	22022012	3002C	April	$256
13	North	New England	22022012	3002C	February	$330
14	North	New England	22022012	3002C	January	$375
15	North	New England	22022012	3002C	March	$290
16	North	New England	22022012	3002C	May	$225
17	North	New England	12011011	3002P	April	$35,734

Tabular layouts are *database-centric*, which means these types of layouts are most commonly found in databases. Database-centric layouts are designed to store and maintain large amounts of data in a well-structured, scalable format.

> **TIP**
> You might work for a manager who demands that the column labels be split into two rows. For example, he might want the heading Gross Margin to be split with Gross in Row 1 and Margin in Row 2. Because pivot tables require a unique heading one row high, your manager's preference can be problematic. To overcome this problem, start typing your heading. For example, type **Gross**. Before leaving the cell, press Alt+Enter and then type **Margin**. The result is a single cell that contains two lines of data.

Avoid Storing Data in Section Headings

Examine the data in Figure 2.2. This spreadsheet shows a report of sales by month and model for the North region of a company. Because the data in Rows 2 through 24 pertains to the North region, the author of the worksheet put a single cell with North in B1. This approach is effective for display of the data, but not effective when used as a pivot table data source.

Figure 2.2
Region and model data are not formatted properly in this data set.

	A	B	C
1		North	
2	Model 2500P	January	33,073
3		February	35,880
4		March	90,258
5		April	13,250
6		May	100,197
7			
8	Model 3002P	January	29,104
9		February	31,574
10		March	79,427
11		April	11,660
12		May	88,173
13			
14	Model 4055T	January	
15		February	25,612
16		March	27,785
17		April	69,896
18		May	10,261
19			
20	Model 4500T	January	
21		February	25,612
22		March	27,785
23		April	69,896
24		May	10,261

Also in Figure 2.2, the author was creative with the model information. The data in Rows 2 through 6 applies to Model 2500P, so the author entered this value once in A2 and then applied a fancy vertical format combined with Merge Cells to create an interesting look for the report. Again, although this is a cool format, it is not useful for pivot table reporting.

Also, the worksheet in Figure 2.2 is missing column headings. You can guess that Column A is Model, Column B is Month, and Column C is Sales. However, for Excel to create a pivot table, this information must be included in the first row of the data.

Avoid Repeating Groups as Columns

The format shown in Figure 2.3 is common. A time dimension is presented across several columns. Although it is possible to create a pivot table from this data, this format is not ideal.

The problem is that the headings spread across the top of the table pull double duty as column labels and actual data values. In a pivot table, this format would force you to manage and maintain six fields, each representing a different month.

Figure 2.3
This matrix format is common but not effective for pivot tables. The Month field is spread across several columns of the report.

	A	B	C	D	E	F	G	H
1								
2	North	MODEL	JANUARY	FEBRUARY	MARCH	APRIL	MAY	JUNE
3		4054T	$2,789	$2,454	$2,160	$1,901	$1,673	$1,472
4		4500C	$32,605	$28,692	$25,249	$22,219	$19,553	$17,207
5		3002P	$52,437	$46,145	$40,607	$35,734	$31,446	$27,673
6		2500P	$17,391	$15,304	$13,468	$11,851	$10,429	$9,178
7		4055T	$2,468	$2,172	$1,911	$1,682	$1,480	$1,302
8		3002C	$375	$330	$290	$256	$225	$198

Eliminate Gaps and Blank Cells in the Data Source

Delete all empty columns within your data source. An empty column in the middle of your data source causes your pivot table to fail on creation because the blank column, in most cases, does not have a column name.

Delete all empty rows within your data source. Empty rows might cause you to inadvertently leave out a large portion of your data range, making your pivot table report incomplete.

Fill in as many blank cells in your data source as possible. Although filling in cells is not required to create a workable pivot table, blank cells are generally errors waiting to happen. Therefore, a good practice is to represent missing values with some logical missing value code wherever possible.

> **NOTE**
> Although this might seem like a step backward for those of you who are trying to create a nicely formatted report, it pays off in the end. After you are able to create a pivot table, there is plenty of time to apply some pleasant formatting. In Chapter 3, "Customizing a Pivot Table," you learn how to apply style formatting to your pivot tables.

Apply Appropriate Type Formatting to Fields

Formatting your fields appropriately helps you avoid a whole host of possible issues from inaccurate reporting to problems with grouping and sorting.

Make certain that any fields to be used in calculations are explicitly formatted as a number, currency, or any other format appropriate for use in mathematical functions. Fields containing dates should also be formatted as any one of the available date formats.

Summary of Good Data Source Design

The attributes of an effective tabular design are as follows:

- The first row of your data source is made up of field labels or headings that describe the information in each column.
- Each column in your data source represents a unique category of data.
- Each row in your data source represents individual items in each column.
- None of the column names in your data source double as data items that will be used as filters or query criteria such as names of months, dates, years, locations, and employees.

CASE STUDY   CLEANING UP DATA FOR PIVOT TABLE ANALYSIS

The worksheet shown in Figure 2.4 is a great-looking report. However, it cannot be used effectively as a data source for a pivot table. Can you identify the problems with this data set?

Figure 2.4
Someone spent a lot of time formatting this report to look good, but what problems prevent it from being used as a data source for a pivot table?

	A	B	C	D	E	F	G
1	Region	Market		Jan	Feb	Mar	Apr
2	Bar Equipment						
3	Midwest	Chicago		132	106	110	90
4		Kansas City		413	504	2,571	505
5		Omaha		332	543	372	424
6	North	Dakotas		130	136	106	90
7		Great Lakes		488	445	4,140	517
8							
9	Commercial Appliances						
10	Midwest	Chicago		780	76	851	76
11		Kansas City		3,352	76	8,442	2,831
12		Omaha		228	17,628	76	304
13	North	Dakotas		0	0	2,608	0
14		Great Lakes		990	76	11,435	76
15							
16	Concession Equipment						
17	Midwest	Chicago		808	0	3,912	0
18		Kansas City		824	1,761	11,181	1,616
19		Omaha		0	8,147	2,968	3,118
20	North	Dakotas		0	0	5,463	2,370
21		Great Lakes		751	808	13,814	1,632

Let's take a look as some of the reasons why this report can't be used as an effective data source for a pivot table.

1. The model information does not have its own column. Product Category information appears in the Region column. To correct this problem, insert a new column for Product Category and include the category name on every row.

2. There are blank columns and rows in the data. Column C should be deleted. The blank rows between models, such as Rows 8 and 15, should also be deleted.

3. Blank cells present the data in an outline format. The person reading this worksheet would probably assume that Cells A4:A5 fall into the Midwest region. These blank cells need to be filled in with the values from above.

> **TIP**
> Here is a trick for filling in the blank cells. Select the entire range of data. Next, select the Home tab on the Ribbon, and then select the Find & Select icon from the Editing group. On the menu that appears, select Go To Special. In the Go To Special dialog box, select Blanks. With all the blank cells selected, begin a formula by typing the equal sign (=), press the up arrow on your keyboard, and then press Ctrl+Enter to fill this formula in all blank cells. Remember to copy and paste special values to convert the formulas to values.

4. The worksheet presents one data column——the data containing the month—among several columns in the worksheet. Columns D through G need to be reformatted as two columns. Place the month name in one column

and the units for that month in the next column. This step either requires a fair amount of copying and pasting or a few lines of VBA macro code.

> **TIP**
>
> For a great book to learn VBA macro programming, read Que Publishing's *VBA and Macros: Microsoft Excel 2010 by Bill Jelen and Tracy Syrstad* (ISBN 0789743140). It is another book in this *MrExcel Library* series.

After you make the four changes described previously, the data is ready to be used as a pivot table data source. As you can see in Figure 2.5, every column has a heading. There are no blank cells, rows, or columns in the data. The monthly data is now presented down Column E instead of across several columns.

Figure 2.5
Although this data takes up six times as many rows, it is perfectly formatted for pivot table analysis.

	A	B	C	D	E
1	Product Category	Region	Market	Month	Units
2	Bar Equipment	Midwest	Chicago	Jan	132
3	Bar Equipment	Midwest	Kansas City	Jan	413
4	Bar Equipment	Midwest	Omaha	Jan	332
5	Bar Equipment	North	Dakotas	Jan	130
6	Bar Equipment	North	Great Lakes	Jan	488
7	Commercial Appliances	Midwest	Chicago	Jan	780
8	Commercial Appliances	Midwest	Kansas City	Jan	3,352
9	Commercial Appliances	Midwest	Omaha	Jan	228
10	Commercial Appliances	North	Dakotas	Jan	0
11	Commercial Appliances	North	Great Lakes	Jan	990
12	Commercial Appliances	North		Jan	
13	Concession Equipment	Midwest	Chicago	Jan	808
14	Concession Equipment	Midwest	Kansas City	Jan	824
15	Concession Equipment	Midwest	Omaha	Jan	0
16	Concession Equipment	North	Dakotas	Jan	0
17	Concession Equipment	North	Great Lakes	Jan	751
18	Bar Equipment	Midwest	Chicago	Feb	106
19	Bar Equipment	Midwest	Kansas City	Feb	504
20	Bar Equipment	Midwest	Omaha	Feb	543
21	Bar Equipment	North	Dakotas	Feb	136
22	Bar Equipment	North	Great Lakes	Feb	445
23	Commercial Appliances	Midwest	Chicago	Feb	76

Creating a Basic Pivot Table

Now that you have a good understanding of the importance of a well-structured data source, let's walk through creating a basic pivot table.

To start, click on any single cell in your data source. This ensures that the pivot table captures the range of your data source by default. Next, select the Insert tab and find the Tables group. In the Tables group, select PivotTable and then select PivotTable from the drop-down list. Figure 2.6 demonstrates how to start a pivot table.

Figure 2.6
Start a pivot table by selecting PivotTable from the Insert tab.

Selecting these options activates the Create PivotTable dialog box, as shown in Figure 2.7.

Figure 2.7
The Create PivotTable dialog box replaces the classic PivotTable and PivotChart Wizard.

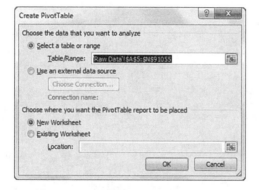

> **NOTE**
> There are other ways to activate the Create PivotTable dialog box. You can click the PivotTable icon on the Insert tab to activate the Create PivotTable dialog box. You can also press the hotkeys Alt+N+V+T to start a pivot table.
>
> A more roundabout way is to format your data set as a table, and then select the Summarize with Pivot command. To do this, place your cursor inside your data set and select Format as Table from the Styles group in the Home tab. After your table has been formatted, place your cursor anywhere inside your data set to activate the Table Tools tab. From the Table Tools tab, you can select the Summarize with Pivot option in the Tools group.

WHERE HAVE ALL THE WIZARDS GONE?

If you are still using Excel 2003, you notice that Figure 2.7 does not look like the PivotTable and PivotChart Wizard you are used to. This is because Microsoft has abandoned the classic multistep wizard for a more streamlined one-step dialog box.

The problem with the classic wizard was that, by the time most first-time users reached step 2, they were either confused or intimidated. Although each subsequent version of Excel has tried to simplify the process of creating a pivot table, the multistep wizard ultimately introduced too much complexity for many users. In contrast, Excel 2010's one-step dialog box presents you with only the minimum requirements necessary to create the pivot table, making for a far less intimidating process.

As you can see in Figure 2.8, the Create PivotTable dialog box essentially asks you two questions: Where is the data that you want to analyze, and where do you want to put the pivot table? The following bullets describe each of these questions:

Figure 2.8
The Create PivotTable dialog box asks you two questions.

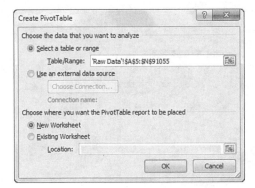

- **Choose the Data That You Want to Analyze**—In response to this question, you tell Excel where your data set is. You can either specify a data set that is located within your workbook, or you can tell Excel to look for an external data set. As you can see in Figure 2.8, Excel is smart enough to read your data set and fill in the range for you. However, you always should take note of this to ensure you are capturing all your data.

- **Choose Where You Want the PivotTable Report to Be Placed**—In response to this question, you tell Excel where you want your pivot table to be placed. This is set to New Worksheet by default, meaning your pivot table will be placed in a new worksheet within the current workbook. You will rarely change this setting because there are relatively few times you need your pivot table to be placed in a specific location.

After you have answered these two questions in the Create PivotTable dialog box, click OK. At this point, Excel adds a new worksheet that contains an empty pivot table report.

Next to that is the PivotTable Field List dialog box, as shown in Figure 2.9. This dialog box helps you build your pivot table.

Figure 2.9
Use the PivotTable Field List dialog box to build your pivot table.

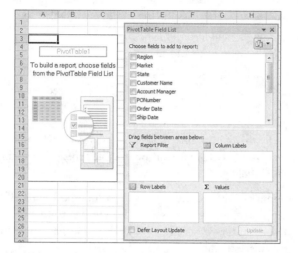

FINDING THE PIVOTTABLE FIELD LIST

The PivotTable Field List dialog box is your main work area in Excel 2010. This is the place where you add fields and make changes to your pivot table report. By default, this dialog box pops up when you place your cursor anywhere inside your pivot table. However, if you explicitly close this dialog box, you override the default and essentially tell the dialog box not to activate when you are in the pivot table.

If clicking on the pivot table does not activate the PivotTable Field List dialog box, you can manually activate it by right-clicking anywhere inside the pivot table and selecting Show Field List. You can also click on the large Field List icon on the Options ribbon.

Adding Fields to the Report

You can add the fields you need into the pivot table by using the four drop zones found in the PivotTable Field List: Report Filter, Column Labels, Row Labels, and Values. These drop zones, which correspond to the four areas of the pivot table, are used to populate your pivot table with data.

> **TIP**
> Review Chapter 1, "Pivot Table Fundamentals," for a refresher on the four areas of a pivot table.

- **Report Filter**—Adding a field to the Report Filter drop zone includes that field in the filter area of your pivot table, which enables you to filter on its unique data items.

- **Column Labels**—Adding a field into the Column Labels drop zone displays the unique values from that field across the top of the pivot table.

- **Row Labels**—Adding a field into the Row Labels drop zone displays the unique values from that field down the left side of the pivot table.

- **Values**—Adding a field into the Values drop zone includes that field in the values area of your pivot table, which enables you to perform a specified calculation using the values in the field.

Because this is generally the point where most new users get stuck, before moving on, let's review some fundamentals of laying out your pivot table report. For example, do you know how to determine which field goes where?

Before you start dropping fields into the various drop zones, ask yourself two questions: What am I measuring? How do I want to see it? The answer to the first question tells you which fields in your data source you need to work with, and the answer to the second question tells you where to place the fields.

For your first pivot table report, you want to measure the dollar sales by region. This tells you automatically that you need to work with the Sales_Amount field and the Region field. How do you want to see it? You want regions to go down the left side of the report and the sales amount to be calculated next to each region.

To achieve this effect, you need to add the Region field to the Row Labels drop zone and add the Sales_Amount field to the Values drop zone.

Find the Region field in the field list, as shown in Figure 2.10.

Figure 2.10
Find the field you want to add to your pivot table.

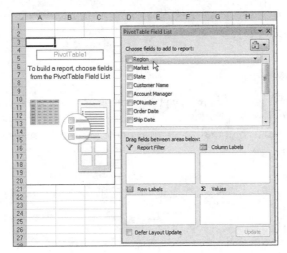

Select the check box next to the field. As you can see in Figure 2.11, not only is the field automatically added to the Row Labels drop zone, but your pivot table is updated to show the unique region names.

Figure 2.11
Select the Region field check box to automatically add that field to your pivot table.

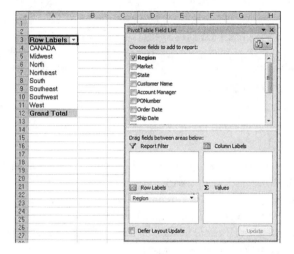

Now that you have regions in your pivot table, it is time to add in the dollar sales. To do that, select the Sales Amount field check box. As Figure 2.12 illustrates, the Sales Amount field is automatically added to the Values drop zone, and your pivot table report now shows the total dollar sales for each region.

Figure 2.12
Select the Sales Amount field check box to add data to your pivot table report.

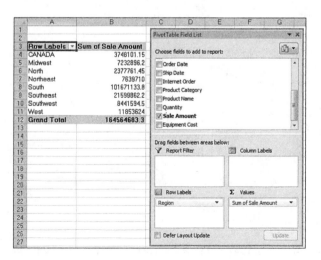

At this point, you have created your first pivot table report!

HOW DOES EXCEL KNOW WHERE FIELDS GO?

As you have just experienced, the new PivotTable Field List interface enables you to add the fields to your pivot table by selecting a check box next to the field name. Excel automatically adds the selected fields to the pivot table. So, how does Excel know in which drop zone to put the selected fields? The answer is that Excel does not really know which drop zone to use. Instead, it makes a decision based on data type. Here is how it works: When you select a check box next to a field, Excel evaluates the data type for that field. If the data type is numeric, Excel places the field into the Values drop zone; otherwise, Excel places the field into the Row Labels drop zone. This placement obviously underlines the importance of correctly assigning the data types for your fields.

Adding Layers to a Pivot Table

Now you can add another layer of analysis to your report. This time you want to measure the amount of dollar sales each region earned by product category. Because your pivot table already contains the Region and Sales Amount fields, all you have to do is select a check box next to the Product Category field. As you can see in Figure 2.13, your pivot table automatically adds a layer for Product Category and refreshes the calculations to include subtotals for each region. Because the data is stored efficiently in the pivot cache, this change took less than a second.

Figure 2.13
Before pivot tables, adding layers to analyses would have required hours of work and complex formulas.

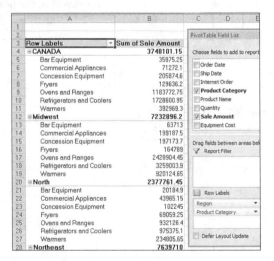

Rearranging a Pivot Table

Suppose this view does not work for your manager because he wants to see Product Categories across the top of the pivot table report. To rearrange these categories, simply drag the Product Category field from the Row Labels drop zone to the Column Labels drop zone, as illustrated in Figure 2.14.

Figure 2.14
Rearranging a pivot table is as simple as dragging fields from one drop zone to another.

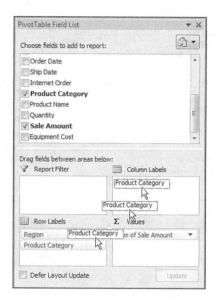

Instantly, the report is restructured, as shown in Figure 2.15.

Figure 2.15
Product categories are now column oriented.

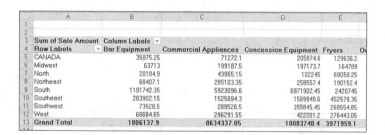

	A	B	C	D	E
1					
2					
3	Sum of Sale Amount	Column Labels			
4	Row Labels	Bar Equipment	Commercial Appliances	Concession Equipment	Fryers	Ov
5	CANADA	35975.25	71272.1	205874.6	129636.2
6	Midwest	63713	199187.5	197173.7	164789
7	North	20184.9	43965.15	102245	69059.25
8	Northeast	68407.1	285103.35	258557.4	190152.4
9	South	1191742.35	5923096.6	6971902.45	2420745
10	Southeast	283902.15	1525894.3	1569948.6	452579.35
11	Southwest	73528.5	289526.5	355845.45	268554.85
12	West	68684.65	296291.55	422201.2	276443.05
13	Grand Total	1806137.9	8634337.05	10083748.4	3971959.1

LONGING FOR DRAG-AND-DROP FUNCTIONALITY?

If you are upgrading from Excel 2003, you notice that you can no longer drag and drop fields directly onto the pivot table layout. This functionality is enabled only within the PivotTable Field List dialog box. However, the good news is that Microsoft has provided the option of working with a classic pivot table layout that enables the drag-and-drop functionality.

To activate the classic pivot table layout, right-click anywhere inside the pivot table and select Table Options. In the Table Options dialog box, select the Display tab, and then select the Classic PivotTable Layout check box, as demonstrated in Figure 2.16. Click OK to apply the change.

At this point, you can drag and drop fields directly onto your pivot table layout.

Unfortunately, this setting is not global. This means you need to go through the same steps to apply the classic layout to each new pivot table you create. However, this setting persists when a pivot table is copied.

Figure 2.16
Select the Classic
PivotTable Layout check
box.

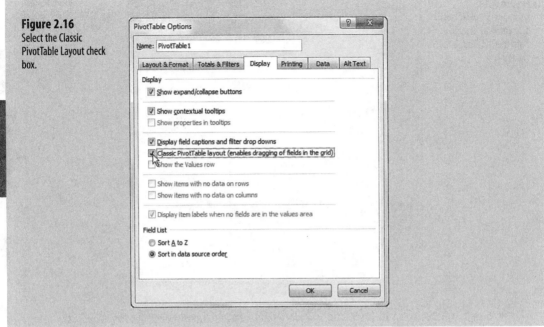

Creating a Report Filter

Often, you might be asked to produce reports for one particular region, market, or product.
Instead of building separate pivot table reports for every possible analysis scenario, you can
use the Filter field to create a report filter. For example, you can create a region filter by
simply dragging the Region field to the Report Filter drop zone. This allows you to analyze
one particular region. Figure 2.17 shows the totals for just the North region.

Figure 2.17
With this setup, you can
see revenues by line of
business and can click
the Region drop-down to
focus on one region.

Introducing Slicers

With Excel 2010, Microsoft introduces a new feature called slicers. *Slicers* enable you to filter your pivot table, similar to the way Filter fields filter a pivot table. The difference is that slicers offer a user-friendly interface that enables you to see the current filter state.

To understand the concept behind slicers, place your cursor anywhere inside your pivot table, then go up to the Ribbon and select the Option tab. On the Option tab, click the Insert Slicer icon (see Figure 2.18).

Figure 2.18
Inserting a slicer in Excel 2010.

This activates the Insert Slicers dialog box, as shown in Figure 2.19. The idea is to select the dimensions you want to filter. In this case, the Region and Market slicers are created when you select these dimensions.

Figure 2.19
Select the dimensions you want filtered using slicers.

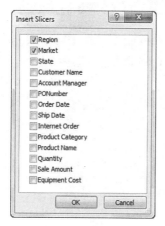

After the slicers are created, you can click the filter values to filter your pivot table. As shown in Figure 2.20, clicking Midwest in the Region slicer not only filters your pivot table, but the Market slicer also responds by highlighting the markets that belong to the Midwest region.

You can also select multiple values by pressing the Ctrl key while selecting the needed filters. In Figure 2.21, pressing the Ctrl key selected Baltimore, California, Charlotte, and

Chicago. This highlights the selected markets in the Market slicer and their associated regions in the Region slicer.

Figure 2.20
Select the dimensions you want filtered using slicers.

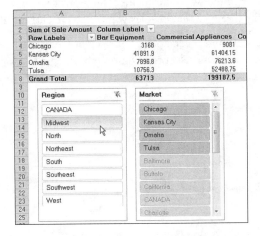

Figure 2.21
The fact that you can visually see the current filter state gives slicers a unique advantage over the Filter field.

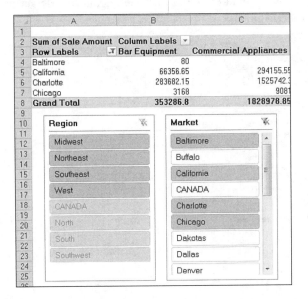

Another advantage gain with slicers is that each slicer can be tied to more than one pivot table. In other words, any filter you apply to your slicer can be applied to multiple pivot tables.

To connect your slicer to more than one pivot table, right-click the slicer, and then select PivotTable Connections (see Figure 2.22).

Figure 2.22
Activating the PivotTable
Connections dialog box.

This activates the PivotTable connections dialog box, as shown in Figure 2.23. Next, select the check box next to any pivot table that you want to filter using the current slicer.

Figure 2.23
Select the pivot tables
that will be filtered by
this slicer.

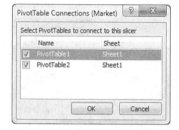

At this point, any filter you apply to the slicer is applied to all the connected pivot tables. Again, slicers have a unique advantage over Filter fields in that they can control the filter state of multiple pivot tables. Filter fields can only control the pivot table in which they live

> **NOTE**
> It is important to note that slicers are not part of the pivot table object. Instead, they are separate objects that can be used in a variety of ways. For a more detailed look at slicers, their functionality, and how to format slicers, see "Using Slicers" in Chapter 4 of Que Publishing's *Microsoft Excel 2010 In Depth* by Bill Jelen (ISBN 0789743086).

CASE STUDY   ANALYZING ACTIVITY BY MARKET

Say your organization has 18 markets that sell products revolving around seven types of products. You have been asked to build a report that breaks out each market, highlighting the dollar sales by each product. You are starting with an intimidating transaction table that contains more than 91,000 rows of data. To start your report, do the following:

1. Place your cursor inside your data set, select the Insert tab, click PivotTable, and then select PivotTable from the drop-down list.

2. When the Create PivotTable dialog box appears, click OK. At this point, you should see an empty pivot table with the field list, as shown in Figure 2.24.

Figure 2.24
The beginnings of your pivot table report.

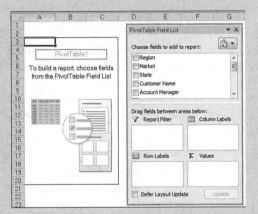

3. Find the Market field in the PivotTable Field List, and then select the check box next to it.

4. Find the Sales Amount field in the PivotTable Field List, and then select the check box next to it.

5. To get the product breakouts, find the Product Category field in the PivotTable Field List and drag it into the Column Labels drop.

In five easy steps, you have calculated and designed a report that satisfies the requirements given to you. After a little formatting, your pivot table report should look similar to the one shown in Figure 2.25.

Figure 2.25
This summary can be created in less than a minute.

Row Labels	Bar Equipment	Commercial Appliances	Concession Equipment	Fryers	
Sum of Sale Amount	Column Labels				
Baltimore	80			352	
Buffalo	37397.9	237297.85	187711	127287.7	
California	66356.65	294155.55	416379.2	261042.05	
CANADA	35975.25	71272.1	205874.6	129636.2	
Charlotte	283682.15	1525742.3	1569948.6	450972.35	
Chicago	3168	9081	18218	9846.8	
Dakotas	3386.5	7287.05	30619.2	18029.45	
Dallas	59580.3	255146	306037	151269.9	
Denver	34558.85	70068.8	75712.8	120087.15	
Florida	1132162.05	5667950.6	6665865.45	2269475.1	
Great Lakes	16798.4	36678.1	71625.8	51029.8	
Kansas City	41891.9	61404.15	57300.7	50395.4	
Knoxville	220	152		1607	
New England	30929.2	47805.5	70846.4	62512.7	
Omaha	7896.8	76213.6	72006.8	42460.15	
Phoenix	38969.65	219457.7	280132.65	148467.7	
Seattle	2328	2136	5822	15401	
Tulsa	10756.3	52488.75	49648.2	62086.65	
Grand Total	1806137.9	8634337.05	10083748.4	3971959.1	

> **NOTE** Lest you lose sight of the analytical power you just displayed, keep in mind that your data source has more than 91,000 rows and 14 columns, which is a hefty set of data by Excel standards. Despite the amount of data, you produced a relatively robust analysis in a matter of minutes.

Keeping Up with Changes in the Data Source

Let's go back to the family portrait analogy. As years go by, your family changes in appearance and probably grows to include some new members. The family portrait that was taken years ago remains static and no longer represents the family today. So another portrait needs to be taken.

The same thing occurs with data. As time goes by, your data might change and grow with newly added rows and columns. However, the pivot cache that feeds your pivot table report is disconnected from your data source, so it cannot represent any of the changes you make to your date source until you take another snapshot.

The action of updating your pivot cache by taking another snapshot of your data source is called *refreshing* your data. There are two reasons you might have to refresh your pivot table report:

■ Changes have been made to your existing data source.

■ Your data source's range has been expanded with the addition of rows or columns.

These two scenarios are handled in different ways that are discussed in the following sections.

Changes Have Been Made to Existing Data Sources

If a few cells in your pivot table's source data have changed due to edits or updates, your pivot table report can be refreshed with a few clicks. To refresh your data source, right-click inside your pivot table report and select Refresh Data. This selection takes another snapshot of your data set and overwrites your previous pivot cache with the latest data.

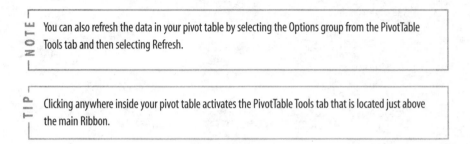

> **NOTE** You can also refresh the data in your pivot table by selecting the Options group from the PivotTable Tools tab and then selecting Refresh.

> **TIP** Clicking anywhere inside your pivot table activates the PivotTable Tools tab that is located just above the main Ribbon.

Data Source's Range Has Expanded

When changes have been made to your data source that affect its range such as when you have added rows or columns, you need to update the range being captured by the pivot cache.

To do this, click anywhere inside your pivot table, and then select Options from the PivotTable Tools tab. From here, select Change Data Source. This selection triggers the dialog box shown in Figure 2.26.

All you have to do in the Change PivotTable Data Source dialog box is update the range to include new rows and columns. After you have specified the appropriate range, click OK.

Figure 2.26
The Change PivotTable Data Source dialog box enables you to redefine the source data for your pivot table.

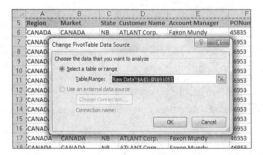

Sharing the Pivot Cache

Many times, you need to analyze the same data set in multiple ways. In most cases, this process requires you to create separate pivot tables from the same data source. Keep in mind that every time you create a pivot table, you are storing a snapshot of your entire data set in a pivot cache. Every pivot cache that is created increases your memory usage and file size. For this reason, you should consider sharing your pivot cache. In other words, in those situations in which you need to create multiple pivot tables from the same data source, you can use the same pivot cache to feed multiple pivot tables. By using the same pivot cache for multiple pivot tables, you gain a certain level of efficiency when it comes to memory usage and files size.

In legacy versions of Excel, when you created a pivot table using a data set that was already being used in another pivot table, Excel actually gave you the option to use the same pivot cache. However, Excel 2010 does not give you such an option.

Instead, each time you create a new pivot table in Excel 2010, a new pivot cache is automatically created even though one might already exist for the data set being used. The side effect of this behavior is that your spreadsheet bloats with redundant data each time you create a new pivot table using the same data set.

You can work around this potential problem by employing copy and paste. That's right; by simply copying a pivot table and pasting it somewhere else, you create another pivot table, *without* duplicating the pivot cache. This enables you to link as many pivot tables as you want to the same pivot cache, with a negligible increase in memory and file size.

Side Effects of Sharing a Pivot Cache

It is important to note that there are a few side effects to sharing a pivot cache. For example, say you have two pivot tables using the same pivot cache. Certain actions affect both pivot tables, including:

- **Refreshing Your Data**—You cannot refresh one pivot table without refreshing the other pivot table. Refreshing affects both tables.

- **Adding a Calculated Field**—If you create a calculated field in one pivot table, your newly created calculated field shows up in the other pivot table's field list.

- **Adding a Calculated Item**—If you create a calculated item in one pivot table, it also shows in the other pivot table.

- **Grouping or Ungrouping Fields**—Any grouping or ungrouping you perform affects both pivot tables. For example, say you group a date field in one pivot table to show months. The same date field in the other pivot table is also grouped to show months.

Although none of these side effects are critical flaws in the concept of sharing a pivot cache, it is important to keep them in mind when determining if sharing a pivot table as your data source is the best option.

Saving Time with New Pivot Table Tools

Microsoft has invested a lot of time and effort in the overall pivot table experience. The results of their efforts are tools that make pivot table functionality more accessible and easier to use. The following sections look at a few of the tools that help you save time when managing your pivot tables.

Deferring Layout Updates

The frustrating part of building a pivot table from a large data source is that each time you add a field to a pivot area, you have to wait while Excel crunches through all that data. This can become a maddeningly time-consuming process if you have to add several fields to your pivot table.

Excel 2010 offers some relief for this problem by providing a way to defer layout changes until you are ready to apply them. You can activate this option by selecting the relatively inconspicuous Defer Layout Update check box on the PivotTable Field List dialog box, as shown in Figure 2.27.

Figure 2.27
Select the Defer Layout Update check box to prevent your pivot table from updating while you add fields.

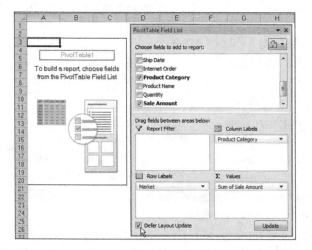

Here is how this feature works: When you select the Defer Layout Update check box, you prevent the pivot table from making real-time updates as you move fields around within the pivot table. In Figure 2.27, notice that fields in the drop zones are not in the pivot table yet. The reason is that the Defer Layout Update check box is selected. When you are ready to apply your changes, simply click the Update button on the lower-right corner of the PivotTable Field List dialog box.

> **NOTE** Remember to clear the Defer Layout Update check box when you have finished building your pivot table. Leaving this check box selected results in your pivot table remaining in a state of manual updates, which prevents you from using the other features of the pivot table such as sorting, filtering, and grouping.

Starting Over with One Click

There are times when you want to start from scratch when working with your pivot table layouts. Excel 2010 provides a straightforward way to essentially start over without deleting your pivot cache. To do this, select Options under the PivotTable Tools tab, and then select the Clear drop-down.

As you can see in Figure 2.28, this command enables you to either clear your entire pivot table layout or remove any existing filters that have been applied in your pivot table.

Figure 2.28
The Clear command enables you to clear your pivot table fields or remove the applied filters in your pivot table.

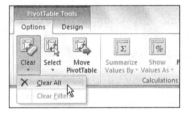

Relocating a Pivot Table

After you have created your pivot table, you might find that you need to move the pivot table to another location. For example, your pivot table might be in the way of other analyses on a worksheet, or you might simply need to move it to another worksheet. Although there are several ways to move your pivot table, Excel 2010 provides a no-frills way to change the location of your pivot table.

To move your pivot table to a different location, select Options under the PivotTable Tools tab, and then select Move PivotTable. This activates the Move PivotTable dialog box illustrated in Figure 2.29. All you have to do in this dialog is specify where you want your pivot table moved.

Figure 2.29
The Move PivotTable
dialog box enables you to
quickly move your pivot
table to another location.

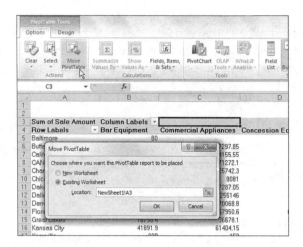

Next Steps

In the next chapter, you learn how to enhance your pivot table reports by customizing
your fields, changing field names, changing summary calculations, applying formats to data
fields, adding and removing subtotals, and using the Show As setting.

Customizing a Pivot Table

3

Although pivot tables provide an extremely fast way to summarize data, sometimes the pivot table defaults are not exactly what you need. In this case, you can use many powerful settings to tweak the information in your pivot table. These tweaks range from making cosmetic changes to changing the underlying calculation used in the pivot table.

In Excel 2010, you find controls to customize the pivot table in a myriad of places: the Options tab, Design tab, Field Settings dialog box, Data Field Settings dialog box, PivotTable Options dialog box, and context menus. Rather than cover each set of controls sequentially, this chapter seeks to cover functional areas in customizing pivot table customization:

- **Minor Cosmetic Changes**—Change blanks to zeros, adjust the number format, and rename a field. Although these changes are minor, they are annoying and affect almost every pivot table that you create.

- **Layout Changes**—Compare three possible layouts, show/hide subtotals and totals, and repeat row labels.

- **Major Cosmetic Changes**—Use table styles to format your table quickly.

- **Summary Calculation**—Change from Sum to Count, Min, Max, and more. If you have a table that defaults to Count of Revenue instead of Sum of Revenue, you need to visit this section.

- **Advanced Calculation**—Use settings to show data as a running total, percent of total, rank, percent of parent item, and more.

- **Other Options**—Review more obscure options found throughout the Excel interface.

- **Impossible Calculation**—If you simply cannot get the calculation you need in a pivot table, use a live pivot table as an intermediate result, and then use GETPIVOTDATA to build the actual formatted report.

Making Common Cosmetic Changes

You need to make a few changes to almost every pivot table to make it easier to understand and interpret. Figure 3.1 shows a typical pivot table. This pivot table has two fields in the Row Labels area and one field in the Column Labels area.

Figure 3.1
A default pivot table.

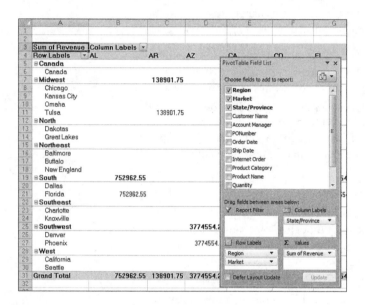

This pivot table contains several annoying items that you might want to change quickly:

- The default table style uses no gridlines that makes it difficult to follow the rows and columns across.

- Numbers in the values area are in a general number format. There are no commas, currency symbols, and so on.

- For sparse data sets, there are many blanks in the values area. The blank cell in B16 indicates that there were no sales in Baltimore. Most people prefer to see a zero instead of blanks.

- Excel renames fields in the values area with the unimaginative name Sum of Revenue. You can change this name.

You can correct each of these annoyances with just a few mouse clicks. The following sections address each issue.

Applying a Table Style to Restore Gridlines

The default pivot table layout contains no gridlines. This format is annoying and a giant step backward. Fortunately, you can apply a table style. Any table style that you choose is better than the default.

Follow these steps to apply a table style:

1. Make sure that the active cell is in the pivot table.
2. From the Ribbon, select the Design tab.
3. Three arrows appear at the right side of the PivotTable Style gallery. Click the bottom arrow to open the complete gallery, as shown in Figure 3.2.

Figure 3.2
The gallery contains 85 styles to choose from.

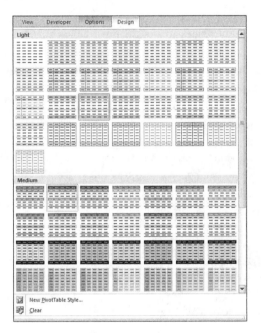

4. Choose any style other than the first style from the drop-down. Styles toward the bottom of the gallery tend to have more formatting.
5. Select the check box for Banded Rows to the left of the PivotTable Styles gallery. This draws gridlines in light styles and adds a row stripe in dark styles.

It does not matter which style you choose from the gallery; any of the 84 other styles are better than the default style.

→ For more details about customizing styles, **see** "Customizing the Pivot Table Appearance with Styles and Themes," **p. 50.**

Changing the Number Format to Add Thousands Separators

If you have gone to the trouble of formatting your underlying data, you might expect that the pivot table would capture some of this formatting. Unfortunately, it does not. Even if your underlying data fields were formatted with a certain numeric format, the default pivot table presents values formatted with a general format.

For example, in the figures in this chapter, the numbers are in the hundreds of thousands. At this level of sales, you would normally have a thousands separator and probably no decimal places. Although the original data had a numeric format applied, the pivot table routinely formats your numbers in an ugly general style.

You can access the numeric format for a field in the Data Field Settings dialog box. There are three ways to display this dialog box:

- Right-click a number in the values area of the pivot table and select Value Field Settings.

- Click the drop-down on the Sum of Revenue field in the drop zones of the PivotTable Field List. Then select Field Settings from the context menu.

- Select any cell in the values area of the pivot table. From the Options tab, select Field Settings from the Active Field group.

As shown in Figure 3.3, the Value Field Settings dialog box is displayed. To change the numeric format, click the Number Format button in the lower-left corner.

Figure 3.3
Display the Value Field Settings dialog box, and then click Number Format.

Number Format

In the Format Cells dialog box, you can choose any built-in number format or choose a custom format. For example, choose Currency, as shown in Figure 3.4.

Figure 3.4
Choose an easier-to-read number format from the Format Cells dialog box.

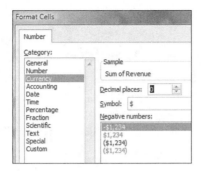

> **NOTE** Although Excel 2010 offers a Live Preview feature for many dialog boxes, the Format Cells dialog box does not offer one. You must assign the number format, and then click OK twice to see the changes.

Replacing Blanks with Zeros

One of the elements of good spreadsheet design is that you should never leave blank cells in a numeric section of the worksheet. Even Microsoft believes in this rule; if your source data for a pivot table contains 1 million numeric cells and 1 blank cell, Excel 2010 treats the entire column as if it were text and will choose to Count the column instead of Sum. This is why it is incredibly annoying that the default setting for a pivot table leaves many blanks in the values area of some pivot tables.

The blank tells you that there were no sales for that particular combination of labels. In the default view, an actual zero is used to indicate that there was activity, but the total sales were zero. This value might mean that a customer bought something and then returned it, resulting in net sales of zero. Although there are limited applications in which you need to differentiate between having no sales and having net zero sales, this seems rare. In 99 percent of the cases, you should fill in the blank cells with zeros.

Follow these steps to change this setting for the current pivot table:

1. Select a cell inside the pivot table.
2. On the Options tab, select the Options icon from the PivotTable Options group to display the PivotTable Options dialog box.
3. On the Layout & Format tab in the Format section, type **0** next to the field labeled For Empty Cells Show (see Figure 3.5).
4. Click OK to accept the change.

The result is that the pivot table is filled with zeros instead of blanks, as shown in Figure 3.6.

Figure 3.5
Enter a zero here to replace the blank cells with zero.

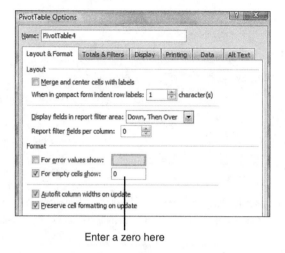

Enter a zero here

Figure 3.6
Your report is now a solid contiguous block of non-blank cells.

Changing a Field Name

Every field in the final pivot table has a name. Fields in the row, column, and report filter areas inherit their names from the heading in the source data. Fields in the data section are given names such as Sum of Revenue. In some instances, you might prefer to print a different name in the pivot table. You might prefer Total Revenue instead of the default name. In these situations, the capability to change your field names comes in quite handy.

Although many of the names are inherited from headings in the original data set, when your data is from an external data source, you might not have control over field names. In these cases, you might want to change the names of the fields as well.

To change a field name in the values area, follow these steps:

1. Select a cell in the pivot table that contains the appropriate type of value. You might have a pivot table with both Sum of Quantity and Sum of Revenue in the values area. Choose a cell that contains a Sum of Revenue value.

2. On the Options tab, select the Field Settings icon from the Active Field group.

3. In the Data Field Settings dialog box, type a new name in the Custom Name field. You can enter any unique name you like, as shown in Figure 3.7.

> **NOTE**
> One common frustration occurs when you would like to rename Sum of Revenue to Revenue. The problem is that this name is not allowed because it is not unique; you already have a Revenue field in the source data. To work around this limitation, you can name the field and add a space to the end of the name. Excel considers "Revenue " (with a space) to be different from "Revenue" (with no space). Because this change is cosmetic, the readers of your spreadsheet do not notice the space after the name.

The new name appears in the pivot table. The name Revenue (with a space) is less awkward than the default Sum of Revenue.

Figure 3.7
The name typed in the Custom Name box appears in the pivot table. Although names should be unique, you can trick Excel into accepting a similar name by adding a space to the end of it.

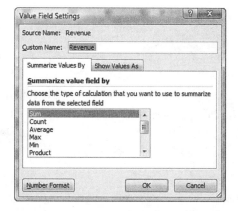

> **TIP**
> If you rename a field in the row, column, or filter areas, the dialog box that opens in response to Field Settings is called Value Field Settings instead of Data Field Settings. This dialog box has different options, but the Custom Name field is located in the same place, as shown in Figure 3.7.

Making Layout Changes

Excel 2010 offers three layout styles instead of the two styles available in legacy versions of Excel. The new style—Compact Layout—is promoted to be the default layout for your pivot tables. In addition, Excel 2010 offers the much-needed Repeat All Item Labels setting. Combined with the option to show subtotals at the top or bottom of the group and to toggle on or off blank rows between items, 16 different layout possibilities are available.

Layout changes are controlled in the Layout group of the Design tab, as shown in Figure 3.8. This group offers four icons:

- **Subtotals**—Moves subtotals to the top or bottom of each group or turns them off.

3

> **NOTE**
> For the statisticians in the audience, you would think that 3 layouts x 2 repeat options x 2 subtotal loca-
> tion options x 2 blank row options would be 24 layouts. However, choosing Repeat All Item Labels does
> not work with the Compact Form, eliminating four combinations. In addition, Subtotals at the Top of
> Each Group does not work with the Tabular layout, eliminating another four combinations.

Figure 3.8
The Layout group on the
Design tab offers differ-
ent layouts and options
for totals.

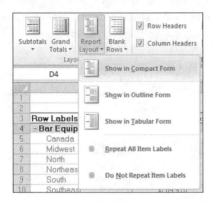

- **Grand Totals**—Turns the grand totals on or off for rows and columns.
- **Report Layout**—Uses the Compact, Outline, or Tabular forms. Offers an option to repeat item labels.
- **Blank Rows**—Inserts or removes blank lines after each group.

Using the New Compact Layout

By default, all new pivot tables use the compact layout shown in Figure 3.6. In this layout, multiple fields in the row area are stacked up in Column A. Note in the figure that the Chicago market and Midwest region are both in Column A.

The compact form is suited for using the Expand and Collapse icons. Select one of the product category cells such as Cell A4 and click the Collapse Entire Field icon on the Options tab. Excel hides all the detail below this field and shows only the product catego-ries, as shown in Figure 3.9.

After a field is collapsed, you can show detail for individual categories by using the plus icons in Column A, or you can click Expand Entire Field on the Options tab to see the detail again.

> **TIP**
> If you select a cell in the innermost row field and click Expand Entire Field on the Options tab, Excel
> displays the Show Detail dialog box, as shown in Figure 3.10, to enable you to add a new innermost
> row field.

Figure 3.9
Click the Collapse Entire
Field icon to hide levels
of detail.

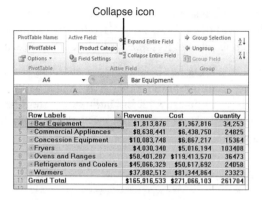

Collapse icon

Figure 3.10
When you attempt to
expand the innermost
field, Excel offers to add a
new innermost field.

Using the Outline Form Layout

When you select Design, Layout, Report Layout, Show in Outline Form, Excel fills Column
A with the outermost row field. Additional row fields occupy Columns B, C, and so on.

A dramatic improvement in Excel 2010 is the option for Repeat All Item Labels. In Figure
3.11, Cells A9:A16 repeat the label from A8. This is a great option if you later plan to reuse
the results of the pivot table in further analysis.

Figure 3.11 shows the pivot table in Outline form with labels repeated.

Figure 3.11
The Outline layout puts
each row field in a sepa-
rate column.

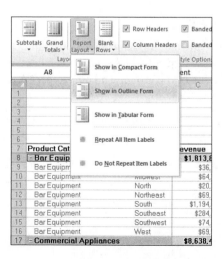

This layout is better suited if you plan to copy the values from the pivot table to a new location for further analysis. Although the Compact layout offers a clever approach by squeezing multiple fields in one column, it is not ideal for reusing the data later.

By default, both the Compact and Outline layouts put the subtotals at the top of each group. You can use the Subtotals drop-down on the Design tab to move the totals to the bottom of each group, as shown in Figure 3.12. In Outline view, this causes a not-really-useful heading row to appear at the top of each group. Cell A9 contains "Bar Equipment" without any additional data in the columns to the right.

Figure 3.12
With subtotals at the bottom of each group, the pivot table occupies several more rows.

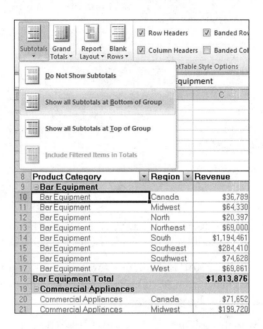

Using the Traditional Tabular Layout

Pivot table veterans will recognize the tabular layout shown in Figure 3.13. This layout is similar to the one that has been used in pivot tables since their invention. In this layout, the subtotals can never appear at the top of the group. The new Repeat All Item Labels works with this layout, as shown in Figure 3.13.

The tabular layout is the best layout if you expect to use the resulting summary data in a subsequent analysis.

Figure 3.13
The tabular layout is similar to pivot tables in legacy versions of Excel.

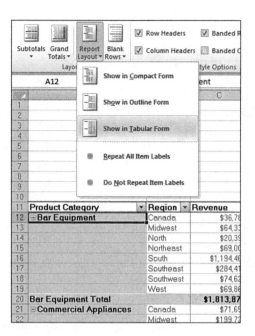

CASE STUDY   CONVERTING A PIVOT TABLE TO VALUES

Say that you want to summarize your data set to show revenue, cost, and quantity by Product Category and Region. Your goal is to export this data for use by another system.

The result in Figure 3.13 is close to the desired output, with a few exceptions:

- ■ The subtotals in Rows 20 and so on should be removed.
- ■ The blank cells in A13:A19, and so on should be filled in.
- ■ The grand totals should be removed.
- ■ The pivot table should be converted from a live pivot table to static values.

To make these changes, follow these steps:

1. Select any cell in the pivot table.
2. From the Design tab, select Grand Totals, Off for Rows and Columns.
3. Select Design, Subtotals, Do Not Show Subtotals.
4. Select Design, Report Layout, Repeat All Item Labels. The report is now a contiguous solid block of data, as shown in Figure 3.14.
5. Select one cell in the pivot table. Press Ctrl+* to select all the data in the pivot table.

Figure 3.14
The pivot table now contains a solid block of data..

A	B	C	D	E
Product Category	**Region**	**Revenue**	**Cost**	**Quantity**
⊟Bar Equipment	Canada	$36,789	$22,064	1122
Bar Equipment	Midwest	$64,330	$73,705	1659
Bar Equipment	North	$20,397	$11,799	639
Bar Equipment	Northeast	$69,000	$45,463	1823
Bar Equipment	South	$1,194,461	$914,990	19387
Bar Equipment	Southeast	$284,410	$214,350	4253
Bar Equipment	Southwest	$74,628	$39,889	2483
Bar Equipment	West	$69,861	$45,555	2887
⊟Commercial Appliances	Canada	$71,652	$54,588	350
Commercial Appliances	Midwest	$199,720	$131,755	527
Commercial Appliances	North	$44,041	$34,378	157
Commercial Appliances	Northeast	$285,407	$209,117	729
Commercial Appliances	South	$5,924,237	$4,468,122	16963

6. Press Ctrl+C to copy the data from the pivot table.

7. Select a blank section of a worksheet.

8. On the Home tab, open the Paste drop-down. Select Paste Values, as shown in Figure 3.15. Excel pastes a static copy of the report to the worksheet.

Figure 3.15
Paste Values to create a static version of the report.

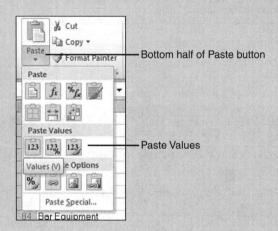

Bottom half of Paste button

Paste Values

The result is a solid block of summary data. These 300 cells are a summary of the 1.3 million cells in the original data set, but they also are suitable for exporting to other systems.

Controlling Blank Lines, Grand Totals, Subtotals, and Other Settings

Additional settings in the pivot table enable you to toggle various elements. For example, subtotals can be moved to the top or bottom of the group or turned off entirely. As noted previously, moving the subtotals to the top of the group saves a few rows in the pivot table. However, top subtotals are available only when the layout is set to Compact or Outline. Use the Subtotals icon on the Design tab to select the subtotals option. Figure 3.16 shows the subtotals at the top of each group.

Grand totals can appear at the bottom of each column and/or at the end of each row or they can be turned off altogether. Settings for grand totals appear in the Grand Totals drop-down of the Layout group on the Design tab. The wording in this drop-down is a bit confusing.

For example, if you would like a grand total column on the right side of the table, select only On for Rows. Keep in mind that even though it is a grand total column, each total is totaling a single row.

Similarly, to add a grand total row, select only On for Rows Columns. In this case, each individual grand total in the total row is totaling the cells in a column.

The Blank Rows drop-down enables you to insert blank lines between groups. In Figure 3.17, the blank lines in Row 13 appear because Insert Blank Line After Each Item was selected in the Blank Rows drop-down.

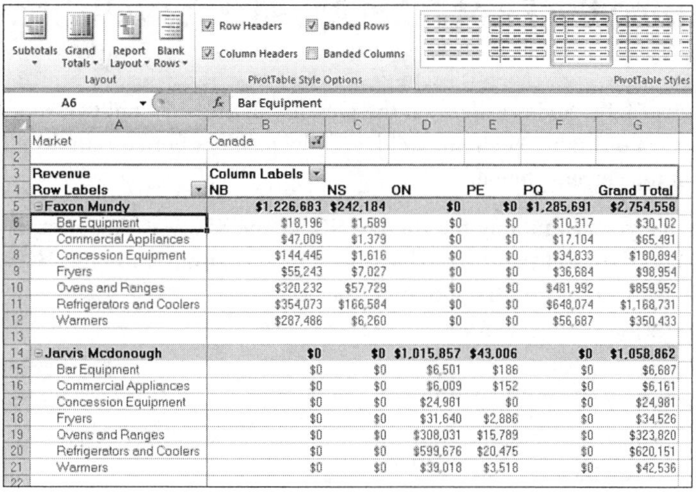

Revenue	Column Labels					
Row Labels	NB	NS	ON	PE	PQ	Grand Total
Faxon Mundy	$1,226,683	$242,184	$0	$0	$1,285,691	$2,754,558
Bar Equipment	$18,196	$1,589	$0	$0	$10,317	$30,102
Commercial Appliances	$47,009	$1,379	$0	$0	$17,104	$65,491
Concession Equipment	$144,445	$1,616	$0	$0	$34,833	$180,894
Fryers	$55,243	$7,027	$0	$0	$36,684	$98,954
Ovens and Ranges	$320,232	$57,729	$0	$0	$481,992	$859,952
Refrigerators and Coolers	$354,073	$166,584	$0	$0	$648,074	$1,168,731
Warmers	$287,486	$6,260	$0	$0	$56,687	$350,433
Jarvis Mcdonough	$0	$0	$1,015,857	$43,006	$0	$1,058,862
Bar Equipment	$0	$0	$6,501	$186	$0	$6,687
Commercial Appliances	$0	$0	$6,009	$152	$0	$6,161
Concession Equipment	$0	$0	$24,981	$0	$0	$24,981
Fryers	$0	$0	$31,640	$2,886	$0	$34,526
Ovens and Ranges	$0	$0	$308,031	$15,789	$0	$323,820
Refrigerators and Coolers	$0	$0	$599,676	$20,475	$0	$620,151
Warmers	$0	$0	$39,018	$3,518	$0	$42,536

Figure 3.16
Subtotals at the top, grand totals for the rows, and blank lines between groups are controlled through icons in the Layout group on the Design tab.

As you examine the pivot table in Figure 3.16, you might wonder why Column B is so much wider than Columns C, D, and E. The text Column Labels in B3 is causing Column B to be too wide. In addition, Row Labels in A4 often makes the column A wider than necessary. These labels were introduced in Excel 2007 to improve readability.

To remove these text entries, click the Field Headers icon in the Show/Hide group on the Options tab. This group also has icons to turn off the plus and minus buttons or to hide the PivotTable Field List. Figure 3.17 shows this section of the Ribbon and the pivot table with all three items turned off.

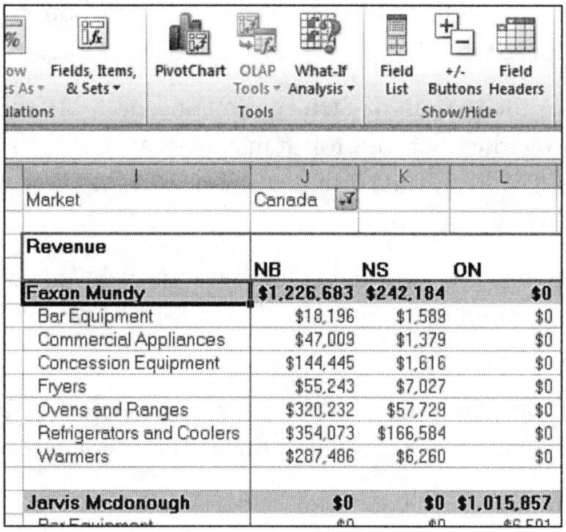

Figure 3.17
In Excel 2010, field headers serve little purpose.

Customizing the Pivot Table Appearance with Styles and Themes

The PivotTable Styles gallery on the Design tab offers 85 built-in styles. Grouped into 28 styles each of Light, Medium, and Dark, the gallery offers variations on the accent colors used in the current theme.

Note that you can modify the thumbnails for the 85 styles shown in the gallery by using the four check boxes in the PivotTable Style Options group. In Figure 3.18, the 85 styles are shown with all four of the option buttons cleared.

Figure 3.18
The 85 thumbnails
appear one way when no
style option check boxes
are selected.

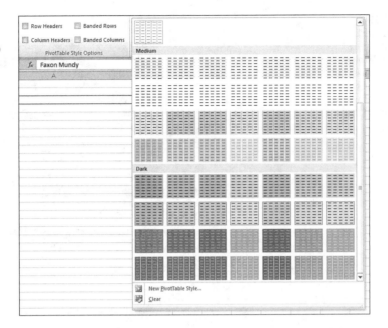

In Figure 3.19, the styles are shown with accents for row headers, column headers, and alternating colors in the columns.

The PivotTable Style Options group appears to the left of the PivotTable Styles gallery. If you want banded rows or columns, it is best to select the Banded Columns option before opening the gallery. Some of the 85 themes do not support banded columns or banded rows.

> **TIP**
>
> By selecting the Banded Columns check box prior to opening the gallery, you can see which styles support the banded columns. If the Banded Columns or Rows check box is selected and the thumbnail in the gallery does not show the effect, you know to avoid that style.

3

Figure 3.19
The 85 thumbnails
appear differently
with four style options
selected. You can see that
many of the styles do not
support banded columns,
even though this option
is selected.

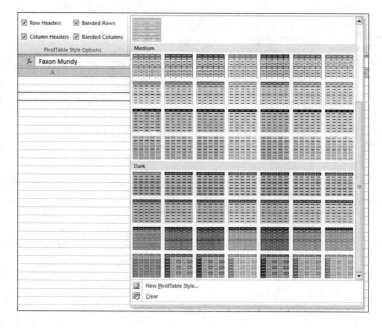

The Live Preview feature in Excel 2010 works in the styles gallery. As you hover your mouse cursor over style thumbnails, the worksheet shows a preview of the style.

Customizing a Style

You can create your own pivot table styles. The new styles are added to the gallery, which means they are available on every new pivot table created on your computer.

Say that you want to create a pivot table style in which the banded colors are two rows high. Follow these steps to create the new style:

1. Find an existing style in the PivotTable Styles gallery that supports banded rows. Right-click the style in the gallery and select Duplicate. Excel displays the Modify PivotTable Quick Style dialog box.

2. Choose a new name for the style. Excel initially appends a *2* to the existing style name, which means you have a name like PivotStyleMedium9 2.

3. In the Table Element list, click First Row Stripe. A new section called Stripe Size appears in the dialog box.

4. Select 2 from the Stripe Size drop-down, as shown in Figure 3.20.

5. If you want to change the stripe color, click the Format button. The Format Cells dialog box appears. Click the Fill tab, and then choose a fill color. Click OK to accept the color and return to the Modify PivotTable Quick Style dialog box.

6. In the Table Element List, click Second Row Stripe. Change the Stripe Size drop-down to 2.

Figure 3.20
Customize the style in the Modify Table Quick Style dialog box.

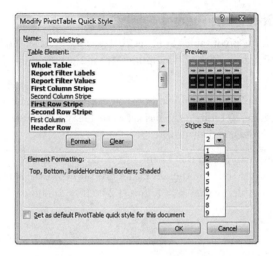

7. Click OK. Prepare to be disappointed that the change did not work. However, this is okay because you actually created a brand-new style when you modified table style Medium 9. The pivot table is still formatted in the original style.

8. Open the PivotTable Styles gallery. Notice that your new style is added to the top of the gallery in the Custom section. Select the new style to apply the formatting, as shown in Figure 3.21.

Figure 3.21
Your new style is available at the top of the gallery.

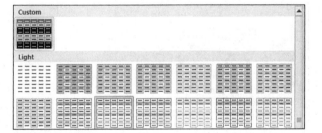

Choosing a Default Style for Future Pivot Tables

You can control which style is the default style to use for all future pivot tables on the computer. The default can either be one of the built-in styles or a new custom style that you modified.

In the PivotTable Styles gallery on the Design tab, right-click the style and select Set as Default.

Modifying Styles with Document Themes

The formatting options for pivot tables in Excel 2010 are impressive. The 84 styles, combined with eight combinations of the Style options, make for hundreds of possible format combinations.

In case you become tired of these combinations, you can visit the Themes drop-down on the Page Layout tab where 20 built-in themes are available. Each theme has a new combination of accent colors, fonts, and shape effects.

To change a document theme, open the Themes drop-down on the Page Layout tab. As you hover the mouse cursor over the themes in the drop-down, Live Preview shows you the colors and fonts in your table, as shown in Figure 3.22. Click a theme to select it.

Figure 3.22
Choose a document theme to modify the colors and fonts in the built-in styles.

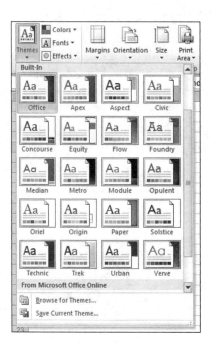

┌ **C A U T I O N** ───

Changing the theme affects the entire workbook. It changes the colors, fonts, and effects of all charts, shapes, tables, and pivot tables on all worksheets of the active workbook.

┌ **T I P** ──

Some of the themes have contemporary fonts. You can apply the colors from a new theme without changing the fonts in your document by using the Colors drop-down in the Themes group on the Page Layout tab.

Changing Summary Calculations

When creating your pivot table report, by default Excel summarizes your data by either counting or summing the items. Instead of Sum or Count, you might want to choose functions such as Min, Max, and Count Numeric. In all, 11 options are available. However, the common reason to change a summary calculation is that Excel incorrectly chose to count instead of sum your data.

Understanding Why One Blank Cell Causes a Count

If all the cells in a column contain numeric data, Excel chooses to sum. If just one cell is either blank or contains text, Excel chooses to count.

In Figure 3.23, the worksheet contains mostly numeric entries in Column M and a single blank cell in M2. The one blank cell is enough to cause Excel to count the data instead of summing.

Figure 3.23
The single blank cell in M2 causes problems in the default pivot table.

	K	L	M	N
1	Product Name	Quantity	Revenue	Cost
2	Pizza Humidified Merchandiser	1		$609
3	Cotton Candy Maker Stainless Ste	1	$824	$512
4	Gas Griddle 3 Burners	2	$1,892	$1,176
5	Open Top Fryer 15 Lb	1	$849	$528
6	Pizza Humidified Merchandiser	2	$1,960	$1,218
7	4 Qt. Cap. Batch Bow	1	$838	$521
8	Built-In Warming Display 1270W	1	$826	$513
9	Commercial Microwave Oven 120	2	$1,688	$1,049

In Excel 2010, the first clue that you have a problem appears when you select the check box for Revenue in the Fields section of the PivotTable Field List. If Excel moves the Revenue field to the Row Labels drop zone, you know that Excel considers the field to be text instead of numeric.

Be vigilant while dragging fields into the Values drop zone. If a calculation appears to be dramatically low, check to see if the field name reads Count of Revenue instead of Sum of Revenue. When you create the pivot table in Figure 3.24, you should notice that your company has only $86 in revenue instead of millions. This should be a hint that the heading in B3 reads Count of Revenue instead of Sum of Revenue. In fact, 86 is the number of records in the data set.

Figure 3.24
Your revenue numbers look anemic. Notice in Cell B3 that Excel chose to count instead of sum the revenue. This often happens if you inadvertently have one blank cell in your Revenue column.

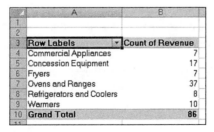

	A	B
1		
2		
3	Row Labels	Count of Revenue
4	Commercial Appliances	7
5	Concession Equipment	17
6	Fryers	7
7	Ovens and Ranges	37
8	Refrigerators and Coolers	8
9	Warmers	10
10	Grand Total	86
11		

To override the incorrect Count calculation, choose one cell in the Revenue column. Open the Summarize Values By drop-down in the Options tab, and then select Sum instead of Count, as shown in Figure 3.25.

Figure 3.25
Change the function from Count to Sum in the Summarize Values By drop-down.

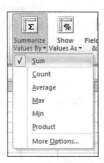

Using Functions Other Than Count or Sum

Excel offers six functions in the drop-down, plus five more options when you select More Options. The options available are as follows:

- **Sum**—Provides a total of all numeric data.

- **Count**—Counts all cells, including numeric, text, and error cells. This is equivalent to the Excel function =COUNTA().

- **Average**—Provides an average.

- **Max**—Shows the largest value.

- **Min**—Shows the smallest value.

- **Product**—Multiplies all the cells together. For example, if your data set has cells with values of 3, 4, and 5, the product would be 60.

- **Count Nums**—Counts only the numeric cells. This is equivalent to the Excel function =COUNT().

- **StdDev and StdDevP**—Calculate the standard deviation. Use StdDevP if your data set contains the complete population. Use StdDev if your data set contains a sample of the population.

- **Var and VarP**—Calculates the statistical variance. Use VarP if your data contains a complete population. If your data contains only a sampling of the complete population, use Var to estimate the variance.

> **NOTE** Standard deviations explain how tightly results are grouped around the mean.

Adding and Removing Subtotals

Subtotals are an essential feature of pivot table reporting. Sometimes you might want to suppress the display of subtotals, and other times you might want to show more than one subtotal per field.

Suppress Subtotals When You Have Many Row Fields

When you have many row fields in your report, subtotals can mire your view. For example, in Figure 3.26 there is no need to show subtotals for each Market because there is only one account manager for each Market.

Figure 3.26
Sometimes you do not need subtotals at every level.

	A	B	C	D
1				
2				
3	Region	Market	Account Manager	Sum of Revenue
4	⊟Midwest	⊟Chicago	Kirstie Paulson	402,698
5	Midwest	Chicago Total		402,698
6	Midwest	⊟Kansas City	Megan Winston	2,299,762
7	Midwest	Kansas City Total		2,299,762
8	Midwest	⊟Omaha	Austen Cope	2,008,287
9	Midwest	Omaha Total		2,008,287
10	Midwest	⊟Tulsa	Maleah Menard	2,649,682
11	Midwest	Tulsa Total		2,649,682
12	Midwest Total			7,360,429
13	⊟North	⊟Dakotas	Annabel Locklear	572,273
14	North	Dakotas Total		572,273

To remove subtotals for the Market field, click the Market field in the drop zone section of the PivotTable Field List. Select Field Settings. In the Field Settings dialog box, select None under Subtotals, as shown in Figure 3.27.

Figure 3.27
Select None to remove subtotals at the Market level.

Notice that the report in Figure 3.28 is easier on the eyes.

> **NOTE** If you want to suppress the subtotals for all the row fields, it is easier to select Design, Layout, Subtotals, Do Not Show Subtotals.

Figure 3.28
After specifying None for the Market, the report has a cleaner look.

	A	B	C	D
1				
2				
3	Region	Market	Account Manager	Sum of Revenue
4	Midwest	Chicago	Kirstie Paulson	402,698
5	Midwest	Kansas City	Megan Winston	2,299,762
6	Midwest	Omaha	Austen Cope	2,008,287
7	Midwest	Tulsa	Maleah Menard	2,649,682
8	Midwest Total			7,360,429
9	North	Dakotas	Annabel Locklear	572,273
10	North	Great Lakes	Norman Stackhouse	1,844,895
11	North Total			2,417,168

Adding Multiple Subtotals for One Field

You can add customized subtotals to a row or column label field. Select the Region field in the drop zone of the PivotTable Field List and select Field Settings.

In the Field Settings dialog box, select Custom and select the types of subtotals you would like to see. The dialog box in Figure 3.29 shows five custom subtotals selected for the Region field.

Figure 3.29
By selecting the Custom option in the Subtotals section, you can specify multiple subtotals for one field.

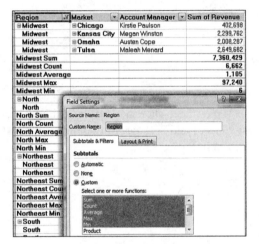

Using Running Total, % of, Rank Options

In the previous section, you learned how to choose from 11 functions such as Sum, Average, and Count. Another dimension to pivot table calculations offers Running Total In, % of Total, Rank options, and so on.

In Excel 2010, Microsoft expanded the options from 9 to 15 that include the badly needed % Running Total In, % of Parent options, and Rank options.

The pivot table in Figure 3.30 includes the Revenue column eight times. Column C shows revenue with no calculations. Columns D through J show other calculations available in the Show Values As drop-down.

Figure 3.30
The Show Values As options offer many different ways to show a value. Columns C:J each shows a different calculation of Revenue.

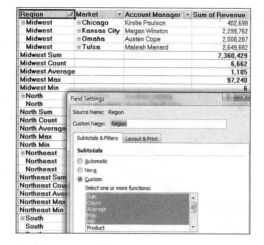

> **NOTE**
> To build the report in Figure 3.30, drag the Revenue field to the Values drop zone many times. Edit the Field Settings for each column one at a time to change the calculation.

As in previous versions of Excel, some of the calculations require no additional information. Five calculations require the definition of a base field. Three calculations require specifying both a base field and a base item.

Table 3.1 summarizes the Show Values As options.

Table 3.1   Calculations in Show Value As

Description	Change in Excel 2010	Additional Required Information	Description
No Calculation	Renamed from Normal	None	
% of Grand Total	Renamed from % of Total	None	Shows percentages so all the detail cells in the pivot table total 100 percent.
% of Column Total	Renamed from % of Column	None	Shows percentages that total up and down the pivot table to 100 percent.
% of Row Total	Renamed from % of Row	None	Shows percentages that total across the pivot table to 100 percent.
% of Parent Row Total	New in 2010	None	With multiple row fields, shows a row's percentage of the parent item's total row.

3

Description	Change in Excel 2010	Additional Required Information	Description
% of Parent Column Total	New in 2010	None	With multiple column fields, shows a column's percentage of the parent column's total.
Index	No Change	None	Calculates the relative importance of items.
% of Parent Total	New in 2010	Base Field Only	With multiple row and/or column fields, calculates a cell's percent of the parent item's total.
Running Total In	No Change	Base Field Only	Calculates a running total.
% Running Total In	New in 2010	Base Field Only	Calculates a running total as a percentage of the total.
Rank Smallest to Largest	New in 2010	Base Field Only	Provides a numeric rank, with 1 as the smallest item.
Rank Largest to Smallest	New in 2010	Base Field Only	Provides a numeric rank, with 1 as the largest item.
% of	No Change	Base Field and Base Item	Expresses the values for one item as a percentage of another item.
Difference From	No Change	Base Field and Base Item	Shows the difference of one item compared to another item or to the previous item.
% Difference From	No Change	Base Field and Base Item	Shows the percent difference of one item compared to another item or to the previous item.

In legacy versions of Excel, these options were found on the Show Values As tab of the Value Field Settings dialog. Although these choices were somewhat hidden, once you found them, the dialog offered all the settings required to define the calculation in a single place. After choosing an option from the initial drop-down, the Base Field and/or Base Item lists would be enabled or disabled as appropriate (see Figure 3.31). You could also rename the field in this dialog.

> **NOTE**
> When you use an option from the Show Data As drop-down list, Excel does not change the headings in any way to indicate that the data is in something other than normal view. Therefore, it is helpful to add a title manually above the pivot table to inform the readers of what they are looking at.

In Excel 2010, Microsoft promoted these choices to the Show Values As drop-down on the Options tab. More people discover the settings here instead of the obscure location in legacy versions of Excel. However, this drop-down is missing options to select a base field, base item, and name the field (see Figure 3.32).

Figure 3.31
You can still access the settings on this second tab of the Value Field Settings dialog.

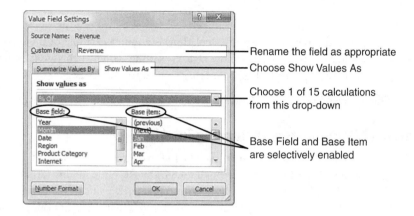

Figure 3.32
Alternatively, you can change the calculation using this new drop-down in Excel 2010.

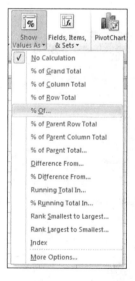

If you choose one of the calculations that require a base field and/or base item, Excel 2010 displays a new dialog box where you can choose one or both fields (see Figure 3.33).

You will still probably want to rename the column to indicate the calculation that is used. To do this, visit the Field Settings dialog to rename the column, and then type a new value in the Active Field box on the Options tab or type a new name directly in the heading cell.

Figure 3.33
If required, choose a base field and possibly a base item.

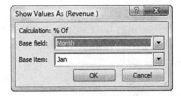

The capability to create custom calculations is another example of the unique flexibility of pivot table reports. With the Show Data As setting, you can change the calculation for a particular data field to be based on other cells in the values area.

The following sections illustrate a number of Show Values As options.

Tracking YTD Numbers with Running Total In

If you need to compare a year-to-date (YTD) total revenue by month, you can do so with the Running Total In option. In Figure 3.34, the Revenue field is set up to show a Running Total In with a base field of Month. With this report, you can see that the company sold a total of $8.7 million through March in 2010. Note that the YTD calculation starts over in Row 17 for the year 2011.

Figure 3.34
The Running Total In option is helpful for calculating YTD totals.

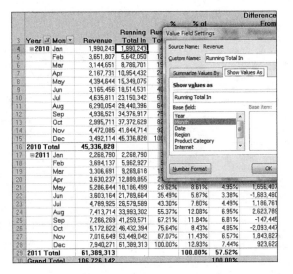

Tracking Percent of Running Total

To calculate a running percent of the total, you can use the new % Running Total In option. To use this option, select a base field. In Figure 3.35, you can see that only 40.84 percent of the 2010 revenue had been shipped by the end of June.

Figure 3.35
A new option in Excel 2010 is calculating a % Running Total In.

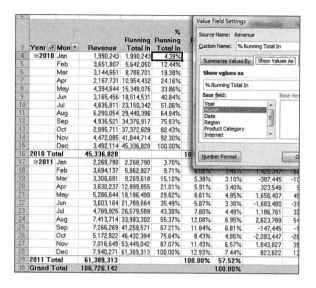

Tracking Percent of Parent Item

Legacy versions of Excel offered a setting for Percentage of Column. As you can see in cell G5 of Figure 3.36, this calculation would say that the February 2010 sales of $3,651,807 represent 3.42 percent of the total revenue shown in Row 30.

People frequently wrote in to the MrExcel.com message board to ask how they could show February 2010 sales as a percentage of the 2010 total. This was impossible in legacy versions of Excel. However, Excel 2010 offers three % of Parent items to enable these calculations. In Figure 3.36, Column F shows a calculation of each month as a percentage of the year. In this case, the February 2010 sales represent 8.05 percent of the total 2010 sales, as shown in Cell F5.

Figure 3.36
A new option in Excel 2010 enables you to calculate a % of the Parent Row.

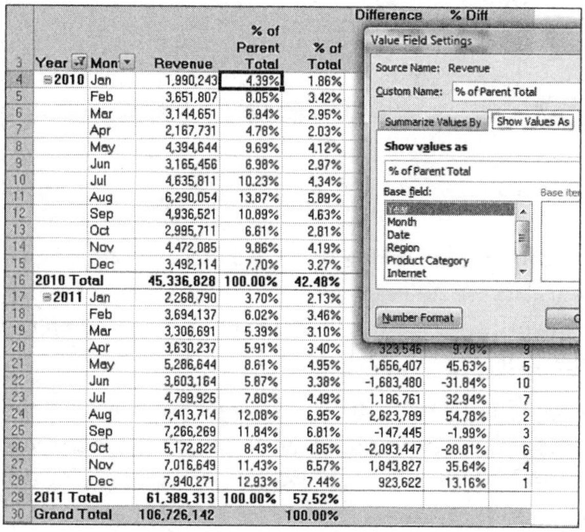

To see a demo of Percent of Parent Item, search for "Pivot Table Data Crunching 3" at YouTube.

Display Change from a Previous Field

The Difference From options require you to specify a base field and a base item. I nearly always choose a base item (Previous) to show the change from a previous period.

In Figure 3.37, Column H is set up to calculate a difference from the previous month. The $3.6 million in February 2010 is $1.6 million more than the $1.99 million in January.

Column I shows a percentage difference from the previous month. The $3.6 million in February 2010 is 83.49 percent more than January.

Column J shows the result of changing the base field from Month to Year. In J4:J12, none of the values for 2010 is shown because there was no data for 2009. The 14 percent in Cell J17 shows that January 2011 is up 14 percent over January 2010.

Figure 3.37
The Difference From options allows you to compare two different time periods.

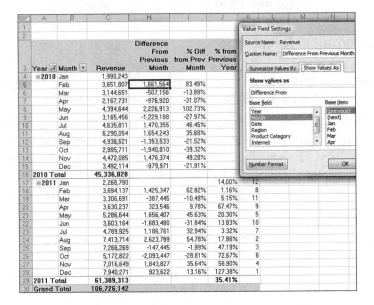

Showing Rank

Also new in Excel 2010 are the ranking options. These options assign a rank of 1, 2, 3 to various rows in your data set. You can choose if the largest number or the smallest number should receive a rank of 1. In Figure 3.38, the Southwest moved up from fifth to third in 2010. However, they fell back to fourth in 2011 and 2012.

These new rank options in Excel 2010 show pivot tables have a strange way of dealing with ties. It is strange because it does not match any of the methods already established by the Excel functions =RANK(), =RANK.AVG(), or =RANK.EQ().

Figure 3.38
The Rank options are new in Excel 2010.

For example, if the top two sales reps have a tie, they are both assigned a rank of 1, while the third sales rep is assigned a rank of 2.

Figure 3.39 compares the pivot table calculation of Rank to the three Excel ranking functons.

Figure 3.39
While in theory ties are rare, the pivot table introduces another way to deal with ties.

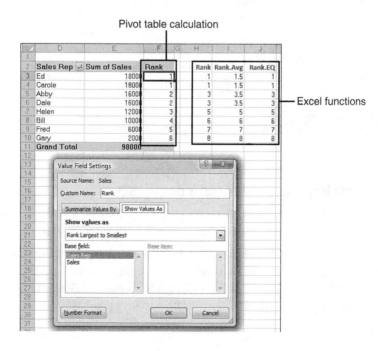

> **NOTE** I really can't complain about this new Rank method because none of the existing RANK functions calculates RANK the way that I would prefer it to be calculated. So, this new calculation is as controversial as any other rank calculations.

Using % of to Compare One Line to Another Line

The % Of option enables you to compare one item to another item. This comparison might be relevant if you want to show each product line compared to your core product line. For example, you can set up a pivot table that compares each product line to Ovens and Ranges revenue. The result is shown in Figure 3.40.

Figure 3.40
This report is created using the % Of option with Ovens and Ranges as the base item.

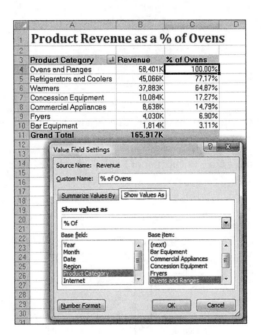

Track Relative Importance with the Index Option

The final option, Index, creates a somewhat obscure calculation. Microsoft claims that this calculation describes the relative importance of a cell within a column.

Consider the normal data at the top of Figure 3.41. To calculate the index for Georgia Peaches, Excel first calculates Georgia Peaches x Grand Total Sales using $180 x $847. Next, Excel calculates Georgia Sales x Peach Sales using $210 x $285. It then divides the first result by the second result to calculate a relative importance index of 2.55.

Figure 3.41
Using the Index function, Excel shows that peach sales are more important in Georgia than in California or Ohio.

Sum of Sales	State			
Crop	Calif	Georgia	Ohio	Grand Total
Apple	100	10	30	140
Banana	200	10	1	211
Kiwi	200	10	1	211
Peach	100	180	5	285
Grand Total	600	210	37	847

Index of Sales	State			
Crop	Calif	Georgia	Ohio	Grand Total
Apple	1.01	0.29	4.91	1.00
Banana	1.34	0.19	0.11	1.00
Kiwi	1.34	0.19	0.11	1.00
Peach	0.50	2.55	0.40	1.00
Grand Total	1.00	1.00	1.00	1.00

The index report shown at the bottom of Figure 3.41 explains that with a relative importance index of 2.55, peaches are more important to Georgia than they are to California, which has a relative importance index of 0.50.

In other words, even though California sold almost as many peaches as Georgia did, a peach predator would be more devastating to Georgia's overall fruit industry.

CASE STUDY HANDLING IMPOSSIBLE CALCULATIONS WITH GETPIVOTDATA

Even with the improved Show Values As calculations in Excel 2010, there are times when you simply cannot get the data needed to produce a certain report. When this occurs, you can still use a live pivot table as an intermediate step toward producing your report.

For example, say that you want to show sales for the four months ending with February 2012 and compare those sales to the same period from the previous period. This requires you to get data from January and February of 2012; January, February, November, and December of 2011; and November and December of 2010. This is beyond the capability of pivot tables.

Follow these steps to produce a solution.

1. Build a pivot table showing sales for all months and years, as shown in Figure 3.42.

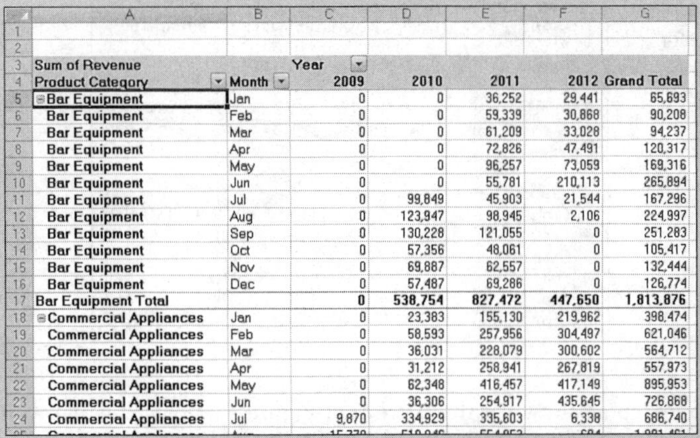

Figure 3.42
Build an ugly pivot table with every possible calculation.

	A	B	C	D	E	F	G
1							
2							
3	Sum of Revenue		Year				
4	Product Category	Month	2009	2010	2011	2012	Grand Total
5	Bar Equipment	Jan	0	0	36,252	29,441	65,693
6	Bar Equipment	Feb	0	0	59,339	30,868	90,208
7	Bar Equipment	Mar	0	0	61,209	33,028	94,237
8	Bar Equipment	Apr	0	0	72,826	47,491	120,317
9	Bar Equipment	May	0	0	96,257	73,059	169,316
10	Bar Equipment	Jun	0	0	55,781	210,113	265,894
11	Bar Equipment	Jul	0	99,849	45,903	21,544	167,296
12	Bar Equipment	Aug	0	123,947	98,945	2,106	224,997
13	Bar Equipment	Sep	0	130,228	121,055	0	251,283
14	Bar Equipment	Oct	0	57,356	48,061	0	105,417
15	Bar Equipment	Nov	0	69,887	62,557	0	132,444
16	Bar Equipment	Dec	0	57,487	69,286	0	126,774
17	Bar Equipment Total		0	538,754	827,472	447,650	1,813,876
18	Commercial Appliances	Jan	0	23,383	155,130	219,962	398,474
19	Commercial Appliances	Feb	0	58,593	257,956	304,497	621,046
20	Commercial Appliances	Mar	0	36,031	228,079	300,602	564,712
21	Commercial Appliances	Apr	0	31,212	258,941	267,819	557,973
22	Commercial Appliances	May	0	62,348	416,457	417,149	895,953
23	Commercial Appliances	Jun	0	36,306	254,917	435,645	726,868
24	Commercial Appliances	Jul	9,870	334,929	335,603	6,338	686,740

2. While you are inside the pivot table, go to the Options tab. On the left side of the Ribbon is an Options button that has a drop-down next to the button. Open the Options drop-down. Verify that the Generate GetPivotData option is selected.

3. On another worksheet, build a formatted report. Make sure that you have headings to identify the year, product, and month. Add formulas to calculate totals and the percentage growth. Leave all the other data points blank.

4. Select the first data point in the report worksheet. As shown in Figure 3.43, this is Cell C4, which should return November 2011 sales of Commercial Appliance.

5. Type an equal sign (=). Click the pivot table worksheet tab to move to that worksheet. Scroll and find the November 2011 sales for Commercial Appliances. Click that cell and press Enter. You might expect a formula such as =CaseStudyPivot!E28. However, Excel inserts the somewhat bizarre formula of =GETPIVOTDATA(...), as shown in the formula bar in Figure 3.43.

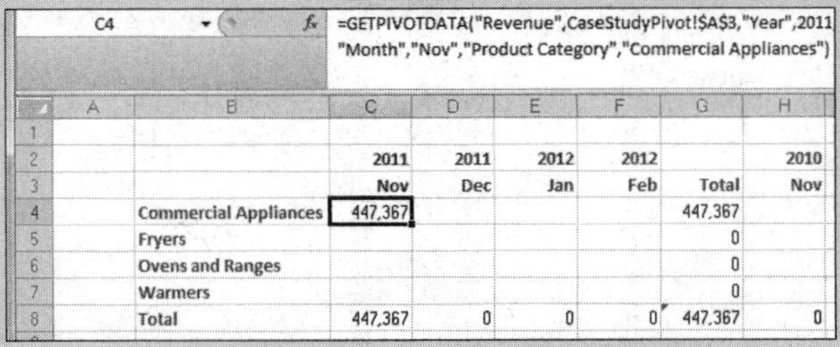

Figure 3.43
Build a formula by typing an equal sign and clicking on the correct cell in the pivot table.

C4   =GETPIVOTDATA("Revenue",CaseStudyPivot!$A$3,"Year",2011
"Month","Nov","Product Category","Commercial Appliances")

	A	B	C	D	E	F	G	H
1								
2			2011	2011	2012	2012		2010
3			Nov	Dec	Jan	Feb	Total	Nov
4		Commercial Appliances	447,367				447,367	
5		Fryers					0	
6		Ovens and Ranges					0	
7		Warmers					0	
8		Total	447,367	0	0	0	447,367	0

The GETPIVOTDATA function that you created in step 5 is always hard-coded to return values from one particular cell of the pivot table. Many people see these functions, but not many people take the time to understand the syntax of the function.

=GETPIVOTDATA("Revenue"—Indicates that you want to return a value from the Revenue field.

CaseStudyPivot!$A$3—Identifies which pivot table to use by specifying any cell within the pivot table. Note that Excel always points to the top left cell of the pivot table.

"Year", 2011—The remaining pairs of arguments consist of a field name and a value to be returned for that value. The second of these arguments is always hard-coded. Changing those arguments to be parameterized is the key to successful use of GETPIVOTDATA.

6. Edit the GetPivotData formula. Change 2011 to point to Cell C$2. Change "Nov" to point to Cell C$3. Change "Commercial Appliances" to point to Cell $B4. Apply a custom number format of #,##0,K. As you can see in Figure 3.44, the result does not change, but you have created a formula that can be copied.

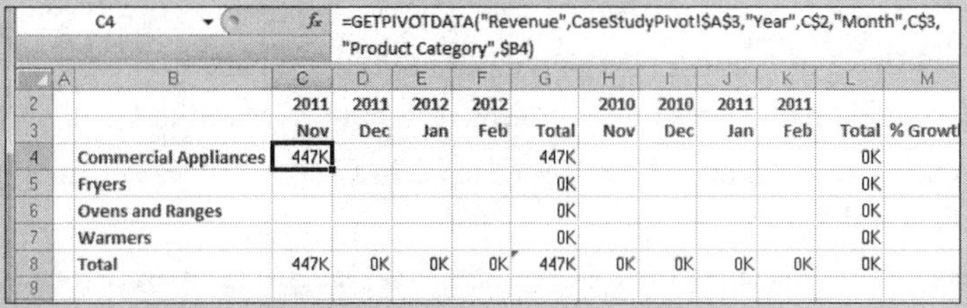

C4 =GETPIVOTDATA("Revenue",CaseStudyPivot!$A$3,"Year",C$2,"Month",C$3,"Product Category",$B4)

	A	B	C	D	E	F	G	H	I	J	K	L	M
2			2011	2011	2012	2012		2010	2010	2011	2011		
3			Nov	Dec	Jan	Feb	Total	Nov	Dec	Jan	Feb	Total	% Growt
4		Commercial Appliances	447K				447K					0K	
5		Fryers					0K					0K	
6		Ovens and Ranges					0K					0K	
7		Warmers					0K					0K	
8		Total	447K	0K	0K	0K	447K	0K	0K	0K	0K	0K	
9													

Figure 3.44
Edit the GETPIVOTDATA function to use parameters in your report.

7. Copy the GETPIVOTDATA formula to all the other core data points in the report.

You now have a nicely formatted report that is drawing results from a live pivot table (see Figure 3.45).

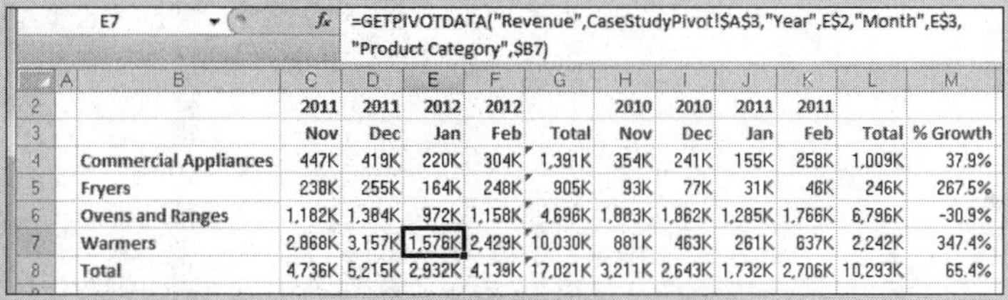

E7 =GETPIVOTDATA("Revenue",CaseStudyPivot!$A$3,"Year",E$2,"Month",E$3,"Product Category",$B7)

	A	B	C	D	E	F	G	H	I	J	K	L	M
2			2011	2011	2012	2012		2010	2010	2011	2011		
3			Nov	Dec	Jan	Feb	Total	Nov	Dec	Jan	Feb	Total	% Growth
4		Commercial Appliances	447K	419K	220K	304K	1,391K	354K	241K	155K	258K	1,009K	37.9%
5		Fryers	238K	255K	164K	248K	905K	93K	77K	31K	46K	246K	267.5%
6		Ovens and Ranges	1,182K	1,384K	972K	1,158K	4,696K	1,883K	1,862K	1,285K	1,766K	6,796K	-30.9%
7		Warmers	2,868K	3,157K	1,576K	2,429K	10,030K	881K	463K	261K	637K	2,242K	347.4%
8		Total	4,736K	5,215K	2,932K	4,139K	17,021K	3,211K	2,643K	1,732K	2,706K	10,293K	65.4%

Figure 3.45
This report is drawing figures from the underlying pivot table.

Even though this report takes a bit more time to build, it is an amazingly powerful concept. The following list includes some advantages of using this report.

- If the underlying data changes, simply refresh the pivot table and the report is accurate.
- Pivot tables frequently lose formatting when you refresh them. However, because this formatted report is not a pivot table, you do not have to worry about constantly reformatting the report.
- If you want to insert a blank column between F and G, you are more than welcome to do so. However, you cannot do that in a regular pivot table.
- While people outside of Microsoft generally despise GETPIVOTDATA, internal employees at Microsoft in all departments use this technique all the time.

However, be aware of the following disadvantages that can create problems:

■ If someone changes the name of the Commercial Appliances category in this report to a new name, you also have to edit the label in Cell B4 or the report will not get the data associated with the new name.

■ GetPivotData is tougher to use with OLAP or PowerPivot pivot tables. In this case, you have to resort to cube functions to create a similar report.

Next Steps

Note that the following pivot table customizations are covered in subsequent chapters:

■ Sorting a pivot table is covered in Chapter 4, "Grouping, Sorting, and Filtering Pivot Data."

■ Filtering records in a pivot table is covered in Chapter 4.

■ Grouping daily dates up to months or years is covered in Chapter 4.

■ Adding new calculated fields is covered in Chapter 5, "Performing Calculations Within Pivot Tables."

■ Using data visualizations and conditional formatting in a pivot table is covered in Chapter 4.

In addition, we discuss the filtering, sorting, and data visualization options available in Excel 2010 in Chapter 4. Using these tools is a great way to focus your pivot table on the largest drivers of success for your business.

Grouping, Sorting, and Filtering Pivot Data

4

Some of the excellent new features that Microsoft added to pivot tables filtering in Excel 2010 include the following:

- Slicers provide a visual way to filter data set. Slicers are far superior to the old Page Filter technology. Yes, they can take up a lot more real estate, but they also vastly improve the multifiltering technology introduced in Excel 2007.

- Sets will someday make an impressive grouping feature in pivot tables. Unfortunately, in Excel 2010, they are limited to OLAP and PowerPivot data sets.

NOTE

Are Sets good enough in Excel 2010 that you should convert your Excel data set to a PowerPivot data set? Read Chapter 10, "Mashing Up Data with PowerPivot" to find out.

These improvements continue the changes to pivot tables that were introduced in Excel 2007:

- Whenever Mike or Bill entertains audiences at a seminar, he could be sure to "wow" the audience with obscure features like the Top 10 AutoShow feature that was buried four menus deep in legacy versions of Excel. In Excel 2007, Microsoft exposed the AutoSort and AutoShow options so they are now just two clicks away from any pivot table.

- Grouping features went from being buried three levels deep in legacy version of Excel to being a button on the Ribbon in Excel 2007.

- Excel 2007 added filtering options for row and column fields that include context-sensitive filters for dates, text, and values.

The remainder of this chapter covers grouping, sorting, filtering, data visualizations, and pivot table options.

Grouping Pivot Fields

Although most of your summarization and calculation needs can be accomplished with standard pivot table settings, you might want reports to be summarized even further in special situations.

For example, transactional data is typically stored with a transaction date. You commonly want to report this data by month, quarter, or year. The Group option provides a straightforward way for you to consolidate transactional dates into a larger group such as month or quarter. Then you can summarize the data in those groups just as you would with any other field in your pivot table.

In the next section, you learn that grouping is not limited to date fields. In fact, you can also group nondate fields to consolidate specific pivot items into a single item.

Grouping Date Fields

4

Figure 4.1 shows a pivot report by date. With two years of transactional data, the report spans more than 500 columns. These columns are a summary of the original 50,563 rows, but managers often want detail by month instead of detail by day.

Excel provides a straightforward way to group date fields. Select any date heading such as Cell B4 in Figure 4.1. On the Options tab, click Group Field in the Group option.

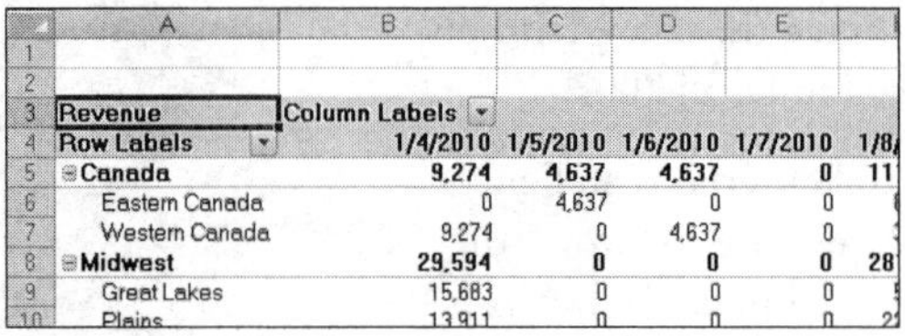

	A	B	C	D	E	
1						
2						
3	Revenue	Column Labels				
4	Row Labels	1/4/2010	1/5/2010	1/6/2010	1/7/2010	1/8/
5	Canada	9,274	4,637	4,637	0	11
6	Eastern Canada	0	4,637	0	0	
7	Western Canada	9,274	0	4,637	0	
8	Midwest	29,594	0	0	0	28
9	Great Lakes	15,683	0	0	0	
10	Plains	13,911	0	0	0	

Figure 4.1
When reported by day, the summary report spans more than 500 columns. It would be meaningful to report by month, quarter, and/or year instead.

When your field contains date information, the Grouping dialog box appears. By default, the Months option is selected. You have choices to group by Seconds, Minutes, Hours, Days, Months, Quarters, and Years. It is possible, and usually advisable, to select more than one field in the Grouping dialog box. In this case, select Months, Quarters, and Years, as shown in Figure 4.2.

There are several interesting points to note about the resulting pivot table. First, notice that Quarters and Years have been added to your Field List. Don't let this fool you. Your source data is not changed to include these new fields, Instead, these fields are now part of your pivot cache in memory. Another interesting point is that, by default, the Years and Quarters

Figure 4.2
Business users of Excel usually group by months, quarters, and years.

fields are automatically added to the same area as the original date field in the pivot table layout, as shown in Figure 4.3.

Figure 4.3
By default, Excel adds the new grouped date fields to your pivot table layout.

	A	B	C	D	E
1					
2					
3	Revenue	Column Labels			
4		⊟2010			
5		⊟Qtr1			⊟Qtr2
6	Row Labels	Jan	Feb	Mar	Apr
7	⊟Canada	183,211	647,545	418,436	158,31
8	Eastern Canada	109,670	527,968	133,457	60,3
9	Western Canada	73,541	119,578	284,979	98,0
10	⊟Midwest	435,891	1,348,312	537,623	583,25
11	Great Lakes	156,309	638,261	280,323	168,5

Including Years When Grouping by Months

Although this point is not immediately obvious, it is important to understand that if you group a date field by month, you also need to include the year in the grouping.

Examine the pivot table shown in Figure 4.4. This table has a date field that has been grouped by month and year. The months in Column A use the generic abbreviations Jan, Feb, and so on. The sales for January 2010 are $1,990,243.

Figure 4.4
This table has a date field that is grouped by both month and year.

Revenue	Column Labels		
Row Labels	2010	2011	Grand Total
Jan	1,990,243	2,222,696	4,212,939
Feb	3,651,807	3,694,137	7,345,944
Mar	3,144,651	3,296,007	6,440,658
Apr	2,212,360	3,640,921	5,853,281
May	4,350,015	5,244,399	9,594,414
Jun	3,165,456	3,619,024	6,784,480
Jul	4,664,039	4,746,256	9,410,295
Aug	6,261,826	7,427,560	13,689,386
Sep	4,936,521	7,359,662	12,296,183
Oct	2,995,711	5,108,017	8,103,729
Nov	4,472,085	6,988,348	11,460,433
Dec	3,538,208	7,996,192	11,534,400
Grand Total	45,382,922	61,343,219	106,726,142

However, if you choose to group the date field only by month, Excel continues to report the date field using the generic Jan abbreviation. The problem is that dates from January 2010 and January 2011 are both rolled up and reported together as Jan.

Having a report that totals Jan 2010 and Jan 2011 might be useful only if you are performing a seasonality analysis. Under any other circumstance, the report of $4,212,939 in January sales is too ambiguous and is likely to be interpreted wrong. To avoid ambiguous reports like the one shown in Figure 4.5, always include a year in the Group dialog box when you are grouping by month.

Figure 4.5

If you fail to include the Year field in the grouping, the report mixes sales from Jan 2010 and Jan 2011 in the same number.

Row Labels	Revenue
Jan	4,212,939
Feb	7,345,944
Mar	6,440,658
Apr	5,853,281
May	9,594,414
Jun	6,784,480
Jul	9,410,295
Aug	13,689,386
Sep	12,296,183
Oct	8,103,729
Nov	11,460,433
Dec	11,534,400
Grand Total	106,726,142

Grouping Date Fields by Week

The Grouping dialog box offers choices to group by Second, Minute, Hour, Day, Month, Quarter, or Year. It is also possible to group on a weekly or biweekly basis.

The first step is to find either a paper calendar or an electronic calendar, such as the Calendar feature in Outlook, for the year in question. If your data starts on January 4, 2010, it is helpful to know that January 4 was a Monday that year. You need to decide if weeks should start on Sunday or Monday or any other day. For example, you can check the paper or electronic calendar to learn that the nearest starting Sunday is January 3, 2010.

Select any date heading in your pivot table. Then select Group Field from the Options tab. In the Grouping dialog box, clear all the By options and select only the Days field. This enables the spin button for Number of Days. To produce a report by week, increase the number of days from 1 to 7.

Next, you need to set up the Starting At date. If you were to accept the default of starting at January 4, 2010, all your weekly periods would run from Monday through Sunday. By checking a calendar before you begin, you know that you want the first group to start on January 3, 2010. Change this setting as shown in Figure 4.6.

The result is a report showing sales by week, as shown in Figure 4.7.

Figure 4.6
The key to accessing the Number of Days spin button is to select only Days from the By field.

Figure 4.7
You have produced a report showing sales by week.

	A	B
1		
2		
3	**Row Labels** ▼	**Revenue**
4	1/3/2010 - 1/9/2010	1,428,386
5	1/10/2010 - 1/16/2010	147,611
6	1/17/2010 - 1/23/2010	220,547
7	1/24/2010 - 1/30/2010	193,699
8	1/31/2010 - 2/6/2010	148,532
9	2/7/2010 - 2/13/2010	3,182,441
10	2/14/2010 - 2/20/2010	206,804
11	2/21/2010 - 2/27/2010	114,939

> **CAUTION**
>
> If you choose to group by week, none of the other grouping options can be selected. You cannot group this or any other field by month or quarter.

Grouping Two Date Fields in One Report

When you group a date field by months and years, Excel repurposes the original date field to show months and adds a new field to show years. The new field is called *Years*. This is simple enough if you have only one date field in the report.

However, if you need to produce a report that has two date fields, and you attempt to group both date fields by months and years, Excel arbitrarily names the first grouped field Years and the second grouped field Years2. This naming convention inevitably leads to confusion. When this occurs, it is important to rename the fields with a meaningful name.

CASE STUDY CREATING AN ORDER LEAD-TIME REPORT

The material schedulers at a manufacturing plant are usually concerned with the lead time, which is the time it takes from when an order arrives until when it needs to ship. The schedulers might know that it takes 60 business days to procure material, schedule production, and build the product. In a perfect world, if all their customers would order 61 or more days in advance, the manufacturing plant would not have to keep any excess raw material inventory on hand.

However, in the real world, the plant always receives orders in which the customer wants the product faster. In these cases, the manufacturing plant might purchase extra inventory of the components with the longest lead time to accommodate rush orders.

If your transactional data source includes a field for date shipped and another field for date ordered, you can produce a report showing the normal order lead time by product. This is a valuable report for the master schedulers in the manufacturing plant. Here are the steps to follow:

1. Build a report with `Ship Date` going across the column area of the report.

2. Group the Ship Date field by month and year.

3. In the PivotTable Field List, drag the Years field to the Report Filter drop zone area of the pivot table. Use the drop-down in B1 to select one year from the data.

4. Drag the Order Date field to the row area of the pivot table.

5. Group the Order Date field by months and years.

6. Excel arbitrarily names the Years field for Order Date as Years2, so rename the field `Order Year`.

7. Choose any cell in the values area of the pivot table. On the Options tab, open the Show Values As drop-down and select % of Column Total.

8. In the Active Field box, type a new name of % of Revenue.

9. Click the Field Settings button. Click the Number Format button. Give the Revenue field a custom number format of **0.0%;;**. The semicolons suppress the display of negative and zero values.

The resulting table is shown in Figure 4.8. Cell C8 indicates that 4.6 percent of the orders shipped in January 2011 were ordered during the month of January. Another 42.8 percent of those orders were received in December 2010. This means that 47.4 percent of the sales from January were received within the manufacturing lead time. This fact dictates that your manufacturing facility needs to increase the amount of inventory to meet these short lead-time orders.

Figure 4.8

The order lead-time report makes use of two fields grouped by month and year.

	A	B	C	D	E
1	Years	2011			
2					
3	% of Revenue		Ship Date		
4	Order Year	Order Date	Jan	Feb	Mar
5	⊟2010	Oct	13.2%		
6		Nov	39.3%	11.0%	
7		Dec	42.8%	36.7%	15.5%
8	⊟2011	Jan	4.6%	39.8%	36.3%
9		Feb		12.6%	37.1%
10		Mar			11.2%

Grouping Numeric Fields

The Grouping dialog box for numeric fields enables you to group items into equal ranges.

In Figure 4.9, the Row Labels field contains the size of each order.

Select any number in Column A, and then select Group Field from the Options dialog box. Excel displays the Grouping dialog box.

In the Grouping dialog box, choose parameters for the group. In Figure 4.9, the dialog is suggesting groups from 0 to 180,000 in increments of 10,000.

Figure 4.9

Select a value and choose Group Field to display the Grouping dialog box.

	A	B	C	D	E
1	Years	2011			
2					
3	% of Revenue		Ship Date		
4	Order Year	Order Date	Jan	Feb	Mar
5	⊟2010	Oct	13.2%		
6		Nov	39.3%	11.0%	
7		Dec	42.8%	36.7%	15.5%
8	⊟2011	Jan	4.6%	39.8%	36.3%
9		Feb		12.6%	37.1%
10		Mar			11.2%

The result shows the number of orders in each group (see Figure 4.10).

Figure 4.10

The numeric row field has been grouped into ranges.

Revenue	Number of Orders	Revenue $
0-10000	48867	58,398,772
10000-20000	702	9,984,136
20000-30000	459	11,433,289
30000-40000	224	7,797,325
40000-50000	114	5,076,657
50000-60000	82	4,468,320
60000-70000	39	2,518,956
70000-80000	24	1,757,286
80000-90000	20	1,688,159
90000-100000	6	560,091
100000-110000	8	830,654
110000-120000	7	796,171
120000-130000	3	379,268
130000-140000	2	266,336
140000-150000	2	294,848
150000-160000	2	307,708
160000-170000	1	168,166
Grand Total	#REF!	106,726,142

Ungrouping

After you have established groups, you can undo the groups by using the Ungroup icon on the Options tab. To undo a group, select one of the grouped cells, and then click the Ungroup icon on the Options tab.

Looking at the PivotTable Field List

The following topics in this chapter involve sorting and filtering your pivot table. Both of these tasks involve subtleties in the PivotTable Field List. The following sections take you through a quick tour of the PivotTable Field List.

Docking and Undocking the PivotTable Field List

The PivotTable Field List starts out docked on the right side of the Excel window.

Grab the gray title bar for the pane and drag to the left to enable the pane to float anywhere in your Excel window.

After you have undocked the PivotTable Field List, you might find that it is difficult to redock it on either side of the screen. To redock the Field List, you must grab the title bar and drag until at least 80 percent of the Field List is off the edge of the window. Pretend that you are trying to remove the floating Field List completely from the screen. Eventually, Excel gets the hint and redocks the Field List. Note that the PivotTable Field List can be either docked on the right or left side of the screen.

CASE STUDY   GROUPING TEXT FIELDS

You get a call from the VP of Sales. Secretly, the Sales department is considering a massive reorganization of the sales regions. The VP would like to see a report showing sales for last year by the new proposed zones. You have been around long enough to know that the proposed zones will change several times before the reorganization happens, so you are not willing to change the Zone field in your source data quite yet.

First, build a report showing revenue by market. The VP of Sales is proposing to build a new zone composed of Atlantic, Carolinas, and Gulf States. Using the Ctrl key, highlight the three zones that make up the new zone. Figure 4.11 shows the pivot table before the first group is created.

Figure 4.11
Use the Ctrl key to select the noncontiguous cells that make up the new zone.

	A	B
1	Ship Date	2010
2		
3	Row Labels	Revenue
4	Atlantic	3,543,292
5	California	3,720,648
6	Carolinas	3,164,057
7	Denver	4,104,292
8	Eastern Canada	2,899,612
9	Great Lakes	5,104,118
10	Gulf States	3,933,254
11	New York	3,969,356
12	Northwest	3,056,328
13	Phoenix	2,824,766
14	Plains	6,665,123
15	Western Canada	2,398,078
16	Grand Total	45,382,922

From the Options tab, click Group Selection. Excel adds a new field called Market2. The three selected cells that are selected together belong to a Market2 grouping that is arbitrarily called Group1, as shown in Figure 4.12.

Figure 4.12
Excel arbitrarily calls the first grouping Group1.

	A	B
1	Ship Date	2010
2		
3	**Row Labels**	**Revenue**
4	**⊟Group1**	
5	Atlantic	3,543,292
6	Carolinas	3,164,057
7	Gulf States	3,933,254
8	**⊟California**	
9	California	3,720,648
10	**⊟Denver**	
11	Denver	4,104,292

Select Group1 in A4. Click the Field Settings icon on the Options tab. Although Excel called this field Zone2, give the field a new name such as Proposed Zones.

Click in Cell A4 and type a meaningful name instead of Group1.

As you repeat these steps to build other regions, Excel continues to assign names such as Group2 or Group3. After creating each region, simply type a meaningful name over the cell containing the arbitrary group name.

You find that the New Region field is a real field. You can use the sorting feature to sequence it alphabetically. The sorting feature is discussed in the "Sorting in a Pivot Table" section later in this chapter.

By default, Excel does not add subtotals for the New Region field. Use the Subtotals drop-down on the Design tab to add subtotals.

Figure 4.13 shows the report that is ready for the VP of Sales. You can probably predict that the Sales department needs to shuffle markets from the Big West region to balance the regions.

Figure 4.13
After you group all the markets into new regions, the report is ready for review.

	A	B
1	Ship Date	2010
2		
3	**Row Labels**	**Revenue**
4	**⊟New South**	**10,640,603**
5	Atlantic	3,543,292
6	Carolinas	3,164,057
7	Gulf States	3,933,254
8	**⊟Big West**	**22,769,234**
9	California	3,720,648
10	Denver	4,104,292
11	Northwest	3,056,328
12	Phoenix	2,824,766
13	Plains	6,665,123
14	Western Canada	2,398,078
15	**⊟Far East**	**11,973,085**
16	Eastern Canada	2,899,612
17	Great Lakes	5,104,118
18	New York	3,969,356
19	**Grand Total**	**45,382,922**

Rearranging the PivotTable Field List

As shown in Figure 4.14, a small drop-down appears near the top right of the PivotTable Field List. Select this drop-down to see the five possible arrangements of the PivotTable Field List. Although the default is to have the Fields section at the top of the list and the areas section at the bottom of the list, four other arrangements are possible.

Figure 4.14
Use this drop-down to rearrange the PivotTable Field List.

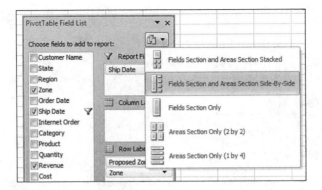

The final three arrangements offered in the drop-down are rather confusing. If someone changes the PivotTable Field List to show only the areas section, you could not see new fields to add to the pivot table.

If you ever encounter a version of the PivotTable Field List with only the areas sections (see Figure 4.15) or only the fields, remember that you can return to a less confusing view of the data by using the arrangement drop-down.

Using the Areas Section Drop-Downs

As shown in Figure 4.16, every field in the areas section has a visible drop-down arrow. When you select this drop-down arrow, you see four categories of choices:

■ The first four choices enable you to rearrange the field within the list of fields in that area of the pivot table.

■ The next four choices enable you to move the field to a new area. This could also be accomplished by dragging the field to a new area.

Figure 4.15
If you encounter this confusing arrangement of the PivotTable Field List, use the drop-down to return to an arrangement showing fields and areas.

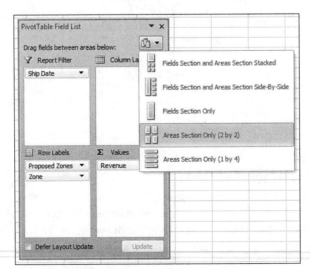

Figure 4.16
The drop-downs in the areas section of the PivotTable Field List are not very useful.

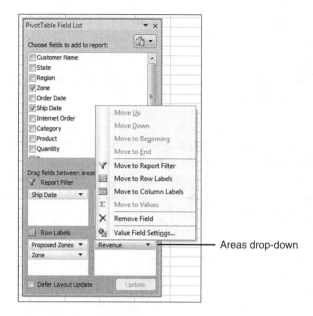

Areas drop-down

■ The next choice enables you to remove the field from the pivot table. This can also be accomplished by dragging the field outside of the field list.

■ The final choice displays the Field Settings dialog box for the field.

Because these drop-down arrows are always visible, you might be more likely to open these drop-downs. However, they are far less powerful than the hidden drop-downs in the Fields section of the list.

Using the Fields Drop-Down

A second set of drop-downs is available in the PivotTable Field List. Hover the mouse cursor over any field in the Fields section of the PivotTable Field List, and a hidden drop-down appears, as shown in Figure 4.17.

Figure 4.17
You have to hover your mouse cursor over a field before you realize that a drop-down is available.

Useful drop-down

4

After you open the drop-down in the Fields section, you can see that all the useful sorting and filtering options are behind the hidden drop-down.

Figure 4.18 shows the drop-down menu for the Product Line field in the top of the PivotTable Field List. Both the Label Filters and Value Filters options open to a flyout menu with many powerful filter choices.

> **CAUTION**
>
> Microsoft has created a catch-22 for anyone trying to teach pivot tables. If this book suggests that you use the Product Line drop-down in the PivotTable Field List, most people tend to use the drop-down visible in the areas section of the PivotTable Field List. For the rest of this chapter, when the text refers to the "Product drop-down in the Fields section of the PivotTable Field List," you should use the hidden drop-down shown in Figure 4.18.

Figure 4.18
You shouldn't be surprised that all the powerful features are in the drop-down that Microsoft hides from view.

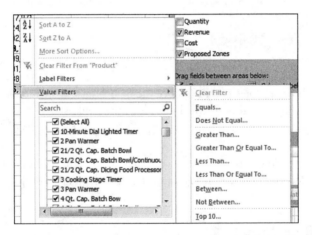

Sorting in a Pivot Table

By default, items in each pivot field are sorted in ascending sequence based on the item name.

Beginning in Excel 2007, Microsoft dramatically simplified pivot table sorting. With these changes, you have the freedom to sort data fields to suit your needs. You can use one of several methods to apply sorting to your pivot table:

- Use the Sorting buttons on the Options tab.
- Use the hidden drop-down in the Fields section of the PivotTable Field List.
- Right-click any item in the row or column section and select Sort.
- Use the manual method.

Sorting Using the Sort Icons on the Options Tab

Three icons appear in the Sort group of the Options tab. The AZ button sorts ascending; the ZA button sorts descending. The Sort icon brings up a dialog box with more options.

To use the Sort icons successfully, pay attention to where you place the cell pointer before clicking the icon.

In Figure 4.19, the pivot table is in the default sort order. The regions are sorted alphabetically (Canada, Midwest, Northeast, Southeast, Southwest, and West). Within each region, the markets are sorted alphabetically.

Figure 4.19
This pivot table is in the default sequence.

There are eight ways to sort this data. You get a different sort depending on whether you have selected A4, B4, A5, or B5 when you click the AZ or ZA buttons. Refer to Figure 4.19 as you read these options:

- If you select Cell A4 and click ZA, the regions are sorted in descending order. The West region appears first. Within the West region, the zones are still sorted in ascending sequence (California, Northwest).

- If you select Cell A5 and click ZA, the markets are sorted in descending order within each region. The zones in the West region appear in descending sequence (Northwest, California).

- If you select Cell B4 and click ZA, the regions are sorted so that the largest region appears first. This is the Midwest region with $27.2 million, followed by the Southeast region with $18.1 million. The zones retain their previous sequence.

- If you select Cell B5 and click ZA, the zones are sorted within each region so that the largest zone appears first. In the Midwest region, the Plains zone appears first, with $15.9 million, followed by the Great Lakes zone with $11.3 million.

In Figure 4.20, the regions are sorted in descending alphabetical order, and the zones are sorted in descending revenue order within the regions.

Figure 4.20
After two sorts, the regions are in descending order alphabetically, and the zones are in descending order by region.

	A	B
1		
2		
3	**Row Labels** ▾	**Revenue**
4	⊟**Canada**	**12,592,297**
5	Western Canada	6,692,980
6	Eastern Canada	5,899,316
7	⊟**Midwest**	**27,225,632**
8	Plains	15,924,109
9	Great Lakes	11,301,523
10	⊟**Northeast**	**17,476,601**
11	New York	8,988,332
12	Atlantic	8,488,270
13	⊟**Southeast**	**18,113,567**
14	Gulf States	10,043,940
15	Carolinas	8,069,627
16	⊟**Southwest**	**15,217,444**
17	Denver	9,600,373
18	Phoenix	5,617,071
19	⊟**West**	**16,100,601**
20	California	9,074,318
21	Northwest	7,026,283
22	**Grand Total**	**106,726,142**

Think about sorting using the Data or Home tab; the sort is a one-time event. If data changes, you must manually choose to sort the data again.

Pivot table sorts are more powerful. When you sort using the pivot table sorting options, Excel sets up a rule for the field. If you change the order of the pivot fields, Excel continues to apply the rule. In Figure 4.21, the Region field was removed from the report. Excel remembered that the Market field should be sorted by descending revenue. Excel correctly re-sorted the data, moving Plains from Row 8 to Row 4.

Figure 4.21
Sort rules applied to a pivot table cause the data to be re-sorted after every pivot or refresh.

	A	B
1		
2		
3	**Row Labels** ▾	**Revenue**
4	Plains	15,924,109
5	Great Lakes	11,301,523
6	Gulf States	10,043,940
7	Denver	9,600,373
8	California	9,074,318
9	New York	8,988,332
10	Atlantic	8,488,270
11	Carolinas	8,069,627
12	Northwest	7,026,283
13	Western Canada	6,692,980
14	Eastern Canada	5,899,316
15	Phoenix	5,617,071
16	**Grand Total**	**106,726,142**

Sorting Using the Field List Hidden Drop-Down

An alternative method for sorting is to use the hidden drop-down in the Fields section of the PivotTable Field List.

Hover the mouse cursor over any field in the top half of the PivotTable Field List, and a drop-down appears. Select this drop-down to access AZ and ZA options and a More Sort Options menu choice.

You can also right-click any label in the pivot table and select Sort from the dialog box.

If you select the More Sort Options choice or the Sort icon in the Options tab, you access the Sort dialog box, as shown in Figure 4.22. In this pivot table version of the Sort dialog box, you can choose to sort the specific field based on another field. In Figure 4.22, you can see that the customer field should be sorted into descending revenue sequence.

Figure 4.22
You can specify complex sort criteria by using this Sort dialog box.

Understanding the Effect of Layout Changes on AutoSort

If you change the report filter, the report automatically re-sorts. Different customers might appear at the top of the list based on their purchases of the filtered items.

If you drop a new field on the report, the pivot table remembers the AutoSort option for the sorted field and does its best to present the data in that order. This might not be in the spirit of your report focusing on the best customers. Say that you add the Zone field as the outer row field. The Zone field is sorted alphabetically by name, but within each region, the customers are arranged in descending order by revenue.

Using a Manual Sort Sequence

Note that the dialog box in Figure 4.23 offers something called a *manual sort*. Rather than using the dialog box, you can invoke a manual sort in a surprising way.

Figure 4.23
Use a manual sort.

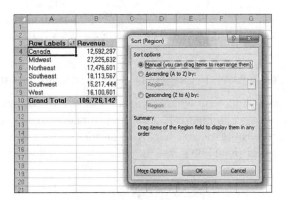

Note that the regions in Figure 4.23 are in the following order: Canada, Midwest, Northeast, Southeast, Southwest, and West. If this company is based in New York, company traditions might dictate that the Northeast region should be shown first, followed by Southeast, Midwest, Southwest, West, and Canada. On the face of it, there is no easy way to sort the Region field into this sequence. An ascending sort would cause the Canada region to be first. A descending sort would cause the West region to be first. Neither sort is in the proper sequence to match the company's standard reporting.

You might try to convince your company to change a decades-long tradition of reporting in the North, South, West, and Midwest sequence. Alternatively, the company could change the region names to accommodate sorting in your pivot table. Both of these concepts would be tough to sell and are not viable options. Fortunately, Microsoft offers a simple solution to this problem, as described below.

Place the cell pointer in Cell A4 and type the word **Northeast**. Excel figures out that you want to move the Northeast column to be first and moves the Northeast values to Row 4. Canada is moved down to Row 9. Next, type **Southeast** in Cell A5. The values for Southeast move to Row 5.

This behavior is completely unintuitive. You should never try this behavior with a regular (nonpivot table) data set in Excel. You would never expect Excel to change the data sequence just by moving the labels.

Figure 4.24 shows the pivot table after typing new column headings in Column A.

Figure 4.24
Simply type a heading in A4 to move a new region to be first

Row Labels	Revenue
Northeast	17,476,601
Southeast	18,113,567
Midwest	27,225,632
Southwest	15,217,444
West	16,100,601
Canada	12,592,297
Grand Total	106,726,142

> **CAUTION**
>
> After you use this technique, any new regions you add to the data source are automatically added to the end of the list because Excel does not know where to add the new region.

You can also reorder labels by dragging them. However, it can be difficult to find the correct place for dragging. Select a label. Hover over the right edge of the cell until the cursor changes to a four-headed arrow. Click and drag the field to resequence it.

Using a Custom List for Sorting

The other solution to the Northeast, Southeast, Midwest, Southwest, West, and Canada sequence problem is to set up a custom list. Custom lists are maintained in the Excel Options dialog box.

Follow these steps to set up a custom list:

1. In an out-of-the-way section of the worksheet, type the regions in their proper sequence. Type one region per cell, going down a column.

2. Select the cells containing the list of regions in the proper sequence.

3. Click the File menu. Select Excel Options from the bottom of the left navigation.

4. Select the Advanced category in the left navigation. Scroll down to the Display group. Click the Edit Custom Lists button.

5. In the Custom Lists dialog box, your selection address is entered in the Import text box. Click Import to bring the regions in as a new list, as shown in Figure 4.25. The new list appears at the bottom of the Custom Lists box.

6. Click OK to close the Custom Lists dialog box. Then click OK to close the Excel Options dialog box.

Figure 4.25
Import a new custom list to enable custom sorts.

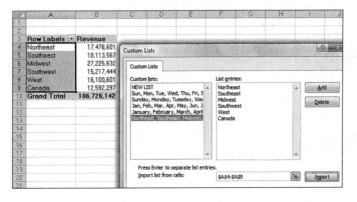

The custom list is now stored on your computer and is available for all future Excel sessions.

To sort the pivot table by the custom list, follow these steps:

1. Select one of the Region cells in the pivot table.
2. From the Options tab, click the Sort icon.
3. In the Sort (Region) dialog box, select Ascending by Region.
4. In the Sort (Region) dialog box, click the More Options button in the lower-left corner.
5. In the More Sort Options dialog box, clear the AutoSort check box.
6. As shown in Figure 4.26, in the More Sort Options dialog box, open the First Key Sort Order drop-down and select Northeast, Southeast, Midwest, Southwest, West, Canada.
7. Click OK twice.

Figure 4.26
Choose to sort by the custom list.

Filtering the Pivot Table

There are five ways to filter a pivot table, as shown in Figure 4.27.

Figure 4.27
Filter drop-downs in B1:B2, A5:B5, and C4 offer various filter options.

- Drop-downs in A5 and B5 offer new row label features, including virtual date filters. These filters were new in Excel 2007.

- Drop-downs in C4 offer new Label filters.

- Drop-downs in B1 and B2 offer what was known as Page Filters in legacy versions of Excel and are now known as Report Filters.

- Cell J5 offers the top-secret AutoFilter location.

- Slicers are a visual method of filtering. They replace the filters in Cells B1:B2 (see Figure 4.28).

Slicers are discussed in the "Using Slicers" section later in this chapter.

Figure 4.28
Slicers are a graphical filter and a great improvement over (Multiple Items) in the old filters.

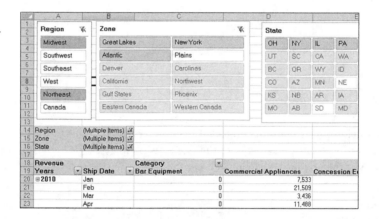

Using Filters in the Label Areas

Click the drop-down for the Region field in Cell C4 of Figure 4.29. Excel offers a list of all values in the field. The Select All button toggles all the other fields on and off. If you need to limit the report to three of the six regions, clear the three unwanted regions, as shown in Figure 4.29.

Figure 4.29
You can filter by selecting or clearing items in the filter.

Text fields offer a flyout menu called Label filters. If you want to filter regions that contain the word "west," you can choose the Contains option (see Figure 4.30). Alternatively, you can type the text in the new Search box.

Figure 4.30
The Label Filters enable you to find labels that match a text pattern.

New Search box —

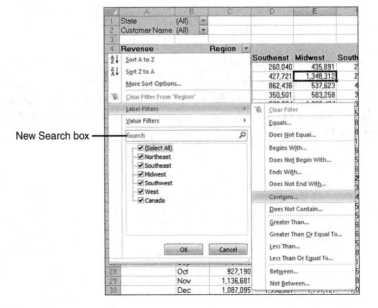

When you choose one of the filter items from the menu, Excel displays the Label Filter dialog box. In this dialog box, you can use wildcard characters. For example, you can use an * to match any series of characters or use ? to match a single character.

You can also choose Regions where the sales match a certain level. When you select the Value Filters flyout, these filters enable you to include or exclude regions based on the revenue values for those filters (see Figure 4.31).

Figure 4.31
The Value Filters enable you to select regions based on their values in a numeric field.

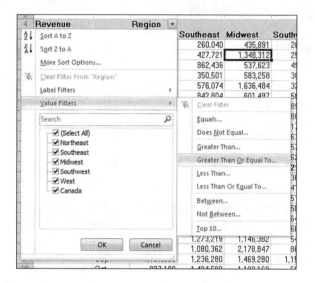

If your label field contains all dates, Excel replaces the Label Filter flyout with a Date Filters flyout. These filters offer many virtual filters such as Next Week, This Month, Last Quarter, and so on (see Figure 4.32).

If you choose Equals, Before, After, or Between, you can specify a date or a range of dates.

Options for the current or past or next day, week, month, quarter, or year occupy 15 options. Combined with Year to Date, these options change day after day. You can pivot a list of projects by due date and always see the projects that are due in the next week using this option. When you open the workbook on another day, the report recalculates.

> **TIP**
> In Microsoft's world, a week runs from Sunday through Saturday. If you select Next Week, the report always shows a period from the next Sunday through the following Saturday.

When you select All Dates in the Period, a new flyout menu offers options such as Each Month and Each Quarter.Case Study

Figure 4.32
The Date Filters offer various virtual date periods.

CAUTION

If you display your report in Compact Layout with multiple row fields, Excel includes all the fields in the first column of the pivot table. In this case, you have one drop-down on the Row Labels cell. To use the Row Labels drop-down, you first need to use the Select Field drop-down at the top of the Row Labels drop-down.

CREATING A TOP 10 REPORT

One of the useful value filters is the Top 10 filter. This value filter can be used to select the Top N, Bottom N, Top N%, or Bottom N%.

For a value filter, you can select text row fields where the corresponding value fields are in the top 10, top 20, and so on.

In Figure 4.33, the pivot table shows revenue by customer.

Figure 4.33
There are too many customers to read the whole report.

Customer Name	Revenue
Agile Adhesive Inc.	42,498
Agile Belt Inc.	85,904
Agile Doorbell Traders	26,918
Agile Hardware Inc.	38,903
Agile Kettle Inc.	22,084
Agile Yardstick Supply	929,921
Alluring Door Inc.	88,206
Alluring Edger Supply	72,458
Alluring Glass Partners	372,620
Alluring Sandal Corporation	164,693
Alluring Shoe Inc.	171,134
Alluring Utensil Corporation	12,936
Alluring Vegetable Company	304,207

Because there are more than 500 customers, your chance of getting a sales manager to read this report is slim. It would be better to show a report of the top 10 customers.

Follow these steps to filter the report:

1. Select the Row Labels drop-down in Cell A4.

2. Select Value Filters from the drop-down.

3. Select Top 10 from the flyout menu. Excel displays the Top 10 Filter (Customer Name) dialog box, as shown in Figure 4.34.

Figure 4.34
Initially, the Top 10 Filter finds the top 10 customers.

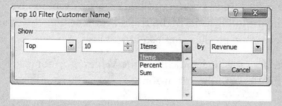

4. Click OK to close the dialog box. Your pivot table then shows only the top 10 customers.

5. If you want the customers to be listed high to low, choose a field in the Revenue column. Click the ZA button in the Options tab. The resulting pivot table is shown in Figure 4.35

Figure 4.35
Specify that the customers should be sorted high to low.

	A	B
1		
2		
3		
4	Customer Name	Revenue
5	Real Juicer Corporation	2,242,374
6	Unusual Flagpole Traders	1,654,376
7	Unique Tackle Company	1,624,493
8	Dependable Utensil Company	1,468,561
9	Handy Kettle Company	1,327,563
10	Tasty Vise Traders	1,293,225
11	Rare Yardstick Company	1,261,981
12	Bright Aerobic Inc.	1,191,582
13	Fascinating Bottle Inc.	1,176,843
14	Stunning Juicer Inc.	1,154,311
15	**Grand Total**	**14,395,308**

Beware that the total in Row 15 is only the total of the top 10 customers.***

Filtering Using the Report Filter Area

Pivot table veterans remember the old page area section of a pivot table. This area has been renamed the report filter area and still operates basically the same as in legacy versions of Excel. Microsoft did add the capability to select multiple items from the report filter area.

Figure 4.36
With multiple fields in the Report Filter area, this pivot table can answer many ad hoc queries.

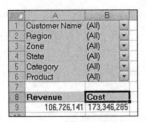

Adding Fields to the Report Filter Area

The pivot table in Figure 4.36 is a perfect ad hoc reporting tool to give to a high-level executive. You can use the drop-downs in B1:B6 to find revenue quickly for any combination of region, zone, state, category, product, or customer. This is a typical use of Report Filters.

To set up the report, drag revenue and cost to the Values drop zone, and then drag as many fields as desired to the Report Filter drop zone.

> **TIP**
>
> If you add many fields to the report filter area, you might want to use one of the obscure pivot table options settings. Click Options on the Options tab. On the Layout & Format tab of the PivotTable Options dialog box, change the Report Filter Fields Per Column from 0 to a positive number. Excel rearranges the filter fields into multiple columns, as shown in Figure 4.37. You can also change Down, Then Over to Over, Then Down to rearrange the sequence of the filter fields.

Figure 4.37
To show the filter fields in multiple columns, change this setting to be nonzero.

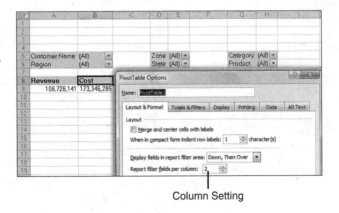

Column Setting

Choosing One Item from a Report Filter

To filter the pivot table, click any drop-down in the report filter area of the pivot table. The drop-down always starts with (All), but then lists the complete unique set of items available in that field.

To filter to a single item, click that item in the list, as shown in Figure 4.38.

Using the Select Multiple Items filter leads to a situation in which the report consumer might not know what items are included in the report. In Figure 4.40, you can see that E5 reports the somewhat cryptic (Multiple Items) label. Slicers solve this problem.

Choosing Multiple Items from a Report Filter

At the bottom of the report filter drop-down is a check box labeled Select Multiple Items. If you select this box, Excel adds a check box next to each item in the drop-down. This enables you to check multiple items from the list.

In Figure 4.39, the pivot table is filtered to show revenue from three zones.

Figure 4.38
After you select this option, the report shows the revenue from the Denver zone.

Figure 4.39
Use the Select Multiple Items check box to enable combination filters.

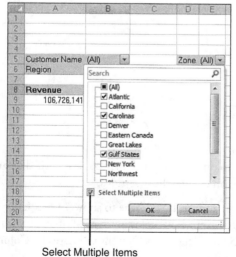

Select Multiple Items

Quickly Selecting or Clearing All Items from a Filter

The (All) check box at the top of the Market drop-down in Figure 4.39 is powerful. Selecting the (All) check box represents a quick way to select or clear all the items in the drop-down.

If the (All) check box is clear, click it to select all items. If the (All) check box is selected, click it to clear all items rapidly.

Figure 4.40
This report includes multiple zones, but which ones?

	A	B	C	D	E
1					
2					
3					
4					
5	Customer Name	(All) ▼		Zone	(Multiple Items) ⊽
6	Region	(All) ▼		State	(All) ▼
7					
8	**Revenue**	**Cost**			
9	26,601,837	40,913,965			

Using Slicers

Slicers are graphical versions of the Report Filter fields. Rather than hiding the items selected in the filter dropdown behind a heading like (Multiple Items), the slicer is a large array of buttons that will show at a glance which items are included or excluded.

To add slicers, click the Insert Slicer icon on the Options tab. Excel displays the Insert Slicers dialog. Choose all the fields for which you want to create graphical filters, as shown in Figure 4.41.

Figure 4.41
Choose fields for slicers.

Initially, Excel chooses one-column slicers of similar color in a tiled arrangement (see Figure 4.42). However, you can change these settings.

You can add more columns to a slicer. If you have to show 50 two-letter state abbreviations, that will look much better as 5 rows of 10 columns instead of 50 rows of one column. Click on the slicer to get access to the Slicer Tools Options tab. Use the Columns spin button to increase the number of columns in the slicer. Use the resize handles in the slicer to make the slicer wider and shorter. To add visual interest, choose a different color from the Slicer Styles gallery for each field.

After formatting the slicers, arrange them in a blank section of the worksheet, as shown in Figure 4.43.

Figure 4.42
The slicers appear with one column each.

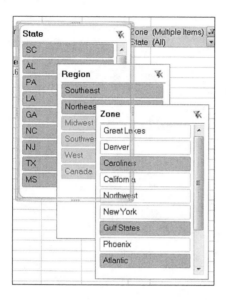

Figure 4.43
After formatting, your slicers might fit on a single screen.

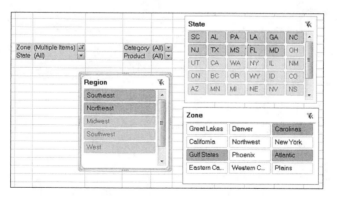

There are three colors that might appear in a slicer. The dark color indicates items that are selected. White boxes often mean the item has no records because of other slicers. Gray boxes indicate items that are not selected.

 To see a demo of slicers, search for "Pivot Table Data Crunching 4" at YouTube.

Next Steps

In Chapter 5, "Performing Calculations Within Pivot Tables," you learn how to use pivot table formulas to add new virtual fields to your pivot table.

4

Performing Calculations Within Pivot Tables

5

Introducing Calculated Fields and Calculated Items

When analyzing data with pivot tables, you often need to expand your analysis to include data based on calculations that are not in your original data set. Excel provides a way to perform calculations within your pivot table through calculated fields and calculated items.

A *calculated field* is a data field you create by executing a calculation against existing fields in the pivot table. Think of a calculated field as adding a virtual column to your data set. This column takes up no space in your source data, contains the data you define with a formula, and interacts with your pivot data as a field—just like all the other fields in your pivot table.

A *calculated item* is a data item you create by executing a calculation against existing items within a data field. Think of a calculated item as adding a virtual row of data to your data set. This virtual row takes up no space in your source data and contains summarized values based on calculations performed on other rows in the same field. Calculated items interact with your pivot data as a data item—just like all the other items in your pivot table.

With calculated fields and calculated items, you can insert a formula into your pivot table to create your own custom field or data item. Your newly created data becomes a part of your pivot table, interacts with other pivot data, recalculates when you refresh, and supplies a calculated metric that does not exist in your source data.

The example in Figure 5.1 demonstrates how a basic calculated field can add another perspective on your data. Your pivot table shows total Sales_Amount and

Contracted Hours for each market. A calculated field that shows you Avg Dollar Per Hour enhances this analysis and adds another dimension to your data.

Figure 5.1
Avg Dollar Per Hour is a calculated field that adds another perspective to your data analysis.

Market	Sales_Amount	Contracted Hours	Avg Dollar Per Hour
BUFFALO	$450,478	6,864	$66
CALIFORNIA	$2,254,735	33,014	$68
CANADA	$776,245	12,103	$64
CHARLOTTE	$890,522	14,525	$61
DALLAS	$467,089	6,393	$73
DENVER	$645,583	8,641	$75
FLORIDA	$1,450,392	22,640	$64
KANSASCITY	$574,899	8,547	$67
MICHIGAN	$678,705	10,744	$63
NEWORLEANS	$333,454	5,057	$66
NEWYORK	$873,581	14,213	$61
PHOENIX	$570,255	10,167	$56
SEATTLE	$179,827	2,889	$62
TULSA	$628,405	9,583	$66
Grand Total	$10,774,172	165,380	$65

Now, when you look at Figure 5.1, you might ask, "Why go through all the trouble of creating calculated fields or calculated items? Why not just use formulas in surrounding cells or even add your calculation directly into the source table to get the information you need?"

To answer these questions, the following sections discuss the three different methods you can use to create the calculated field shown in Figure 5.1.

Method 1: Manually Add the Calculated Field to the Data Source

You can manually add a calculated field to your data source, as shown in Figure 5.2, which allows the pivot table to pick up the field as a regular data field.

On the surface, this option looks straightforward. However, this method of precalculating metrics and incorporating them into your data source is impractical on several levels.

For example, if the definitions of your calculated fields change, you have to go back to the data source, recalculate the metric for each row, and then refresh your pivot table. If you add a metric, you have go back to the data source, add a new calculated field, and then change the range of your pivot table to capture the new field.

Method 2: Use a Formula Outside the Pivot Table to Create the Calculated Field

You can add a calculated field by performing the calculation in an external cell with a formula. In the example shown in Figure 5.3, the Avg Dollar Per Hour column is created with formulas referencing the pivot table.

Figure 5.2
Precalculating calculated fields in your data source is both cumbersome and impractical.

	N	O	P	Q	R
R2			f_x	=N2/O2	
1	Sales_Amount	Contracted Hours	Sales_Period	Sales_Rep	Avg Dollar Per Hour
2	$197.95	2	P08	5060	$98.98
3	$197.95	2	P08	5060	$98.98
4	$191.28	3	P08	5060	$63.76
5	$240.07	4	P11	44651	$60.02
6	$147.22	2	P08	160410	$73.61
7	$163.51	2	P02	243	$81.76
8	$134.01	3	P02	243	$44.67
9	$134.01	3	P02	243	$44.67
10	$134.01	3	P02	243	$44.67
11	$239.00	3	P01	4244	$79.67
12	$215.87	4	P02	5030	$53.97
13	$180.57	4	P02	64610	$45.14
14	$240.07	4	P02	213	$60.02
15	$180.57	4	P02	55031	$45.14
16	$180.57	4	P02	55031	$45.14
17	$180.57	4	P02	55031	$45.14
18	$180.57	4	P02	55031	$45.14

Figure 5.3
Typing a formula next to your pivot table essentially gives you a calculated field that refreshes when your pivot table is refreshed.

	A	B	C	D	E
D4			f_x	=B4/C4	
1					
2					
3	Market	Sales_Amount	Contracted Hours	Avg Dollar Per Hour	
4	BUFFALO	$450,478	6,864	$65.63	<< This is a formula
5	CALIFORNIA	$2,254,735	33,014	$68.30	
6	CANADA	$776,245	12,103	$64.14	
7	CHARLOTTE	$890,522	14,525	$61.31	
8	DALLAS	$467,089	6,393	$73.06	
9	DENVER	$645,583	8,641	$74.71	
10	FLORIDA	$1,450,392	22,640	$64.06	
11	KANSASCITY	$574,899	8,547	$67.26	
12	MICHIGAN	$678,705	10,744	$63.17	
13	NEWORLEANS	$333,454	5,057	$65.94	
14	NEWYORK	$873,581	14,213	$61.46	
15	PHOENIX	$570,255	10,167	$56.09	
16	SEATTLE	$179,827	2,889	$62.25	
17	TULSA	$628,405	9,583	$65.57	
18	Grand Total	$10,774,172	165,380	$65.15	

Although this method gives you a calculated field that updates when your pivot table is refreshed, any changes in the structure of your pivot table have the potential of rendering your formula useless.

As you can see in Figure 5.4, moving the Market field to the report filter area changes the structure of your pivot table, which exposes the weakness of makeshift calculated fields that use external formulas.

Method 3: Insert a Calculated Field Directly into the Pivot Table

Inserting the calculated field directly into your pivot table is the best option because this method provides the following advantages:

- Eliminates the need to manage formulas
- Provides for scalability when your data source grows or changes
- Allows for flexibility in the event that your metric definitions change
- Alters a pivot table's structure

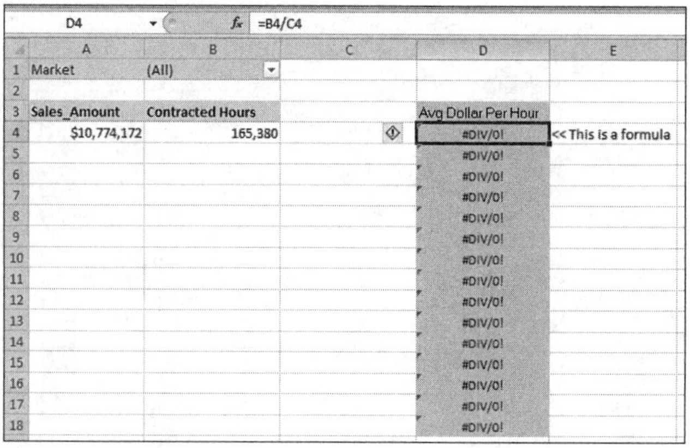

D4 =B4/C4

	A	B	C	D	E
1	Market	(All)			
2					
3	Sales_Amount	Contracted Hours		Avg Dollar Per Hour	
4	$10,774,172	165,380		#DIV/0!	<< This is a formula
5				#DIV/0!	
6				#DIV/0!	
7				#DIV/0!	
8				#DIV/0!	
9				#DIV/0!	
10				#DIV/0!	
11				#DIV/0!	
12				#DIV/0!	
13				#DIV/0!	
14				#DIV/0!	
15				#DIV/0!	
16				#DIV/0!	
17				#DIV/0!	
18				#DIV/0!	

Figure 5.4
External formulas run the risk of errors when the pivot table structure is changed.

- Measures different data fields against a calculated field without worrying about errors in formulas or losing cell references

The pivot table report shown in Figure 5.5 is the same one you see in Figure 5.1, except it has been restructured so you get the Avg Dollar Per Hour by market and product.

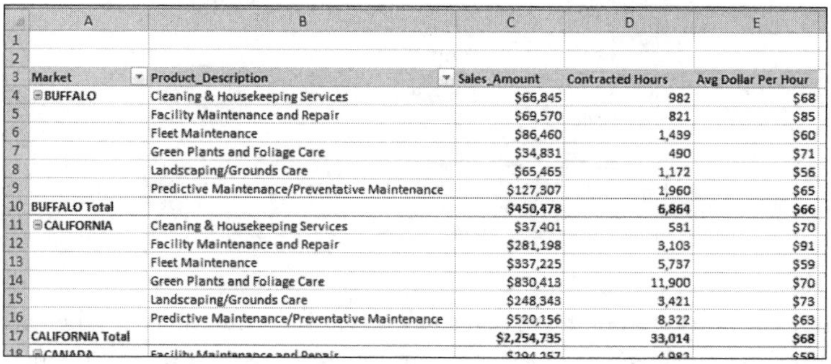

	A	B	C	D	E
1					
2					
3	Market	Product_Description	Sales_Amount	Contracted Hours	Avg Dollar Per Hour
4	BUFFALO	Cleaning & Housekeeping Services	$66,845	982	$68
5		Facility Maintenance and Repair	$69,570	821	$85
6		Fleet Maintenance	$86,460	1,439	$60
7		Green Plants and Foliage Care	$34,831	490	$71
8		Landscaping/Grounds Care	$65,465	1,172	$56
9		Predictive Maintenance/Preventative Maintenance	$127,307	1,960	$65
10	BUFFALO Total		$450,478	6,864	$66
11	CALIFORNIA	Cleaning & Housekeeping Services	$37,401	531	$70
12		Facility Maintenance and Repair	$281,198	3,103	$91
13		Fleet Maintenance	$337,225	5,737	$59
14		Green Plants and Foliage Care	$830,413	11,900	$70
15		Landscaping/Grounds Care	$248,343	3,421	$73
16		Predictive Maintenance/Preventative Maintenance	$520,156	8,322	$63
17	CALIFORNIA Total		$2,254,735	33,014	$68
18	CANADA	Facility Maintenance and Repair	$294,257	4,983	$59

Figure 5.5
Your calculated field remains viable even when your pivot table's structure changes to accommodate new dimensions.

5

The bottom line is that there are significant benefits to integrating your custom calculations into your pivot table, which include the following:

- The elimination of potential formula and cell reference errors
- The capability to add and remove data from your pivot table without affecting your calculations
- The capability to auto-recalculate when your pivot table is changed or refreshed
- The flexibility to change calculations easily when your metric definitions change
- The capability to manage and maintain your calculations effectively

Creating Your First Calculated Field

Before you create a calculated field, you must first have a pivot table. Therefore, begin by building the pivot table shown in Figure 5.6.

Figure 5.6
Create the pivot table shown here.

	A	B	C
1			
2			
3	Market	Sales_Amount	Contracted Hours
4	BUFFALO	$450,478	6,864
5	CALIFORNIA	$2,254,735	33,014
6	CANADA	$776,245	12,103
7	CHARLOTTE	$890,522	14,525
8	DALLAS	$467,089	6,393
9	DENVER	$645,583	8,641
10	FLORIDA	$1,450,392	22,640
11	KANSASCITY	$574,899	8,547
12	MICHIGAN	$678,705	10,744
13	NEWORLEANS	$333,454	5,057
14	NEWYORK	$873,581	14,213
15	PHOENIX	$570,255	10,167
16	SEATTLE	$179,827	2,889
17	TULSA	$628,405	9,583
18	Grand Total	$10,774,172	165,380

Now that you have a pivot table, it is time to create your first calculated field. To do this, you must activate the Insert Calculated Field dialog box. Select Options under the PivotTable Tools tab, and then select Fields, Items & Sets from the Tools group. Selecting this option activates a drop-down menu from which you can select Calculated Field, as shown in Figure 5.7.

Figure 5.7
Start the creation of your calculated field by selecting Calculated Field.

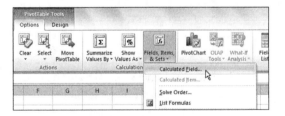

Excel activates the Insert Calculated Field dialog box, as shown in Figure 5.8.

Notice the two input boxes, Name and Formula, at the top of the dialog box. Give your calculated field a name, and then build the formula by selecting the combination of data fields and mathematical operators that provide the metric for which you are looking.

Figure 5.8
The Insert Calculated
Field dialog box assists
you in creating a calcu-
lated field in your pivot
table.

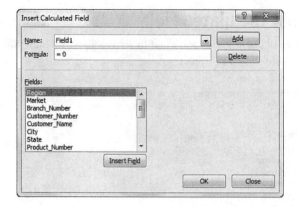

As shown in Figure 5.9, first give your calculated field a descriptive name. For example,
you might choose a name that describes the utility of the mathematical operation. In this
example, enter **Average Dollar Per Hour** in the Name input box.

Figure 5.9
Give the calculated field a
descriptive name.

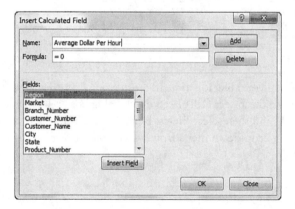

Next, go to the Fields list and double-click the Sales_Amount field. Enter / to let Excel
know you plan to divide the Sales_Amount field by something.

> ┌ CAUTION ──
> │ By default, the Formula input box in the Insert Calculated Field dialog box contains = 0. Be sure to
> │ delete the 0 before continuing with your formula.

At this point, your dialog box should look similar to the one shown in Figure 5.10.

Next, double-click the Contracted Hours field to finish your formula, as shown in Figure
5.11.

Figure 5.10
Start your formula with =
Sales_Amount .

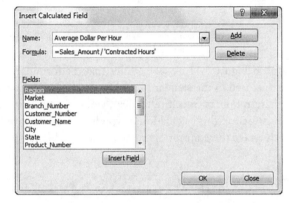

Figure 5.11
The full formula,
= Sales_Amount/
'Contracted Hours', gives
you the calculated field
you need.

Finally, select Add and then click OK to create your newly created calculated field.

As you can see in Figure 5.12, not only does your pivot table create a new field called Sum of Average Dollar Per Hour, but the PivotTable Field List includes your new calculated field as well.

> **NOTE**
> The resulting values from a calculated field are not formatted. However, you can apply any desired formatting using some of the techniques you learned in Chapter 3, "Customizing a Pivot Table."

Does this mean you have just added a column to your data source? The answer is no. Calculated fields are similar to the pivot table's default subtotal and grand total calculations in that they are all mathematical functions that recalculate when the pivot table changes or is refreshed. Calculated fields merely mimic the hard fields in your data source, enabling you to drag them, change field settings, and use them with other calculated fields.

Figure 5.12
Although your calculated fields don't go to your source data, they will show in your PivotTable Field List.

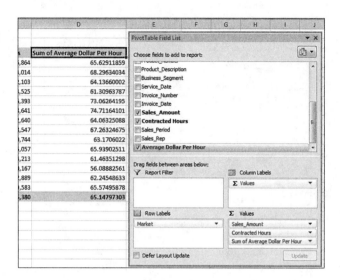

Take a moment to look at Figure 5.11 closely. Notice that the formula you entered uses a format similar to the one used in the standard Excel formula bar. The obvious difference is that instead of using hard numbers or cell references, you are referencing pivot data fields to define the arguments used in this calculation. If you have worked with formulas in Excel before, you will quickly grasp the concept of creating calculated fields.

CASE STUDY   SUMMARIZING NEXT YEAR'S FORECAST

Say that all the branch managers in your company have submitted their initial revenue forecasts for next year. Your task is to take the first-pass numbers they submitted and create a summary report showing the following:

- Total revenue forecast by market
- Total percent growth over last year
- Total contribution margin by market

Because these numbers are first-pass submissions and you know they will change over the course of the next two weeks, you decide to use a pivot table to create the requested forecast summary.

Start by building the initial pivot table that includes Revenue Last Year and Forecast Next Year for each market (see Figure 5.13). After creating the pivot table, notice that by virtue of adding the Forecast Next Year field in the data area, you have met your first requirement—to show total revenue forecast by market.

Figure 5.13
The initial pivot table is basic, but it provides the data for your first requirement—show total revenue forecast by market.

	A	B	C
1			
2			
3		Values	
4	MARKET ▾	Revenue Last Year	Forecast Next Year
5	BUFFALO	$450,478	$411,246
6	CALIFORNIA	$2,254,735	$2,423,007
7	CANADA	$776,245	$746,384
8	CHARLOTTE	$890,522	$965,361
9	DALLAS	$467,089	$510,635
10	DENVER	$645,583	$722,695
11	FLORIDA	$1,450,392	$1,421,507
12	KANSASCITY	$574,899	$607,226
13	MICHIGAN	$678,705	$870,447
14	NEWORLEANS	$333,454	$366,174
15	NEWYORK	$873,581	$953,010
16	PHOENIX	$570,255	$746,721
17	SEATTLE	$179,827	$214,621
18	TULSA	$628,405	$661,726
19	Grand Total	$10,774,172	$11,620,760

The next metric you need is percent growth over last year. To get this data, you need to add a calculated field that calculates the following formula:

(Forecast Next Year / Revenue Last Year) - 1

To accomplish this, do the following:

1. Activate the Insert Calculated Field dialog box and name your new field **Percent Growth** (see Figure 5.14).

Figure 5.14
Name your new field Percent Growth.

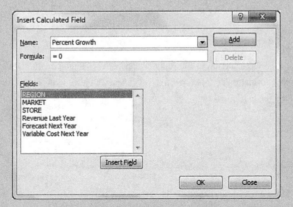

2. Delete the 0 in the Formula input box.
3. Enter **(** (an open parenthesis).
4. Double-click the Forecast Next Year field.

5. Enter **/** (a division sign).

6. Double-click the Revenue Last Year field.

7. Enter **)** (a close parenthesis).

8. Enter **-** (a minus sign).

9. Enter the number **1**.

> **TIP**
> You can use any constant in your pivot table calculations. Constants are static values that do not change. In this example, the number 1 is a constant. Though the value of Revenue Last Year or Forecast Next Year might change based on the available data, the number 1 will always have the same value.

After you have entered the full formula, your dialog box should look similar to the one shown in Figure 5.15.

Figure 5.15
With just a few clicks, you have created a variance formula!

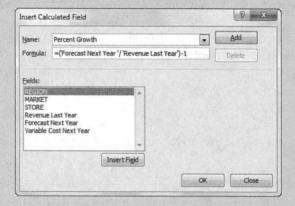

With your formula typed in, you can click OK to add your new field. After changing the format of the resulting values to percent, you have a nicely formatted Percent Growth calculation in your pivot table. At this point, your pivot table should look like the one shown in Figure 5.16.

Figure 5.16
You have added a Percent Growth calculation to your pivot table.

MARKET	Revenue Last Year	Forecast Next Year	Sum of Percent Growth
BUFFALO	$450,478	$411,246	-8.7%
CALIFORNIA	$2,254,735	$2,423,007	7.5%
CANADA	$776,245	$746,384	-3.8%
CHARLOTTE	$890,522	$965,361	8.4%
DALLAS	$467,089	$510,635	9.3%
DENVER	$645,583	$722,695	11.9%
FLORIDA	$1,450,392	$1,421,507	-2.0%
KANSASCITY	$574,899	$607,226	5.6%
MICHIGAN	$678,705	$870,447	28.3%
NEWORLEANS	$333,454	$366,174	9.8%
NEWYORK	$873,581	$953,010	9.1%
PHOENIX	$570,255	$746,721	30.9%
SEATTLE	$179,827	$214,621	19.3%
TULSA	$628,405	$661,726	5.3%
Grand Total	$10,774,172	$11,620,760	7.9%

With this newly created view into your data, you can see that three markets need to resubmit their forecasts to reflect positive growth over last year, as shown in Figure 5.17.

Figure 5.17
You can already discern some information from the calculated field that identifies three problem markets.

	A	B	C	D
1				
2				
3		**Values**		
4	**MARKET**	**Revenue Last Year**	**Forecast Next Year**	**Sum of Percent Growth**
5	BUFFALO	$450,478	$411,246	-8.7%
6	CALIFORNIA	$2,254,735	$2,423,007	7.5%
7	CANADA	$776,245	$746,384	-3.8%
8	CHARLOTTE	$890,522	$965,361	8.4%
9	DALLAS	$467,089	$510,635	9.3%
10	DENVER	$645,583	$722,695	11.9%
11	FLORIDA	$1,450,392	$1,421,507	-2.0%
12	KANSASCITY	$574,899	$607,226	5.6%
13	MICHIGAN	$678,705	$870,447	28.3%
14	NEWORLEANS	$333,454	$366,174	9.8%
15	NEWYORK	$873,581	$953,010	9.1%
16	PHOENIX	$570,255	$746,721	30.9%
17	SEATTLE	$179,827	$214,621	19.3%
18	TULSA	$628,405	$661,726	5.3%
19	**Grand Total**	$10,774,172	$11,620,760	7.9%

Now it is time to focus on your last requirement, which is to find total contribution margin by market. To get this data, you need to add a calculated field that calculates the following formula:

Forecast Next Year + Variable Cost Next Year

> **NOTE**
> A quick look at Figure 5.17 confirms that the Variable Cost Next Year field is not displayed in the pivot table report. Can you build pivot table formulas with fields that are not currently in the pivot table? The answer is yes. You can use any field that is available to you in the PivotTable Field List, even though that the field is not shown in the pivot table.

To create this field, do the following:

1. Activate the Insert Calculated Field dialog box and name your new field **Contribution Margin**.
2. Delete the 0 in the Formula input box.
3. Double-click the Forecast Next Year field.
4. Enter + (a plus sign).
5. Double-click the Variable Cost Next Year field.

After you have entered the full formula, your dialog box should look similar to the one shown in Figure 5.18.

Figure 5.18
With just a few clicks, you have created a formula that calculates contribution margin.

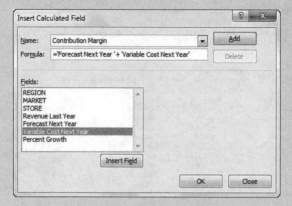

With the creation of the contribution margin, this report is ready to be delivered (see Figure 5.19).

Figure 5.19
Contribution margin is now a data field in your pivot table report thanks to your calculated field.

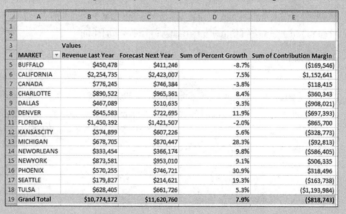

MARKET	Revenue Last Year	Forecast Next Year	Sum of Percent Growth	Sum of Contribution Margin
	Values			
BUFFALO	$450,478	$411,246	-8.7%	($169,546)
CALIFORNIA	$2,254,735	$2,423,007	7.5%	$1,152,641
CANADA	$776,245	$746,384	-3.8%	$118,415
CHARLOTTE	$890,522	$965,361	8.4%	$360,343
DALLAS	$467,089	$510,635	9.3%	($908,021)
DENVER	$645,583	$722,695	11.9%	($697,393)
FLORIDA	$1,450,392	$1,421,507	-2.0%	$865,700
KANSASCITY	$574,899	$607,226	5.6%	($328,773)
MICHIGAN	$678,705	$870,447	28.3%	($92,813)
NEWORLEANS	$333,454	$366,174	9.8%	($586,405)
NEWYORK	$873,581	$953,010	9.1%	$506,335
PHOENIX	$570,255	$746,721	30.9%	$318,496
SEATTLE	$179,827	$214,621	19.3%	($163,738)
TULSA	$628,405	$661,726	5.3%	($1,193,984)
Grand Total	$10,774,172	$11,620,760	7.9%	($818,743)

Now that you have built your pivot table report, you can analyze any new forecast submissions by refreshing your report with the new updates.

Creating Your First Calculated Item

As you learned at the beginning of this chapter, a calculated item is a virtual data item you create by executing a calculation against existing items within a data field. Calculated items come in especially handy when you need to group and aggregate a set of data items.

For example, the pivot table in Figure 5.20 gives you sales amount by Sales_Period. Imagine that you need to compare the average performance of the most recent six Sales_Periods to the average of the prior seven periods. In other words, you want to take the average of P01–P07 and compare it to the average of P08–P13.

To do this, place your cursor on any data item in the Sales_Period field and then select Fields, Items & Sets from the Tools group. Next, select Calculated Item, as shown in Figure 5.21.

Selecting this option opens the Insert Calculated Item dialog box. Figure 5.22 shows that the top of the dialog box identifies with which field you are working. In this case, it is the Sales_Period field. In addition, notice the Items list box is filled with all the items in the Sales_Period field automatically.

Your goal is to give your calculated item a name, and then build its formula by selecting the combination of data items and operators that provide the metric you are looking for.

Figure 5.20
You want to compare the most recent six Sales_Periods to the average of the prior seven periods.

	A	B
1		
2		
3	Row Labels ▾	Sum of Sales_Amount
4	P01	$681,865
5	P02	$1,116,916
6	P03	$657,611
7	P04	$865,498
8	P05	$925,802
9	P06	$868,930
10	P07	$640,587
11	P08	$1,170,262
12	P09	$604,552
13	P10	$891,253
14	P11	$949,605
15	P12	$887,665
16	P13	$513,625
17	**Grand Total**	**$10,774,172**

Figure 5.21
Start the creation of your calculated item by selecting Calculated Item.

Figure 5.22
The Insert Calculated Item dialog box is populated to reflect the field with which you are working automatically.

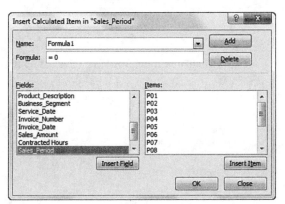

In this example, name your first calculated item **Avg P1-P7 Sales**, as shown in Figure 5.23.

Next, you can build your formula in the Formula input box by selecting the appropriate data items from the Items list. In this scenario, you want to create the following formula:

= Average(P01, P02, P03, P04, P05, P06, P07)

Enter this formula into the Formula input box, as demonstrated in Figure 5.24.

Figure 5.23
Give calculated items descriptive names.

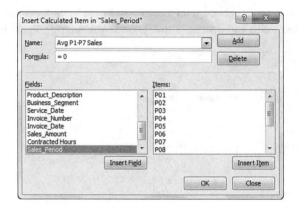

Figure 5.24
Enter a formula that gives you the average of P01–P07.

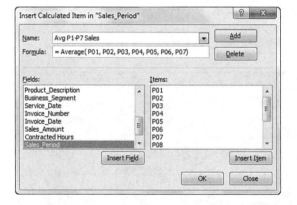

Click OK to activate your new calculated item. You now have a data item called Avg P1-P7 Sales, as shown in Figure 5.25.

Figure 5.25
A calculated item has
been added successfully
to your pivot table.

	A	B
1		
2		
3	**Row Labels** ▾	**Sum of Sales_Amount**
4	P01	$681,865
5	P02	$1,116,916
6	P03	$657,611
7	P04	$865,498
8	P05	$925,802
9	P06	$868,930
10	P07	$640,587
11	P08	$1,170,262
12	P09	$604,552
13	P10	$891,253
14	P11	$949,605
15	P12	$887,665
16	P13	$513,625
17	Avg P1-P7 Sales	$822,458
18	**Grand Total**	**$11,596,630**

> **TIP**
> You can use any worksheet function in both a calculated field and a calculated item. The only restriction is that the function you use cannot reference external cells or named ranges. In effect, this means you can use any worksheet function that does not require cell references or defined names to work (such as COUNT, AVERAGE, IF, OR).

Create a calculated item to represent the average sales for P08–P13, as shown in Figure 5.26.

Figure 5.26
Create a second calcu-
lated item.

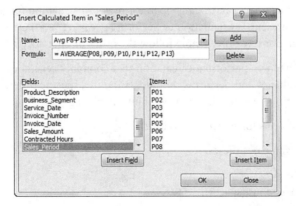

Now you can hide the individual sales periods, leaving only your two calculated items. After a little formatting, your calculated items enable you to compare the average performance of the six most recent Sales_Periods to the average of the prior seven periods (see Figure 5.27).

5

Figure 5.27
The most recent six Sales_Periods can be compared to the average of the prior seven periods.

	A	B
1		
2		
3	Row Labels ▼	Sum of Sales_Amount
4	Avg P1-P7 Sales	$822,458
5	Avg P8-P13 Sales	$836,160

> **CAUTION**
>
> If you do not hide the data items used to create your calculated item, your grand totals and subtotals might show incorrect amounts.

Understanding Rules and Shortcomings of Pivot Table Calculations

Although there is no better way to integrate your calculations into a pivot table than using calculated fields and calculated items, they come with their own set of drawbacks. It is important that you understand what goes on behind the scenes when you use pivot table calculations. It is even more important for you to be aware of the boundaries and limitations of calculated fields and calculated items to avoid potential errors in your data analysis.

The following sections highlight the rules around calculated fields and calculated items that you will most likely encounter when working with pivot table calculations.

Remembering the Order of Operator Precedence

Just as in a spreadsheet, you can use any operator in your calculation formulas, meaning any symbol that represents a calculation to perform (+, - , *, /, %, ^). Moreover, just as in a spreadsheet, calculations in a pivot table follow the order of operator precedence.

In other words, when you perform a calculation that combines several operators, as in (2+3) * 4/50%, Excel evaluates and performs the calculation in a specific order. Understanding the order of operations ensures that you avoid miscalculating your data.

The order of operations for Excel is as follows:

- Evaluate items in parentheses.
- Evaluate ranges (:).
- Evaluate intersections (spaces).
- Evaluate unions (,).
- Perform negation ([-]).
- Convert percentages (%).
- Perform exponentiation (^).
- Perform multiplication (*) and division (/), which are of equal precedence.
- Perform addition (+) and subtraction (-), which are of equal precedence.

- Evaluate text operators (&).
- Perform comparisons (=, <>, <=, >=).

> **NOTE**
> Operations that are equal in precedence are performed left to right.

Consider this basic example. The correct answer to (2+3)*4 is 20. However, if you leave off the parentheses, as in 2+3*4, Excel performs the calculation like this: 3*4 = 12 + 2 = 14. The order of operator precedence mandates that Excel perform multiplication before subtraction. Entering 2+3*4 gives you the wrong answer. Because Excel evaluates and performs all calculations in parentheses first, placing 2+3 inside parentheses ensures the correct answer.

Here is another widely demonstrated example. If you enter 10^2, which represents the exponent 10 to the 2nd power as a formula, Excel returns 100 as the answer. If you enter -10^2, you expect -100 to be the result. Instead, Excel returns 100 yet again. The reason is that Excel performs negation before exponentiation. This means that Excel converts 10 to -10 before the exponentiation, which effectively calculates -10*-10, which indeed equals 100. However, using parentheses in the formula, - (10^2), ensures that Excel calculates the exponent before negating the answer, which gives you -100.

Using Cell References and Named Ranges

When you create calculations in a pivot table, you are essentially working in a vacuum. The only data available to you is the data that exists in the pivot cache. Therefore, you cannot reach outside the confines of the pivot cache to reference cells or named ranges in your formula.

Using Worksheet Functions

You can use any worksheet function that does not require cell references or defined names as an argument. In effect, this means you can use any worksheet function that does not require cell references or defined names to work. Of the many functions that fall into this category, some include COUNT, AVERAGE, IF, AND, NOT, AND OR.

Using Constants

You can use any constant in your pivot table calculations. Constants are static values that do not change. For example, in the formula [Units Sold]*5, 5 is a constant. Though the value of Units Sold might change based on the available data, 5 will always have the same value.

Referencing Totals

Your calculation formulas cannot reference a pivot table's subtotals or grand total. This means that you cannot use the result of a subtotal or grand total as a variable or argument in your calculated field.

Rules Specific to Calculated Fields

Calculated field calculations are always performed against the sum of your data. In basic terms, Excel always calculates data fields, subtotals, and grand totals before evaluating your calculated field. This means that your calculated field is always applied to the sum of the underlying data.

The example shown in Figure 5.28 demonstrates how this can adversely affect your data analysis.

In each quarter, you need to get the total revenue for every product by multiplying the number of units sold by the price. If you look at Q1 first, you can immediately see the problem. Instead of returning the sum of 220+150+220+594, which would give you $1,184, the subtotal is calculating the sum of number of units times the sum of price, which returns the wrong answer.

Figure 5.28
Although the calculated field is correct for the individual data items in your pivot table, the subtotal is mathematically incorrect.

	A	B	C	D	E	F	G	H
1			Data					
2	Qtr	Product	Number of Units	Price	CalcField Unit*Price			
3	Q1	A	10	22	$220			
4		B	5	30	$150			
5		C	5	44	$220			
6		D	11	54	$594			
7	Grand Total		31	150	$4,650			$1,184 <<Real Q1 SubTotal

As you can see in Figure 5.29, including the whole year in your analysis compounds the problem.

Figure 5.29
The grand total for the year as a whole is completely wrong.

	A	B	C	D	E	F	G	H
1			Data					
2	Qtr	Product	Number of Units	Price	CalcField Unit*Price			
3	Q1	A	10	22	$220			
4		B	5	30	$150			
5		C	5	44	$220			
6		D	11	54	$594			
7	Q1 Total		31	150	$4,650			$1,184 <<Real Q1 SubTotal
8	Q2	A	7	19	$133			
9		B	12	25	$300			
10		C	9	39	$351			
11		D	5	52	$260			
12	Q2 Total		33	135	$4,455			$1,044 <<Real Q2 SubTotal
13	Q3	A	6	17	$102			
14		B	8	21	$168			
15		C	6	40	$240			
16		D	7	55	$385			
17	Q3 Total		27	133	$3,591			$895 <<Real Q3 SubTotal
18	Q4	A	8	22	$176			
19		B	7	31	$217			
20		C	6	35	$210			
21		D	10	49	$490			
22	Q4 Total		31	137	$4,247			$1,093 <<Real Q4 SubTotal
23	Grand Total		122	555	$67,710			$4,216 <<Real Grand Total

Unfortunately, there is no solution to this problem, but there is a workaround. In worst-case scenarios, you can configure your settings to eliminate subtotals and grand totals, and then calculate your own Totals. Figure 5.30 demonstrates this workaround.

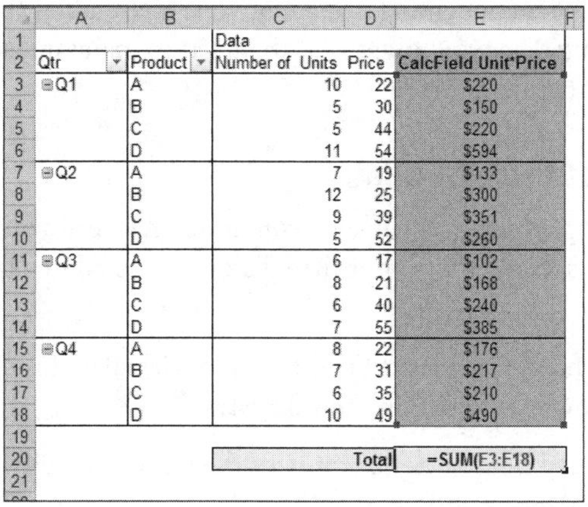

Figure 5.30

Calculating your own totals can prevent reporting incorrect data.

	A	B	C	D	E	F
1			Data			
2	Qtr ▾	Product ▾	Number of Units	Price	CalcField Unit*Price	
3	⊟ Q1	A	10	22	$220	
4		B	5	30	$150	
5		C	5	44	$220	
6		D	11	54	$594	
7	⊟ Q2	A	7	19	$133	
8		B	12	25	$300	
9		C	9	39	$351	
10		D	5	52	$260	
11	⊟ Q3	A	6	17	$102	
12		B	8	21	$168	
13		C	6	40	$240	
14		D	7	55	$385	
15	⊟ Q4	A	8	22	$176	
16		B	7	31	$217	
17		C	6	35	$210	
18		D	10	49	$490	
19						
20				Total	=SUM(E3:E18)	
21						

Rules Specific to Calculated Items

You cannot use calculated items in a pivot table that uses averages, standard deviations, or variances. Conversely, you cannot use averages, standard deviations, or variances in a pivot table that contains a calculated item.

You cannot use a Report Filter field to create a calculated item, nor can you move any calculated item to the report filter area.

You cannot add a calculated item to a report that has a grouped field, nor can you group any field in a pivot table that contains a calculated item.

When building your calculated item formula, you cannot reference items from a field other than the one you are working with.

As you think about the section you have just read, do not be put off by these shortcomings of pivot tables. Despite the clear limitations mentioned in this section, the capability to create custom calculations directly into your pivot table remains a powerful and practical feature that can enhance your data analysis. Now that you are aware of the inner workings of pivot table calculations and understand the limitations of calculated fields and items, you can avoid the pitfalls and use this feature with confidence.

5

Managing and Maintaining Pivot Table Calculations

In your dealings with pivot tables, you might find that sometimes you will not keep a pivot table for more than the time it takes to say, "Copy, Paste Values." However, other times it can be more cost effective to keep your pivot table and all its functionality intact.

When you find yourself maintaining and managing your pivot tables through changing requirements and growing data, you might find the need to maintain and manage your calculated fields and calculated items.

Editing and Deleting Pivot Table Calculations

When your calculation's parameters change or you no longer need your calculated field or calculated item, you can activate the appropriate dialog box to edit or remove the calculation.

To do this, activate the Insert Calculated Field or Insert Calculated Item dialog box and select the Name drop-down, as shown in Figure 5.31.

After you select a calculated field or item, you have the option of deleting the calculation or modifying the formula, as shown in Figure 5.32.

Figure 5.31
Opening the drop-down list under Name reveals all the calculated fields or items in the pivot table.

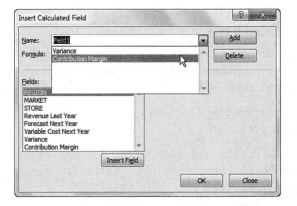

Figure 5.32
After selecting the appropriate calculated field or item, you can either delete or modify the calculation.

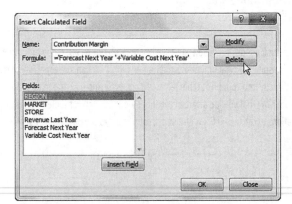

Changing the Solve Order of Calculated Items

If the value of a cell in your pivot table is dependent on the results of two or more calculated items, you have the option to change the solve order of the calculated items. In other words, you can specify the order in which the individual calculations are performed.

To get to the Solve Order dialog box, place your cursor anywhere in the pivot table, select Fields, Items, & Sets from the Tools group, and then select Solve Order, as shown in Figure 5.33.

Figure 5.33
Activate the Solve Order dialog box by selecting Formulas and then Solve Order.

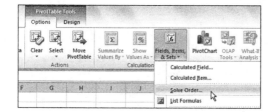

The Solve Order dialog box lists all the calculated items that currently exist in your pivot table (see Figure 5.34). Select any of the calculated items you see listed to enable the Move Up, Move Down, and Delete command buttons. The order you see the formulas in this list is the exact order the pivot table performs each operation.

Figure 5.34
After identifying the calculated item you are working with, move the item up or down to change the solve order. You also have the option of deleting the item in this dialog box.

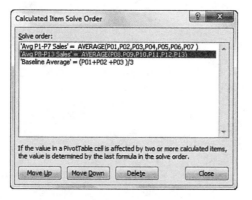

5

Documenting Formulas

Excel provides a nice function that lists the calculated fields and calculated items used in your pivot table. This function can also provide details of the solve order and formulas. This feature comes in especially handy when you need to determine which calculations are applied in a pivot table and the fields or items those calculations affect.

To use this function to list your pivot table calculations, place your cursor anywhere in the pivot table to select Fields, Items, & Sets, and then select List Formulas. Excel creates a new tab in your workbook that lists the calculated fields and calculated items in the current pivot table. Figure 5.35 shows a sample output of the List Formulas command.

Figure 5.35

The List Formulas command enables you to document the details of your pivot table calculations quickly.

Calculated Field		
Solve Order	Field	Formula
Calculated Item		
Solve Order	Item	Formula
1	'Avg P1-P7 Sales'	= AVERAGE(P01,P02,P03,P04,P05,P06,P07)
2	'Avg P8-P13 Sales'	= AVERAGE(P08,P09,P10,P11,P12,P13)
3	'Baseline Average'	=(P01+P02 +P03)/3
Note:	When a cell is updated by more than one formula,	
	the value is set by the formula with the last solve order.	
	To change formula solve orders,	
	use the Solve Order command on the Pivot Formulas drop down menu.	

Next Steps

In the next chapter, you learn the fundamentals of pivot charts and the basics of representing your pivot data graphically. You also gain a firm understanding of the limitations of pivot charts and alternatives to using pivot charts.

Using Pivot Charts and Other Visualizations

What Is a Pivot Chart...Really?

When sharing your analyses with others, you find there is no way to get around the fact that people want charts. Pivot tables are nice, but they leave so many annoying numbers that take time to absorb. On the other hand, charts enable users to make a split-second determination about what your data actually reveals. Charts offer instant gratification by enabling users to immediately see relationships, point out differences, and observe trends.

The bottom line is that managers want to absorb data as fast as possible, and nothing delivers that capability faster than a chart. This is where pivot charts come into play. While pivot tables offer the analytical, pivot charts offer the visual.

A common definition of a *pivot chart* is a graphical representation of the data in your pivot table. Although this definition is technically correct, it somehow misses the mark on what a pivot chart truly does.

When you create a standard chart from data that is not in a pivot table, you feed the chart a range made up of individual cells holding individual pieces of data. Each cell is an individual object with its own piece of data, so your chart treats each cell as an individual data point, charting each one separately.

However, the data in your pivot table is part of a larger object. The pieces of data you see inside your pivot table are not individual pieces of data that occupy individual cells. Instead, they are items inside a larger pivot table object that is occupying space on your worksheet.

When you create a chart from your pivot table, you are not feeding it individual pieces of data inside individual cells. Instead, you are feeding the pivot chart the entire pivot table layout. Therefore, a true definition of a *pivot chart* is a chart that uses a PivotLayout Object to view and control the data in your pivot table.

Using the PivotLayout Object enables your pivot chart to interactively add, remove, filter, and refresh data fields inside the chart just like your pivot table. The result of this action is a graphical representation of the data you see in your pivot table.

Creating Your First Pivot Chart

With all the complexity behind the make-up of a pivot chart, you might have the impression that it is difficult to create a pivot chart. The reality is that it is quite a straightforward task.

The pivot table in Figure 6.1 shows how straightforward it is to create a pivot chart. This pivot table provides for a simple view of revenue by market. The Business Segment field in the report filter area lets you parse out revenue by line of business.

Figure 6.1
This basic pivot table shows revenue by market and enables filtering by line of business.

Creating a pivot chart from this data not only provides an instant view of the performance of each market, but it also permits you to retain the ability to filter by line of business.

To start the process, place your cursor anywhere inside the pivot table and click the Insert tab on the Application ribbon. On the Insert tab, you can see the Charts group displaying the various types of charts you can create. Here, you can choose the chart type you would like to use. For this example, click the Column chart icon and select the first 2-D column chart, as shown in Figure 6.2.

As you can see in Figure 6.3, choosing the chart type causes a chart to appear.

Figure 6.2
Select the chart type you want to use.

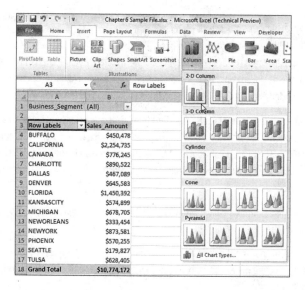

Figure 6.3
Excel creates your pivot chart on the same sheet as your pivot table.

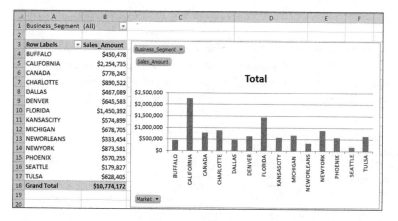

> **TIP**
>
> Notice that by default pivot charts are placed on the same sheet as the source pivot table. If you long for the days when pivot charts were located on their own chart sheet, you are in luck. All you have to do is place your cursor inside your pivot table and then press F11. This creates a pivot chart on its own sheet.
>
> By the way, you can change the location of your pivot charts by right-clicking the chart outside of the plot area, and then select Move Chart. This activates the Move Chart dialog box, where you can specify the new location.

6

A WORD ABOUT PIVOT FIELD BUTTONS

In Excel 2003, pivot charts displayed the available pivot field buttons directly on the charts. Pivot field buttons are the gray buttons and drop-downs you see on the pivot charts. Using these pivot field buttons, a user could rearrange a chart and apply filters to the underlying pivot table simply by clicking and dragging the pivot field buttons.

In Excel 2007, Microsoft chose to remove pivot field buttons from pivot charts. Presumably this was done to give pivot charts a cleaner look. In place of the pivot field buttons, Excel 2007 provided the PivotChart Filter Pane. Like the old pivot field buttons, the PivotChart Filter Pane enabled users to limit the data shown in the pivot chart by applying filters to the underlying pivot table. However, most users never caught on to the idea of using a separate pane to do the same things the pivot field buttons used to do.

For this reason, the pivot field buttons are back with Excel 2010. As shown in Figure 6.3, you can now control pivot fields directly on the chart using the gray pivot field buttons.

If you are not too keen about showing the pivot field buttons directly on your pivot charts, you can remove them by clicking your chart, and then selecting the Analyze tab. On the Analyze tab, use the Field Buttons drop-down to hide some or all of the pivot field buttons.

You now have a chart that is a visual representation of your pivot table. More than that, because the pivot chart is tied to the underlying pivot table, changing the pivot table in any way changes the chart. For example, adding the Region field to the pivot table adds a region dimension to your chart, as shown in Figure 6.4.

Figure 6.4
The pivot chart displays the same fields your underlying pivot table displays.

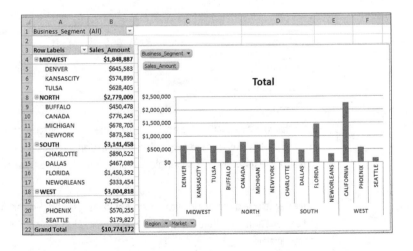

NOTE The pivot chart in Figure 6.4 does not display the subtotals shown in the pivot table. When creating a pivot chart, Excel ignores subtotals and grand totals.

In addition, selecting a Business Segment from the page field filters not only the pivot table, but also the pivot chart. All this behavior occurs because pivot charts use the same pivot cache and pivot layout as their corresponding pivot tables. This means that if you add or remove data from your data source and then refresh your pivot table, your pivot chart updates to reflect the changes.

> **TIP**
>
> You can also use slicers with your pivot charts. To do this, click your pivot chart, and then select the Analyze tab where you find the Insert Slicer icon. Click this icon to take advantage of all the benefits of slicers with your pivot chart!
>
> Refer back to Chapter 2, "Creating a Basic Pivot Table," for a quick refresher on slicers.

Take a moment and think about the possibilities. Essentially, you can create a fairly robust interactive reporting tool based on the power of one pivot table and one pivot chart—no programming necessary.

CREATING A PIVOT CHART FROM SCRATCH

You do not have to build your pivot table before creating a pivot chart. Instead, you can go straight from your raw data to a pivot chart. To do this, click any single cell in your data source and select the Insert tab. Select PivotTable from the Tables group, and then select PivotChart from the drop-down list. This activates the Create PivotChart dialog box. At this point, you go through the same steps you take to build a pivot table.

Keeping Pivot Chart Rules in Mind

As with other aspects of pivot table technology, pivot charts come with their own set of rules and limitations. The following sections provide an understanding of the boundaries and restrictions of pivot charts.

How Changes in Underlying Pivot Tables Affect Pivot Charts

The primary rule you should be cognizant of is that your pivot chart is merely an extension of your pivot table. If you refresh, move a field, add a field, remove a field, hide a data item, show a data item, or apply a filter, your pivot chart reflects your changes.

Placement of Data Fields in a Pivot Table Might Not Be Suited for a Pivot Chart

One common mistake people make when using pivot charts is assuming that Excel places the values in the column area of the pivot table in the x-axis of the pivot chart. For instance, the pivot table in Figure 6.5 is in a format that is easy to read and comprehend. The structure chosen shows Sales Periods in the column area and the Region in the row area. This structure works fine in the pivot table view.

Figure 6.5
The placement of your data fields works for a pivot table view.

	A	B	C	D	E	F
1						
2						
3	Sum of Sales_Amount	Sales_Period				
4	Region	P01	P02	P03	P04	P05	P0
5	MIDWEST	$109,498	$207,329	$101,861	$155,431	$159,298
6	NORTH	$180,772	$260,507	$183,151	$214,665	$235,369
7	SOUTH	$198,415	$334,189	$189,493	$255,558	$283,012
8	WEST	$193,180	$314,891	$183,106	$239,843	$248,124
9	Grand Total	$681,865	$1,116,916	$657,611	$865,498	$925,802

Suppose you decide to create a pivot chart from this pivot table. You would instinctively expect to see fiscal periods across the x-axis and lines of business along the y-axis. However, as you can see in Figure 6.6, your pivot chart comes out with Region in the x-axis and Sales Period in the y-axis.

Figure 6.6
Creating a pivot chart from your nicely structured pivot table does not yield the results you were expecting.

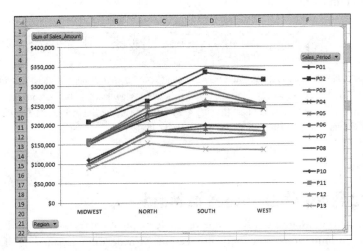

Why does the structure in your pivot table not translate to a clean pivot chart? The answer has to do with the way pivot charts handle the different areas of your pivot table.

In a pivot chart, both the x-axis and y-axis correspond to a specific area in your pivot table:

- **X-axis**—Corresponds to the row area in your pivot table and makes up the x-axis of your pivot chart.

- **Y-axis**—Corresponds to the column area in your pivot table and makes up the y-axis of your pivot chart.

Given this information, look at the pivot table in Figure 6.5 again. This structure says that the Sales_Period field will be treated as the y-axis because it is in the column area. The Region field will be treated as the x-axis because it is in the row area.

Now suppose you rearrange the pivot table to show fiscal periods in the row area and lines of business in the column area, as shown in Figure 6.7.

Figure 6.7
This format makes for slightly more difficult reading in a pivot table view but enables your pivot chart to give you the effect you are looking for.

	A	B	C	D	E	F
1						
2						
3	Sum of Sales_Amount	Region ▾				
4	Sales_Period ▾	MIDWEST	NORTH	SOUTH	WEST	Grand Total
5	P01	$109,498	$180,772	$198,415	$193,180	$681,865
6	P02	$207,329	$260,507	$334,189	$314,891	$1,116,916
7	P03	$101,861	$183,151	$189,493	$183,106	$657,611
8	P04	$155,431	$214,665	$255,558	$239,843	$865,498
9	P05	$159,298	$235,369	$283,012	$248,124	$925,802
10	P06	$149,426	$221,791	$249,258	$248,456	$868,930
11	P07	$101,809	$184,350	$180,146	$174,282	$640,587
12	P08	$207,278	$277,905	$345,842	$339,236	$1,170,262
13	P09	$98,129	$172,271	$163,153	$171,000	$604,552
14	P10	$156,974	$227,469	$251,042	$255,769	$891,253
15	P11	$159,130	$246,435	$293,184	$250,855	$949,605
16	P12	$154,276	$221,242	$261,113	$251,034	$887,665
17	P13	$88,448	$153,083	$137,053	$135,041	$513,625
18	Grand Total	$1,848,887	$2,779,009	$3,141,458	$3,004,818	$10,774,172

This arrangement generates the pivot table shown in Figure 6.8.

Figure 6.8
With the new arrangement in your pivot table, you get a pivot chart that makes sense.

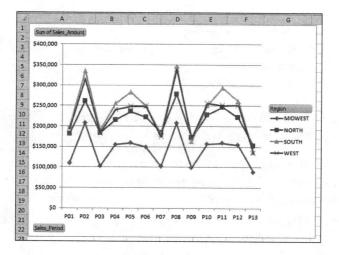

A Few Formatting Limitations Still Exist in Excel 2010

With legacy versions of Excel, many users avoided using pivot charts because of the formatting limitations that came with them. These limitations included the following:

■ Inability to resize or move key components of the pivot chart

- Loss of formatting when underlying pivot tables were changed
- Inability to use certain chart types

These limitations led to pivot charts being viewed by most users as too clunky and impractical to use.

Beginning with Excel 2007, Microsoft introduced substantial improvements to the pivot chart functionality. For example, it gave users the ability to format almost every property and component of a pivot chart. In addition, pivot charts in Excel 2007 no longer lost their formatting when the underlying pivot table changes. Pivot charts were also placed on the same worksheet as the source pivot table.

Excel 2010 continues to offer the functionality introduced in Excel 2007, with a few additions such as pivot field buttons and slicers. Overall, the look and feel of pivot charts in Excel 2010 is like that of standard charts, which makes them a more viable reporting option.

However, a few limitations persist in Excel 2010 that you should keep in mind:

- You still cannot use XY (scatter) charts, bubble charts, or stock charts when creating a pivot chart.
- Applied trend lines are often lost when adding or removing fields in the underlying pivot table.
- The chart titles in the pivot chart cannot be resized.

> **TIP**
> Although you cannot resize the chart titles in a pivot chart, making the font bigger or smaller indirectly resizes the chart title.

CASE STUDY CREATING A REPORT SHOWING INVOICE FREQUENCY AND REVENUE DISTRIBUTION BY PRODUCT

Say you have been asked to provide both region and market managers with an interactive reporting tool that will allow them to see the frequency and distribution of revenues across products easily. Your solution needs to give managers the flexibility to filter out a region or market if needed.

Given the amount of data in your source table and the possibility that this will be a recurring exercise, you decide to use a pivot chart. Start by building the pivot chart you see in Figure 6.9.

Figure 6.9
The initial pivot table meets all the data requirements.

	A	B	C
1	Region	(All)	
2	Market	(All)	
3			
4	Product_Description	Count of Invoice_Number	Sum of Sales_Amount
5	Cleaning & Housekeeping Services	2,534	$1,138,593
6	Facility Maintenance and Repair	21,351	$2,361,158
7	Fleet Maintenance	18,623	$2,627,798
8	Green Plants and Foliage Care	8,357	$1,276,783
9	Landscaping/Grounds Care	6,077	$1,190,915
10	Predictive Maintenance/Preventative Maintenance	11,672	$2,178,925

Next, place your cursor anywhere inside the pivot table and click Insert. On the Insert tab, you can see the Charts menu displaying the various types of charts you can create. Select the Column chart icon, and then select the first 2-D column chart. You immediately see the chart in Figure 6.10.

Figure 6.10
The raw pivot chart needs some formatting to meet requirements.

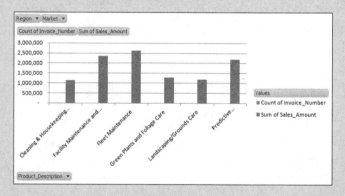

> **TIP**
> The next few steps in this case study expose you to some basic chart formatting techniques. To keep the focus of this book on pivot tables, any explanation on the techniques shown here is in the context of this case study. For a detailed look at creating, formatting, and managing charts in Excel 2010, refer to *Charts and Graphs for Microsoft Office Excel 2010* by Bill Jelen, Que, ISBN: 0789743124.

The first thing you notice is that only one of the two data series is visible, which is the series that represents Sales_Amount. The reason is that the two series are on such different scale ranges that the scale on the bigger series actually represses the other.

To fix this problem, you need to place one of the series on a secondary axis. To do this, right-click the Sales_Amount data series, and then select Format Data Series. After the Format Data Series dialog box activates, select the Secondary Axis radio button, as shown in Figure 6.11.

6

Figure 6.11
Place the Sales_Amount series on a secondary axis.

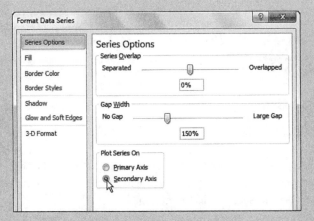

Next, right-click the Sales_Amount series again and select Change Series Chart Type. Select the Line with Markers chart type, as shown in Figure 6.12.

Figure 6.12
Change the chart type for the Sales_Amount data series to a line chart.

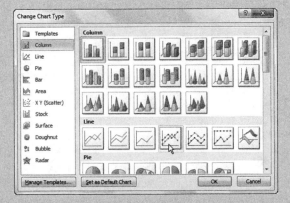

At this point, your pivot chart should look similar to the one in Figure 6.13. As you can see, the bars represent the number of invoices generated for each product, and the line represents the revenue for each product.

Figure 6.13
All that is required now is some final formatting.

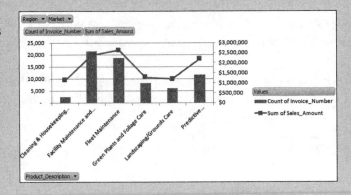

Next, change the data series names to be a bit more user-friendly. Activate the PivotTable Field List and change the names of the data fields in the pivot table from Count of Invoice_Number and Sum of Sales_Amount to something more appropriate. As you can see in Figure 6.14, Invoice Count and Revenue work well for this scenario.

Figure 6.14
The names on the data series are now a bit more user-friendly.

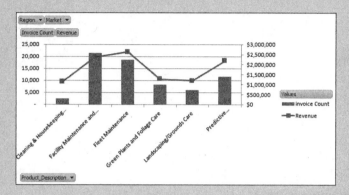

On an aesthetic note, the x-axis labels are difficult to read. This can be fixed by rotating the x-axis labels so they are vertical. To do this, right-click the x-axis labels and select Format Axis. When the Format Axis dialog box opens (see Figure 6.15), go to the Alignment section, and then use the Text Direction drop-down to rotate the text vertically.

Figure 6.15
Rotate the x-axis labels vertically.

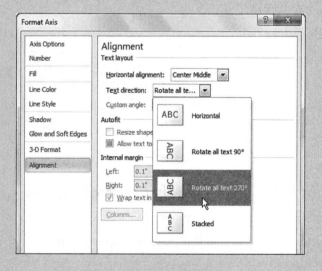

The final step is to remove any superfluous pivot field buttons from the chart because you only need the Region and Market drop-downs. These buttons give your users an interactive way to filter the pivot chart. The other gray buttons you see on the chart are not necessary.

You can remove superfluous pivot field buttons by clicking the chart and selecting the Analyze tab in the Ribbon. Use the Field Buttons drop-down to choose the field buttons you want visible in the chart. In this case, because you only want the Report Filter Field Buttons to be visible, select only that option. Figure 6.16 demonstrates how this is done.

Figure 6.16
Use the Field Buttons drop-down to hide any unwanted pivot field buttons on the chart.

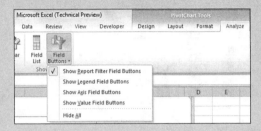

Your final pivot chart should look similar to the one in Figure 6.17.

Figure 6.17
Your final report meets all the requirements of content and interactivity.

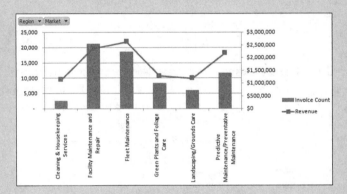

You now have a pivot chart that allows a manager to see the frequency a product is invoiced and the revenue it generates. This pivot chart also gives anyone using this report the ability to filter by region and market.

Examining Alternatives to Using Pivot Charts

There are generally two reasons why you would need an alternative to using pivot charts.

■ You do not want the overhead that comes with a pivot chart.

■ You want to avoid some of the formatting limitations of pivot charts.

In fact, sometimes you might create a pivot table simply to summarize and shape your data in preparation for charting. In these situations, you usually do not plan to keep your source data, and you definitely do not want a pivot cache taking up memory and file space.

In the example in Figure 6.18, you can see a pivot table that summarizes revenue by quarter for each product.

The idea in Figure 6.18 is that you created this pivot table only to summarize and shape your data for charting. However, you do not want to keep the source data, and you do not want to keep the pivot table with all its overhead. The problem is if you try to create a chart using the data in the pivot table, you inevitably create a pivot chart. This effectively means you have all the overhead of the pivot table looming in the background. This could be problematic if you do not want to share your source data with end users or if you do not want to inundate them with unnecessarily large files.

Figure 6.18
This pivot table was created to summarize and chart revenue by quarter for each product.

	A	B	C	D	E
1					
2	Sum of Sales_Amount	Invoice_Date			
3	Product_Description	Qtr1	Qtr2	Qtr3	Qtr4
4	Cleaning & Housekeeping Services	$257,218	$290,074	$297,251	$294,049
5	Facility Maintenance and Repair	$563,799	$621,715	$600,810	$574,834
6	Fleet Maintenance	$612,496	$691,440	$674,592	$649,269
7	Green Plants and Foliage Care	$293,194	$325,276	$329,787	$328,527
8	Landscaping/Grounds Care	$288,797	$310,670	$303,086	$288,363
9	Predictive Maintenance/Preventative Maintenance	$533,127	$567,391	$552,380	$526,027

The good news is there are a few simple techniques that enable you to create a chart from a pivot table, but not end up with a pivot chart. Any one of the following methods does the trick.

Method 1: Turn the Pivot Table into Hard Values

After you have created and structured your pivot table appropriately, select the entire pivot table and copy it. Then, select Paste Values from the Insert tab, as shown in Figure 6.19.

Figure 6.19
The Paste Values functionality is useful when you want to create hard-coded values from pivot tables.

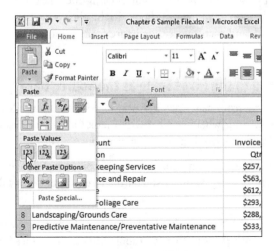

This action essentially deletes your pivot table, leaving you with the last values that were displayed in the pivot table. These values can subsequently be used to create a standard chart.

> **NOTE**   This technique effectively disables the dynamic functionality of your pivot chart. That is, your pivot chart becomes a standard chart that cannot be interactively filtered or refreshed. This is also true for Method 2 and Method 3, which are discussed next.

Method 2: Delete the Underlying Pivot Table

If you have already created your pivot chart, you can turn it into a standard chart by deleting the underlying pivot table. To do this, select the entire pivot table and press the Delete key. Keep in mind that unlike Method 1, with this method you are not left with any of the values that made up the source data for the chart. In other words, if anyone asks for the data that feeds the chart, you do not have it.

> **TIP**   Here is a handy tip to keep in the back of your mind. If you ever find yourself in a situation in which you have a chart but the data source is not available, activate the chart's data table. The data table lets you see the data values that feed each series in the chart.

Method 3: Distribute a Picture of the Pivot Chart

It might seem strange to distribute pictures of pivot chart, but this is an entirely viable method of distributing your analysis without a lot of overhead. In addition to small file sizes, you also get the added benefit of controlling what your clients get to see.

To use this method, copy the pivot chart by right-clicking the chart itself outside of the plot area, select Copy, and then open a new workbook. Right-click anywhere in the new workbook, select Paste Special, and then select the picture format you prefer. A picture of your pivot chart is placed in the new workbook.

Method 4: Use Cells Linked to the Pivot Table as the Source Data

Many Excel users shy away from using pivot charts solely based on the formatting restrictions and issues they encounter when working with them. Often these users give up the functionality of a pivot table to avoid the limitations of pivot charts.

However, if you want to retain key functionality in your pivot table, such as report filters and top 10 ranking, there is a way to link a standard chart to your pivot table without creating a pivot chart.

In the example in Figure 6.20, a pivot table shows the top 10 markets by contracted hours along with their total revenue. Notice that the report filter area enables you to filter by business segment so you can see the top 10 markets segment.

Suppose you want to turn this view into an XY scatter chart to point out the relationship between the contracted hours and revenues. You need to keep the functionality of filtering out 10 records by model number. However, you want to avoid the inability to create XY.

In this case, a pivot chart is definitely out because you cannot build pivot charts with certain chart types such as XY scatter charts. The techniques outlined in Methods 1, 2, and 3 are also out because those methods disable the interactivity you need. So, what is the solution?

The answer is to use the cells around the pivot table to link back to the data you need, and then chart those cells. In other words, you can build a mini data set that feeds your standard chart. This data set links back to the data items in your pivot table, so when your pivot table changes, so does your data set.

Figure 6.20

This pivot table enables you to filter by business segment to see the top 10 markets by total contracted hours and revenue.

	A	B	C
1	Business_Segment (All)		
2			
3	**Market**	**Contracted Hours**	**Sales_Amount**
4	CALIFORNIA	33,014	$2,254,735
5	CANADA	12,103	$776,245
6	CHARLOTTE	14,525	$890,522
7	DENVER	8,641	$645,583
8	FLORIDA	22,640	$1,450,392
9	KANSASCITY	8,547	$574,899
10	MICHIGAN	10,744	$678,705
11	NEWYORK	14,213	$873,581
12	PHOENIX	10,167	$570,255
13	TULSA	9,583	$628,405
14			

To do this, click your cursor in a cell next to your pivot table, as shown in Figure 6.21. Reference the first data item that you need to create the range you will feed your standard chart.

Figure 6.21

Start your linked data set by referencing the first data item you need to capture.

SUM		X ✓ fx	=B4		
	A	B	C	D	E
1	Business_Segment (All)				
2					
3	**Market**	**Contracted Hours**	**Sales_Amount**		
4	CALIFORNIA	33,014	$2,254,735		=B4
5	CANADA	12,103	$776,245		
6	CHARLOTTE	14,525	$890,522		
7	DENVER	8,641	$645,583		
8	FLORIDA	22,640	$1,450,392		
9	KANSASCITY	8,547	$574,899		
10	MICHIGAN	10,744	$678,705		
11	NEWYORK	14,213	$873,581		
12	PHOENIX	10,167	$570,255		
13	TULSA	9,583	$628,405		
14					

Next, copy the formula you just entered and paste that formula down and across to create your complete data set. At this point, you should have a data set that looks similar to Figure 6.22.

Figure 6.22
Copy the formula and paste it down and across to create your complete data set.

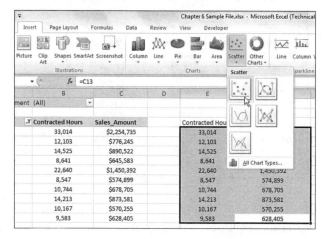

	Market	Contracted Hours	Sales_Amount		Contracted Hours	Sales_Amount
1	Business_Segment (All)					
3	Market	Contracted Hours	Sales_Amount		Contracted Hours	Sales_Amount
4	CALIFORNIA	33,014	$2,254,735		33,014	2,254,735
5	CANADA	12,103	$776,245		12,103	776,245
6	CHARLOTTE	14,525	$890,522		14,525	890,522
7	DENVER	8,641	$645,583		8,641	645,583
8	FLORIDA	22,640	$1,450,392		22,640	1,450,392
9	KANSASCITY	8,547	$574,899		8,547	574,899
10	MICHIGAN	10,744	$678,705		10,744	678,705
11	NEWYORK	14,213	$873,581		14,213	873,581
12	PHOENIX	10,167	$570,255		10,167	570,255
13	TULSA	9,583	$628,405		9,583	628,405

After your linked data set is complete, you can use it to create a standard chart. In this example, you are creating an XY scatter chart with this data (see Figure 6.23). You could never do this with a pivot chart.

Figure 6.23
Use your completed linked data set to create a standard chart.

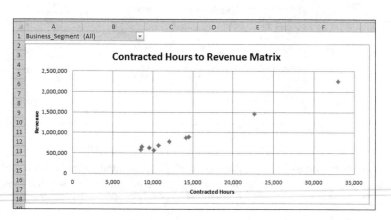

Figure 6.24 demonstrates how this solution offers the best of both worlds. You have kept the ability to filter out a particular business segment using the page field, and you have all the formatting freedom of a standard chart without any of the issues related to using a pivot chart.

Figure 6.24
This solution enables you to continue using the functionality of your pivot table without any of the formatting limitations you would have with a pivot chart.

Using Conditional Formatting with Pivot Tables

One of the most impressive new features of Excel 2010 is the conditional formatting functionality. In legacy versions of Excel, conditional formatting simply enabled you to change the color or formatting of a value or a range of cells dynamically based on a set of conditions you defined.

In Excel 2010, conditional formatting includes a more robust set of visualizations including data bars, color scales, and icon sets. These new visualizations enable users to build dashboard-style reporting that goes far beyond the traditional red, yellow, and green designations. What's more, conditional formatting has been extended to integrate with pivot tables. This means that in Excel 2010, conditional formatting is applied to a pivot table's structure, not just the cells it occupies.

In this section, you learn how to leverage the magic combination of pivot tables and conditional formatting to create interactive visualizations that serve as an alternative to pivot charts.

To start the first example, create the pivot table shown in Figure 6.25.

Figure 6.25
Create this pivot table.

◢	A	B	C
1	Market	(All) ▾	
2			
3	Sales_Period ▾	Sales_Amount	
4	P01	$681,865	
5	P02	$1,116,916	
6	P03	$657,611	
7	P04	$865,498	
8	P05	$925,802	
9	P06	$868,930	
10	P07	$640,587	
11	P08	$1,170,262	
12	P09	$604,552	
13	P10	$891,253	
14	P11	$949,605	
15	P12	$887,665	
16	P13	$513,625	
17			
18			

Say you want to create a report that allows your managers to see the performance of each sales period graphically. You could build a pivot chart, but you decide to use conditional formatting. In this example, take the easy route and apply some data bars.

First, select all the Sales_Amount values in the values area. After you have highlighted the revenue for each Sales_Period, click the Home tab, and then select Conditional Formatting in the Styles group to data bars, as shown in Figure 6.26.

As shown in Figure 6.27, you now have a set of bars that correspond to the values in your pivot table. This visualization looks similar to a sideways chart. What is more impressive is that as you filter the markets in the report filter area, the data bars dynamically update to correspond with the data for the selected market.

6

Figure 6.26
Apply data bars to the
values in your pivot table.

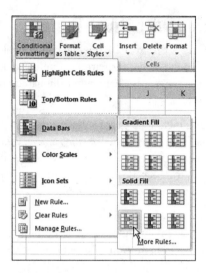

Figure 6.27
You have applied condi-
tional data bars with just
three easy clicks!

	A	B	C
1	Market	(All)	
2			
3	Sales_Period	Sales_Amount	
4	P01	$681,865	
5	P02	$1,116,916	
6	P03	$657,611	
7	P04	$865,498	
8	P05	$925,802	
9	P06	$868,930	
10	P07	$640,587	
11	P08	$1,170,262	
12	P09	$604,552	
13	P10	$891,253	
14	P11	$949,605	
15	P12	$887,665	
16	P13	$513,625	
17			
18			

Notice that you did not have to trudge through a dialog box to define the condition levels. This occurs because Excel 2010 has a handful of preprogrammed scenarios that can be leveraged when you want to spend less time configuring conditional formatting and more time analyzing data. For example, to create the data bars you just employed, Excel uses a predefined algorithm that takes the largest and smallest values in the selected range and calculates the condition levels for each bar.

Other examples of preprogrammed scenarios include:

- Top Nth Items
- Top Nth %
- Bottom Nth Items
- Bottom Nth %

- Above Average
- Below Average

Excel 2010 makes an effort to offer the conditions that are most commonly used in data analysis.

> **NOTE** To remove the applied conditional formatting, place your cursor inside the pivot table, click the Home tab, and select Conditional Formatting in the Styles group. Next, select Clear Rules, and then select Clear Rules from This PivotTable.

It is important to note that you are not limited to these preprogrammed scenarios. You can still create your own custom conditions. To help illustrate this, create the pivot table shown in Figure 6.28.

Figure 6.28
This pivot table shows Sales_Amount, Contracted Hours, and a calculated field that calculates Dollars Per Hour.

Market	Sales_Amount	Contracted Hours	Dollars Per Hour
Product_Description (All)			
BUFFALO	$450,478	6,864	$66
CALIFORNIA	$2,254,735	33,014	$68
CANADA	$776,245	12,103	$64
CHARLOTTE	$890,522	14,525	$61
DALLAS	$467,089	6,393	$73
DENVER	$645,583	8,641	$75
FLORIDA	$1,450,392	22,640	$64
KANSASCITY	$574,899	8,547	$67
MICHIGAN	$678,705	10,744	$63
NEWORLEANS	$333,454	5,057	$66
NEWYORK	$873,581	14,213	$61
PHOENIX	$570,255	10,167	$56
SEATTLE	$179,827	2,889	$62
TULSA	$628,405	9,583	$66
Grand Total	$10,774,172	165,380	$65

In the scenario shown in Figure 6.28, you want to evaluate the relationship between total revenue and dollars per hour. The idea is that some strategically applied conditional formatting helps identify opportunities for improvement.

To do this, begin by placing your cursor in the Sales_Amount column. Click the Home tab and select Conditional Formatting. Then, select New Rule. This activates the New Formatting Rule dialog box, as shown in Figure 6.29.

The objective in this dialog box is to identify the cells where the conditional formatting will be applied, specify the rule type to use, and define the details of the conditional formatting.

First, you must identify the cells where your conditional formatting will be applied. You have three choices:

- **Selected Cells**—Applies conditional formatting to only the selected cells.

6

- **All Cells Showing "Sales_Amount" Values**—Applies conditional formatting to all values in the Sales_Amount column including all subtotals and grand totals. This selection is ideal for use in analyses in which you are using averages, percentages, or other calculations where a single conditional formatting rule makes sense for all levels of analysis.

- **All Cells showing "Sales_Amount" Values for "Market"**—Applies conditional formatting to all values in the Sales_Amount column at the Market level only, except the subtotals and grand totals. This selection is ideal for use in analyses where you are using calculations that make sense only within the context of the level being measured.

Figure 6.29
The New Formatting Rule dialog box.

> **NOTE** The words Sales_Amount and Market are not permanent fixtures of the New Formatting Rule dialog box. These words change to reflect the fields in your pivot table. Sales_Amount is used because your cursor is in that column. Market is used because the active data items in the pivot table are in the Market field.

In this example, select the All Cells Showing "Sales_Amount" Values for "Market" radio button because it makes the most sense, as shown in Figure 6.30.

Next, in the Select a Rule Type section, specify the rule type you want to use for the conditional format by selecting one of the following five rule types:

- **Format All Cells Based on Their Values**—Enables you to apply conditional formatting based on some comparison of the actual values of the selected range. In other words, the values in the selected range are measured against each other. This selection is ideal when you want to identify general anomalies in your data set.

- **Format Only Cells That Contain**—Enables you to apply conditional formatting to those cells that meet specific criteria you define. Keep in mind that the values in your range are not measured against each other when you use this rule type. This selection is useful when you are comparing your values against a predefined benchmark.

- **Format Only Top or Bottom Ranked Values**—Enables you to apply conditional formatting to those cells that are ranked in the top or bottom *N*th number or percent of all the values in the range.

- **Format Only Values That Are Above or Below the Average**—Enables you to apply conditional formatting to those values that are mathematically above or below the average of all values in the selected range.

- **Use a Formula to Determine Which Cells to Format**—Enables you to specify your own formula and evaluate each value in the selected range against that formula. If the values evaluate as true, then the conditional formatting is applied. This selection comes in handy when you are applying conditions based on the results of an advanced formula or mathematical operation.

Figure 6.30
Select the All Cells Showing "Sales_Amount" Values for "Market" radio button.

> **NOTE**
> Data bars, color scales, and icon sets can be used only when the selected cells are formatted based on their values. This means that if you want to use data bars, color scales, and icon sets, you must select the Format All Cells Based on Their Values rule type.

In this scenario, you want to identify problem areas using icon sets. With this in mind, format the cells based on their values.

Finally, you need to define the details of the conditional formatting in the Edit the Rule Description section. Again, you want to identify problem areas using the slick new icon sets that are offered by Excel 2010. In that light, select Icon Sets from the Format Style drop-down box.

After selecting Icon Sets, select a style appropriate to your analysis. The style selected in Figure 6.31 is ideal in situations in which your pivot tables cannot always be viewed in color.

Figure 6.31
Select Icon Sets from the Format Style drop-down.

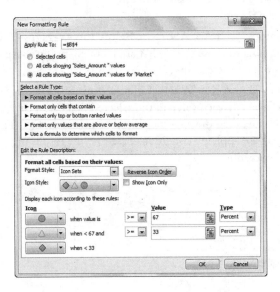

With this configuration, Excel applies the sign icons based on the percentile bands >=67, >=33, and <33. Keep in mind that the actual percentile bands could be changed based on your needs. In this scenario, the default percentile bands are sufficient.

Click OK to apply the conditional formatting. As you can see in Figure 6.32, you now have icons that enable you to determine where each market falls in relation to other markets as it pertains to revenue.

Next, apply the same conditional formatting to the Dollars Per Hour field. When you are done, your pivot table should look similar to the one shown in Figure 6.33.

Take a moment to analyze the report you have created. With this view, a manager can analyze the relationship between total revenue and dollars per hour. For example, the Dallas market manager can see that he is in the bottom percentile for revenue but in the top percentile for dollars per hour. With this information, he immediately sees that his dollars per hour rates might be too high for his market. Conversely, the New York market manager can see that she is in the top percentile for revenue but in the bottom percentile for dollars per hour. This tells her that her dollars per hour rates might be too low for her market.

Figure 6.32
You have applied your first custom conditional formatting!

	A	B	C	D
1	Product_Description	(All)		
2				
3	Market	Sales_Amount	Contracted Hours	Dollars Per Hour
4	BUFFALO	◆ $450,478	6,864	$66
5	CALIFORNIA	● $2,254,735	33,014	$68
6	CANADA	◆ $776,245	12,103	$64
7	CHARLOTTE	△ $890,522	14,525	$61
8	DALLAS	◆ $467,089	6,393	$73
9	DENVER	◆ $645,583	8,641	$75
10	FLORIDA	△ $1,450,392	22,640	$64
11	KANSASCITY	◆ $574,899	8,547	$67
12	MICHIGAN	◆ $678,705	10,744	$63
13	NEWORLEANS	◆ $333,454	5,057	$66
14	NEWYORK	△ $873,581	14,213	$61
15	PHOENIX	◆ $570,255	10,167	$56
16	SEATTLE	◆ $179,827	2,889	$62
17	TULSA	◆ $628,405	9,583	$66
18	Grand Total	$10,774,172	165,380	$65

Figure 6.33
You have successfully created an interactive visualization.

	A	B	C	D
1	Product_Description	(All)		
2				
3	Market	Sales_Amount	Contracted Hours	Dollars Per Hour
4	BUFFALO	◆ $450,478	6,864	△ $66
5	CALIFORNIA	● $2,254,735	33,014	△ $68
6	CANADA	◆ $776,245	12,103	△ $64
7	CHARLOTTE	△ $890,522	14,525	◆ $61
8	DALLAS	◆ $467,089	6,393	● $73
9	DENVER	◆ $645,583	8,641	● $75
10	FLORIDA	△ $1,450,392	22,640	△ $64
11	KANSASCITY	◆ $574,899	8,547	△ $67
12	MICHIGAN	◆ $678,705	10,744	△ $63
13	NEWORLEANS	◆ $333,454	5,057	△ $66
14	NEWYORK	△ $873,581	14,213	◆ $61
15	PHOENIX	◆ $570,255	10,167	◆ $56
16	SEATTLE	◆ $179,827	2,889	△ $62
17	TULSA	◆ $628,405	9,583	△ $66
18	Grand Total	$10,774,172	165,380	$65

NOTE

Remember that this in an interactive report. This means that each manager can view the same analysis by product by filtering the report filter area.

Next Steps

In the next chapter, you learn how to bring together disparate data sources into one pivot table. You also create a pivot table from multiple data sets, and you learn the basics of creating pivot tables from other pivot tables.

Analyzing Disparate Data Sources with Pivot Tables

7

Until this point, you have been working with one local table located in the worksheet within which you are operating. Indeed, it would be wonderful if every data set you came across were neatly packed in one easy-to-use Excel table. Unfortunately, the business of data analysis does not always work out that way.

The reality is that some of the data you encounter comes from disparate data sources—meaning sets of data that are from separate systems, stored in different locations, or saved in a variety of formats. In an Excel environment, disparate data sources generally fall into one of two categories: external data and multiple ranges.

External data is exactly what it sounds like—data that is not located in the Excel workbook in which you are operating. Some examples of external data sources are text files, Access tables, SQL Server tables, and other Excel workbooks.

Multiple ranges are separate data sets located in the same workbook but separated either by blank cells or by different worksheets. For example, if your workbook has three tables on three different worksheets, each of your data sets covers a range of cells. You are therefore working with multiple ranges.

A pivot table can be an effective tool when you need to summarize data that is not neatly packed into one table. With a pivot table, you can quickly bring together either data found in an external source or data found in multiple tables within your workbook. In this chapter, you discover how to work with external data sources and data sets located in multiple ranges within your workbook.

Using Multiple Consolidation Ranges

If you need to analyze data dispersed in multiple ranges, your options are somewhat limited. For example, the data in Figure 7.1 shows you three ranges that you need to bring together to analyze as a group.

Figure 7.1
Someone passed you a file that has three ranges of data. You need to bring the three ranges together so you can analyze them as a group.

	A	B	C	D	E	F	
1	NORTH						
2	Line of Business	Lob Manager	Jan	Feb	Mar	Apr	
3	Copier Sale	Jim Graham	$1,670,642	$1,908,785	$2,185,037	$2,239,371	$2
4	Parts	Mike Alexander	$2,378,240	$2,372,974	$2,537,793	$2,429,561	$2
5	Printer Sale	Allan Howe	$1,443,106	$1,628,517	$1,745,271	$1,545,072	$1
6	Service Plan	Kelly Richardson	$17,098,331	$17,045,471	$17,497,027	$16,903,477	$1
7							
8	SOUTH						
9	Line of Business	Lob Manager	Jan	Feb	Mar	Apr	
10	Copier Sale	Jim Graham	$2,703,264	$2,923,311	$2,869,761	$2,892,764	$3
11	Parts	Mike Alexander	$2,457,824	$2,658,591	$2,736,089	$2,493,456	$2
12	Printer Sale	Allan Howe	$2,016,462	$2,378,109	$2,467,409	$2,089,987	$2
13	Service Plan	Kelly Richardson	$18,922,385	$19,240,187	$19,100,783	$19,072,738	$1
14							
15	WEST						
16	Line of Business	Lob Manager	Jan	Feb	Mar	Apr	
17	Copier Sale	Jim Graham	$1,672,342	$1,913,201	$2,000,897	$2,073,048	$1
18	Parts	Mike Alexander	$1,840,374	$2,041,408	$1,899,784	$2,028,641	$2
19	Printer Sale	Allan Howe	$1,383,284	$1,630,537	$1,676,003	$1,495,751	$1
20	Service Plan	Kelly Richardson	$12,840,822	$12,878,362	$12,728,642	$12,405,450	$1

You essentially have three paths you can take to get to the point where you can analyze all three ranges together:

- You can obtain the original data used to create this summary. This seems like a good choice, but in most cases, you could find another solution by the time it took you to obtain the original data—if you have access to it at all.
- You can manually shape the data into a proper tabular data set and then do your analysis. In reality, this option would be the best one if you had the time to spare or you were planning to use this data on an ongoing basis. However, if this is a one-time analysis or if you're in a crunch, you would not want to spend the time to manually format this data.
- You can create a pivot table using multiple consolidation ranges. With this pivot table option, you can quickly and easily consolidate all the data from your selected ranges into a single pivot table. This is the best option if you need to perform only a one-time analysis on multiple ranges or if you need to analyze multiple ranges in a hurry.

To start the process of bringing this data together with a pivot table, you have to activate the classic PivotTable and PivotChart Wizard.

ACTIVATING THE CLASSIC PIVOTTABLE AND PIVOTCHART WIZARD

As you learned in Chapter 2, "Creating a Basic Pivot Table," Microsoft has abandoned the classic PivotTable and PivotChart Wizard for a streamlined dialog box. Unfortunately, some of the functionality exposed in the classic wizard was not brought over with the new pivot table interfaces. The capability to create multiple consolidation range pivot tables is one example of functionality that did not make its way to Excel's new UI.

The good news is that Excel does enable you to activate the classic wizard (complete with all the old functionality) through a custom toolbar command. The idea is to add the PivotTable and PivotChart Wizard custom toolbar command to the Quick Access toolbar. After it's on the Quick Access toolbar, you can call up the classic wizard simply by clicking on the icon.

Follow these steps to add the PivotTable and PivotChart Wizard custom toolbar command to the Quick Access toolbar:

1. Click the File tab on the Ribbon.
2. Select Options to open the Options dialog box.
3. Select Quick Access Toolbar to bring up all the available commands that can be added to the Quick Access toolbar.
4. In the Choose Commands From drop-down box, select Commands Not in the Ribbon.
5. Select the PivotTable and PivotChart Wizard from the list of commands and click the Add button.
6. Click OK.

As you can see in Figure 7.2, your reward is an easily accessible icon that calls the classic PivotTable and PivotChart Wizard.

> **TIP**
> You can also activate the classic PivotTable and PivotChart Wizard by pressing Alt+D+P on your keyboard. Keep in mind this approach does not add an icon to the Quick Access toolbar.

Figure 7.2
Add the PivotTable and PivotChart Wizard command to the Quick Access toolbar.

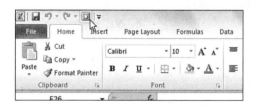

After you have access to the PivotTable and PivotChart Wizard, activate it and then select Multiple Consolidation Ranges, as demonstrated in Figure 7.3. Then, select Next.

In the next step, you specify if you want Excel to create one page field for you or if you would like to create your own. In most cases, the page fields that Excel creates are ambiguous and of no value. Therefore, in almost all cases, you should select the option of creating your own page fields, as illustrated in Figure 7.4. Then, select Next.

Next, you need to point Excel to each of your individual data sets one by one. Simply select the entire range of your first data set and select Add, as shown in Figure 7.5.

7

Figure 7.3
Start the PivotTable and PivotChart Wizard and select Multiple Consolidation Ranges. Select Next to move to the next step.

Figure 7.4
Specify that you want to create your own page fields, and then select Next.

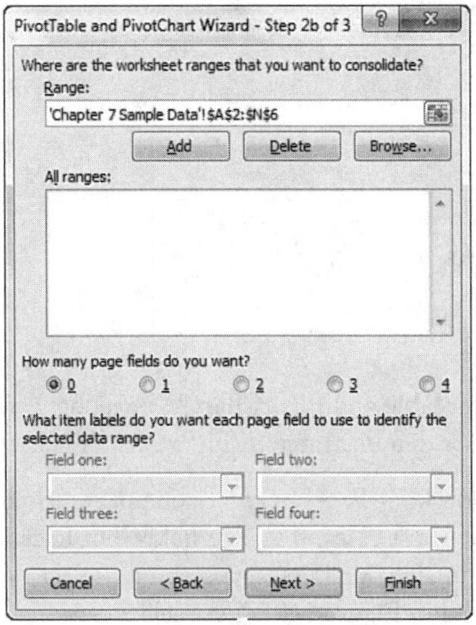

Figure 7.5
Select the entire range of your first data set and select Add.

> **CAUTION**
>
> For your pivot table to generate properly, the first line of each range must include column labels.

Select the rest of your ranges and add them to your list of ranges. At this point, your dialog box should look similar to the one in Figure 7.6.

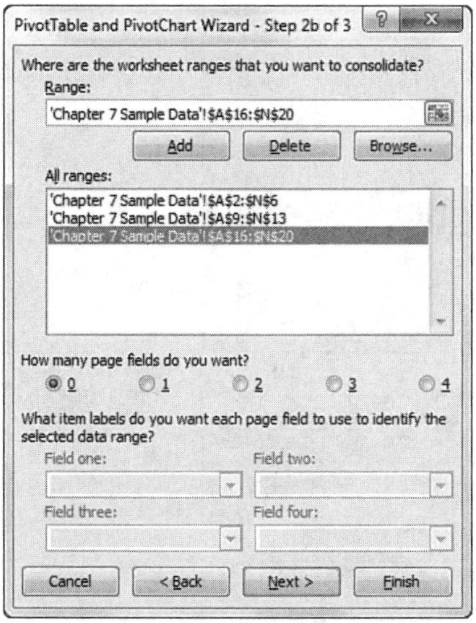

Figure 7.6
Add the other two data set ranges to your range list.

Notice that each of your data sets belongs to a Region (North, South, or West). When your pivot table brings your three data sets together, you need a way to parse out each Region again.

To ensure you have that capability, you need to tag each range in your list of ranges with a name identifying which data set that range came from. The result is the creation of a Page field that enables you to filter each region as needed.

The first thing you have to do to create your Region page field is specify how many page fields you want to create. In your case, you want to create only one page field for your region identifier, so simply click the radio button next to the number 1, as demonstrated in Figure 7.7. This action enables the Field One input box. As you can see, you can create up to four page fields.

You have to tag each range one by one, so click the first range in your range list to highlight it. Enter the region name into the Field One input box. As you can see in Figure 7.8, the first range is made up of data from the North region, so you enter **North** in the input box.

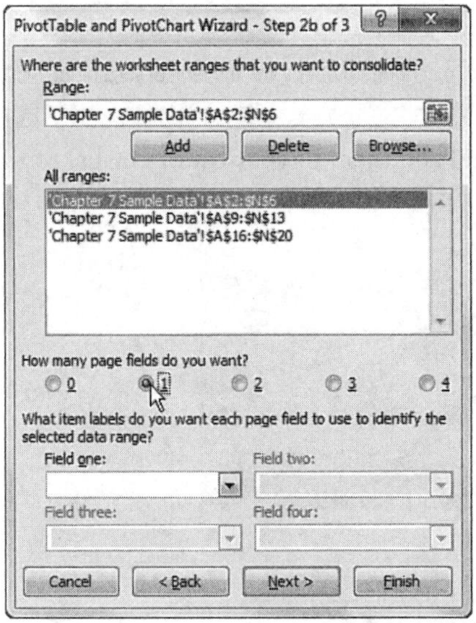

Figure 7.7
To be able to filter by Region when your pivot table is complete, you have to create a page field. Click the radio button next to the number 1 to create one page field. This action enables the Field One input box.

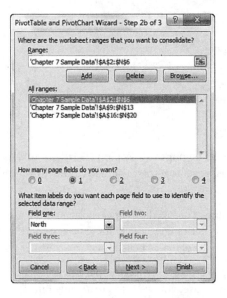

Figure 7.8
Select the first range that represents the data set for the North region and enter the word North in the input box.

Repeat the process for the other regions, as illustrated in Figure 7.9. When you're done, select Next.

The last step is to choose the destination of your new pivot table. In this case, select the New worksheet option, and then click Finish.

You have successfully brought three data sources together into one pivot table, as shown in Figure 7.10.

Figure 7.9
Repeat the process until you have tagged all your data sets. When you're done, select Next.

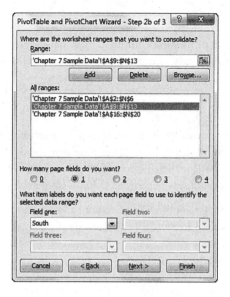

Figure 7.10
You now have a pivot table that contains data from three data sources.

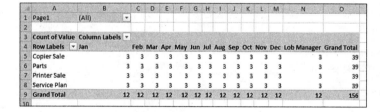

Analyzing the Anatomy of a Multiple Consolidation Range Pivot Table

Take a moment to analyze your new pivot table. You might notice a few interesting things. First, your field list includes a field called Row, a field called Column, a field called Value, and a field called Page1.

It is important to keep in mind that pivot tables using multiple consolidation ranges as their data source can have only three base fields: Row, Column, and Value. In addition to these base fields, you can create up to four page fields.

> **TIP**
> Notice that the fields generated with your pivot table have fairly generic names (Row, Column, Value, and Page). You can customize the field settings for these fields to rename and format them to better suit your needs.

→ See Chapter 3, "Customizing a Pivot Table," for a more detailed look at customizing field settings.

7

The Row Field

The Row field is always made up of the first column in your data source. Note that in Figure 7.1, the first column in your data source is Line of Business. Therefore, the Row field in your newly created pivot table contains Line of Business.

The Column Field

The Column field contains the remaining columns in your data source. Pivot tables that use multiple consolidation ranges combine all the fields in your original data sets (minus the first column, which is used for the Row field) into a kind of super field called the Column field. The fields in your original data sets become data items under the Column field.

Notice that your pivot table initially applies Count to your Column field. If you change the field setting of the Column field to Sum, all the data items under the Column field are affected. Figure 7.11 shows the same data as Figure 7.10, except the summarize type is set to Sum instead of the default Count.

Figure 7.11
The data items under the Column field are treated as one entity. When you change the calculation of the Column field from Count to Sum, the change applies to all items under the Column field.

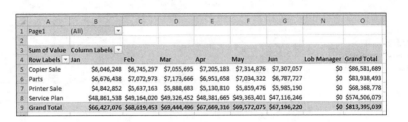

	A	B	C	D	E	F	G	N	O
1	Page1	(All)							
2									
3	Sum of Value	Column Labels							
4	Row Labels	Jan	Feb	Mar	Apr	May	Jun	Lob Manager	Grand Total
5	Copier Sale	$6,046,248	$6,745,297	$7,055,695	$7,205,183	$7,314,876	$7,307,057	$0	$86,581,689
6	Parts	$6,676,438	$7,072,973	$7,173,666	$6,951,658	$7,034,322	$6,787,727	$0	$83,938,493
7	Printer Sale	$4,842,852	$5,637,163	$5,888,683	$5,130,810	$5,859,476	$5,985,190	$0	$68,368,778
8	Service Plan	$48,861,538	$49,164,020	$49,326,452	$48,381,665	$49,363,401	$47,116,246	$0	$574,506,079
9	Grand Total	$66,427,076	$68,619,453	$69,444,496	$67,669,316	$69,572,075	$67,196,220	$0	$813,395,039

The Value Field

The Value field contains the value for all data items under the Column field. Notice that even fields that were originally text fields in your data set are treated as numerical values. An example is Lob Manager in Column N, which is shown in Figure 7.11. Although this field contained manager names in the original data set, it is now treated as a number in your pivot table.

As mentioned before, pivot tables that use multiple consolidation ranges merge the fields in your original data sets (minus the first field), making them data items in the Column field. Although you might recognize fields like Lob Manager as text fields that contain their own individual data items, they no longer hold data of their own. They have been transformed into data items themselves—data items with a value.

The net effect of this behavior is that fields originally holding text or dates show up in your pivot table as a meaningless numerical value. It's usually a good idea to simply hide these fields to avoid confusion.

→ See Chapter 3, "Customizing a Pivot Table," for a more detailed look at customizing field settings.

7

The Page Fields

Page fields are the only fields in multiple consolidation range pivot tables that you have direct control over. You can create and define up to four page fields. The useful feature of these fields is that you can drag them to the row area or column area to add layers to your pivot table.

The Page1 field shown in the pivot table in Figure 7.11 was created to filter by region. However, if you move the Page1 field to the row area of your pivot table, you can create a one-shot view of all your data by region. Figure 7.12 demonstrates this view.

> **TIP**
> Your pivot table might have a different layout than Figure 7.12. You can achieve the same layout by selecting Design from the PivotTable Tools tab, and then selecting Report Layout in the Layout group. Then, you can select Show in Tabular Form to get the same layout.

Figure 7.12
Moving the Page1 field to the row area adds a layer to your pivot table report, giving you a one-shot view of all your data by region.

	A	B	C	D	E	F	G	N	O	P
3	Sum of Value		Column							
4	Page1	Row	Jan	Feb	Mar	Apr	May	Dec	Lob Manager	Grand Total
5	North	Copier Sale	$1,670,642	$1,908,785	$2,185,037	$2,239,371	$2,121,648	$2,210,070	$0	$25,893,618
6		Parts	$2,378,240	$2,372,974	$2,537,793	$2,429,561	$2,419,169	$2,480,289	$0	$29,063,171
7		Printer Sale	$1,443,106	$1,628,517	$1,745,271	$1,545,072	$1,808,141	$1,701,849	$0	$20,621,317
8		Service Plan	$17,098,331	$17,045,471	$17,497,027	$16,903,477	$17,157,864	$16,408,849	$0	$201,414,511
9	North Total		$22,590,319	$22,955,747	$23,965,128	$23,117,481	$23,506,822	$22,801,057	$0	$276,992,617
10	South	Copier Sale	$2,703,264	$2,923,311	$2,869,761	$2,892,764	$3,203,760	$2,887,451	$0	$36,711,470
11		Parts	$2,457,824	$2,658,591	$2,736,089	$2,493,456	$2,583,428	$2,558,530	$0	$31,205,269
12		Printer Sale	$2,016,462	$2,378,109	$2,467,409	$2,089,987	$2,351,109	$2,217,202	$0	$28,153,264
13		Service Plan	$18,922,385	$19,240,187	$19,100,783	$19,072,738	$19,193,191	$18,262,758	$0	$223,750,307
14	South Total		$26,099,935	$27,200,198	$27,174,042	$26,548,945	$27,331,488	$25,925,941	$0	$319,820,310
15	West	Copier Sale	$1,672,342	$1,913,201	$2,000,897	$2,073,048	$1,989,468	$1,938,033	$0	$23,976,601
16		Parts	$1,840,374	$2,041,408	$1,899,784	$2,028,641	$2,031,725	$1,874,497	$0	$23,670,053
17		Printer Sale	$1,383,284	$1,630,537	$1,676,003	$1,495,751	$1,700,226	$1,512,818	$0	$19,594,197
18		Service Plan	$12,840,822	$12,878,362	$12,728,642	$12,405,450	$13,012,346	$12,055,176	$0	$149,341,261
19	West Total		$17,736,822	$18,463,508	$18,305,326	$18,002,890	$18,733,765	$17,380,524	$0	$216,582,112
20	Grand Total		$66,427,076	$68,619,453	$69,444,496	$67,669,316	$69,572,075	$66,107,522	$0	$813,395,039

Redefining Your Pivot Table

You might run into a situation in which you need to redefine your pivot table. That is, you need to add a data range, remove a data range, or redefine your page fields. To redefine your pivot table, simply activate the classic PivotTable and PivotChart Wizard, and then select the Back button until you get to the dialog box you need.

Building a Pivot Table Using External Data Sources

There is no argument that Excel is good at processing and analyzing data. In fact, pivot tables themselves are a testament to the analytical power of Excel. However, despite all its strengths, Excel makes for a poor data management platform, primarily for three reasons:

- A data set's size has a significant impact on performance, making for less efficient data crunching. The reason for this is the fundamental way Excel handles memory. When you open an Excel file, the entire file is loaded into RAM to ensure quick data processing and access. The drawback to this behavior is that Excel requires a great deal of RAM to process even the smallest change in your spreadsheet (typically giving you a "Calculating" indicator in the status bar). So although Excel 2010 offers over 1 million rows and over 16,000 columns, creating and managing large data sets causes Excel to slow down considerably, making data analysis a painful endeavor.

- The lack of a relational data structure forces the use of flat tables that promote redundant data. It also increases the chance for errors.

- There is no way to index data fields in Excel to optimize performance when you're attempting to retrieve large amounts of data.

In smart organizations, the task of data management is not performed by Excel; rather, it is primarily performed by relational database systems such as Microsoft Access and SQL Server. These databases are used to store millions of records that can be rapidly searched and retrieved.

The effect of this separation in tasks is that you have a data management layer (your database) and a presentation layer (Excel). The trick is to find the best way to get information from your data management layer to your presentation layer for use by your pivot table.

Managing your data is the general idea behind building your pivot table using an external data source. Building your pivot tables from external systems enables you to leverage environments that are better suited to data management. This means you can let Excel do what it does best: analyze and create a presentation layer for your data. The following sections walk you through several techniques that enable you to build pivot tables using external data.

Building a Pivot Table with Microsoft Access Data

Often Access is used to manage a series of tables that interact with each other, such as a Customers table, an Orders table, and an Invoices table. Managing data in Access provides the benefit of a relational database where you can ensure data integrity, prevent redundancy, and easily generate data sets via queries.

The modus operandi of most Excel users is to use an Access query to create a subset of data and then import that data into Excel. From there, the data can be analyzed with pivot tables. The problem with this method is that it forces the Excel workbook to hold two copies of the imported data sets: one on the spreadsheet and one in the pivot cache. Holding two copies obviously causes the workbook to be twice as big as it needs to be, and it introduces the possibility of performance issues.

Excel 2010 offers a surprisingly easy way to use your Access data without creating two copies of your data. To see how easy it is, open Excel and start a new workbook. Then, click the Data tab and look for the group called Get External Data. Here, you find the From Access selection, as shown in Figure 7.19.

Figure 7.19
Click the From Access button to get data from your Access database.

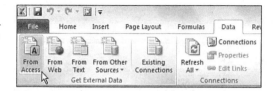

The sample database used in this chapter is available for download from www.MrExcel.com/pivotbookdata2010.html.

Selecting the From Access button activates a dialog box asking you to select the database you want to work with. Select your database.

After your database has been selected, the dialog box shown in Figure 7.20 activates. This dialog box lists all the tables and queries available. In this example, select the query called Sales_By_Employee and click OK.

Figure 7.20
Select the table or query you want to analyze.

NOTE In Figure 7.20, notice that the Select Table dialog box contains a column called Type. There are two types of Access objects you can work with: Views and Tables. View indicates that the data set listed is an Access query, and Table indicates that the data set is an Access table.

In this example, notice that Sales_By_Employee is actually an Access query. This means that you import the results of the query. This is true interaction at work; Access does all the backend data management and aggregation, and Excel handles the analysis and presentation!

Next, you see the Import Data dialog box, where you select the format in which you want to import the data. As you can see in Figure 7.21, you have the option of importing the data as a table, as a pivot table, or as a pivot chart with an accompanying pivot table. You also have the option to tell Excel where to place the data.

Select the radio button next to PivotTable Report and click OK.

At this point, you should see the PivotTable Field List shown in Figure 7.22. From here, you can use this pivot table just as you normally would.

7

Figure 7.21
Select the radio button next to PivotTable Report.

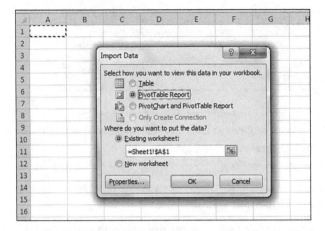

Figure 7.22
Your pivot table is ready to use.

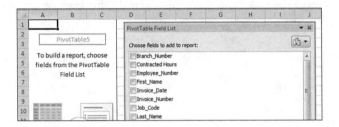

The wonderful thing about this technique is that the only copy of the data resides inside the pivot cache. You won't find the data in any of the other tabs. Does this present a problem when you need to get to the raw data in the pivot cache? The answer is no.

You can tell the pivot cache to output a raw data set for any dimension in the pivot table simply by double-clicking on the data for that dimension. For example, Figure 7.23 illustrates how double-clicking the Grand Total for Mr. Gall outputs all the raw records that make up his Grand Total. The output is automatically placed into a separate tab.

Figure 7.23
Double-clicking on the totals in the data area of a pivot table outputs the raw records that make up that total into a separate tab.

> **CAUTION**
>
> If you create a pivot table that uses an Access database as its source, you can refresh that pivot table only if the table or view is available. That is, deleting, moving, or renaming the database used to create the pivot table destroys the link to the external data set, thus destroying your ability to refresh the data. Deleting or renaming the source table or query has the same effect.
>
> Following that reasoning, any clients using your linked pivot table cannot refresh the pivot table unless the source is available to them. If you need your clients to be able to refresh, you might want to make the data source available via a shared network directory.

Building a Pivot Table with SQL Server Data

In the spirit of collaboration, Excel 2010 vastly improves your ability to connect to transactional databases such as a SQL Server. With its new connection functionality found in Excel, creating a pivot table from SQL Server data is as easy as ever.

Start on the Data tab and select From Other Sources to see the drop-down menu shown Figure 7.24. Then, select From SQL Server.

Figure 7.24
Select From SQL Server from the drop-down menu.

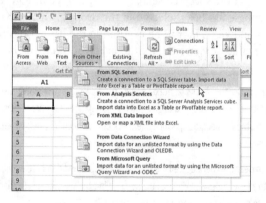

Selecting this option activates the Data Connection Wizard, as shown in Figure 7.25. The idea here is that you configure your connection settings so Excel can establish a link to the server.

> **NOTE**
> There is no sample file for this case study. The essence of this demonstration is the interaction between Excel and a SQL Server data source. The actions you take to connect to your particular database are the same as demonstrated here.

The first step in this endeavor is to provide Excel with some authentication information. As you can see in Figure 7.25, you enter the name of your server, your username, and your password.

7

Figure 7.25
Enter your authentication information and click Next.

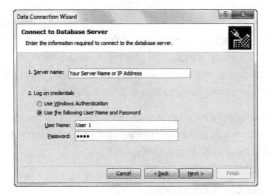

> **NOTE**
> If you are typically authenticated via Windows authentication, you simply select the Use Windows Authentication option.

Next, you select the database with which you are working from a drop-down menu containing all available databases on the specified server. As you can see in Figure 7.26, a database called Facility_Svcs_Database has been selected in the drop-down box. Selecting this database causes all the tables and views in it to be exposed in the list of objects below the drop-down menu. Choose the table or view you want to analyze, and then click Next.

> **TIP**
> In Figure 7.26, notice the check box titled Connect to a Specific Table. In most cases, you connect to one table or view that has been created to give you an aggregation or a smaller subset of data for analysis. For this reason, the Connect to a Specific Table check box is selected by default, enabling you to make only one selection.
>
> If you were to clear the check box, all the objects in the specified database would be selected, giving you access to all the tables and views available. Enabling the selection of all objects in the database enables you to create your own aggregations and queries using MS Query.

Figure 7.26
Specify your database, and then choose the table or view you want to analyze.

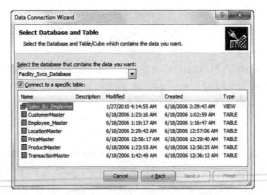

The next screen in the wizard, as shown in Figure 7.27, enables you to enter some descriptive information about the connection you've just created.

Figure 7.27
Edit descriptive information for your connection.

The fields that you use most often are:

- **File Name**—In the File Name input box, you can change the filename of the .odc (Office Data Connection) file generated to store the configuration information for the link you just created.

- **Save Password in File**—Under the File Name input box, you have the option of saving the password for your external data in the file itself via the Save Password in File check box. Selecting this check box enters your password in the file.

> **CAUTION**
>
> Keep in mind that this password is not encrypted, so anyone interested enough could potentially get the password for your data source simply by viewing your file with a text editor.

- **Description**—In the Description field, you can enter a plain description of what this particular data connection does.

- **Friendly Name**—The Friendly Name field enables you to specify your own name for the external source. You typically enter a name that is descriptive and easy to read.

7

When you are satisfied with your descriptive edits, click Finish to finalize your connection settings. You immediately see the Import Data dialog box, as shown in Figure 7.28. From here, you select a pivot table, and then click OK to start building your pivot table.

Figure 7.28
When your connection is finalized, you can start building your pivot table.

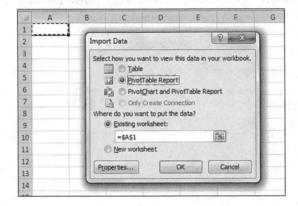

Next Steps

Chapter 8, "Sharing Pivot Tables with Others," covers the ins and outs of sharing your pivot tables with the world. You learn how you can distribute your pivot tables to the Web, publish your pivot tables to Excel services, and render your pivot tables through other Microsoft Office applications.

Sharing Pivot Tables with Others

As pivot tables evolved in Excel 2007 and Excel 2010, certain incompatibilities were introduced when you share your pivot table with people using legacy versions of Office.

Office 2003 had offered a way to share pivot tables with interactivity to a web page using Office Web Services. This ability was removed in Excel 2007 and is now replaced in Excel 2010 using the Excel Web Application. The Excel Web Application offers interactivity with slicers. The Excel Web Application is actually a hosted version of the Excel Services functionality introduced in Excel 2007 for people using SharePoint.

8

Sharing a Pivot Table with Other Versions of Office

A version property is attached to every pivot table. This property controls certain behaviors for compatibility with previous versions of Excel.

New pivot tables created in Excel 2010 have a version number of 14, whereas pivot tables created in Excel 2007 have a version number of 12. Pivot tables that were created originally in Excel 2002 or 2003 have a version number of 10. This section explains the compatibility issues you encounter when opening a pivot table created with a different version of Excel.

Compatibility Issues Between Excel 2007 and Excel 2010

You should be thrilled that Microsoft continues to invest heavily in pivot tables. The downside of this investment is that pivot tables created in Excel 2010 will not play well with people who are using Excel 2007. Several issues are explained here.

Slicers Disappear in Excel 2007

Slicers were not available in Excel 2007. For this reason, if you create a slicer in Excel 2010, and then open that workbook in Excel 2007, a box appears where the slicer used to be. The box indicates that this shape represents a slicer created in a newer version of Excel and cannot be used in this version.

However, the problem is a bit more insidious. In Figure 8.1, a slicer in an Excel 2010 pivot table limits the pivot table to only the East region. Sales are $2.4 million.

Figure 8.1
An Excel 2010 pivot table uses a slicer to show only the East region.

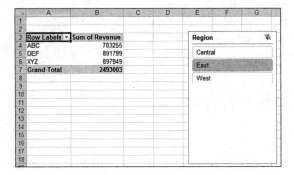

If someone opens the workbook in Excel 2007, an Excel Shape object appears where the slicer used to be. The shape warns that slicers cannot be used in this version of Excel. However, because you were using the slicer to filter instead of using the Report Filter, there is no visible reason to explain why sales are only $2.4 million (see Figure 8.2).

Figure 8.2
When opened in Excel 2007, the slicer is gone. Someone might mistakenly assume the total revenue was only $2.4 million.

If the person using Excel 2007 refreshes the pivot table, they see the Grand Total changes without any apparent reason (see Figure 8.3). The underlying reason is that the filter applied through the slicer is no longer stored in the pivot table.

Figure 8.3
After a refresh, the revenue changes for no apparent reason.

	A	B
1		
2		
3	Row Labels ▾	Sum of Revenue
4	ABC	2101370
5	DEF	2163714
6	XYZ	2442728
7	Grand Total	6707812

In another example, say you build a pivot table in Excel 2010. You add a slicer for Region and move the region field to the Report Filter. You also limit the report to the West region. Save the file in Excel 2010. Open it in Excel 2007. Change the Report Filter from the West region to the Central region. If you save the file in Excel 2007 and then open it in Excel 2010, the slicer returns, but the file is corrupt. The slicer says West, but the filter says Central, and the actual numbers in the table show all regions (see Figure 8.4).

Figure 8.4
If you round-trip this pivot table from 2010 to 2007 and then back to 2010, the slicer remains, but the file is corrupt.

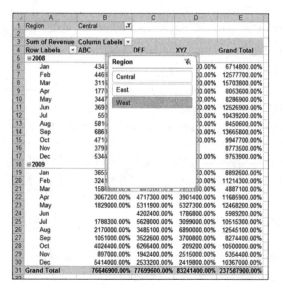

Percent of Parent Item Calculations Will Not Refresh

Certain calculations in the Show Values As were not available in previous versions of Excel. For example, if you use % of Parent Item, Rank, or % Running Total, the pivot table opens in Excel 2007 and even shows the results. However, the field setting in 2007 indicates that the calculation should be Normal. This means that any change to the pivot table causes the pivot table to begin showing the value field as Normal instead of the correct setting.

Repeat All Labels Is Lost After Any Change in 2007

Repeat All Item Labels on the Report Layout is not available in Excel 2007. An Excel 2010 pivot table with this setting initially appears with the item labels repeated. After any change to the pivot table, the repeated items labels disappear and the setting is lost when you return to Excel 2010.

Excel 2007 Pivot Tables Work Fine in Excel 2010

If you create a pivot table in Excel 2007 and then open it in Excel 2010, you should find no limitations. In addition, you can add Excel 2010 features to pivot tables created in Excel 2007.

Features Unavailable When a Legacy Pivot Table Is Opened in Excel 2010

If you open a pivot table created in Excel 2003 in Excel 2010, the following features are not available:

- Label filtering is grayed out. For example, this is the menu item where you can choose all customers whose names start with A.
- Most Value filtering is unavailable. The only exception is the Top 10 filter.
- Manual Inclusive filtering is unavailable.
- Slicers are unavailable.
- Certain items in the Show Values As menu are unavailable. These include % of Parent, % Running Total In, and Rank options.
- Formatting of hidden items is unavailable. In Excel 2010, if you format a field, remove the field from the table, and then later add it back to the table, the format is remembered. This functionality is not present in Excel 2003 version 10 pivot tables.
- The capability to hide intermediate levels of hierarchies in OLAP data sources is not available.
- The use of key performance indicators from a SQL Server Analysis Services data set is disabled.
- The number of rows is limited to 64,000 instead of 1 million.
- The number of columns is limited to 255 instead of 16,000.
- The maximum number of unique items in a pivot table is limited to 32,000 instead of 1 million.
- Field labels are truncated after 255 characters instead of 32,000 characters.
- The number of fields in the field list is limited to 255 instead of 16,000.

Excel 2010 Compatibility Mode

To a certain extent, version number is controlled in Excel 2010 by compatibility mode. If you create a new pivot table in a workbook that is still in compatibility mode, the pivot table is created as a version 10 pivot table.

When you save the workbook from compatibility mode to one of the new file formats, all the pivot tables are marked for upgrade. You must go through and refresh each pivot table to convert the pivot table to a version 14 pivot table.

No Downgrade Path Available from Version 12 and Version 14 Pivot Tables

After a pivot table has been upgraded to version 12 or 14, it no longer functions in legacy versions of Excel. Even if you save the file in compatibility mode, the pivot table is no longer refreshable.

Strategies for Sharing Pivot Tables

Version 12 and 14 pivot tables cannot be refreshed by anyone using legacy versions of Excel. Therefore, if you want to share a pivot table with someone using a legacy version of Excel, you must take extra care to make sure that the pivot table never existed as a version 12 or 14 pivot table.

You can follow these steps to create a version 10 pivot table:

1. Open a new Excel workbook.
2. Save the workbook as Excel 97–2003 format. Close and reopen the workbook.
3. Copy and paste your data set from the Excel 2010 workbook to the Excel 2003 workbook.
4. Create the pivot table in the Excel 2003 workbook while in compatibility mode.

Saving Pivot Tables to the Web

Unless you had an expensive SharePoint configuration, there was no way to interact with pivot tables in a browser using Excel 2007. It is slick that the new Excel 2010 Web Application will render slicers and pivot tables, but this still does not offer all the interactivity that used to be available in Excel 2003's Save As Webpage command.

Using Web Services in Excel 2003

The interactivity available in Excel 2003 might be a reason to keep one computer in the office that still has Excel 2003 installed. In Excel 2003, you would select File, Save As Web Page, Publish. Specify that the web page should have pivot table functionality, as shown in Figure 8.5.

When you open the resulting Web page in a browser, you had an amazing selection of pivot table functionality. You could drag fields to new drop zones. You use the collapse and

Figure 8.5
In Excel 2003, you can save the pivot table with pivot table interactivity.

Figure 8.6
When opened in Internet Explorer, the Web page offered pivot table functionality when using Excel 2003.

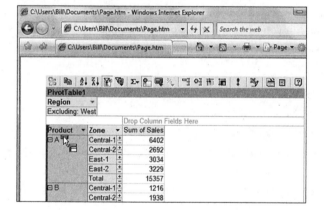

expand buttons to zoom out or zoom in. You could choose from the report filters. You could even double-click a cell to drill down. The browser version even allowed you to choose multiple items from a Page Filter even though Excel 2003 would not.

Figure 8.6 shows the pivot table rendered in a browser.

Using Save As HTML in Excel 2010 Provides a Static Image

You can still use File, Save As, HTML to save the workbook as an HTML page. Microsoft quit investing in this technology after Excel 2003. The Save With Interactivity feature is gone. You will get a static view of your pivot table rendered as a report in the browser. There will be no slicers, no charts, no graphics.

Follow these steps to create a static image of the pivot table:

1. From the File menu, select Save As.
2. In the Save as Type drop-down, select Web Page.
3. Click the Publish button to display the Publish as Web Page dialog box, as shown in Figure 8.7.

Figure 8.7
In the Publish as Web Page dialog box, you can specify a few options for the Web page.

4. Click the Title button to specify a title for the Web page.
5. If you want the Web page updated every time the file is saved, select the AutoRepublish check box.
6. Specify a filename for the resulting Web page.
7. Click Publish. Excel writes out a static view of the Web page, as shown in Figure 8.8.

Publishing Pivot Tables to Excel Services in Excel 2010

Starting in Excel 2007, Microsoft revealed their replacement for Office Web Services. The Excel Services product in Excel 2007 required an expensive SharePoint installation.

Excel services supports loading, calculating, and rendering Excel spreadsheets on servers. The person reading the Excel spreadsheet can access the file through his browser.

As the author of the file, you can specify certain cells that the end user can change in the browser. These fields can even be filter fields in your pivot table. Imagine the possibilities for creating fantastic ad hoc reporting tools that people can use to query your data.

Figure 8.8
The resulting Web page is a static view of the data.

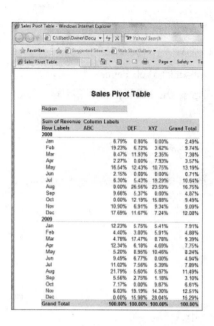

Even better, if your Excel spreadsheet is querying an SQL Server database, every time the browser is refreshed, the Excel file pulls new data from the SQL Server, providing real-time business intelligence.

There are three likely scenarios when you want to use Office Services:

- Allow everyone to have read-only access to a single version of an important spreadsheet. This eliminates the problem of multiple versions of the spreadsheet floating around.

- Encapsulate several ranges of various spreadsheets into an executive dashboard running in a browser.

- Build a custom application in the browser that reuses logic already designed in the Excel spreadsheet.

Requirements to Render Spreadsheets with Excel Services

The requirements for Excel Services are fairly high-end. Your organization needs to provide a server running Windows Server 2008R2. You need the Enterprise Editions of SharePoint Server and Excel Services for SharePoint.

As the author of the spreadsheet, you need read-write access to the server.

Preparing Your Spreadsheet for Excel Services

You need to decide carefully which cells in your spreadsheet can be edited by the end user. In a pivot table spreadsheet, these fields are likely the value fields in the Report Filter section of the report.

You need to assign each of these cells a name. To assign a name, follow these steps:

1. Select the desired cell.

2. To the left of the formula bar is the Name box. Typically, this box shows the cell address, such as A1. Click in this box and type a name for the cell. Do not use spaces in the name. "WhichYear" or "Which_Year" are valid. "Which Year" is not valid.

3. Press the Enter key to accept the name.

If you need to later change or delete a name, use the Name Manager icon on the Formulas tab.

Publishing Your Spreadsheet to Excel Services

The first time you publish your spreadsheet, you have to go through a few extra steps to specify the parameter cells. Make sure you have assigned range names to the parameter cells before starting this process. Then do the following:

1. From the File menu, select Share, and then Publish to Excel Services, as shown in Figure 8.9.

Figure 8.9
Access Excel Services through the Share category in the File menu.

2. Specify a path and filename in the Save As dialog box.

3. If this is the first time you are publishing the workbook, click the Excel Services Options button, as shown in Figure 8.10. Excel displays the Excel Services Options dialog box.

4. There are two tabs in the Excel Services Options dialog box. On the Show tab, choose which spreadsheet(s) you want to include in the browser.

Figure 8.10
Click the Excel Services
Options button to access
the parameter selection.

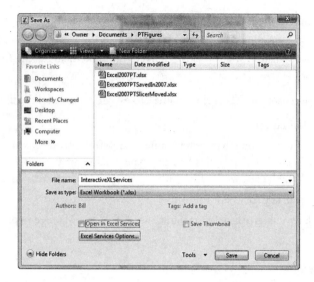

5. Click the Parameters tab. Click the Add button to display the Add Parameters dialog box.

6. On the Add Parameters dialog box, you see a list of all named ranges in the worksheet. Click the ranges that you want to specify as parameters (see Figure 8.11).

Figure 8.11
On the Add Parameters
dialog box, choose which
named ranges to use as
parameters.

7. Click OK to close the Add Parameters dialog box.

8. Click OK to close the Excel Services Options dialog box.

9. Click Save to save the worksheet for Excel Services.

What the End User Sees in Excel Services

The goals of Excel Services are:

- Enable the end user to view data in the spreadsheet
- Navigate around the spreadsheet
- Perform further exploration of the data in the spreadsheet
- Change parameters to facilitate what-if analysis

Microsoft has enabled a limited subset of features that allow the end user to achieve these four goals.

Excel Services is not designed to enable someone to author a new spreadsheet. To do this, the user would need to own Excel 2010. Instead, Excel Services allows:

- Support for basic Excel formatting (row height, column width, font, color, gridlines, text rotation). Excel Services also supports data bars, color scales, and table style formatting.
- Capability to switch between sheets in the workbook.
- Support for the use of expand and collapse buttons, either in pivot tables or when using the group and outline buttons.
- Support for querying external data and refreshing that data.
- Support for the Find utility.
- Support for displaying charts.
- Support for filtering and sorting within a defined table.
- Support for filtering and sorting within a pivot table.

As the author of the worksheet, you have a certain amount of control in this support. For example, you can specify that you do not want interactivity to be enabled for the spreadsheet.

> **NOTE** One difference between Excel and Excel Services is that Excel Services creates sections of the worksheet and serves up only one section at a time. A typical section contains 75 rows and 20 columns. This is primarily a performance consideration; you do not want the browser attempting to render 20 million cells at once.

What You Cannot Do with Excel Services

Although Excel Services handles many aspects of Excel files, it does not support several features. Any of the items discussed in this section causes the Excel workbook not to load in Excel Services:

■ Spreadsheets with code. This includes spreadsheets with VBA macros, forms controls, toolbox controls, Microsoft Excel 5.0 dialog boxes, and XLM sheets.

■ IRM-protected spreadsheets

■ ActiveX controls

■ Embedded SmartTags

■ Pivot tables based on "multiple consolidation" ranges

■ External references (links to other spreadsheets)

■ Spreadsheets saved in formula view

■ XML expansion packs

■ XML maps

■ Data validation

■ Query tables, SharePoint lists, Web queries, and text queries

■ Spreadsheets that reference add-ins

■ Spreadsheets that use the RTD() function

■ Spreadsheets that use spreadsheet and sheet protection

■ Embedded pictures or clip art

■ Cell and Sheet background pictures

■ AutoShapes and WordArt

■ Ink annotations

■ Organization charts and diagrams

■ DDE links

Other items are not displayed by Excel Services. For example, if a worksheet contains items in the following list, the worksheet is still displayed, but the item in question is ignored:

■ Split and freeze panes

■ Headers and footers

■ Page layout view

■ Cell patterns

■ Zoom

■ Analysis Services' member properties in ToolTips

■ Some cell formatting (for example, diagonal borders and border types are not supported by HTML)

Viewing the Pivot Table in the Browser

After publishing the file to Excel Services, you can open the workbook with Internet Explorer or Firefox. Navigation aids in the browser include the following:

- Sheet tabs in the lower-left corner
- Filter button to control the pivot table filter fields in Cell B1
- Drop-down in Cell B3

> **TIP** The report in Figure 8.12 still looks like a spreadsheet. If you are trying to use spreadsheet logic in a quick application, you might want to turn off gridlines and row and column headers in the original workbook before publishing to Excel Services.

Figure 8.12
This Web page has a surprising amount of spreadsheet-like functionality.

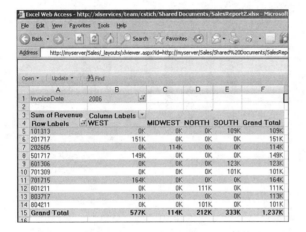

Viewing Your Excel 2010 Pivot Table on the SkyDrive

The new Excel Web App in Excel 2010 will allow you to save a pivot table complete with slicers and charts to the Windows Live SkyDrive. You can view the pivot table in the browser, interact with the slicers, and see the pivot table and pivot charts update.

On the one hand, rendering of charts and slicers is a tremendous improvement over the options available in Excel 2003. On the other hand, the Excel 2003 interactivity would allow you to drag fields around the pivot table. The Excel 2010 web application is not there yet.

To access the SkyDrive, you need to sign up for a free account in Live.com.

Once you are signed in to the SkyDrive, open the More drop-down and choose SkyDrive.

By default, the My Documents folder is a private folder. You can create new folders on the SkyDrive and either make these public or share them with a specific list of Windows Live accounts.

Figure 8.13 shows a worksheet in Excel 2010. A pivot table in A3:A12 summarizes 6000 rows of data. One slicer controls the pivot table and the chart is based on the results of the pivot table.

Figure 8.13
This workbook in Excel 2010 includes a pivot table, slicers, and a chart.

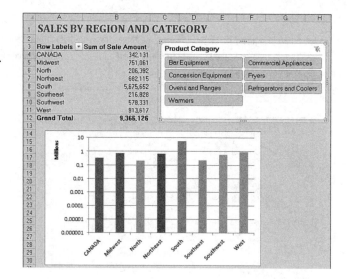

Choose File, Share, Save to Web. Sign in to your SkyDrive account and then use the Save As button to save the workbook on your SkyDrive (see Figure 8.14).

Figure 8.14
Choose to save to your SkyDrive.

In the SkyDrive, choose View. The pivot table, the slicers, and the chart all render in the browser. You can select new categories from the slicer. The pivot table and the chart all render in a few seconds. This is an impressive dashboard created using Excel 2010. (see Figure 8.15).

Figure 8.15
This workbook, complete with working slicers, is rendered in a browser with no need for Excel on the computer.

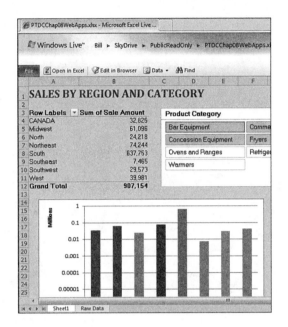

> **TIP**
> If you have saved the workbook in a public folder, you can share it by sharing the URL from the address bar.

To see a demo of saving a pivot table to the Excel Web App, search for "Pivot Table Data Crunching 8" at YouTube.

The Row Labels dropdown in cell A3 of Figure 8.15 offers choices to let you sort the regions by region name or the sales value.

Although the Excel Web App will let you edit the worksheet in the browser, you can not create a new pivot table nor rearrange fields in the Excel Web App.

Next Steps

In the next chapter, you learn about running pivot tables on data stored outside Excel including OLAP data sources and SQL Server.

Working with and Analyzing OLAP Data

9

What Is OLAP?

Online Analytical Processing (OLAP) is a category of data warehousing that enables you to mine and analyze vast amounts data with ease and efficiency. Unlike other types of databases, OLAP databases are designed specifically for reporting and data mining. In fact, there are several key differences between your standard transactional databases, such as Access or SQL Server, and OLAP databases.

Records within a transactional database are routinely added, deleted, or updated. OLAP databases, on the other hand, contain only snapshots of data. The data in an OLAP database is typically archived data, stored solely for reporting purposes. Although new data might be appended on a regular basis, existing data is rarely edited or deleted.

Another difference between transactional databases and OLAP databases is structure. Transactional databases typically contain many tables; each table usually contains multiple relationships with other tables. Indeed, some transactional databases contain so many tables that it can be difficult to determine how each table relates to another. In an OLAP database, however, all the relationships between the various data points have been predefined and stored in *OLAP cubes*. These cubes already contain the relationships and hierarchies you need to easily navigate the data within. Consequently, you can build reports without the need to know how the data tables relate to one another.

The biggest difference between OLAP and transactional databases is the way the data is stored. The data in an OLAP cube is rarely stored in raw form. OLAP cubes typically store data in preorganized and preaggregated views. That is, grouping, sorting, and aggregations are all predefined and ready to use.

This makes querying and browsing for data far more efficient than in a transactional database, where you would have to group, aggregate, and sort records on the fly.

> **NOTE** An OLAP database is typically set up and maintained by the database administrator in your IT department. *If your organization does not utilize OLAP databases, you might want to speak with your database administrator to discuss the possibility of some OLAP reporting solutions.*

Connecting to an OLAP Cube

Before you can browse OLAP data, you must first establish a connection to an OLAP cube. Start on the Data tab and select From Other Sources to see the drop-down menu shown in Figure 9.1. Then, select the From Analysis Services option.

Figure 9.1
Select From Analysis Services.

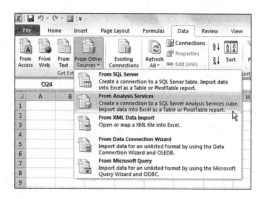

Selecting this option activates the Data Connection Wizard, as shown in Figure 9.2. Follow these steps to configure your connection settings so Excel can establish a link to the server:

> **NOTE** The examples you see in this chapter have been created using the Analysis Services Tutorial cube that comes with SQL Server Analysis Services 2005. The actions you take to connect to and work with your OLAP database are the same as demonstrated here because *the concepts are applicable to any OLAP cube you might be using.*

1. The first step in this endeavor is to provide Excel with some authentication information. Enter the name of your server, your username, and your password, as demonstrated in Figure 9.2. Then, click Next.

> **NOTE** If you are typically authenticated via Windows authentication, you simply select the Use Windows Authentication option.

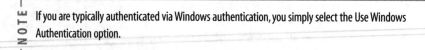

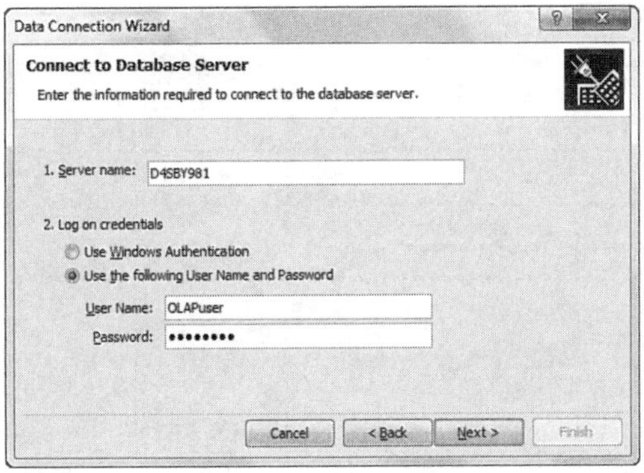

Figure 9.2
Enter your authentication information and click Next.

2. Next, you select the OLAP database with which you are working from the drop-down box. In Figure 9.3, the database called OLAP_Database is selected for this scenario. Selecting this database causes all the available cubes to be exposed in the list of objects below the drop-down menu. In this case, there is one cube available. However, the idea is that you would choose the cube you want to analyze, and then click Next.

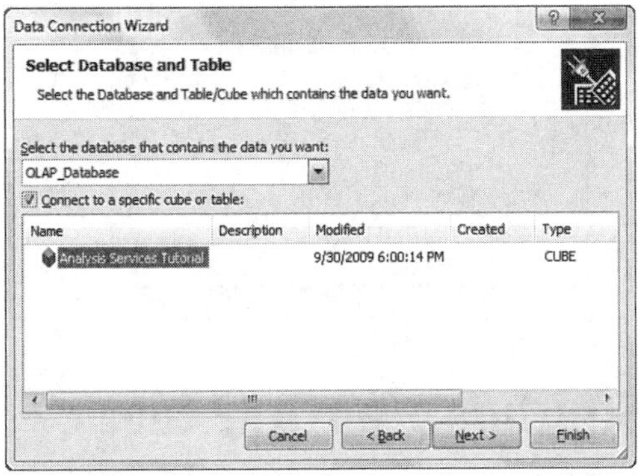

Figure 9.3
Specify your database and then choose the OLAP cube you want to analyze.

3. The next screen, shown in Figure 9.4, enables you to enter some descriptive information about the connection you've just created.

> **NOTE** All the fields shown in Figure 9.4 are optional edits only. That is, you can bypass this screen with-out editing anything, and your connection works fine.

4. Click Finish to finalize your connection settings. You immediately see the Import Data dialog box, as shown in Figure 9.5. From here, you select PivotTable Report, and then click OK to start building your pivot table.

Figure 9.4
Edit descriptive information for your connection.

Figure 9.5
When your connection is finalized, you can start building your pivot table.

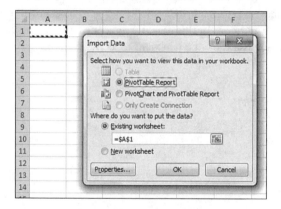

Understanding the Structure of an OLAP Cube

When your pivot table is created, you might notice that the PivotTable Field List looks somewhat different from that of a standard pivot table. The reason is that the PivotTable Field List for an OLAP pivot table is arranged to represent the structure of the OLAP cube you are connected to.

To effectively browse an OLAP cube, you need to understand the component parts of OLAP cubes and the way they interact with one another. Figure 9.6 illustrates the basic structure of a typical OLAP cube.

As you can see, the main components of an OLAP cube are dimensions, hierarchies, levels, members, and measures:

- **Dimensions** are major classifications of data that contain the data items that are analyzed. Some common examples of dimensions are Products dimension, Customer dimension, and Employee dimension. In Figure 9.6, the structure you see is that of the Products dimension.

- **Hierarchies** are predefined aggregations of levels within a particular dimension. A hierarchy enables you to pivot and analyze multiple levels at one time without any previous knowledge of the relationships between the levels. In the example in Figure 9.6, the Products dimension has three levels that are aggregated into one hierarchy called Product Categories.

- **Levels** are categories of data that are aggregated within a hierarchy. You can think of Levels as data fields that can be queried and analyzed individually. In Figure 9.6, note that there are three levels: Category, SubCategory, and Product Name.

- **Members** are the individual data items within a dimension. Members are typically accessed via the OLAP structure of dimension, hierarchy, level, and member. In the example shown in Figure 9.6, the members you see belong to the Product Name level. The other levels have their own members and are not shown here.

- **Measures** are the actual data values within the OLAP cube. Measures are stored within their own dimension appropriately called the Measures Dimension. The idea is that you can use any combination of dimension, hierarchy, level, and member to query the measures. This is called *slicing the measures*.

Figure 9.6
The basic structure of an OLAP cube.

Now that you understand how the data in an OLAP cube is structured, take a look at the PivotTable Field List again. The arrangement of the available fields starts to make sense. Figure 9.7 illustrates what the PivotTable Field List for an OLAP pivot table might look like.

As you can see, the measures are listed first under the Sigma icon. These are the only items you can drop into the values area of your pivot table. Next, you see dimensions represented next to the table icon. In this example, you see the Product dimension. Under the Product dimension, you see the Product Categories hierarchy that can be drilled into. Drilling into the Product Categories hierarchy enables you to see the individual levels.

The cool thing is that you are able to browse the entire cube structure by simply navigating through your PivotTable Field List! From here, you can build your OLAP pivot table report just as you would build a standard pivot table.

Figure 9.7
The PivotTable Field List
for an OLAP pivot table.

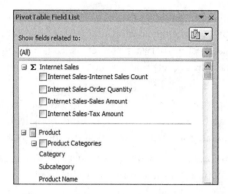

Understanding Limitations of OLAP Pivot Tables

When working with OLAP pivot tables, you must remember that the source data is maintained and controlled in the Analysis Services OLAP environment. This means that every aspect of the cube's behavior, from the dimensions and measures included in the cube to the capability to drill into the details of a dimension, is controlled via Analysis Services. This reality translates into some limitations to the actions you can take with your OLAP pivot tables.

When your pivot table report is based on an OLAP data source:

- You cannot place any field other than measures into the values area of the pivot table.
- You cannot change the function used to summarize a data field.
- You cannot create a calculated field or a calculated item.
- Any changes you make to field names are lost when you remove the field from the pivot table.
- The page field settings are not available.
- The Show Pages command is disabled.
- The Show Items with No Data option is disabled.
- The Subtotal Hidden Page Items setting is disabled.
- The Background Query option is not available.
- The Optimize Memory check box in the PivotTable Options dialog box is disabled.

Creating Offline Cubes

With a standard pivot table, the source data is typically stored on your local drive. This way, you can work with and analyze your data while disconnected from the network. However, this is not the case with OLAP pivot tables. With an OLAP pivot table, the pivot cache is never brought to your local drive. This means that while you are disconnected from the

network, your pivot table is out of commission. You can't even move a field while disconnected.

If you need to analyze your OLAP data while disconnected from your network, you need
to create an offline cube. An *offline cube* is essentially a file that acts as a pivot cache, locally
storing OLAP data so that you can browse that data while disconnected from the network.

To create an offline cube, start with an OLAP-based pivot table. Place your cursor anywhere inside the pivot table and click the OLAP Tools drop-down menu button on the
PivotTable Tools Options tab. Then, select Offline OLAP, as demonstrated in Figure 9.8.

Figure 9.8
Select Offline OLAP to
start the creation of an
offline cube.

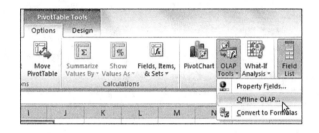

Selecting this option activates the Offline OLAP Settings dialog box, where you click the
Create Offline Data File button.

The Create Cube File Wizard activates, as shown in Figure 9.9. Click Next to start the
process.

Figure 9.9
Start the Create Cube File
Wizard.

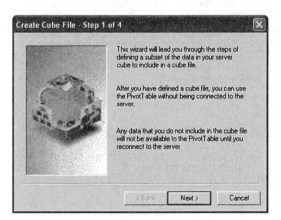

As you can see in Figure 9.10, you first select the dimensions and levels you want included
in your offline cube. This dialog box tells Excel which data you want imported from the
OLAP database. The idea is to select only the dimensions that you need available to you

while disconnected from the server. The more dimensions you select, the more disk space your offline cube file takes up.

Figure 9.10
Select the dimensions and levels you want included in your offline cube.

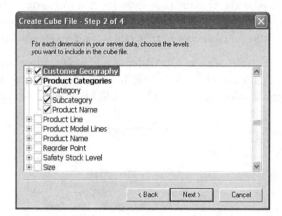

Clicking Next moves you to the next dialog box, as shown in Figure 9.11. Here, you are given the opportunity to filter out any members or data items that you do not want included. For instance, the Internet Sales-Extended Amount measure is not needed, so this dialog box is cleared. Clearing this box ensures that this measure is not imported and does not take up unnecessary disk space.

Figure 9.11
Clear any members you do not need to see offline.

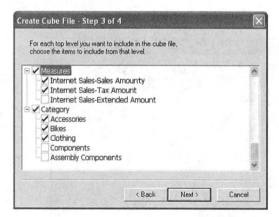

The final step is to specify a name and location for your cube file. In Figure 9.12, the cube file is named MyOfflineCube.cub, and it is placed in a directory called MyDirectory.

After a few moments of crunching, Excel outputs your offline cube file to your chosen directory. To test it, simply double-click the file to automatically generate an Excel workbook that is linked to the offline cube via a pivot table.

Figure 9.12
Specify a name and location for your cube file.

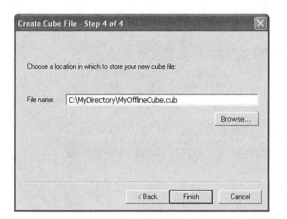

> **NOTE**
> The file extension for all offline cubes is .cub.

After your offline cube file has been created, you can distribute it to others and use it while disconnected from the network.

Breaking Out of the Pivot Table Mold with Cube Functions

Cube functions are Excel functions that can be used to access OLAP data outside a pivot table object. In legacy versions of Excel, you could find cube functions only if you installed the Analysis Services Add-In. In Excel 2010, cube functions have been brought into the native Excel environment. To fully understand the benefit of cube functions, take a moment to walk through an example.

One of the easiest ways to start exploring cube functions is to e Excel to convert your OLAP-based pivot table into cube formulas. Converting a pivot table to cube formulas is a delightfully easy way to create a few cube formulas without doing any of the work yourself. The idea is to tell Excel to replace all cells in the pivot table with a formula that connects back to the OLAP database. Figure 9.13 shows a pivot table connected to an OLAP database.

With just a few clicks, you can convert any OLAP pivot table into a series of cube formulas. Place the cursor anywhere inside the pivot table and click the OLAP Tools drop-down menu button on the PivotTable Tools Options tab. Then, select Convert to Formulas, as demonstrated in Figure 9.14.

If your pivot table contains a report filter field, the dialog box shown in Figure 9.15 activates. This dialog box gives you the option of converting your filter drop-down selectors to cube formulas. If you select this option, the drop-down selectors are removed, leaving a static formula. If you need to have your filter drop-down selectors intact so that you can continue to interactively change the selections in the filter field, leave the Convert Report Filters option cleared.

Figure 9.13
A normal OLAP pivot
table.

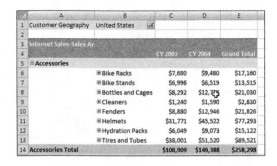

Figure 9.14
Select Convert to
Formulas to convert
your pivot table to cube
formulas.

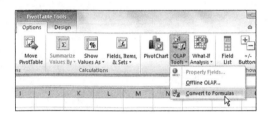

NOTE   If you are working with a pivot table in compatibility mode, Excel automatically converts the filter fields
to formulas.

Figure 9.15
Excel gives you the option
of converting your report
filter fields.

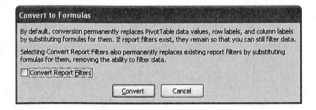

After a second or two, the cells that used to house a pivot table are now homes for cube formulas. Note that, as in Figure 9.16, any styles that you might have applied are removed.

So why is this capability useful? Now that the values you see are no longer part of a pivot
table object, you can insert rows and columns; you can add your own calculations; you can
combine the data with other external data; and you can modify the report in all sorts of
ways by simply moving the formulas around. For instance, Figure 9.17 illustrates a report in
which specific data items from Accessories and Bikes have been combined and formatted to
create a new Bike Products report. Again, note that all cells displaying values for each product are formulas that read directly from the OLAP cube via the connection you created.

Figure 9.16
Note in the formula bar, these cells are now a series of cube formulas!

	A	B	C	D	E
	C6			=CUBEVALUE("AdventureWorks OLAP Cube",$B$1,$A$3,$B6,C$4)	
1	Customer Geography	United States			
2					
3	Internet Sales-Sales Amount				
4			CY 2003	CY 2004	Grand Total
5	Accessories				
6		Bike Racks	$7,680.00	$9,480.00	$17,160.00
7		Bike Stands	$6,996.00	$6,519.00	$13,515.00
8		Bottles and Cages	$8,292.26	$12,738.04	$21,030.30
9		Cleaners	$1,240.20	$1,590.00	$2,830.20
10		Fenders	$8,879.92	$12,946.22	$21,826.14
11		Helmets	$31,770.92	$45,521.99	$77,292.91
12		Hydration Packs	$6,048.90	$9,073.35	$15,122.25
13		Tires and Tubes	$38,001.19	$51,519.83	$89,521.02
14	Accessories Total		$108,909.39	$149,388.43	$258,297.82

Figure 9.17
A Bike Products report built using cube formulas from a converted OLAP pivot table.

	A	B	C	D	E	F
	D6			=CUBEVALUE("AdventureWorks OLAP Cube",$B$1,$D$1,$A6,D$4)		
1	Customer Geography	United States		Internet Sales-Sales Amount		
2						
3	**Bike Products**					
4			CY 2003	CY 2004	Grand Total	
5						
6		Bike Racks	$7,680	$9,480	$17,160	
7		Bike Stands	$6,996	$6,519	$13,515	
8		Mountain Bikes	$1,387,330	$1,474,746	$2,862,076	
9		Road Bikes	$862,974	$797,771	$1,660,746	
10		Touring Bikes	$456,283	$849,374	$1,305,657	
11		Helmets	$31,771	$45,522	$77,293	
12		Total	$2,753,034	$3,183,412	$5,936,447	

Next Steps

In Chapter 10, "Mashing Up Data with PowerPivot," you learn how to use the PowerPivot add-in for Excel 2010 to mash up millions of rows of data into a single pivot table.

Mashing Up Data with PowerPivot

PowerPivot is a free add-in for Excel 2010 brought to you by the SQL Server Analysis Services team at Microsoft. One of the themes for the 2010 release of Office was to improve Excel as a Business Intelligence tool. PowerPivot makes it possible to do jaw-dropping analyses in Excel.

10

Benefits and Drawbacks to PowerPivot

There are some pluses to PowerPivot, but also a few minuses. This chapter starts with the mega-pluses, which are the things that make you love PowerPivot.

Mega-Benefits of PowerPivot

Here are five mega-benefits to using PowerPivot. Any one of these benefits are enough to make me upgrade to Excel 2010.

- **Process far more than a million rows of data**—You have probably seen demos with 100 million rows. If you have data sets that extend beyond row 1,048,576, you can now sort, filter, scroll, and pivot those data sets in PowerPivot.

- **Create pivot tables from multiple tables without writing a VLOOKUP**—You no longer have to write processor-intensive VLOOKUP formulas to join data from two worksheets before creating a pivot table. PowerPivot takes your various Excel tables and mashes them together without having to code VLOOKUPs.

- **Mash-up data from disparate sources**—The PowerPivot window can import text, Access, RSS, SQL Server, and Excel data and present it in a single pivot table.

■ **Get access to sets**—Microsoft added a cool Set feature to Excel 2010 pivot tables that enables asymmetric reporting. One problem: It only works with OLAP pivot tables, not regular Excel data. The good news: Take your regular data through PowerPivot and you have just created an OLAP pivot table. The heads of the Excel team will spin when I say it, but just having access to sets is enough to make me run every future pivot table through PowerPivot!

■ **Do calculations that make Excel's calculated fields look like they were designed by someone in kindergarten**—Microsoft introduced a new formula language in PowerPivot called Data Analysis Expressions (DAX). DAX is comprised of 117 functions that enable you to do two types of calculations. There are 81 typical Excel functions that can be used to add a calculated column to a table in the PowerPoint window. Then, there are 54 functions that are used to create a new measure in the pivot table. These 54 functions add incredible power to pivot tables. Some examples: COUNTROWS(DISTINCT()) finally lets you count the number of distinct rows. CALCULATE(Expression,Filter1, Filter2,...FilterN) is like SUMIFS but for any expression. (Think MAXIFS and more....) There are 34 time intelligence functions that let you compare TOTALYTD sales versus a PARALLELPERIOD.

Moderate Benefits of PowerPivot

The following benefits are nice, but not jaw-dropping amazing:

■ **Compression**—Excel workbooks with PowerPivot data are smaller than workbooks that use traditional PivotCache pivot tables. The data is still stored inside the .xlsx workbook file, but the PowerPivot team came up with better ways to compress the data.

■ **Join two pivot tables with a single set of slicers**—You can have one set of slicers that controls two separate PowerPivot tables.

■ **Slicer autolayout**—Slicers created in regular Excel are always one column and always start at the same size. Slicers created in PowerPivot attempt to use some intellisense to be sized appropriately. It is not full-proof, but at least you see that the PowerPivot team is trying to be thoughtful about your slicers.

■ **PivotCharts without PivotTables**—Well, not really. However, it looks like it. PowerPivot can automatically build a chart on your presentation worksheet, and then tuck the linked pivot table away on another worksheet.

Why Is This Free?

Until Excel 2010, what was the greatest innovation in spreadsheets? Your answer depends on the type of work that you have to do, but some possible answers might be:

■ **Pivot Tables**—When Pito Salas brought the pivot table concept to Lotus 1-2-3, it meant that you never had to do @DSUM and /Data Table 2 anymore.

- **VLOOKUP**—Join data from two tables. It is what enables people to do things in Excel that should be done in Access.
- **IF, SUMIFS, AGGREGATE**—These functions enable various conditional calculations.
- **1,048,576 Rows in Excel 2007**—This feature could mean you never again have to open Microsoft Access.

With Excel 2010, you now have a new add-in that is as good as all four of those innovations wrapped into one. The PowerPivot add-in provides the following advantages:

- You can do analysis of massive data sets, even data 100 times larger than Excel 2007.
- You can join tables without writing a VLOOKUP.
- You have aggregation and time series functions that have been lacking in Excel.
- You have the ability to do all of this in a pivot table.

It is not an exaggeration to say that PowerPivot is the best spreadsheet improvement to come out of Microsoft since pivot tables debuted in 1993.

Why then would the price for this be free?

Because there are 500 million people using Excel. That is a massive market of people. If you could somehow sell a book to just one-hundredth of one percent of that market, you would have a bestseller on your hands.

The SQL Server Analysis Services team is giving the client side version of PowerPivot to 500 million people because they figure that some small tiny percentage of those people will upgrade to the server version of PowerPivot. To get a server version, you have to buy SharePoint, SQL Server, and other expensive technologies. By empowering Excel pros with these amazing tools, they figure that they might double their existing customer base of SQL Server customers.

This chapter does not cover the server version of PowerPivot. However, it mentions some benefits of the server version.

Benefits of the Server Version of PowerPivot

If your IT folks install the PowerPivot Server, the following additional benefits are available to you:

- **Automatic Refresh**—In the client side, you have to open PowerPivot every day and click Refresh to have PowerPivot read the updated data sources. With the server version, this can automatically happen overnight.
- **Publish to Report Gallery**—With the server version, you can publish your PowerPivot pivot tables to a SharePoint server. Someone without Excel can open your workbook in a Web page and use the slicers to filter the data. Those people have a

nice gallery of report thumbnails from which to choose. The people in IT can monitor which reports are used and by whom.

Drawbacks to Using PowerPivot

As you start using PowerPivot, you might run into a few annoyances.

- **No grouping**—PowerPivot cannot use the Group feature of pivot tables. This feature is used a lot to roll daily dates up to months, quarters, and years. You can work around this by using the DAX language to define year, quarter, and month columns, but it is not as simple as using the Group feature.

- **You lose Undo**—PowerPivot is an add-in. Traditionally, when you run a macro or some external code, the Undo stack is cleared. Thus, anytime you deal with PowerPivot, you are going to lose the ability to undo anything before you went in to PowerPivot.

- **No VBA**—You can automate regular pivot tables with VBA. You cannot use VBA to control PowerPivot.

- **No drilldown**—Usually, you can double-click a cell in a pivot table and see the rows that make up that cell. This feature is not in the first version of PowerPivot.

- **Excel 2010 only**—PowerPivot only works with Excel 2010. You cannot use it with Excel 2007 or with files that are stored in compatibility mode.

Installing PowerPivot

The main trick is to get the PowerPivot add-in that matches your version of Office. Office 2010 ships in 32-bit and 64-bit versions. If you have a new computer running 64-bit Windows, it is possible that you have 32-bit or 64-bit office.

Go to the File menu in Excel 2010 and select Help. The right side of the backstage view shows a version number. If the version number ends with (64-bit), then you need the 64-bit add-in version.

If you plan on dealing with millions of records, then you want to go with the 64-bit versions of Office and PowerPivot. You are still constrained to a 2GB file size limit, but because PowerPivot can compress data, it is possible to fit 10 times that amount of data in a PowerPivot file. The 64-bit version of Office can make use of memory sizes beyond the 4GB limit in 32-bit Windows.

After installing the add-in, you should see a PowerPivot tab on the Excel 2010 ribbon, as shown in Figure 10.1.

Figure 10.1
After successful installation, you have a PowerPivot tab in the ribbon.

Building a PowerPivot Report

This case study walks you through your first PowerPivot data mash up. In this example, you create a report that merges a 1.8 million row CSV file with a store identifying data in Excel.

Your main table is a 1.8 million record CSV file called demo.txt. This file is shown in Notepad in Figure 10.2. It is important that you have column headings in Row 1 of the CSV file. The point-of-sale vendor who provides this data usually had a "Run on mm/dd/ yyyy" row at the top of the file, a blank row, and then headings in Row 3. This does not work for PowerPivot. You need to get rid of those extraneous rows at the top of the data set.

Figure 10.2
This 1.8 million row file is too big for Excel.

Import a Text File

To import the 1.8 million row file into PowerPivot, follow these steps:

1. Select the PowerPivot tab in Excel 2010.

2. Select the PowerPivot Window icon. A new PowerPivot application window appears. PowerPivot offers two tabs: Home and Design. The Home tab is shown in Figure 10.3.

Figure 10.3
The Home tab of the PowerPivot application.

3. You want to import your main table first. This is the large CSV file shown in Figure 10.2. From the Get External Data group, select From Text. PowerPivot shows the Table Import Wizard.

4. Select a Friendly Connection Name, such as Sales History. Click the Browse button and locate your text file. PowerPivot does not default to see the first row as column

headers, so the data preview is offering five unfriendly column names of F1, F2, F3, and so on (see Figure 10.4).

Figure 10.4
Initially, the headers are not recognized.

Use headers

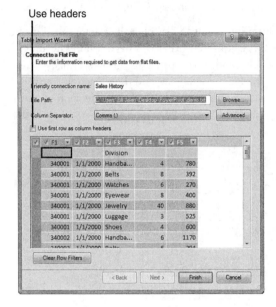

5. Verify that your delimiter is a comma. The drop-down offers standard delimiters such as comma, semicolon, vertical bar, and so on.

6. Select the check box for Use First Row as Column Headers. The preview now shows the real column names.

7. If there are any columns that you do not need to import, clear those check boxes. The entire file is going to be read into memory. If you have extraneous columns or particular columns with long text values, you can save memory by clearing them. Figure 10.5 shows the data preview with Units cleared.

> **TIP**
> Note that there are filter drop-downs for each field. You can actually sort and filter this 1.8 million row data set. However, it is slower than it will be in a few steps from now. If you open a filter field, you can select to exclude certain values from the import.

8. Click Finish and PowerPivot begins loading the file into memory. The Wizard shows how many rows have been fetched so far (see Figure 10.6).

9. When the file is imported, the Wizard confirms how many rows have been imported, as shown in Figure 10.7. Click Close to return to the PowerPivot window.

Figure 10.5
Choose which columns to import.

Uncheck to skip

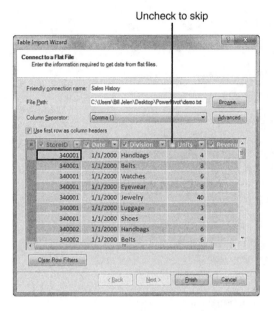

Figure 10.6
In less than a minute, PowerPivot is up to 1.5 million rows.

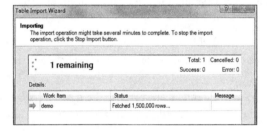

Figure 10.7
Success!

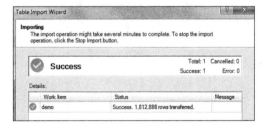

10. The 1.8 million row data set is shown in the PowerPivot Window. Grab the vertical scroll bar and scroll through the records. You can also Sort, change the number format, or filter (see Figure 10.8).

Differences Between PowerPivot and Excel

Even though it might feels like you are working with Excel, it is not Excel. The following lists some of the ways PowerPivot is different from Excel:

Figure 10.8
1.8 million records are in a grid that feels a lot like Excel.

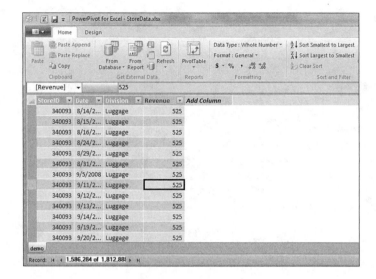

■ You cannot edit an individual cell.

■ If you add a calculation in what amounts to Cell E1 in Figure 10.8, that calculation is automatically copied to all rows.

■ If you format the revenue in one cell, all the cells in that column are formatted.

■ You can change column widths by dragging the border between the column names just like in Excel.

■ The Filters in PowerPivot are not as powerful as the new filters introduced in Excel 2007. In particular, the date columns do not show a hierarchical filter where you can choose a year or month.

■ If you right-click a column, a menu appears where you can rename, freeze, copy, hide, or unhide the columns (see Figure 10.9).

Figure 10.9
Right-click a column to rename, copy, or hide it.

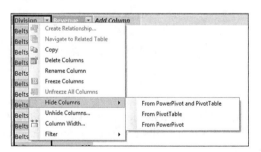

The bottom line is that you have 1.8 million records that you can sort, filter, and later, pivot. This is cool!

Add Excel Data by Copying and Pasting

The previously imported file only has StoreID as a field. It does not have store name or location. However, you probably have a small Excel file that maps StoreID to store name and other relevant data. You can add this data as a new tab in PowerPivot. Follow these steps:

1. Open this workbook in Excel.
2. Select the data with Ctrl+*.
3. Copy it with Ctrl+C.
4. Click the PowerPivot tab. On the left side of the ribbon is an icon to return to PowerPivot (see Figure 10.10).

Figure 10.10
Copy Excel data.

	A	B	C
1	StoreID	Selling SF	Mall Developer
2	340001	603	Westfield
3	340002	654	Westfield
4	340003	998	Simon Property Group
5	340004	858	General Growth Properties
6	340005	746	Westfield
7	340006	1633	Simon Property Group
8	340007	725	Irvine Retail Group
9	340008	535	Westfield

5. Click the PowerPivot Window icon. PowerPivot returns, and you see your 1.8 million row data set.
6. Click the Paste icon on the left side of the PowerPivot Home tab. You see a Paste Preview window.
7. Give the new table a better name than Table, like StoreInfo (see Figure 10.11). Click OK.

Figure 10.11
Give the pasted table a name.

Figure 10.12
You now have two
unrelated tables in the
PowerPivot window.

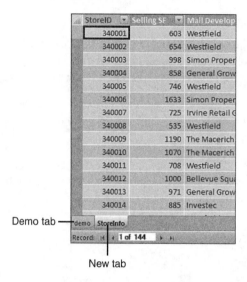

Demo tab ——
New tab

You now see the store information in a new StoreInfo tab. Notice that there are now two
worksheet tabs at the bottom of the PowerPivot window, as shown in Figure 10.12.

Add Excel Data By Linking

In the previous example, you added the StoreInfo table by using Copy and Paste. This actually creates two copies of the data. One is stored in an Excel worksheet somewhere, and the
other is stored in the PowerPivot window. If the original worksheet changes, those changes
do not make it through to PowerPivot. Alternatively, you can use the following steps to link
the data from Excel to PowerPivot:

> **TIP** To link to Excel data, that data must be converted to the Table Format introduced in Excel 2007.

1. If you start with an Excel worksheet, make sure that you have single-row headings at
   the top (no blank rows or blank columns).
2. Select one cell in the worksheet and press Ctrl+T. Excel asks you to confirm the extent
   of your table and if your data has headers (see Figure 10.13).
3. The table gets a default format. You can use the Table Tools Design tab to change that
   format if the dark blue-banded rows are too much for you.
4. Go to the Table Tools Design tab. On the left side of the ribbon, you see that this table
   is called Table1. Type a new name such as StoreInfo.
5. On the PowerPivot tab, select Create Linked Table, as shown in Figure 10.14.

The table appears in the PowerPivot window.

Figure 10.13
Convert your regular Excel
data to a Table.

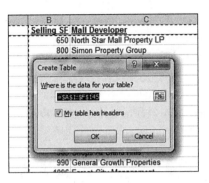

Figure 10.14
Use the Create Linked
Table to get this data into
PowerPivot.

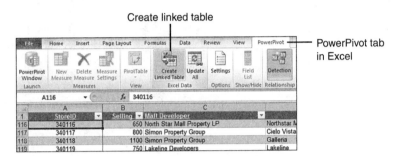

Define Relationships

Normally, in regular Excel, you would be creating VLOOKUPs to match the two tables. It is far easier in PowerPivot. Follow these steps:

1. You are linking from one column in your main table to a column in another table. To simplify the relationship process, navigate to your main table and select a cell in the column from which you are linking.

2. Click on the Design tab in the PowerPivot ribbon.

3. Select Create Relationship. The Create Relationship dialog appears. By default, the selected table and column appears in the first two fields, as shown in Figure 10.15.

Figure 10.15
Define a relationship
between tables. By selecting the key column before
starting, two of the four
fields are populated.

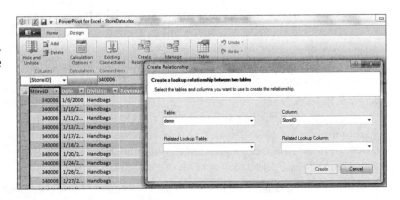

4. If you skipped step 1 and the correct table is not shown in the Table drop-down, then select Demo from the Table drop-down.

5. If you did not select the correct column in step 1, then open the Column drop-down. Select StoreID.

6. Open the Related Lookup table drop-down. Select StoreInfo.

7. Because the column names match, PowerPivot automatically changes the Related Lookup Column to say StoreID, as shown in Figure 10.16.

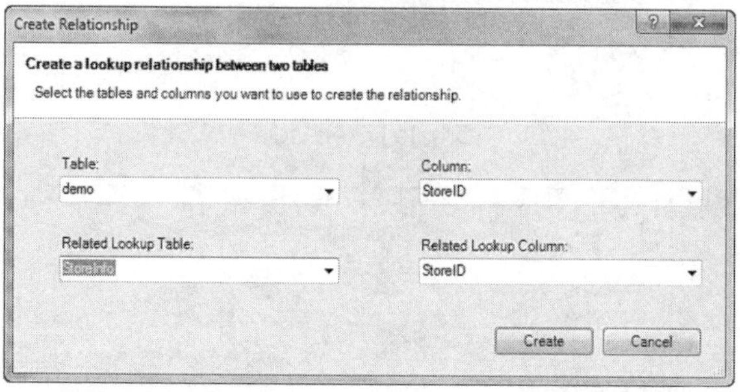

Figure 10.16
This simple dialog replaces the VLOOKUP.

8. Click Create.

You have now created a relationship between the two tables.

Add Calculated Columns Using DAX

One downside to pivot tables created from PowerPivot data is that they cannot automatically group daily data up to years. Before building the pivot table, use the DAX formula language to add a new calculated column to the Demo table.

Follow these steps to add a Year field to the Demo table:

1. Click on the Demo worksheet tab at the bottom of the PowerPivot window.

2. The column to the right of Revenue has an Add Column heading. Click in the first cell of this blank column.

3. Click the fx icon to the left of the formula bar. The Insert Function dialog appears with categories for All, Date & Time, Math & Trig, Statistical, Text, Logical, and Filter. Select Date & Time from the drop-down. You instantly notice that this is not the same list of functions in Excel. Five of the first six functions that appear in the window are exotic and new (see Figure 10.17).

4. Luckily, some familiar old functions are in the list as well. Scroll down and select the YEAR function. Click on the first date in the Date column. PowerPivot proposes a formula of =year(demo[Date]. Complete the formula by typing a closing parenthesis and pressing Enter. Excel fills in the column with the year associated with the date, as shown in Figure 10.18.

5. Right-click the column and select Rename Column. Type a name such as Year.

Figure 10.17
DAX offers a different list of functions than Excel.

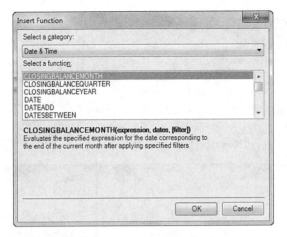

Figure 10.18
A new calculated column is added. You want to rename this.

Sto...	Date	Division	Revenue	CalculatedColumn1	Add Column
340001	1/1/2000	Handbags	780	2000	
340008	1/1/2000	Handbags	780	2000	
340006	1/1/2000	Handbags	780	2000	
340005	1/1/2000	Handbags	780	2000	
340007	1/1/2000	Handbags	975	2000	
340004	1/1/2000	Handbags	1,170	2000	

[CalculatedColur ▾] f_x =year(demo[Date])

There are many more columns that you might think of adding, but let's move on to using the pivot table.

Build a Pivot Table

One of the advantages of PowerPivot is that multiple tables can share the same data and slicers. Open the PivotTable drop-down on the Home tab of the PowerPivot ribbon. As shown in Figure 10.19, you have choices for a single pivot table, a single chart, a chart and a table, two charts, and so on.

Figure 10.19
You have many options beyond a single table or chart.

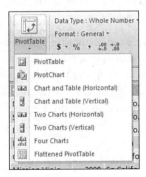

→ To learn how to deal with two or more pivot charts, **see** the "Combination Layouts" section later in this chapter.

Figure 10.20
Choose the location for
the pivot table.

Figure 10.21
The PowerPivot field list is
different from the regular
pivot table field list.

Original pivot table tabs   Multiple tables

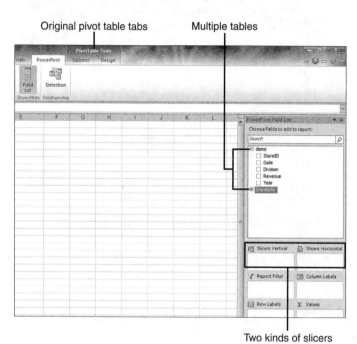

Two kinds of slicers

Follow these steps:

1. Select PivotTable. You now see the PowerPivot tab back in the Excel window.

2. Choose to put the pivot table on a new worksheet (see Figure 10.20).

   Figure 10.21 shows the initial screen. There are many things to notice. The
   PowerPivot Field List is a third variation of the pivot table field list. It is actually a new
   entry in the Task Pane. Both tables are available in the top of the Field List. The main
   table is expanded to show the field names, but you can expand the other table and add
   those fields to this pivot table. Two new sections in the drop zones offer vertical or
   horizontal slicers. Because you are in a pivot table, the PivotTable Tools tabs are available.

3. Select Revenue from the PowerPivot Field List. Expand the StoreInfo table. Select
   Region from the StoreInfo table. Excel builds a pivot table showing sales by region (see
   Figure 10.22). At this point, you have a pivot table from 1.8 million rows of data with a
   virtual link to a lookup table.

Figure 10.22
This pivot table summarizes 1.8 million rows and data from two tables.

You might want to go to the PivotTable Tools tabs to further format the pivot table. You could apply a currency format and rename the Sum of Revenue field, choose a format with banded rows, and so on.

To show some more features of the PowerPivot pivot table, add some slicer functionality.

Slicers in PowerPivot

Slicers are new in Excel 2010. The slicers in PowerPivot are slightly different from slicers in regular Excel.

1. First, you notice that the PowerPivot Field List offers boxes for Slicers Vertical and Slicers Horizontal. Vertical slicers are placed to the left of your pivot table. They are great for long lists that might need a scroll bar. Horizontal slicers go above your pivot table.

2. Drag the Year field to the Slicers Horizontal drop zone. The years appear in a small 3-column slicer surrounded by a big box, as shown in Figure 10.23. Your first reaction is to make that big box smaller, but do not do this.

Figure 10.23
Microsoft draws a big box around a small slicer.

That big box is the slicer parent control. It is actually a drawing object that defines the boundary for all the horizontal slicers. If you make the slicer parent control box small, there will not be room for additional slicers.

3. Add Division and Era to the Slicers Horizontal. All of a sudden, the box around the three slicers looks almost the right size. It's as if Microsoft knew that you were going to add two more slicers!

4. Add Mall Developer to the vertical slicer. Because it has a long list of relatively long names, it fits well as the only vertical slicer.

5. Slicers work the same as they do in regular Excel pivot tables. Click one item to select it. Ctrl+click additional items to select them as well.

Figure 10.24 shows the default slicers after applying a few filters.

Figure 10.24
PowerPivot chooses the number of columns for each slicer.

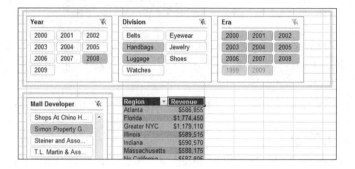

You probably like the PowerPivot slicers better than regular Excel slicers. The PowerPivot spec calls for some intellisense to choose how many columns might work for each slicer. The fact that the PowerPivot takes a guess at arranging the slicers means that you might not have to adjust the slicers. In regular Excel, you find yourself always adjusting the slicers.

The slicer parent control box disappears after you click outside of the pivot table. It comes back when the PowerPivot Field List is displayed. You can resize that box if you want the slicers to take up more or less room. Click the box once and resizing handles appear.

To format the slicers, you have to click on the slicer, not on the bounding box.

Some Things Are Different

If you have spent your whole Excel life building pivot tables out of regular Excel data, you are going to find some annoyances with these PowerPivot pivot tables. Many of these issues are not because of PowerPivot. They are because any PowerPivot pivot table automatically is an OLAP pivot table. This means that it behaves like an OLAP pivot table.

The following lists some items that you should keep in mind when working with PowerPivot pivot tables:

■ Days of the week do not automatically sort into Monday, Tuesday, Wednesday, and so on sequence. It takes eight clicks to get them to sort into custom list sequence.

To see how to force a PowerPivot report to sort into custom list sequence, search for "Pivot Table Data Crunching 10" at YouTube.

■ There is a trick in regular Excel pivot tables that you can do instead of dragging field names to the right place. You can go to a cell that contains the word Friday and type Monday there. When you press Enter, the Monday data moves to that new column. This does not work in PowerPivot pivot tables. Decide between Compact, Tabular, and Outline layouts before you drag fields to the correct location. Otherwise, everything snaps back to the original sequence.

■ The PowerPivot Field List looks like the regular Field List, but there is a lot of functionality missing. You cannot access filters by hovering over fields in the top of the field list. You cannot rearrange the field list. If you add multiple fields to the Values drop zone, you cannot access the Values field to move it to a new position. The good news: the real PivotTable Field List is available. Turn it back on using PivotTable Tools Options, Field List. You can then move the Values field to the proper location.

■ When you are entering a formula in the Excel interface, you can point to a cell to include that cell in the formula. You can do this using the mouse or the arrow keys. Apparently, the PowerPivot team is made up of mouse people because they support building a formula using the mouse in PowerPivot. Old-time Lotus 1-2-3 customers who build their formulas using arrow keys will be disappointed to find that the arrow key method does not work.

■ There are two types of refresh with these pivot tables. If you go to the PowerPivot tab and Update All, new data is read from the data sources. This does not automatically refresh the pivot tables. You then have to go to the PivotTable Tools Options tab to click Refresh. Certainly, the Customer Experience Improvement Program data shows that everyone immediately goes from one Refresh to the other Refresh in quick succession. You might complain loudly that these are two separate steps, but remember that you are dealing with two different products, which makes this acceptable.

Two Kinds of DAX Calculations

You have already seen an example where you used a DAX function to add a calculated column to a table in the PowerPivot window. There are 81 functions that are mostly copied straight from Excel for doing these types of calculations. The RELATED function can also be used in a calculated column to grab a value from a different table.

DAX can also be used to create new measures in the pivot table. These functions do not calculate a single cell value. They are all aggregate functions that calculate a value for the filtered rows behind any cell in the pivot table. There are 54 new DAX functions to enable these calculations. The real power is in these functions.

DAX Calculations for Calculated Columns

You have already seen one example of a calculated column. The functions are remarkably similar to the same function in Excel. Therefore, most do not require a lot of explanation.

In the Date & Time category, there are 17 functions. The first 16 are identical to Excel's function. The rarely-documented DATEDIF function in Excel is now renamed as YEARFRAC and is rewritten to actually work:

```
DATE(<year>, <month>, <day>)
DATEVALUE(date_text)
DAY(<date>)
EDATE(<start_date>, <months>)
EOMONTH(<start_date>, <months>)
HOUR(<datetime>)
MINUTE(<datetime>)
MONTH(<datetime>)
NOW()
SECOND(<time>)
TIME(hour, minute, second)
TIMEVALUE(time_text)
TODAY()
WEEKDAY(<date>, <return_type>)
WEEKNUM(<date>, <return_type>)
YEAR(<date>)
YEARFRAC(<start_date>, <end_date>, <basis>)
```

In the Information category, six functions are from Excel:

```
ISBLANK(<value>)
ISERROR(<value>)
ISLOGICAL(<value>)
ISNONTEXT(<value>)
ISNUMBER(<value>)
ISTEXT(<value>)
```

In the Logical Functions, seven are Excel functions. Do not be concerned that SUMIFS is not in this list. See a discussion on CALCULATE later:

```
AND(<logical1>,<logical2>,...)
FALSE()
IF(<logical_test>,<value if true>,<value if false>)
IFERROR(value,value if error)
NOT(<logical>)
OR(<logical1>,<logical2>,...)
TRUE()
```

Math and Trig offers 22 familiar functions:

```
ABS(<number>)
CEILING(<number>, <significance>)
EXP(<number>)
FACT(<number>)
FLOOR(<number>, <significance>)
```

```
INT(<number>)
LN(<number>)
LOG(<number>,<base>)
LOG10(<number>)
MOD(<number>, <divisor>)
MROUND(<number>, <multiple>)
PI()
POWER(<number>, <power>)
QUOTIENT(<numerator>, <denominator>)
RAND ()
RANDBETWEEN(<bottom>, <top>)
ROUND(<number>, <num_digits>)
ROUNDDOWN(<number>, <num_digits>)
ROUNDUP(<number>, <num_digits>)
SIGN(<number>)
SQRT(<number>)
TRUNC(<number>, <num_digits>)
```

In the Statistical category, there are 10 functions:

```
AVERAGE(<column>)
AVERAGEA(<column>)
COUNT(<column>)
COUNTA(<column>)
COUNTBLANK(<column>)
MAX(<column>)
MAXA(<column>)
MIN(<column>)
MINA(<column>)
SUM(<column>)
```

There are some items to note in the Text category.

First, the CONCATENATE function only lets you join two items. Use the & operator instead. Because PowerPivot cannot join two tables based on two fields in each table, you find that you are using concatenation frequently to join fields together.

Second, the Excel TEXT function has been renamed to FORMAT. It still works the same. Apparently, the PowerPivot team wanted a more descriptive explanation of what TEXT actually does:

```
CODE(<text>)
CONCATENATE(<text1>, <text2>,...)
EXACT(<text1>, <text2>)
FIND(<find_text, within_text, start_num)
FIXED(<number>, <decimals>, <no_commas>)
FORMAT(<value>, <format_string>)
LEFT(<text>, <num_chars>)
LEN(<text>)
LOWER(<text>)
MID(<text>, <start_num>, <num_chars>)
REPLACE(<old_text>, <start_num>, <num_chars>, <new_text>)
REPT(<text>, <num_times>)
RIGHT(<text>, <num_chars>)
SEARCH(<search_text>, <within_text>, [start_num])
SUBSTITUTE(<text>, <old_text>, <new_text>, <instance_num>)
TRIM(<text>)
```

```
UPPER (<text>)
VALUE(<text>)
```

Most of the items in the Filter and Value Functions category are used for creating new measures. There are two items that are of use in calculated columns:

- DAX introduces the `BLANK()` function. Because some of the aggregation functions are able to base a calculation on either the `ALLNONBLANKROW` or `FIRSTNONBLANK`, you can use the `BLANK()` function in an `IF()` function to exclude certain rows from measure calculations.

- You have the `RELATED()` function. This is described next.

Using RELATED ( ) to Base a Column Calculation on Another Table

The next several examples make use of a sample file called Ch10WeatherMashup.xlsx. This file started out with a generic sales by day and by store data set. A company sells products both in a mall location and at an airport. The two stores are less than 10 miles apart, but they might show different sales trends.

Say you used a Web query and a macro to download weather data for the three years of daily dates. Several examples in the DAX Measure calculation mash up the sales and weather data to look for trends.

While preparing this workbook, you use DAX to create the following calculated columns:

- WeekdayName uses `=FORMAT(Sales[Date],"dddd")` to convert the date to the day of the week.

> **TIP**
> You might be disappointed to find that PowerPivot pivot tables do not respect the custom list when presenting weekdays. For this reason, you should add a new WeekdayID column.

- WeekdayID uses `=WEEKDAY(Sales[Date],2)`. The 2 argument matches the same function in Excel. 2 numbers the days starting with 1 for Monday through 7 for Sunday. The Weekday table is a seven row table that maps 1 to 1-Mon and so on. This way, the day names would sort correctly.

- LocationDays is `=CONCATENATE(Sales[Location],Sales[Date])`. You see this used later when calculating the distinct number of store days.

Next, you need to calculate sales per store associate. The two locations have different scheduling requirements. The airport location usually operates with one associate, but staffs up to two on the busy travel days of Sunday, Monday, and Friday. The mall location has extra staff on Friday and Saturday. To calculate the number of staff on a given day, you need to concatenate Location and Weekday. The formula for LocationWeek is `=Concatenate(Sales[Location],Sales[WeekdayName])`. Note that calculated columns have no problem referring to other calculated columns.

A relationship links this column to the staffing table.

You might think that because PowerPivot understands the relationship between the Sales table and the Staffing table that you could write a formula such as `=Sales[Net Sales]/ Staffing[Staff Level]`, as shown in Figure 10.25. Unfortunately, this evaluates to an error.

Figure 10.25
Calculated columns do not automatically use the defined relationship.

The problem is that the calculation is trying to divide this row's sales of 2202 by all 14 values in the staffing table.

The solution is to use the Related function. Rewrite the formula as `=Sales[Net Sales]/ Related(Staffing[StaffLevel])`. The related function tells DAX that you do not want to divide 2202 by all 14 values in the table, but only by the one value that is related to AirportSunday.

Figure 10.26 shows the result. In the first row, the airport location had two people staffing the store. Thus, the sales per person is half of the 2202. On Tuesday, only one person staffs the store, so SalesPerPerson is the same as Net Sales.

Figure 10.26
The Related function is like a 1-argument VLOOKUP.

				LocationDays	LocationWe...	SalesPerPerson
port	Sunday		7	Airport1/1/2006	AirportSunday	1101
port	Monday		1	Airport1/2/2006	AirportMonday	1448
port	Tuesday		2	Airport1/3/2006	AirportTuesday	2659
port	Wednesday		3	Airport1/4/2006	AirportWednesday	3389

`=Sales[Net Sales]/Related(Staffing[StaffLevel])`

Using these calculated columns and relationships, you can create some interesting pivot tables.

Figure 10.27 shows an analysis of sales by weekday at the two locations. You can see in Cell I10 that sales peak at the Mall on Saturday. At the airport, you would think that sales would peak on Friday when business travelers need a gift on their way back home. Instead, they peak on Sunday when business travelers are purchasing new items for their upcoming business meetings.

The percentages in Rows 9 and 10 of Figure 10.27 work out because over three years, there are roughly the same number of Mondays as Fridays in the data set.

Figure 10.27
Sales at the airport location peak on Sunday.

Values	Location	Day							
		1 - Mon	2 - Tue	3 - Wed	4 - Thu	5 - Fri	6 - Sat	7 - Sun	Grand Total
Net Sales									
	Airport	402,729	368,299	369,055	383,688	402,217	416,262	448,157	2,790,407
	Mall	450,320	437,546	456,181	432,157	553,421	800,635	413,661	3,543,921
% of Sales									
	Airport	14%	13%	13%	14%	14%	15%	16%	100%
	Mall	13%	12%	13%	12%	16%	23%	12%	100%

As you continue to do other analyses, the results are not as meaningful. In Figure 10.28, a report of sales by the amount of rain shows that most sales happened on sunny days. However, this could just be telling you that it is sunny a lot more in Florida than rainy.

Figure 10.28
Do people hit the mall more often on sunny days? You cannot tell from this report.

Net Sales	Location		
Rain	Airport	Mall	Grand Total
0-None	1,743,909	2,268,816	4,012,725
1-Trace	726,746	947,691	1,674,437
2-Moderate Rain	171,848	186,903	358,751
3-Heavy Rain	67,751	53,320	121,071
4-Rainforest Rain	55,389	57,110	112,499
5-Hurricane Rain	24,764	30,081	54,845
Grand Total	2,790,407	3,543,921	6,334,328

The answer is to use DAX to create new measures that calculate sales per store per day.

Using DAX to Create New Measures

A measure is the OLAP term for a Calculated Field. However, DAX measures can run circles around calculated fields. Before you dive in, you need to remember one mantra, "Filter first, and then calculate." To understand this mantra, consider Cell C15 in Figure 10.29.

Figure 10.29
How many filters are on Cell C15?

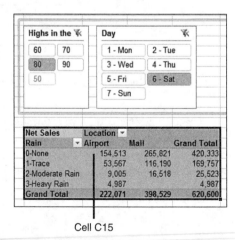

Cell C15

Think about how many filters are applied to Cell C15. You might think that the answer is two, but it is probably four.

Everyone would agree that Cell C15 is filtered to show only records that fell on a Saturday with high temperatures in the 80s. That is two filters.

In addition, the row and column fields are really filters as well. For Cell C15, you only want records with sales at the airport location. You also only want days where there was no rain. That is two additional filters for Cell C15.

As you start to think about DAX measures, remember to figure out the measure for a particular cell in the pivot table; they first filter, and then calculate the result using the DAX formula.

Count Distinct Using DAX

DAX lets you count how many distinct values meet the filter.

Wait—that is so good, it warrants repeating.

DAX lets you count how many distinct values meet the filter! Do you understand the gravity of that statement? People who are creating advanced pivot tables always are tripped up because pivot tables cannot come up with a distinct count of something. In Chapter 12 on VBA, the ridiculous formula =1/COUNTIFS(...) is offered to try to replicate the Count Distinct. DAX now lets you count how many distinct values meet the filter.

To create a new measure in DAX, use the New Measure icon in the PowerPivot tab. It seems confusing, but keep in mind that this is not a tab in the PowerPivot window, it is the PowerPivot tab in the Excel ribbon. To be clear, click the New Measure icon shown in Figure 10.30.

Figure 10.30
New Measure is on the Excel ribbon on the PowerPivot tab.

When you click New Measure, you get the Measure Settings dialog, as shown in Figure 10.31:

1. The Table Name should be the base table where your main numerical data is located. Change the first drop-down from Weather to Sales.

2. For the Measure Name, use a name such as DayCount.

3. Use the same name for Custom Name.

Figure 10.31
Edit measures in this
dialog.

4. Measures are always aggregate functions, not cell-level functions. Thus, you must use an aggregate function such as SUM or COUNTROWS.

5. The magic function here is Distinct(Sales[Date]). For any cell in the pivot table, the distinct function returns a list of the distinct values for the rows that match the filter.

> **TIP** Note that distinct must be used on a column in the home table. It cannot be applied to a value in a linked table. It is affected by filters applied to linked tables, but you must be using a value in the home table. Distinct actually returns a one-column table with a list of the distinct values. To count how many items there are, use =CountRows(Distinct(Sales[Date]).

6. After typing the formula, click the Check Formula button to make sure that your syntax is correct (see Figure 10.32).

Think of DayCount as an intermediate result to illustrate the concept of using Distinct.

Figure 10.32
Build a formula and then
check the syntax.

You could then define a measure of Net Sales divided by DayCount. However, you could also skip DayCount altogether and build Sales Per Day with a single formula:

```
=SUM(Sales[Net Sales])/COUNTROWS(Distinct(Sales[Date]))
```

Figure 10.33 shows Sales Per Day based on the amount of rain and the location.

Figure 10.33
Both locations do better on sunny days.

Sales Per Day	Location		
Rain	Airport	Mall	Grand Total
0-None	2,845	5,008	6,329
1-Trace	2,550	4,175	5,638
2-Moderate Rain	2,322	3,398	4,659
3-Heavy Rain	2,053	2,962	3,669
4-Rainforest Rain	1,910	3,006	3,879
5-Hurricane Rain	1,905	2,735	3,428
Grand Total	2,665	4,526	5,833

You might have thought that sales would pick up in the airport on rainy days due to rain delays. Apparently, people are too stressed out when their flights are delayed to shop.

> **CAUTION**
>
> There is something wrong with the totals in Figure 10.33. The Grand Total row for the airport is accurate; there is an average of $2665 in sales per day at the airport. However, if the airport is averaging $2665 a day and the mall is averaging $4526 a day, how can the Grand Total column be showing $5833?

Fortunately, you have the intermediate Day Count column available. Figure 10.34 shows a test report showing sales, days, and sales per day.s

Figure 10.34
Something is wrong in Cell J12.

	Location	Values								
	Airport			Mall				Total Sales	Total # Days	Total Sales Per Day
Rain	Sales	# Days	Sales Per Day	Sales	# Days	Sales Per Day				
0-None	1,743,909	613	2,845	2,268,816	453	5,008	4,012,725	634	6,329	
1-Trace	726,746	285	2,550	947,691	227	4,175	1,674,437	297	5,638	
2-Moderate Rain	171,848	74	2,322	186,903	55	3,398	358,751	77	4,659	
3-Heavy Rain	67,751	33	2,053	53,320	18	2,962	121,071	33	3,669	
4-Rainforest Rain	55,389	29	1,910	57,110	19	3,006	112,499	29	3,879	
5-Hurricane Rain	24,764	13	1,905	30,081	11	2,735	54,845	16	3,428	
Grand Total	2,790,407	1047	2,665	3,543,921	783	4,526	6,334,328	1086	5,833	

The airport location was open for all three years. The mall location opened late in 2006 so there are less days for the mall location. The airport is open on Christmas, but the mall is not. Thus, there are many days where only one store is open.

Column I shows total sales of both stores. The Day Count in Column J counts a day when either one store or the other was open. Thus, both stores did sell $6.3 million over the course of the data set. However, because both stores were not open for the entire period, the calculation of $6.3 million divided by 1086 days is wrong.

The solution is to count the distinct number of a concatenated column of location and date. The Location Days column is a calculated column in the PowerPivot window. To see this, refer back to Figure 10.25. In Figure 10.35, two new measures appear:

```
LocationDayCount =CountRows(Distinct(Sales[LocationDays]))
Sales Per Store Per Day =Sum(Sales[Net Sales])/ CountRows(Distinct(Sales[Locat
ionDays]))
```

Although these new measures produce the exact same results for the Airport or Mall Sales Per Day, the improvement is that Column K shows the true average sales per store per day.

Figure 10.35
This calculation works better.

Sales	Location DayCount	Sales Per Store Per Day	Total Sales	Total Location DayCount	Total Sales Per Store Per Day
2,268,816	453	5,008	4,012,725	1066	3,764
947,691	227	4,175	1,674,437	512	3,270
186,903	55	3,398	358,751	129	2,781
53,320	18	2,962	121,071	51	2,374
57,110	19	3,006	112,499	48	2,344
30,081	11	2,735	54,845	24	2,285
3,543,921	783	4,526	6,334,328	1830	3,461

When "Filter, Then Calculate" Does Not Work in DAX Measures

Say that you create a DAX measure for SUM(Sls[Sales]). By definition, all filters are taken into account before PowerPivot starts calculating. To get the 851 in Cell D6 of Figure 10.36, the program filters the data to where Rep=Bill, Date = 6/2/2011. The remaining rows are added to get the 851.

Figure 10.36
Excel applies a filter to calculate the 851.

Sum of Sales	Rep					
Date	Amber	Bill	Chris	Dale	Eddy	Grand Total
6/1/2011	1083	346	49	88		1566
6/2/2011	1094	851	429	359	671	3404
6/3/2011	1444	765	1028	236	295	3768
6/4/2011	954	659	851		149	2613
6/5/2011	900	1304	578	137	136	3055
6/6/2011	533	1201	526	153	347	2760
6/7/2011	1184	976	558	143	37	2898

In essence, without the DAX calculation specifying any filters, the result for Cell D6 in the pivot table is automatically going to sum up the rows shown by the arrows in Figure 10.37.

Incidentally, the formula in Cell E12 of Figure 10.37 is =SUMIFS(Sls[Sales],Sls[Rep],"Bil l",Sls[Date],40696) and also returns 851. The DAX formula of =SUM(Sls[Sales]) is a bit shorter.

Figure 10.37
The answer in Figure 10.36 adds up all the arrow rows.

C12 fx 299

	Date	Rep	Sales	D	E
12	6/1/2011	Amber	299		851
13	6/1/2011	Amber	36		
14	6/2/2011	Dale	82		
15	6/2/2011	Bill	107	←	
16	6/2/2011	Bill	278	←	
17	6/2/2011	Bill	37	←	
18	6/2/2011	Bill	134	←	
19	6/2/2011	Chris	145		
20	6/2/2011	Eddy	190		
21	6/2/2011	Amber	217		
22	6/2/2011	Eddy	250		
23	6/2/2011	Amber	752		
24	6/2/2011	Dale	218		
25	6/2/2011	Bill	32	←	
26	6/2/2011	Eddy	109		
27	6/2/2011	Bill	66	←	
28	6/2/2011	Bill	117	←	
29	6/2/2011	Eddy	122		
30	6/2/2011	Amber	60		
31	6/2/2011	Amber	65		
32	6/2/2011	Dale	59		
33	6/2/2011	Chris	200		
34	6/2/2011	Bill	80	←	
35	6/2/2011	Chris	84		

You should appreciate that for most calculations, you never have to specify a filter.

However, this assumption leads to trouble when you need part of your formula to look at all rows, not just the filtered rows.

Say that you want to see how the sales compared to the total sales for the month. You need to calculate a fraction. The numerator of the fraction is going to be `SUM(Sls[Sales])`. The denominator of the fraction needs to be all the records in the sales table. That is going to be tougher.

In DAX, instead of using `SUMIFS`, you need to use Calculate. Calculate asks for an expression and then one or more filters. For those filters, you are going to use a special function called `ALL`. If you ask for `Calculate(Sum(Sls[Sales]),ALL(Sls))` then the filter is almost an anti-filter. Rather than further limiting the calculation, `ALL` says that you want it to look not just at Bill's sales for 6/2/2011, but all the sales in the table.

In Figure 10.38, a new measure calculates % of Grand Total sales by using `=SUM(Sls[Sales])/Calculate(Sum(Sls[Sales]),All(Sls))`. The % of Grand Total for Cell F7 says that Bill's $851 in sales on June 2 represents 0.9 percent of the grand total sales.

Figure 10.38
The denominator of these calculations is always the tough part.

	Rep / Values				
	Amber		Bill		Chris
Date	Sum of Sales	% of Grand Total	Sum of Sales	% of Grand Total	Sum of
6/1/2011	1083	1.1%	346	0.4%	
6/2/2011	1094	1.1%	851	0.9%	
6/3/2011	1444	1.5%	765	0.8%	
6/4/2011	954	1.0%	659	0.7%	
6/5/2011	900	0.9%	1304	1.3%	
6/6/2011	533	0.5%	1201	1.2%	
6/7/2011	1184	1.2%	976	1.0%	

CAUTION

The past example might seem trivial because you could replace that calculation with Show Values As, % of the Total. However, do not skip over understanding the ALL(Sls) syntax. After you understand that syntax, you can replace the first argument in Calculate with Max, Min, Average, or any function. Therefore, Calculate becomes like SUMIFS, AVERAGEIFS, MINIFS, MAXIFS, and so on.

Early on in the days of the PowerPivot beta, many people blogged an example or two that calculated the % of the total using Calculate and All. This is not the most powerful use of calculated measures.

Say that you want to calculate how Bill's $851 sale on June 2 compared to all sales on June 2. The numerator of the DAX Measure is =Sum(Sls[Sales]). Again, the denominator is going to be the hard part.

For the denominator, you want to say, "Look at all the sales that match today, but do not pay any attention to the sales rep filter. Give me all sales reps."

If you asked for ALL(Sls), the calculation would throw out all the filters.

This time, you need to ask for AllExcept(Sls,Sls[Date]). I cannot even count if this is a quadruple or a quintuple negative, but I can tell you that it takes some time to wrap your head around this. You might think of it like this: "DAX is already going to be filtering by date and sales rep. Go ahead and throw out all the filters except for the Date filter. Keep filtering by date."

In Figure 10.39, the DAX measure calculates =SUM(Sls[Sales])/Calculate(Sum(Sls[Sales]),AllExcept(Sls,Sls[Date])). This calculation shows you the percentage of each day's sales achieved by a certain rep.

Figure 10.39

All Except says to ignore all filters except the Date filter.

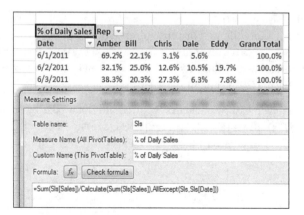

You can also override the filters by specifying other filters in the Calculate function. The actual syntax of the Calculate function is Calculate(Expresion,[filter 1], [filter 2], [filter 3], [filter 4], ...). Just like SUMIFS in Excel 2010, you can keep adding additional filters.

=Calculate(Sls[Sales],Sls[Rep]="Amber") gets all Amber's sales for this row. If Amber is the sales star in the store, perhaps someone would want to show everyone's sales as a percentage of Amber's Sales.

=SUM(Sls[Sales])/ Calculate(Sls[Sales],Sls[Rep]="Amber") shows sales as a percentage of Amber's total sales for that day. If the store manager posted this report from Figure 10.40, Chris might call home on the 16th to say, "Guess what! I sold 259.2 percent of what Amber sold."

Figure 10.40
Show all values as a percentage of Amber is not one of the built-in selections, but it is possible with the DAX formula language.

	K21			fx	259.183673469388%			
	B	C	F	H	I	K	L	
3		Rep						
4		Amber	Bill		Chris		Dale	
5	Date	Sum of Sales	Sum of Sales	% of Amber	Sum of Sales	% of Amber	Sum of	
15	6/10/2011	1105	201	18.2%	436	39.5%		
16	6/11/2011	2495	1197	48.0%	702	28.1%		
17	6/12/2011	1113	435	39.1%	29	2.6%		
18	6/13/2011	1845	1572	85.2%	1550	84.0%		
19	6/14/2011	1667	520	31.2%	534	32.0%		
20	6/15/2011	1951	186	9.5%	736	37.7%		
21	6/16/2011	441	773	175.3%	1143	259.2%		
22	6/17/2011	556	1157	208.1%	478	86.0%		
23	6/18/2011	660	1458	220.9%	831	125.9%		
24	6/19/2011	758	518	68.3%	1422	187.6%		
25	6/20/2011	969	773	79.8%	272	28.1%		

Mix in Those Amazing Time Intelligence Functions

Remember that you can apply many filters in the Calculate function. As you saw in the last example, you could filter to show total sales for the rep named Amber. You can also filter to all dates that match a certain date function.

There are 34 Time Intelligence functions. Say that you want to calculate a running MTD total. You can use the Calculate function and specify a filter of DatesMTD(Sls[Date]). That is the complete filter. You do not need to say, "This row's date falls within the MTDDates compared to the current date in the report." You just have to say DatesMTD(Sls[Date]).

In pseudo code you would say, "I want a formula that adds up all the sales for dates that fall in the MTD period compared to the current row, but only for reps that match the current column."

To add up all the sales, use =Calculate(Sum(sls[Sales]).

For dates that are MTD, use DatesMTD(Sls[Date]).

But only for reps that match, use AllExcept(Sls,Sls[Rep]).

The complete formula in Figure 10.41 is =Calculate(Sum(sls[Sales]), DatesMTD(Sls[Date])),AllExcept(Sls,Sls[Rep])).

10

Figure 10.41
MTD Sales for each rep.

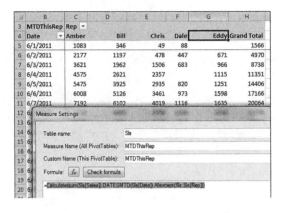

10

CAUTION

Notice that Dale did not work on June 4 and thus gets no calculation for MTD Sales on that date. If you use pivot tables a lot, you understand that empty cells usually show up as blank, and you generally change the pivot table options to have empty cells show up as 0. The same thing is happening here. Because there was no data for Dale for June 4, none of the DAX measures are calculated for that cell. The solution would be to go back to the original data and add in a zero-sale record for every person for every day.

If you download the sample files for this book and look at Ch10DAXMeasures.xlsx, you see other calculated measures in the field list.

Note that a measure can refer to another measure. To get to This Rep's Percentage of MTD Sales versus all MTD Sales, first you need to build MTDThisRep, as previously shown. Next, you need to build MTD All Reps using =Calculate(Sum(Sls[Sales]),Dates MTD(Sls[Date]),All(Sls)). When it comes time to create the formula to divide those two, you can simply build the formula as =Sls[MTDThisRep]/Sls[MTD All Reps], as shown in Figure 10.42.

Figure 10.42
You can use previously defined measures to simplify the calculation for another measure.

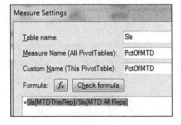

TIP

The filtering techniques such as All() and AllExcept() are going to work well in the home table. If you need to have a calculation ignore or respect a filter in a linked table, your results might vary. It is always best to have the filter fields in the home table. One workaround is to use the =Related() function in the PowerPivot window to bring a copy of the field from the linked table into the home table.

The following is a complete list of Time Intelligence Functions:

```
CLOSINGBALANCEMONTH(<expression>, <dates>, <filter>)
CLOSINGBALANCEQUARTER(<expression>, <dates>, <filter>)
CLOSINGBALANCEYEAR(<expression>, <dates>, <filter>)
DATEADD(<date_column>, <number_of_intervals>, <interval>)
DATESBETWEEN(<column>, <start_date>, <end_date>
DATESINPERIOD(<date_column>, <start_date>,
<number_of_intervals>, <intervals>)
DATESMTD(<date_column>)
DATESQTD (<date_column>)
DATESYTD (<date_column>, [,<YE_date>])
ENDOFMONTH(<date_column>)
ENDOFQUARTER(<date_column>)
ENDOFYEAR(<date_column>)
FIRSTDATE (<datecolumn>)
LASTDATE (<datecolumn>)
LASTNONBLANK (<datecolumn>, <expression>)
NEXTDAY(<date_column>)
NEXTMONTH(<date_column>)
NEXTQUARTER (<date_column>)
NEXTYEAR(<date_column>, [,<YE_date>])
OPENINGBALANCEMONTH(<expression>, <dates>, <filter>)
OPENINGBALANCEQUARTER(<expression>, <dates>,
<filter>)
OPENINGBALANCEYEAR(<expression>, <dates>, <filter>)
PARALLELPERIOD(<date_column>, <number_of_intervals>,
<intervals>)
PREVIOUSDAY(<date_column>)
PREVIOUSMONTH(<date_column>)
PREVIOUSQUARTER(<date_column>)
PREVIOUSYEAR(<date_column>)
SAMEPERIODLASTYEAR(<dates>)
STARTOFMONTH (<date_column>)
STARTOFQUARTER (<date_column>)
STARTOFYEAR(<date_column>[,<YE_date>])
TotalMTD(<expression>, <dates>, <filter>)
TotalQTD(<expression>, <dates>, <filter>)
TotalYTD(<expression>, <dates>,<filter>)
```

> **NOTE** Check out the optional Year Ending date parameter in DatesYTD and other arguments. You can finally deal with fiscal years other than those ending on December 31!

For completeness, these are the remaining functions supported by DAX:

```
BLANK()
RELATED(<column>)
ALL(<table_or_column>)
DISTINCT(<column>)
EARLIER(<column>, <number>)
EARLIEST(<table_or_column>)
VALUES(<column>)
ALLEXCEPT(<table>, <column1>, <column2>, ...)
```

```
CALCULATE(<expression>, <filter1>, <filter2>, ...)
CALCULATETABLE(<expression>, <filter1>, <filter2>, ...)
FILTER(<table>, <filter>)
RELATEDTABLE(<table>)
ALLNONBLANKROW(<column>)
FIRSTNONBLANK(<column>, <expression>)
AVERAGEX(<table>, <expression>)
COUNTAX(<table>, <expression>)
COUNTROWS(<table>)
COUNTX(<table>, <expression>)
MAXX(<table>, <expression>)
MINX(<table>, < expression>)
SUMX(<table>, <expression>)
```

Using PowerPivot To Access Named Sets For Asymmetric Reporting

Back in the summer of 2009, I read a post in the Excel team blog about named sets and how they would allow asymmetric reporting. This would enable you to report actual sales for all of the months that have passed and forecast numbers for the future months. I was nearly drooling at the end of the article until they said, "Oh, by the way, this only works for OLAP pivot tables in Excel 2010." I was crushed.

All the pivot tables created by PowerPivot are automatically OLAP pivot tables. If you need to do asymmetric reporting, take your Excel data to PowerPivot and create the pivot table from there.

→ A detailed example of using a Named Set for Asymmetric reporting can be found in Chapter 12,"Using VBA to Create Pivot Tables."

Other Notes

The topic of PowerPivot deserves a whole book. In fact, you can read my whole book on the subject, *PowerPivot for the Data Analyst* (Que Publishing, ISBN: 978-0789743152).

Here are a few miscellaneous topics that did not make it elsewhere in this chapter.

Combination Layouts

The PivotTable drop-down in the PowerPivot Window offers eight choices.

The first choice is a single pivot table and has been used throughout this chapter.

The last choice is a flattened pivot table. That is a pivot table that starts in Outline layout instead of compact layout. The Repeat All Row Labels feature is turned on. If you plan to convert the pivot table to values to reuse it, choosing a flattened pivot table saves you a few clicks along the way.

The other six layouts include pivot charts, which does not make sense to me. PivotCharts look great in Microsoft demos, but no one actually uses them. I see why Microsoft put them here because it gives them something to demo. However, I cannot figure out why they give you six different versions. If one PivotChart is bad, why would anyone ever want four of them?

However, now assume you are trying to create several pivot charts and you found this section in the index. When you choose a combination of multiple elements, you have multiple outlines on the worksheet. In Figure 10.43, the pivot table on the right is the active table. You can tell because the cell pointer is inside the outline for that pivot table. Any changes that you make to the PowerPivot Field list affects that pivot table first.

Figure 10.43
A combination report offers one or more pivot tables or charts.

Active element

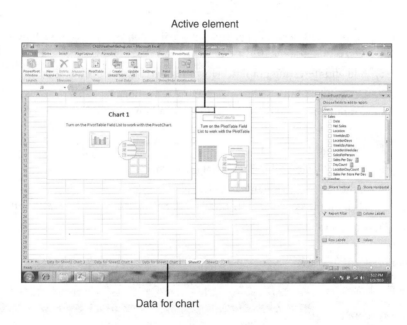

Data for chart

When you are ready to work on another element in the combination, click on that element. The Field List resets to blank, and you can design that element. All elements share the same slicers.

Note that for each chart on your layout, Microsoft inserted a new worksheet to hold the actual pivot table for the chart.

Report Formatting

PowerPivot is exciting because it lets people who cannot do VLOOKUPs mash up data and do reports that have never been imagined before. However, Microsoft blogs are busy showing the exact same layout for their PowerPivot demos. They all look like Figure 10.44. You have probably seen many of them. The following steps show how to replicate the layouts shown in the blogs and press:

1. Insert a new worksheet to hold the workbook.

2. Create a combo of two or four pivot charts. Choose a location rather than letting them default. Choose a spot on Row 5 of the new workbook.

3. Add as many slicers as possible to the top and left of the chart.

4. Build the charts.

5. Make Row 1 very tall, perhaps 270 to 300 points tall. Use Insert, Screenshot to add an interesting graphic to Row 1.

6. Add an interesting graphic below the charts to balance the graphic on top of the charts.

7. Go to File, Options, Advanced, Display Options for This Worksheet. Clear the Gridlines check box. If you want to go all out, scroll up and also clear the scroll bars, sheet tabs, and formula bars.

8. Minimize the ribbon.

9. Add a fill color behind the whole worksheet.

10. Although the pivot table is active, click on the bounding box around each slicer. Right-click on the border. Select properties. Select Move and Size with cells.

11. Click away from the pivot table.

Figure 10.44
This dashboard tracks how many publications have shown this style of dashboard generated by PowerPivot.

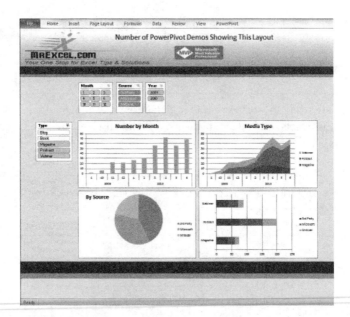

If your layout contains an actual pivot table, consider converting the pivot table to formulas. You can then actually insert extra rows between the pivot table rows, adding color, and so on.

Refreshing PowerPivot Versus Refreshing Pivot Table

Say your underlying data changes. If it is stored in an Excel linked table, you go to the PowerPivot tab in the Excel ribbon and click Refresh All. If it is stored in an External Data Source, you go to the PowerPivot window and select Refresh. If the data was pasted to PowerPivot, you can Paste Append new data or do a Paste Replace.

This does not refresh the pivot table! When you return to Excel, you have to remember to go to the PivotTable Tools Options tab and select Refresh.

Getting Your Data into PowerPivot with SQL Server

Data coming from SQL Server already has many relationships defined. Find the main Fact table, choose that table, and then click the button for Choose Related Tables. PowerPivot reads the database schema and brings in all the tables with relationships predefined. It is, of course, then possible to add in additional Excel or text data to mash up with the SQL Server data.

Other Issues

Can there be multiple relationships between two tables? No. If you need two relationships, import the lookup table twice and link to each copy separately.

Will PowerPivot ever be available for Excel 200n? No. PowerPivot relies on a number of features added to Excel 2010.

Next Steps

In the next chapter, you learn how macros can help you enhance your pivot table reports and empower users to do their own Excel analysis.

Enhancing Pivot Table Reports with Macros

Why Use Macros with Your Pivot Table Reports?

Imagine that you could be in multiple locations at one time, with multiple clients at one time, helping them with their pivot table reports. Suppose you could help multiple clients refresh their data, extract top 20 records, group by months, or sort by revenue The fact is you can do just that by using Excel macros.

A *macro* is a series of keystrokes that have been recorded and saved. After saved, the macro can be played back on command. In other words, you can record your actions in a macro, save the macro, and then allow your clients to play back your actions with the touch of a button. It would be as though you were there with them! This functionality is exceptionally useful when you're distributing pivot table reports.

For example, suppose you want to give your clients the option of grouping their pivot table report by month, quarter, or year. Although the process of grouping can be technically performed by anyone, some of your clients might not have a clue how to do it. In this case, you could record a macro to group by month, a macro to group by quarter, and a macro to group by year. Then, you could create three buttons, one for each macro. In the end, your clients, having little experience with pivot tables, need only to click a button to group their pivot table report.

A major benefit of using macros with your pivot table reports is the power you can give your clients to easily perform pivot table actions that they would not normally be able to perform on their own, empowering them to more effectively analyze the data you provide.

11

Recording Your First Macro

Look at the pivot table in Figure 11.1. You know that you can refresh this pivot table by right-clicking inside the pivot table and selecting Refresh Data. Now, if you were to record your actions with a macro while you refreshed your pivot table, you, or anyone else, could replicate your actions and refresh this pivot table by running the macro.

Figure 11.1

This basic pivot table can easily be refreshed by right-clicking and selecting Refresh Data, but if you recorded your actions with a macro, you could also refresh this pivot table simply by running the macro.

	A	B
1	Region	(All)
2		
3	Row Labels	Sum of Sales_Amount
4	ACASCO Corp.	$675
5	ACECUL Corp.	$593
6	ACEHUA Corp.	$580
7	ACOPUL Corp.	$675
8	ACORAR Corp.	$2,232
9	ACSBUR Corp.	$720
10	ADACEC Corp.	$345
11	ADADUL Corp.	$690
12	ADANAS Corp.	$345
13	ADCOMP Corp.	$553
14	ADDATI Corp.	$379
15	ADDOUS Corp.	$5,209
16	ADFARM Corp.	$357

The first step in recording a macro is to initiate the Record Macro dialog box. Select the Developer tab on the Ribbon, and then select Record Macro.

> **TIP**
> Can't find the Developer tab on the Ribbon? Click the File tab on the Ribbon, and then select the Options selection. This opens the Excel Options dialog box, where you click Customize Ribbon. In the ListBox to the far right, you select the Developer check box. Selecting this option enables the Developer tab.

When the Record Macro dialog box activates, you can fill in a few key pieces of information about the macro:

- **Macro Name**—Enter a name for your macro. You should generally enter a name that describes the action being performed.

- **Shortcut Key**—You can enter any letter into this input box. That letter becomes part of a set of keys on your keyboard that can be pressed (in conjunction with the Ctrl key) to play back the macro. This is optional.

- **Store Macro In**—Specify where you want the macro to be stored. If you are distributing your pivot table report, you should select This Workbook so that the macro is available to your clients.

- **Description**—In this input box, you can enter a few words that give more detail about the macro.

Because this macro refreshes your pivot table when it is played, name your macro **RefreshData**. Also assign a shortcut key of R. Notice that the dialog box gives you a full key of Ctrl+Shift+R. Keep in mind that you use the full key to play your macro after it is created. Be sure to store the macro in This Workbook. Click OK to continue. When this is done, your dialog box should look like the one shown in Figure 11.2.

Figure 11.2
Fill in the Record Macro dialog box as shown here, and then click OK to continue.

When you click OK in the Record Macro dialog box, you initiate the recording process. At this point, any action you perform is being recorded by Excel. In that case, you want to record the process of refreshing your pivot table.

Right-click anywhere inside the pivot table, and then select Refresh Data. After you have refreshed your pivot table, you can stop the recording process by going up to the Developer tab and selecting the Stop Recording button.

Congratulations! You have just recorded your first macro. You can now play your macro by pressing Ctrl+Shift+R.

A WORD ON MACRO SECURITY

You should be aware that when you record a macro yourself, your macro runs fine on your PC with no security restrictions. However, when you distribute workbooks that contain macros, your clients have to let Excel know that your workbook is not a security risk, thus enabling your macros to run.

Indeed, you note that the sample file that comes with this chapter does not run unless you tell Excel to enable the macros within.

The best way to do this is to use the workbook in a *trusted location*, a directory that is deemed a safe zone where only trusted workbooks are placed. A trusted location enables you and your clients to run a macro-enabled workbook with no security restrictions, as long as the workbook is in that location.

To set up a trusted location, follow these steps:

1. Select the Macro Security button on the Developer tab. This activates the Trust Center dialog box.
2. Select the Trusted Locations button.
3. Select Add New Location.
4. Click Browse to specify the directory to be considered a trusted location.

After you specify a trusted location, all workbooks opened from that location are, by default, opened with macros enabled.

> **NOTE**
>
> In Excel 2010, Microsoft has enhanced the security model to remember files that you've deemed trustworthy. That is, when you open an Excel workbook and click the Enable button, Excel remembers that you trusted that file. Each time you open the workbook after that, Excel automatically trusts it.
>
> For information on macro security in Excel 2010, pick up Que Publishing's *Microsoft Excel 2010 In Depth* by Bill Jelen (ISBN 0789743086).

Creating a User Interface with Form Controls

Allowing your clients to run your macro with shortcut keys like Ctrl+Shift+R can be a satisfactory solution if you have only one macro in your pivot table report. However, suppose you want to allow your clients to perform several macro actions. In this case, you should give your clients a clear and easy way to run each macro without having to remember a gaggle of shortcut keys. A basic user interface provides the perfect solution. You can think of a user interface as a set of controls such as buttons, scrollbars, and other devices that enable users to run macros with a simple click of the mouse.

In fact, Excel offers a set of controls designed specifically for creating user interfaces directly on a spreadsheet. These controls are called *form controls*. The general idea behind form controls is that you can place one on a spreadsheet and then assign a previously recorded macro to it. After a macro is assigned to the control, that macro is executed, or played, when the control is clicked.

Form controls can be found in the Controls group on the Developer tab. To get to the form controls, simply select the Insert icon in the Controls group, as demonstrated in Figure 11.3.

Figure 11.3
To see the available form controls, click Insert in the Controls group on the Developer tab.

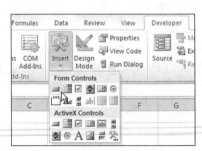

Here, you can select the control that best suits your needs. In this example, you want your clients to be able to refresh their pivot table with the click of a button. Click the Button control, and then drop the control onto your spreadsheet by clicking the location you would like to place the button.

After you drop the button control onto your spreadsheet, the Assign Macro dialog box, as shown in Figure 11.4, opens and asks you to assign a macro to this button. Select the macro you want to assign to the button, in this case RefreshData, and then click OK.

> **NOTE** Notice that there are form controls and ActiveX controls. Although they look similar, they are quite different. Form controls, with their limited overhead and easy configuration settings, are designed specifically for use on a spreadsheet. Meanwhile, ActiveX controls are typically used on Excel userforms. As a general rule, you always want to use form controls when working on a spreadsheet.

Figure 11.4
Select the macro you want to assign to the button, and then click OK. In this case, you want to select RefreshData.

> **NOTE** Keep in mind that all the controls in the Forms toolbar work in the same way as the command button; in that, you assign a macro to run when the control is selected.

As you can see in Figure 11.5, you can assign each macro in your workbook to a different form control, and then name the controls to distinguish between them.

Figure 11.6 demonstrates that after you have all the controls you need for your pivot table report, you can format the controls and surrounding spreadsheet to create a basic interface.

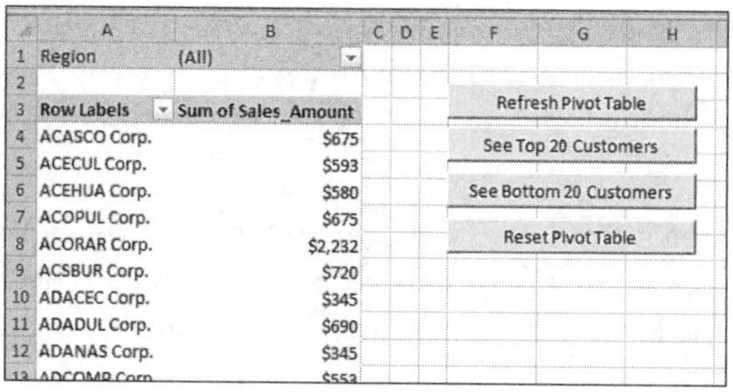

Figure 11.5
You can create a different button for each one of your macros.

Figure 11.6
You can easily create the feeling of an interface with a handful of macros, a few form controls, and a little formatting.

Altering a Recorded Macro to Add Functionality

When you record a macro, Excel creates a module that stores the recorded steps of your actions. These recorded steps are actually lines of Visual Basic for Applications (VBA) code that make up your macro. You can add some interesting functionality to your pivot table reports by tweaking your macro's VBA code to achieve various effects.

To get a better understanding of how this process works, start by creating a new macro that extracts the top five records by customer. Go to the Developer tab, and select Record Macro. Set up the Record Macro dialog box, as shown in Figure 11.7. Name your new macro **TopNthCusts**, and specify that you want to store the macro in This Workbook. Click OK to start recording.

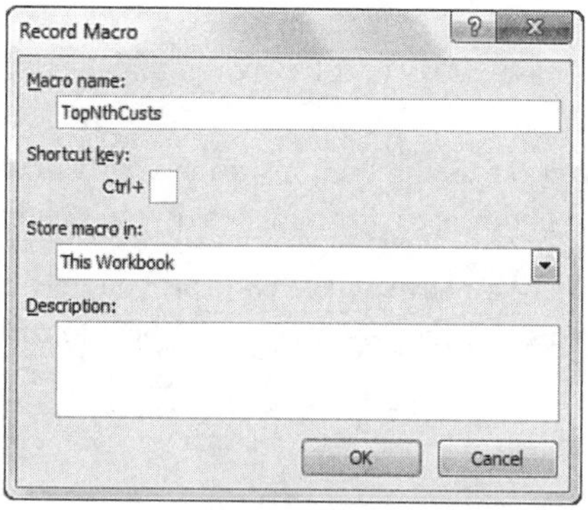

Figure 11.7
Name your new macro, and then specify where you want to store it.

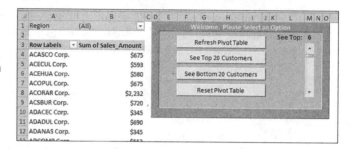

After you have started recording, right-click the Customer field and select Filter. Then, select Top 10. Selecting this option opens the Filter dialog box, where you specify that you want to see the top five customers by sales amount. Enter the settings shown in Figure 11.8, and then click OK.

Figure 11.8
Enter the settings you see here to get the top five customers by revenue.

After successfully recording the steps to extract the top five customers by revenue, select Stop Recording from the Developer tab.

You now have a macro that, when played, filters your pivot table to the top five customers by revenue. The plan is to tweak this macro to respond to a scrollbar. That is, you force the macro to base the number used to filter the pivot table on the number represented by a scrollbar in your user interface. In other words, a user can get the top 5, top 8, or top 32 simply by moving a scrollbar up or down.

To get a scrollbar onto your spreadsheet, select the Insert icon on Developer tab, and then select the scrollbar control from the form controls. Place the scrollbar control onto your spreadsheet by clicking the location you would like to see it.

Right-click the scrollbar, and then select Format Control. This activates the Format Control dialog box. Here, you make the following setting changes: Set Minimum Level to 1 so the scrollbar cannot go below 1; set Maximum Level to 200 so the scrollbar cannot go above 200; and set Cell Link to $M$2 so that the number represented by the scrollbar outputs to cell M2. After you have completed these steps, your dialog box should look like the one shown in Figure 11.9.

Next, assign the TopNthCusts macro you just recorded to your scrollbar, as demonstrated in Figure 11.10. Right-click the scrollbar, and then select Assign Macro. Select the TopNthCusts macro from the list, and then click OK. Assigning this macro ensures that it plays each time the scrollbar is clicked.

At this point, test your scrollbar by clicking on it. When you click your scrollbar, two things should happen: The TopNthCusts macro should play, and the number in cell M2 should change to reflect your scrollbar's position. The number in cell M2 is important because that is the number you are going to reference in your TopNthCusts macro.

The only thing left to do is to tweak your macro to respond to the number in cell M2, effectively tying it to your scrollbar. To do this, you have to get to the VBA code that makes up the macro. There are several ways to get there, but for the purposes of this example, go to the Developer tab and select Macros. Selecting this option opens the Macro dialog

11

Figure 11.9
After you have placed a scrollbar on your spreadsheet, configure the scrollbar as shown here.

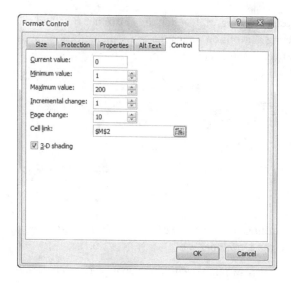

Figure 11.10
Select the macro from the list.

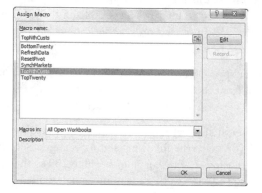

box, exposing several options. From here, you can run, delete, step into, or edit a selected macro. To get to the VBA code that makes up your macro, select the macro, and then select Edit, as demonstrated in Figure 11.11.

The Visual Basic Editor opens with a detailed view of all the VBA code that makes up this macro (see Figure 11.12). Notice that the number 5 is hard-coded as part of your macro. The reason is that you originally recorded your macro to filter the top five customers by revenue. Your goal here is to replace the hard-coded number 5 with the value in cell M2, which is tied to your scrollbar.

You delete the number 5 and replace it with the following:

```
ActiveSheet.Range("M2").Value
```

Your macro's code should now look similar to the code shown in Figure 11.13.

Figure 11.11
To get to the VBA code that makes up the TopNthCusts macro, select the macro, and then select Edit.

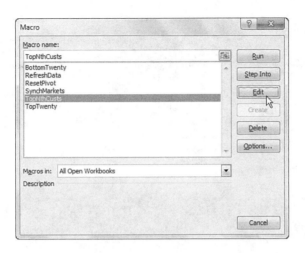

Figure 11.12
Your goal is to replace the hard-coded number 5, as specified when you originally recorded your macro, with the value in cell M2.

```
Sub TopNthCusts()
'
' TopNthCusts Macro
'

    Range("A4").Select
    ActiveSheet.PivotTables("PivotTable1").PivotFields("Customer_Name").ClearAllFilters

    ActiveSheet.PivotTables("PivotTable1").PivotFields("Customer_Name"). _
        PivotFilters.Add Type:=xlTopCount, DataField:=ActiveSheet.PivotTables( _
        "PivotTable1").PivotFields("Sum of Sales_Amount"), Value1:=5
End Sub
```

Figure 11.13
Simply delete the hard-coded number 5 and replace it with a reference to cell M2.

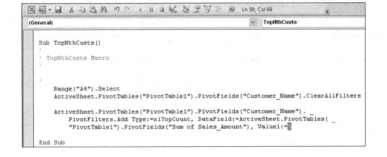

```
Sub TopNthCusts()
'
' TopNthCusts Macro
'

    Range("A4").Select
    ActiveSheet.PivotTables("PivotTable1").PivotFields("Customer_Name").ClearAllFilters

    ActiveSheet.PivotTables("PivotTable1").PivotFields("Customer_Name"). _
        PivotFilters.Add Type:=xlTopCount, DataField:=ActiveSheet.PivotTables( _
        "PivotTable1").PivotFields("Sum of Sales_Amount"), Value1:=ActiveSheet.Range("M2").Value
End Sub
```

Close the Visual Basic Editor to get back to your pivot table report. Test your scrollbar by setting the scrollbar to 11. Your macro should play and filter out the Top 11 customers by revenue, as shown in Figure 11.14.

Figure 11.14

After a little formatting, you have a clear and easy way for your clients to get the top customers by revenue.

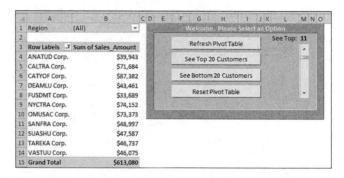

CASE STUDY SYNCHRONIZING TWO PIVOT TABLES WITH ONE COMBO BOX

The report in Figure 11.15 contains two pivot tables. Each pivot table has a filter field to enable you to select a market. The problem is that every time you select a market from the filter field in one pivot table, you have to select the same market from the filter field in the other pivot table to ensure you are analyzing the correct Units Sold versus Revenue.

Not only is it a bit of a hassle to have to synchronize both pivot tables every time you want to analyze a new market's data, but there is a chance you, or your clients, might forget to do so.

Figure 11.15

This pivot table report contains two pivot tables with filter fields that filter out a market. The issue is that you have to synchronize the two pivot tables when analyzing data for a particular market.

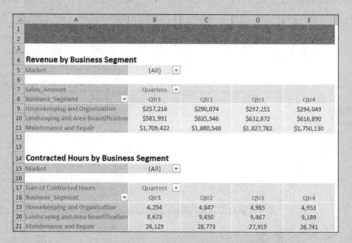

One way to synchronize these pivot tables is to use a combo box. The idea is to record a macro that selects a market from the Market field of both tables. Then you can create a combo box and fill it with the market names that exist in your two pivot tables. Finally, you can alter your macro to filter both pivot tables, using the value from your combo box. To do so, follow these steps:

1. Create a new macro and call it **SynchMarkets**. When recording starts, select the California market from the Market field in both pivot tables, and then stop recording.

2. Activate the Forms toolbar and place a combo box onto your spreadsheet.

3. Create a hard-coded list of all the markets that exist in your pivot table. Note that the first entry in your list is (All). You must include this entry if you want to select all markets with your combo box.

As you can see in Figure 11.16, you place the combo box and your list of markets directly in your spreadsheet.

Figure 11.16
At this point, you should have all the tools you need: a macro that changes the Market field of both pivot tables, a combo box on your spreadsheet, and a list of all the markets that exist in your pivot table.

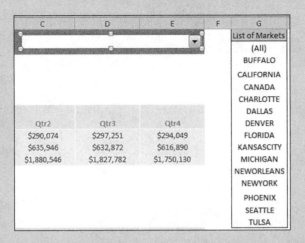

4. Right-click your combo box and select Format Control to perform the initial setup. First, specify an input range for the list you are using to fill your combo box. In this case, this means the market list you created in step 3. Next, specify a cell link—that is, the cell that shows the index number of the item you select. (Cell H1 is the cell link in this example.) After you have configured your combo box, your dialog box should look similar to the one shown in Figure 11.17.

Figure 11.17
The settings for your combo box should reference your market list as the input range and specify a cell link close to your market list. In this case, the cell link is cell H1.

11

At this point, you should now be able to select a market from your combo box and see the associated index number in cell H1. Why an index number instead of the name of the selected market? Well, the only output of a combo box form control is an index number. This is the position number of the selected item. For instance, in Figure 11.18, the selection of Charlotte from the combo box results in the number 5 in cell H1. This means that Charlotte was the fifth item in the combo box.

Figure 11.18
Your combo box, now filled with market names, outputs an index number in cell H1 when a market is selected.

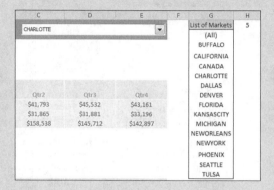

To make use of this index number, you have to pass it through the INDEX function. The INDEX function converts an index number to a value that can be recognized.

5. Enter an INDEX function that converts the index number in cell H1 to a value (See Figure 11.19).

An INDEX function requires two arguments to work properly. The first argument is the range of the list you are working with. In most cases, you use the same range that is feeding your combo box. The second argument is the index number. If the index number is in a cell such as cell H1, you can simply reference the cell.

Figure 11.19
The index function in cell I1 converts the index number in cell H1 to a value. You will eventually use the value in cell I1 to alter your macro.

6. Edit the SynchMarkets macro using the value in cell I1, instead of a hard-coded value. To get to the VBA code that makes up your macro, click the Macros button on the Developer tab. This activates the Macro dialog box, as shown in Figure 11.20. From here, select the SynchMarkets macro, and then select Edit.

Figure 11.20
In the Macro dialog box, select the SynchMarkets macro, and then select Edit.

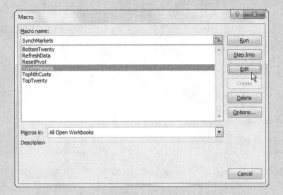

When you recorded your macro originally, you selected the California market from the Market field in both pivot tables. As you can see in Figure 11.21, California is hard-coded in your macro's VBA code.

Figure 11.21
The California market is hard-coded in your macro's VBA code.

```
(General)                                    SynchMarkets

    Option Explicit

    Sub SynchMarkets()

        ActiveSheet.PivotTables("PivotTable1").PivotFields("Market").ClearAllFilters
        ActiveSheet.PivotTables("PivotTable1").PivotFields("Market").CurrentPage = "CALIFORNIA"

        ActiveSheet.PivotTables("PivotTable2").PivotFields("Market").ClearAllFilters
        ActiveSheet.PivotTables("PivotTable2").PivotFields("Market").CurrentPage = "CALIFORNIA"

    End Sub
```

Replace `California` with `ActiveSheet.Range("I1").Value`, as demonstrated in Figure 11.22. This code references the value in cell I1. After you have edited the macro, close the Visual Basic Editor to get back to the spreadsheet.

Figure 11.22
Replace `California` with a pointer to Range I1 and then close the Visual Basic Editor.

```
(General)                                    SynchMarkets

    Option Explicit

    Sub SynchMarkets()

        ActiveSheet.PivotTables("PivotTable1").PivotFields("Market").ClearAllFilters
        ActiveSheet.PivotTables("PivotTable1").PivotFields("Market").CurrentPage = ActiveSheet.Range("I1").Value

        ActiveSheet.PivotTables("PivotTable2").PivotFields("Market").ClearAllFilters
        ActiveSheet.PivotTables("PivotTable2").PivotFields("Market").CurrentPage = ActiveSheet.Range("I1").Value

    End Sub
```

7. All that is left to do is ensure that the macro plays when you select a market from the combo box. Right-click the combo box, and then select Assign Macro. Select the SynchMarkets macro, and then click OK.

8. Clean up the formatting on your newly created report by hiding the rows and columns that hold the filter fields in your pivot tables, the market list you created, and any unseemly formulas.

As you can see in Figure 11.23, this setup provides your clients with an attractive interface that enables them to make selections in multiple pivot tables using one control.

Figure 11.23
Your pivot table report is ready to use!

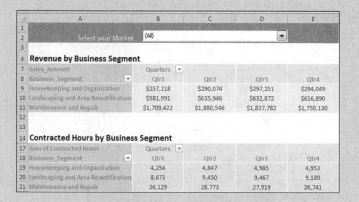

TIP

When you select a new item from your combo box, the pivot tables automatically adjust the columns to fit the data. This behavior can be annoying when you have a formatted template. You can suppress this behavior by right-clicking on each pivot table, and then selecting Table Options. Selecting this option activates the PivotTable Options dialog box, where you can clear the Autofit Column Widths check box on Update selection.

Next Steps

In the next chapter, you go beyond recording macros. Chapter 12, "Using VBA to Create Pivot Tables," shows how to utilize VBA to create powerful, behind-the-scenes processes and calculations using pivot tables.

Using VBA to Create Pivot Tables

12

Introducing VBA

Version 5 of Excel introduced a powerful new macro language called Visual Basic for Applications (VBA). Every copy of Excel shipped since 1993 has had a copy of the powerful VBA language hiding behind the worksheets. VBA enables you to perform steps that you normally perform in Excel quickly and flawlessly. I have seen a VBA program change a process that would take days each month and turn it into a single button click and a minute of processing time.

Do not be intimidated by VBA. The VBA macro recorder tool gets you 90 percent of the way to a useful macro, and I get you the rest of the way using examples in this chapter.

Every example in this chapter is available for download from www.mrexcel.com/pivot2010data.html/.

Enabling VBA in Your Copy of Excel

By default, VBA is disabled in Office 2010. Before you can start using VBA, you need to enable macros in the Trust Center. Follow these steps:

1. Click the File menu to show the Backstage View.
2. In the left navigation, select Options. The Excel Options dialog displays.
3. In the left navigation of Excel Options, select Customize Ribbon.
4. The right listbox has a list of main tabs available in Excel. By default, the checkbox for the Developer tab is unchecked. Select this tab to include it in the ribbon. Click OK to close Excel Options.

5. Click the Developer tab in the ribbon. As shown in Figure 12.1, the Code group on the left side of the ribbon includes icons for the Visual Basic Editor, Macros, Macro Recorder, and Macro Security.

Figure 12.1
Enable the Developer tab to access the VBA tools.

6. Click the Macro Security icon. Excel opens the Trust Center where you have four security choices. These choices use different words than those used in Excel 97 through Excel 2003. Step 7 explains the choices.

7. Choose one of the following options:

- **Disable all macros with notification**—This setting is equivalent to medium macro security in Excel 2003. When you open a workbook that contains macros, a message appears alerting you that macros are in the workbook. If you expect macros to be in the workbook, you should click Options, Enable to allow the macros to run. This is the safest setting because it forces you to explicitly enable macros in each workbook.

- **Enable all macros**—This setting is not recommended because potentially dangerous code can run. However, this setting is equivalent to low macros security in Excel 2003. Because it can enable rogue macros to run in files that are sent to you by others, Microsoft recommends that you do not use this setting.

Using a File Format That Enables Macros

The default Excel 2010 file format is initially the Excel Workbook (.xlsx). This workbook is defined to disallow macros. You can build a macro in a .xlsx workbook, but they will never be allowed to run and won't be saved with the workbook.

You have several options for saving workbooks that enables macros:

- **Excel Macro-Enabled Workbook (.xlsm)**—This uses the new xml-based method for storing workbooks and enables macros. I prefer this file type because it is compact and less prone to becoming corrupt.

- **Excel Binary Workbook (.xlsb)**—This is a binary format and always enables macros.

- **Excel 97-2003 Workbook (.xls)**—There are billions of .xls files in existence and all of them are capable of storing macros. The downside, particularly with pivot tables, is that .xls files force Excel into compatibility mode. You lose access to Slicers, new Filters, and other pivot table improvements.

When you create a new workbook, you can use File, Save As to choose the appropriate file type.

> **TIP**
>
> If you routinely work with macros, you can change a default setting in Excel 2010 to always save files in your preferred file format. Go to File, Options, Save. In the Save Files In This Format drop-down, select Excel Macro-Enabled Workbook (.xlsm). Click OK.

Visual Basic Editor

From Excel, press Alt+F11 or select Developer, Visual Basic to open the Visual Basic Editor, as shown in Figure 12.2. The three main sections of the VBA Editor are described here. If this is your first time using VBA, some of these items might be disabled. Follow the instructions given in the following list to make sure that each is enabled.

Figure 12.2
The Visual Basic Editor window is lurking behind every copy of Excel shipped since 1993.

Project Explorer

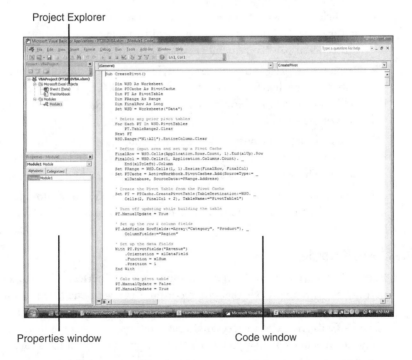

Properties window   Code window

- **Project Explorer**—This pane displays a hierarchical tree of all open workbooks. Expand the tree to see the worksheets and code modules present in the workbook. If the Project Explorer is not visible, enable it by pressing Ctrl+R.

- **Properties window**—The Properties window is important when you begin to program user forms. It has some use when you are writing normal code, so enable it by pressing F4.

- **Code window**—This is the area where you write your code. Code is stored in one or more code modules attached to your workbook. To add a code module to a workbook, select Insert, Module from the VBA menu.

Visual Basic Tools

Visual Basic is a powerful development environment. Although this chapter cannot offer a complete course on VBA, if you are new to VBA, you should take advantage of these important tools:

- As you begin to type code, Excel might offer a drop-down with valid choices. This feature, known as AutoComplete, enables you to type code faster and eliminate typing mistakes.

- For assistance on any keyword, put the cursor in the keyword and press F1. You might need your installation DVDs because the VBA help file can be excluded from the installation of Office 2010.

- Excel checks each line of code as you finish it. Lines in error appear in red. Comments appear in green. You can add a comment by typing a single apostrophe. Use lots of comments so you can remember what each section of code is doing.

- Despite the aforementioned error checking, Excel might still encounter an error at runtime. If this happens, click the Debug button. The line that caused the error is highlighted in yellow. Hover your mouse cursor over any variable to see the current value of the variable.

- When you are in Debug mode, use the Debug menu to step line by line through code. If you have a wide monitor, try arranging the Excel window and the VBA window side by side. This way, you can see the effect of running a line of code on the worksheet.

- Other great debugging tools are breakpoints, the Watch window, the Object Browser, and the Immediate window. Read about these tools in the Excel VBA Help menu.

The Macro Recorder

Excel offers a macro recorder that is about 90 percent perfect. Unfortunately, the last 10 percent is frustrating. Code that you record to work with one data set is hard-coded to work only with that data set. This behavior might work fine if your transactional database occupies Cells A1:L87601 every single day, but if you are pulling in a new invoice register every day, it is unlikely that you will have the same number of rows each day. Given that you might need to work with other data, it would be a lot better if Excel could record selecting cells using the End key. This is one of the shortcomings of the macro recorder.

In reality, Excel pros use the macro recorder to record code but then expect to have to clean up the recorded code.

Understanding Object-Oriented Code

VBA is an object-oriented language. Most lines of VBA code follow the Noun.Verb syntax. However, in VBA, it is called Object.Method. Examples of objects are workbooks, worksheets, cells, or ranges of cells. Methods can be typical Excel actions, such as .Copy, .Paste, and .PasteSpecial.

Many methods allow adverbs—parameters you use to specify how to perform the method. If you see a construct with a := (colon and equal signs), you know that the macro recorder is describing how the method should work.

You also might see the type of code in which you assign a value to the adjectives of an object. In VBA, adjectives are called properties. If you set `ActiveCell.Font.ColorIndex = 3`, you are setting the font color of the active cell to red. Note that when you are dealing with properties, there is only an = (equal sign), not a := (colon and equal signs).

Learning Tricks of the Trade

You need to master a few simple techniques to write efficient VBA code. These techniques help you make the jump to writing effective code.

Writing Code to Handle Any Size Data Range

The macro recorder hard-codes the fact that your data is in a range, such as A1:L87601. Although this hard-coding works for today's data set, it might not work as you get new data sets. You need to write code that can deal with different size data sets.

The macro recorder uses syntax such as Range("H12") to refer to a cell. However, it is more flexible to use Cells(12, 8) to refer to the cell in Row 12, Column 8. Similarly, the macro recorder refers to a rectangular range as Range("A1:L87601"). However, it is more flexible to use the Cells syntax to refer to the upper-left corner of the range, and then use the Resize() syntax to refer to the number of rows and columns in the range. The equivalent way to describe the preceding range is Cells(1, 1).Resize(87601,12). This approach is more flexible because you can replace any of the numbers with a variable.

In the Excel user interface, you can use the End key on the keyboard to jump to the end of a range of data. If you move the cell pointer to the final row on the worksheet and press the End key followed by the up-arrow key, the cell pointer jumps to the last row with data. The equivalent of doing this in VBA is to use the following code:

```
Range("A1048576").End(xlUp).Select
```

You do not need to select this cell; you just need to find the row number that contains the last row. The following code locates this row and saves the row number to a variable named FinalRow:

```
FinalRow = Range("A1048576").End(xlUp).Row
```

There is nothing magic about the variable name FinalRow. You could call this variable x, y, or even your dog's name. However, because VBA enables you to use meaningful variable names, you should use something such as FinalRow to describe the final row.

> **NOTE**
> Excel 2010 files offer 1,048,576 rows and 16,384 columns. Files saved in the Excel 2003 compatibility mode offer 65,536 rows and 256 columns. Because you won't know in advance if the active workbook is from Excel 2010 or 2003, you can generalize the preceding code like so:
>
> ```
> FinalRow = Cells(Rows.Count, 1).End(xlUp).Row
> ```

You also can find the final column in a data set. If you are relatively sure that the data set begins in Row 1, you can use the End key in combination with the left-arrow key to jump from Cell XFD1 to the last column with data. To generalize for the possibility that the code is running in legacy versions of Excel, you can use the following code:

```
FinalCol = Cells(1, Columns.Count).End(xlToLeft).Column
```

END+DOWN VERSUS END+UP

You might be tempted to find the final row by starting in Cell A1 and using the End key in conjunction with the down-arrow key. Avoid this approach. Data coming from another system is imperfect. If your program imports 500,000 rows from a legacy computer system every day for the next five years, a day will come when someone manages to key a null value into the data set. This value will cause a blank cell or even a blank row to appear in the middle of your data set. Using Range("A1").End(xlDown) stops prematurely at the blank cell instead of including all your data. This blank cell causes that day's report to miss thousands of rows of data, a potential disaster that calls into question the credibility of your report. Take the extra step of starting at the last row in the worksheet to greatly reduce the risk of problems.

Using Super-Variables: Object Variables

In typical programming languages, a variable holds a single value. You might use x = 4 to assign a value of 4 to the variable x.

Think about a single cell in Excel. Many properties describe a cell. A cell might contain a value such as 4, but the cell also has a font size, a font color, a row, a column, possibly a formula, possibly a comment, a list of precedents, and more. It is possible in VBA to create a super-variable that contains all the information about a cell or about any object. A statement to create a typical variable such as x = Range("A1") assigns the current value of A1 to the variable x.

However, you can use the Set keyword to create an object variable:

```
Set x = Range("A1")
```

You have now created a super-variable that contains all the properties of the cell. Instead of having a variable with only one value, you have a variable in which you can access the value of many properties associated with that variable. You can reference x.Formula to learn the formula in A1 or x.Font.ColorIndex to learn the color of the cell.

> **TIP** The examples in this chapter frequently set up an object variable called PT to refer to the entire pivot table. This way, any time that the code would generally refer to ActiveSheet.PivotTables("PivotTable1"), you can specify PT to avoid typing the longer text.

Using With and End With to Shorten Code

You will frequently find that you are making several changes to the pivot table. Although the following code is explained later in this chapter, all these lines of code are changing settings in the pivot table:

```
PT.NullString = 0
PT.RepeatAllLabels xlRepeatLabels
PT.ColumnGrand = False
PT.RowGrand = False
PT.RowAxisLayout xlTabularRow
PT.TableStyle2 = "PivotStyleMedium10"
PT.TableStyleRowStripes = True
```

For all those lines of code, the VBA engine has to figure out what you mean by PT. Your code executes faster if you only refer to PT once. Add an initial line of With PT. Then, all the remaining lines do not need to start with PT. Any line that starts with a period is assumed to be referring to the object in the With statement. Finish the code block using an End With statement:

```
With PT
    .NullString = 0
    .RepeatAllLabels xlRepeatLabels
    .ColumnGrand = False
    .RowGrand = False
    .RowAxisLayout xlTabularRow
    .TableStyle2 = "PivotStyleMedium10"
    .TableStyleRowStripes = True
End With
```

Understanding Versions

Pivot tables have been evolving. They were introduced in Excel 5 and perfected in Excel 97. In Excel 2000, pivot table creation in VBA was dramatically altered. Some new parameters were added in Excel 2002. A few new properties such as PivotFilters and TableStyle2 were added in Excel 2007. Slicers and new choices for Show Values As have been added in Excel 2010. Therefore, you need to be extremely careful when writing code in Excel 2010 that might be run in Excel 2007 or legacy versions of Excel.

> **NOTE**
> Much of the code in this chapter is backwards-compatible back to Excel 2000. Pivot table creation in Excel 97 required using the PivotTableWizard method. Although this book does not include code for Excel 97, one example has been included in the sample file for this chapter. See the macro, PivotExcel97Compatible.

New in Excel 2010

Excel 2010 offers many new features in pivot tables. If you use any of these features in VBA, the code works in Excel 2010, but crashes in any previous versions of Excel.

Table 12.1 shows items that are in Excel 2010 VBA for pivot tables. The following items cause incompatibilities when run in Excel 2007.

Table 12.1   Excel 2010 VBA Elements That Are Incompatible with Excel 2007

Feature	Properties and Method
Slicers	Anything with the word Slicer does not work in Excel 2007. This includes SlicerCaches, Slicers, and SlicerItems.
Write-Back	You can now write-back to OLAP data sets. Properties include AllocateChanges, Allocation, Allocation Method, AllocationValue, AllocationWeightExpression, ChangeList, and EnableWriteback. Methods include AllocateChanges, CommitChanges, DiscardChanges, and RefreshDataSourceValues. Objects include PivotTableChangeList, PivotCell.AllocateChange, PivotCell.CellChanged, PivotCell. DataSourceValue, PivotCell.DiscardChange, and PivotCell.MDX.
Repeat Labels	Excel 2010 will fill in the blank cells in the outer row fields. Any code that usesRepeatAllLabels method or RepeatLabels property will fail in Excel 2007.
Sets	Named sets only work in Excel 2010 OLAP pivot tables. All of these elements will fail in previous versions of Excel: AlternativeText, CalculatedMembersInFilters, DisplayContextTooltips, ShowValuesRow, Summary, and VisualTotalsForSets.
Show Values As	These values from xlPivotFieldCalculation are new in Excel 2010: xlPercentOfParentColumn, xlPercentOfParentRow, xlPercentRunningTotal, xlRankAscending, and xlRankDescending.

Concepts Introduced in Excel 2007

If there is some chance that your code runs in Excel 2003, there are even more possible incompatibilities. Many concepts on the Design tab were introduced in Excel 2007, such as subtotals at the top, the report layout options, blank rows, and the new PivotTable styles. Excel 2007 offered better filters than legacy versions. If you are hoping to share your pivot table macro with people running legacy versions of Excel, you need to avoid these methods. Your best bet is to open an Excel 2003 workbook in compatibility mode and record the macro while the workbook is in compatibility mode. If you are using the macro only in Excel 2007 or later, you can use any of these new features.

Table 12.2 shows the methods that were introduced in Excel 2007. If you record a macro that uses these methods, you cannot share the macro with someone using a legacy version of Excel.

Table 12.2   Methods Introduced in Excel 2007

Type	Description
ClearAllFilters	Clears all filters in the pivot table.
ClearTable	Removes all fields from the pivot table, but keeps the pivot table intact.
ConvertToFormulas	Converts a pivot table to cube formulas. This method is valid only for pivot tables based on OLAP data sources.
DisplayAllMember PropertiesInTooltip	Equivalent to Options, Display, Show Properties in ToolTips.
RowAxisLayout	Changes the layout for all fields in the row area. Valid values are xlCompactRow, xlTabularRow, or xlOutlineRow.
SubtotalLocation	Controls whether subtotals appear at the top or bottom of each group. Valid arguments are xlAtTop or xlAtBottom.

Table 12.3 lists the properties that were new in Excel 2007. If you record a macro that refers to these properties, you cannot share the macro with someone using a legacy version of Excel.

Table 12.3   Properties New in Excel 2010

Property	Description
ShowTableStyleColumnHeaders	Controls whether table style 2 should affect the column headers.
ShowTableStyleColumnStripes	Controls whether table style 2 should show banded columns.
ShowTableStyleLastColumn	Controls whether table style 2 should format the final column.
ShowTableStyleRowHeaders	Controls whether table style 2 should affect the row headers.
ShowTableStyleRowStripes	Controls whether table style 2 should show banded columns.
SortUsingCustomLists	Controls whether custom lists are used for sorting items of fields, both initially and later when applying a sort. Setting this property to False can optimize performance for fields with many items and enables you to avoid using custom-list based sorting.
TableStyle2	Specifies the pivot table style currently applied to the pivot table. Note that legacy versions of Excel offered a weak AutoFormat option. That feature's settings were held in the TableStyle property, so Microsoft had to use TableStyle2 as the property name for the new pivot table styles. The property might have a value such as PivotStyleLight17.

12

Building a Pivot Table in Excel VBA

This chapter does not mean to imply that you use VBA to build pivot tables to give to your clients. Instead, the purpose of this chapter is to remind you that pivot tables can be used as a means to an end. You can use a pivot table to extract a summary of data and then use that summary elsewhere.

> **TIP**
>
> The code listings from this chapter are available for download at `www.MrExcel.com/pivot-2010data.html`.

> **CAUTION**
>
> Beginning with Excel 2007, the user interface has new names for the various sections of a pivot table. Even so, VBA code will continue to refer to the old names. Microsoft had to make this decision, otherwise millions of lines of code would stop working in Excel 2007 when they referred to a page field instead of a filter field. While the four sections of a pivot table in the Excel user interface are Report Filter, Column Labels, Row Labels, and Values, VBA continues to use the old terms of Page fields, Column fields, Row fields, and Data fields.

In Excel 2000 and newer, you first build a pivot cache object to describe the input area of the data:

```
Dim WSD As Worksheet
Dim PTCache As PivotCache
Dim PT As PivotTable
Dim PRange As Range
Dim FinalRow As Long
Dim FinalCol As Long
Set WSD = Worksheets("Data")

' Delete any prior pivot tables
For Each PT In WSD.PivotTables
    PT.TableRange2.Clear
Next PT
' Define input area and set up a Pivot Cache
FinalRow = WSD.Cells(Rows.Count, 1).End(xlUp).Row
FinalCol = WSD.Cells(1, Columns.Count).End(xlToLeft).Column
Set PRange = WSD.Cells(1, 1).Resize(FinalRow, FinalCol)
Set PTCache = ActiveWorkbook.PivotCaches.Add(SourceType:=xlDatabase, _
    SourceData:=PRange)
```

After defining the pivot cache, use the `CreatePivotTable` method to create a blank pivot table based on the defined pivot cache:

```
Set PT = PTCache.CreatePivotTable(TableDestination:=
WSD.Cells(2, FinalCol + 2).TableName:="PivotTable1")
```

In the `CreatePivotTable` method, you specify the output location and optionally give the table a name. After running this line of code, you have a strange-looking blank pivot table, like the one shown in Figure 12.3. You now have to use code to drop fields onto the table.

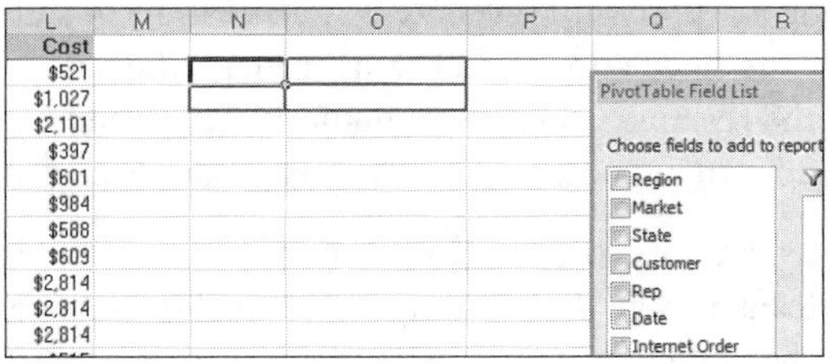

Figure 12.3
Immediately after you use the CreatePivotTable method, Excel gives you a four-cell blank pivot table that is not useful.

If you choose the Defer Layout Update setting in the user interface to build the pivot table, Excel does not recalculate the pivot table after you drop each field onto the table. By default in VBA, Excel calculates the pivot table as you execute each step of building the table. This could require the pivot table to be executed a half-dozen times before you get to the final result.

To speed up your code execution, you can temporarily turn off calculation of the pivot table by using the `ManualUpdate` property:

```
PT.ManualUpdate = True
```

You can now run through the steps needed to lay out the pivot table. In the `.AddFields` method, you can specify one or more fields that should be in the row, column, or filter area of the pivot table.

The `RowFields` parameter enables you to define fields that appear in the Row Labels layout area of the PivotTable Field List. The `ColumnFields` parameter corresponds to the Column Labels layout area. The `PageFields` parameter corresponds to the Report Filter layout area.

The following line of code populates a pivot table with two fields in the row area and one field in the column area:

```
' Set up the row & column fields
PT.AddFields RowFields:=Array("Category", "Product"), _
    ColumnFields:="Region"
```

> **NOTE** If you are adding a single field to an area such as Region to the Column area, you only need to specify the name of the field in quotes. If you are adding two or more fields, you have to include that list inside the array function.

Although the row, column, and page fields of the pivot table can be handled with the .AddFields method, it is best to add fields to the Data area using the code described in the next section.

12

Adding Fields to the Data Area

When you are adding fields to the Data area of the pivot table, there are many settings that you would rather control rather than let Excel's intellisense decide.

Say that you are building a report with revenue. You likely want to sum the revenue. If you do not explicitly specify the calculation, Excel scans through the data in the underlying data. If 100 percent of the revenue columns are numeric, Excel sums. If one cell is blank or contains text, Excel decides to count the revenue. This produces confusing results.

Because of this possible variability, you should never use the DataFields argument in the AddFields method. Instead, change the property of the field to xlDataField. You can then specify the Function to be xlSum.

While you are setting up the data field, you can change several other properties within the same With...End With block.

The Position property is useful when adding multiple fields to the data area. Specify 1 for the first field, 2 for the second field, and so on.

By default, Excel renames a Revenue field to have a strange name like Sum of Revenue. You can use the .Name property to change that heading back to something normal. Note that you cannot reuse the word Revenue as a name, but you can use "Revenue " (with a space).

You are not required to specify a number format, but it can make the resulting pivot table easier to understand and only takes an extra line of code:

```
' Set up the data fields
With PT.PivotFields("Revenue")
    .Orientation = xlDataField
    .Function = xlSum
    .Position = 1
    .NumberFormat = "#,##0"
    .Name = "Revenue "
End With
```

Formatting the Pivot Table

Microsoft introduced the Compact Layout for pivot tables in Excel 2007. This means that there are three layouts available in Excel 2010. Excel should default to using the Tabular layout. This is good because tabular view is the one that makes the most sense. It cannot hurt to add one line of code to ensure that you get the desired layout:

```
PT.RowAxisLayout xlTabularRow
```

In tabular layout, each field in the row area is in a different column. Subtotals always appear at the bottom of each group. This is the layout that has been around the longest and is most conducive to reusing the pivot table report for further analysis.

The Excel user interface frequently defaults to Compact layout. In this layout, multiple columns fields are stacked up into a single column on the left side of the pivot table. To create this layout, use the following code:

```
PT.RowAxisLayout xlCompactRow
```

The one limitation of tabular layout is that you cannot show the totals at the top of each group. If you would need to do this, you want to switch to the Outline layout and show totals at the top of the group:

```
PT.RowAxisLayout xlOutlineRow
PT.SubtotalLocation xlAtTop
```

Your pivot table inherits the table style settings selected as the default on whatever computer happens to run the code. If you would like control over the final format, you can explicitly choose a table style. The following code applies banded rows and a medium table style:

```
' Format the pivot table
PT.ShowTableStyleRowStripes = True
PT.TableStyle2 = "PivotStyleMedium10"
```

At this point, you have given VBA all the settings required to correctly generate the pivot table. If you set `ManualUpdate` to `False`, Excel calculates and draws the pivot table. Thereafter, you can immediately set this back to `True` by using this code:

```
' Calc the pivot table
PT.ManualUpdate = False
PT.ManualUpdate = True
```

At this point, you have a complete pivot table like the one shown in Figure 12.4.

Figure 12.4
Fewer than 50 lines of code create this pivot table in less than a second.

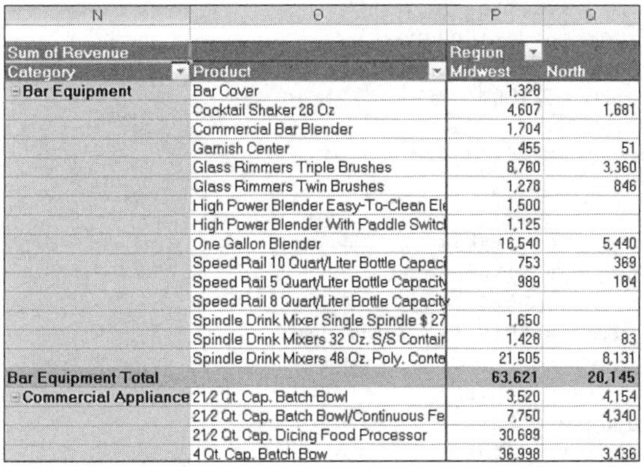

N	O	P	Q
Sum of Revenue		Region	
Category	Product	Midwest	North
- Bar Equipment	Bar Cover	1,328	
	Cocktail Shaker 28 Oz	4,607	1,681
	Commercial Bar Blender	1,704	
	Garnish Center	455	51
	Glass Rimmers Triple Brushes	8,760	3,360
	Glass Rimmers Twin Brushes	1,278	846
	High Power Blender Easy-To-Clean El	1,500	
	High Power Blender With Paddle Switc	1,125	
	One Gallon Blender	16,540	5,440
	Speed Rail 10 Quart/Liter Bottle Capac	753	369
	Speed Rail 5 Quart/Liter Bottle Capacity	989	184
	Speed Rail 8 Quart/Liter Bottle Capacity		
	Spindle Drink Mixer Single Spindle $ 27	1,650	
	Spindle Drink Mixers 32 Oz. S/S Contair	1,428	83
	Spindle Drink Mixers 48 Oz. Poly. Conte	21,505	8,131
Bar Equipment Total		63,621	20,145
- Commercial Appliance	21/2 Qt. Cap. Batch Bowl	3,520	4,154
	21/2 Qt. Cap. Batch Bowl/Continuous Fe	7,750	4,340
	21/2 Qt. Cap. Dicing Food Processor	30,689	
	4 Qt. Cap. Batch Bow	36,998	3,436

Listing 12.1 shows the complete code used to generate the pivot table.

Listing 12.1 Code to Generate a Pivot Table

```
Sub CreatePivot()
    '
    Dim WSD As Worksheet
    Dim PTCache As PivotCache
    Dim PT As PivotTable
```

```
Dim PRange As Range
Dim FinalRow As Long
Set WSD = Worksheets("Data")

' Delete any prior pivot tables
For Each PT In WSD.PivotTables
    PT.TableRange2.Clear
Next PT
WSD.Range("N1:AZ1").EntireColumn.Clear

' Define input area and set up a Pivot Cache
FinalRow = WSD.Cells(Application.Rows.Count, 1).End(xlUp).Row
FinalCol = WSD.Cells(1, Application.Columns.Count). _
    End(xlToLeft).Column
Set PRange = WSD.Cells(1, 1).Resize(FinalRow, FinalCol)
Set PTCache = ActiveWorkbook.PivotCaches.Add(SourceType:= _
    xlDatabase, SourceData:=PRange.Address)

' Create the Pivot Table from the Pivot Cache
Set PT = PTCache.CreatePivotTable(TableDestination:=WSD. _
    Cells(2, FinalCol + 2), TableName:="PivotTable1")

' Turn off updating while building the table
PT.ManualUpdate = True

' Set up the row & column fields
PT.AddFields RowFields:=Array("Category", "Product"), _
    ColumnFields:="Region"

' Set up the data fields
With PT.PivotFields("Revenue")
    .Orientation = xlDataField
    .Function = xlSum
    .Position = 1
    .NumberFormat = "#,##0"
End With

' Format the pivot table
PT.RowAxisLayout xlTabularRow
PT.ShowTableStyleRowStripes = True
PT.TableStyle2 = "PivotStyleMedium10"

' Calc the pivot table
PT.ManualUpdate = False
PT.ManualUpdate = True

WSD.Activate
Cells(2, FinalCol + 2).Select

End Sub
```

Dealing with Limitations of Pivot Tables

As with pivot tables in the user interface, Microsoft maintains tight control over a live pivot table. You need to be aware of these issues as your code is running on a sheet with a live pivot table.

Filling Blank Cells in the Data Area

It is always a bit annoying that Excel puts blank cells in the data area of a pivot table. In Figure 12.4, the North region had no sales of a Bar Cover, so that cell appears blank instead of with a zero.

You can override this in the Excel interface by using the For Empty Cells Show setting in the PivotTable Options dialog. The equivalent code is shown here:

```
PT.NullString = "0"
```

> **NOTE** Note that the Excel macro recorder always wraps that zero in quotation marks. No matter whether you specify "0" or just 0, the blank cells in the data area of the pivot table has numeric zeroes.

Filling Blank Cells in the Row Area

Excel 2010 added a much needed setting to fill in the blank cells along the left columns of a pivot table. This problem happens any time that you have two or more fields in the row area of a pivot table. Rather than repeating a label such as "Bar Equipment" in Cells N5:N18, Microsoft traditionally left those cells blank.

To solve that problem in Excel 2010, use:

```
PT.RepeatAllLabels xlRepeatLabels
```

Learning Why You Cannot Move or Change Part of a Pivot Report

You cannot use many Excel commands inside of a pivot table. Inserting rows, deleting rows, and cutting and pasting parts of a pivot table are all against the rules.

Say that you tried to delete the Grand Total column from Column W in a pivot table. If you try to delete or clear Column W, the macro comes to a screeching halt with an error 1004, as shown in Figure 12.5.

Figure 12.5
You cannot delete just part of a pivot table.

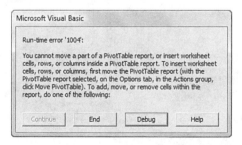

There are two strategies to get around this limitation. The first strategy is to find if there is already an equivalent command in the pivot table interface. For example, there is code to do any of these items:

- Remove the grand total column
- Remove the grand total row
- Add blank rows between each section
- Suppress subtotals for outer row fields

The second strategy is to convert the pivot table to values. You can then insert, cut, and clear as necessary.

Both strategies are discussed in the following sections.

Controlling Totals

The default pivot table includes a grand total row and a grand total column. You can choose to hide one or both of these elements.

To remove the grand total column from the right side of the pivot table, use:

```
PT.ColumnGrand = False
```

To remove the grand total row from the bottom of the pivot table, use:

```
PT.RowGrand = False
```

Turning off the subtotals rows is surprisingly complex. This issue comes up when you have multiple fields in the row area. Excel automatically turns on subtotals for the outermost row fields.

> **TIP**
>
> Did you know that you can have a pivot table show multiple subtotal rows? I have never seen anyone actually do this, but you can use the Field Settings dialog to specify that you want to see a Sum, Average, Count, Max, Min, and so on. Figure 12.6 shows this setting in the user interface.

Figure 12.6
It is rarely used, but the fact that you can specify multiple types of subtotals for a single field complicates the VBA code for suppressing subtotals.

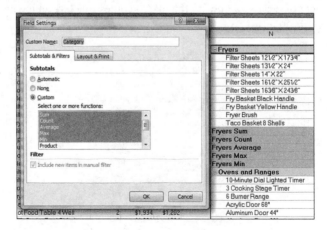

To suppress the subtotals for a field, you must set the Subtotals property equal to an array of 12 False values. The first False turns off automatic subtotals, the second False turns off the Sum subtotal, the third False turns off the Count subtotal, and so on. This line of code suppresses the Category subtotal:

```
PT.PivotFields("Category").Subtotals = Array(False, False, False, False, _
    False, False, False, False, False, False, False, False)
```

A different technique is to turn on the first subtotal. This method automatically turns off the other 11 subtotals. You can then turn off the first subtotal to make sure that all subtotals are suppressed:

```
PT.PivotFields("Category").Subtotals(1) = True
PT.PivotFields("Category").Subtotals(1) = False
```

Determining Size of a Finished Pivot Table to Convert the Pivot Table to Values

If you plan on converting a live pivot table to values, you need to copy the entire pivot table. This might be tough to predict. If you summarize transactional data every day, you might find that on any given day you do not have sales from one region. This can cause your table to be perhaps seven columns wide on some days and only six columns wide on other days.

Excel provides two range properties that you can use to refer to a pivot table. The .TableRange2 property includes all the rows of the pivot table including any page field drop-downs at the top of the pivot table.

The .TableRange1 property starts just below the filter fields. It does often include the unnecessary row with Sum of Revenue at the top of the pivot table.

If your goal is to convert the pivot table to values and not move the pivot table to a new place, you can use this code:

```
PT.TableRange2.Copy
PT.TableRange2.PasteSpecial xlPasteValues
```

If you want to copy only the data section of the pivot table to a new location, you frequently use the .Offset property to start one row lower than the top of .TableRange2:

```
PT.TableRange2.Offset(1,0).Copy
```

This reference copies the data area plus one row of headings.

Notice in the figure that using .OFFSET without .RESIZE causes one extra row to be copied. However, because that row is always blank, there is no need to use .RESIZE to not copy the extra blank row.

The code copies PT.TableRange2 and uses PasteSpecial on a cell six rows below the current pivot table. At that point in the code, your worksheet appears as shown in Figure 12.7. The table in Cell N2 is a live pivot table, and the table in Cell N58 contains the copied results.

12

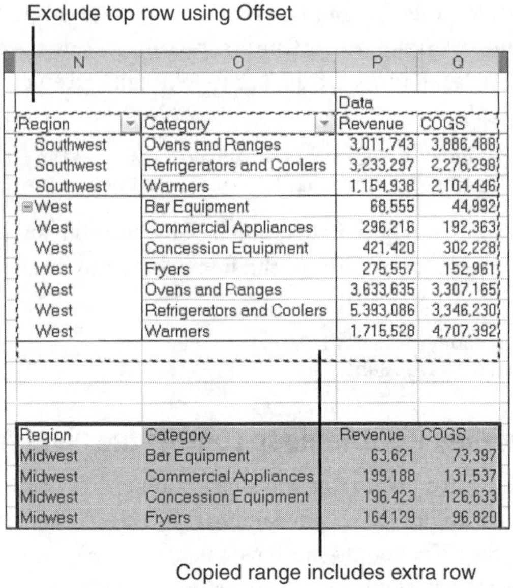

Figure 12.7
An intermediate result of the macro. The data at the bottom has been converted to values.

Exclude top row using Offset

Copied range includes extra row

You can then eliminate the pivot table by applying the Clear method to the entire table. If your code is then going on to do additional formatting, you should remove the pivot cache from memory by setting PTCache equal to Nothing.

Listing 12.2 uses a pivot table to produce a summary from the underlying data. More than 80,000 rows are reduced to a tight 50 row summary. The resulting data is properly formatted for additional filtering, sorting, and so on. At the end of the code, the pivot table is copied to static values, and the pivot table is cleared.

Listing 12.2   Code to Produce a Static Summary from a Pivot Table

```
Sub UsePivotToCreateValues()
'
    Dim WSD As Worksheet
    Dim PTCache As PivotCache
    Dim PT As PivotTable
    Dim PRange As Range
    Dim FinalRow As Long
    Set WSD = Worksheets("Data")

    ' Delete any prior pivot tables
    For Each PT In WSD.PivotTables
        PT.TableRange2.Clear
    Next PT
    WSD.Range("N1:AZ1").EntireColumn.Clear

    ' Define input area and set up a Pivot Cache
    FinalRow = WSD.Cells(Application.Rows.Count, 1).End(xlUp).Row
    FinalCol = WSD.Cells(1, Application.Columns.Count). _
        End(xlToLeft).Column
    Set PRange = WSD.Cells(1, 1).Resize(FinalRow, FinalCol)
```

```vba
Set PTCache = ActiveWorkbook.PivotCaches.Add(SourceType:= _
    xlDatabase, SourceData:=PRange.Address)

' Create the Pivot Table from the Pivot Cache
Set PT = PTCache.CreatePivotTable(TableDestination:=WSD. _
    Cells(2, FinalCol + 2), TableName:="PivotTable1")

' Turn off updating while building the table
PT.ManualUpdate = True

' Set up the row & column fields
PT.AddFields RowFields:=Array("Region", "Category"), _
    ColumnFields:="Data"

' Set up the data fields
With PT.PivotFields("Revenue")
    .Orientation = xlDataField
    .Function = xlSum
    .Position = 1
    .NumberFormat = "#,##0"
    .Name = "Revenue "
End With

With PT.PivotFields("Cost")
    .Orientation = xlDataField
    .Function = xlSum
    .Position = 2
    .NumberFormat = "#,##0"
    .Name = "COGS"
End With

' Settings to create a solid block of data
With PT
    .NullString = 0
    .RepeatAllLabels Repeat:=xlRepeatLabels
    .ColumnGrand = False
    .RowGrand = 0
    .PivotFields("Region").Subtotals(1) = True
    .PivotFields("Region").Subtotals(1) = False
End With

' Calc the pivot table
PT.ManualUpdate = False
PT.ManualUpdate = True

' Copy the pivot table as values below the pivot table
PT.TableRange2.Offset(1, 0).Copy
PT.TableRange1.Cells(1, 1).Offset(PT.TableRange1.Rows.Count + _
    4, 0).PasteSpecial xlPasteValuesAndNumberFormats
StartRow = PT.TableRange1.Cells(1, 1) _
    .Offset(PT.TableRange1.Rows.Count + 5, 0).Row


PT.TableRange1.Clear
Set PTCache = Nothing
```

12

```
    WSD.Activate
    Cells(StartRow, FinalCol + 2).Select

End Sub
```

The preceding code creates the pivot table. It then copies the results as values and pastes them below the original pivot table. In reality, you probably want to copy this report to another worksheet or another workbook. Examples later in this chapter introduce the code necessary for this.

So far, this chapter has walked you through building the simplest of pivot table reports. Pivot tables offer far more flexibility. Read on for more complex reporting examples.

Pivot Table 201: Creating a Report Showing Revenue by Category

A typical report might provide a list of markets by category with revenue by year. This report could be given to product line managers to show them which markets are selling well. The report in Figure 12.8 is not a pivot table, but the macro to create the report used a pivot table to summarize the data. Regular Excel commands such as Subtotal then finish off the report.

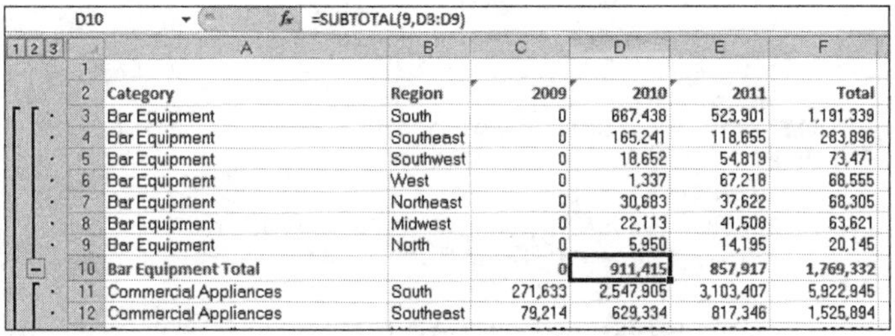

D10 =SUBTOTAL(9,D3:D9)

	A	B	C	D	E	F
1						
2	**Category**	**Region**	**2009**	**2010**	**2011**	**Total**
3	Bar Equipment	South	0	667,438	523,901	1,191,339
4	Bar Equipment	Southeast	0	165,241	118,655	283,896
5	Bar Equipment	Southwest	0	18,652	54,819	73,471
6	Bar Equipment	West	0	1,337	67,218	68,555
7	Bar Equipment	Northeast	0	30,683	37,622	68,305
8	Bar Equipment	Midwest	0	22,113	41,508	63,621
9	Bar Equipment	North	0	5,950	14,195	20,145
10	**Bar Equipment Total**		**0**	**911,415**	**857,917**	**1,769,332**
11	Commercial Appliances	South	271,633	2,547,905	3,103,407	5,922,945
12	Commercial Appliances	Southeast	79,214	629,334	817,346	1,525,894

Figure 12.8
This report started as a pivot table, but finished as a regular data set.

In this example, you want to show the markets in descending order by revenue with years going across the columns. A sample pivot table report is shown in Figure 12.9.

There are some tricky issues required to create this pivot table:

- You have to roll the daily dates in the original data set up to years.
- You want to control the sort order of the row fields.
- You want to fill in blanks throughout the pivot table, use a better number format, and suppress the subtotals for the category field.

The key to producing this data quickly is to use a pivot table. The default pivot table has a number of quirky problems which you can correct in the macro.

Figure 12.9

A typical request is to take transactional data and produce a summary by product for product line managers.

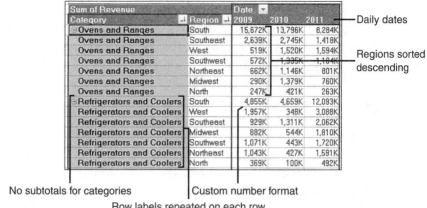

Daily dates

Regions sorted descending

No subtotals for categories

Custom number format

Row labels repeated on each row

To start, use VBA to build a pivot table with Category and Region as the row fields. Add Date as a column field. Add Revenue as a data field using this code:

```
PT.AddFields RowFields:=Array("Category", _
    "Region"), ColumnFields:="Date"

' Set up the data fields
With PT.PivotFields("Revenue")
    .Orientation = xlDataField
    .Function = xlSum
    .Position = 1
    .NumberFormat = "#,##0"
End With
```

Figure 12.10 shows the default pivot table created with these settings.

Figure 12.10

By default, the initial report has many problems.

Sum of Revenue		Date		
Category	Region	01/02/09	01/03/09	01/04/09
⊟ Bar Equipment	Midwest			
	North			
	Northeast			
	South			
	Southeast			
	Southwest			
	West			
Bar Equipment Total				
⊟ Commercial Appliances	Midwest	838		
	North			
	Northeast			
	South	3,310		
	Southeast	4,064		
	Southwest			
	West	829		
Commercial Appliances Total		9,041		
⊟ Concession Equipment	Midwest			
	North			

Here are just a few of the annoyances that most pivot tables present in their default state:

- The Outline view is horrible. In Figure 12.10, the value Bar Equipment appears in the product column only once and is followed by six blank cells. Thankfully, Excel 2010 now offers the RepeatAllLabels method to correct this problem. If you intend to repurpose the data, you need the row labels to be repeated on every row.

- Because the original data set contains daily dates, the default pivot table has over a thousand columns of daily data. No one is able to process this report. You need to roll those daily dates up to years. Pivot tables make this easy.

- The report contains blank cells instead of zeros. In Figure 12.10, the entire visible range of Bar Equipment is blank. These cells should contain zeroes instead of blanks.

- The title is boring. Most people would agree that Sum of Revenue is an annoying title.

- Some captions are extraneous. Date floating in the first row of Figure 12.10 does not belong in a report.

- The default alphabetical sort order is rarely useful. Product line managers are going to want the top markets at the top of the list. It would be helpful to have the report sorted in descending order by revenue.

- The borders are ugly. Excel draws in a myriad of borders that make the report look awful.

- Pivot tables offer no intelligent page break logic. If you want to produce one report for each Category manager, there is no fast method for indicating that each product should be on a new page.

- Because of the page break problem, you might find it is easier to do away with the pivot table's subtotal rows and have the Subtotal method add subtotal rows with page breaks. You need a way to turn off the pivot table subtotal rows offered for Category in Figure 12.10. These rows show up automatically whenever you have two or more row fields. If you had four row fields, you would want to turn off the automatic subtotals for the three outermost row fields.

Even with all these problems in default pivot tables, they are still the way to go. You can overcome each complaint either by using special settings within the pivot table or by entering a few lines of code after the pivot table is created and then copied to a regular data set.

Ensuring Tabular Layout Is Utilized

In legacy versions of Excel, multiple row fields appeared in multiple columns. Three layouts are now available. The Compact layout squeezes all the row fields into a single column.

To prevent this outcome and ensure that your pivot table is in the classic table layout, use this code:

```
PT.RowAxisLayout xlTabularRow
```

Rolling Daily Dates Up to Years

With transactional data, you often find your date-based summaries having one row per day. Although daily data might be useful to a plant manager, many people in the company want to see totals by month or quarter and year.

The great news is that Excel handles the summarization of dates in a pivot table with ease. For anyone who has ever had to use the arcane formula =A2+1-Day(A2) to change daily dates into monthly dates, you will appreciate the ease with which you can group transactional data into months or quarters.

Creating a date group with VBA is a bit quirky. The .Group method can be applied to only a single cell in the pivot table, and that cell must contain a date or the Date field label.

In Figure 12.10, you would have to select either the Date heading in Cell P2 or one of the dates in Cells P3:APM3. Selecting one of these specific cells is risky, particularly if the pivot table later starts being created in a new column. Two other options are more reliable.

If you will never use a different number of row fields, then you can assume that the Date heading is in Row 1, Column 3 of the area known as TableRange2. The following line of code would select this cell:

```
PT.TableRange2.Cells(1, 3).Select
```

You should probably add a comment that you need to edit the 3 in that line to another number any time that you change the number of row fields.

Another solution is to use the LabelRange property for the Date field. The following code always selects the cell containing the Date heading:

```
PT.PivotFields("Date").LabelRange.Select
```

To group the daily dates up to yearly dates, you should define a pivot table with Date in the row field. Turn off ManualCalculation to enable the pivot table to be drawn. You can then use the LabelRange property to locate the date label.

Use the .Group method on the date label cell. You specify an array of seven Boolean values for the Periods argument. The seven values correspond to seconds, minutes, hours, days, months, quarters, and years. For example, to group by years, you would use:

```
PT.PivotFields("Date"),LabelRange.Group _
    Periods:=(False, False, False, False, False, False, True)
```

After grouping by years, the field is still called Date. This differs from the results when you group by multiple fields.

To group by months, quarters, and years, you would use:

```
PT.PivotFields("Date"),LabelRange.Group _
    Periods:=(False, False, False, False, True, True, True)
```

After grouping up to months, quarters, and years, the Date field starts referring to months. Two new virtual fields are available in the pivot table: Quarters and Years.

12

To group by weeks, you choose only the Day period, and then use the By argument to group into seven-day periods:

```
PT.PivotFields("Date"),LabelRange.Group By:=7_
    Periods:=(False, False, False, True, False, False, False)
```

In Figure 12.10, the goal is to group the daily dates up to years, so the following code is used:

```
PT.PivotFields("Date"),LabelRange.Group _
    Periods:=(False, False, False, False, False, False, True)
```

Figure 12.11 shows the pivot table after grouping daily dates up to years.

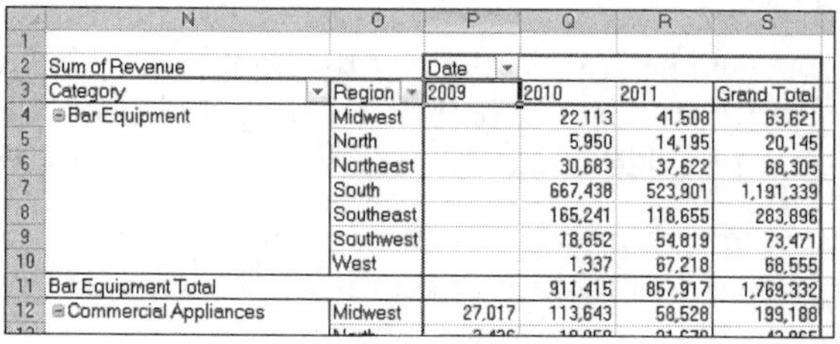

Figure 12.11
Daily dates have been rolled up to years using the Group method.

	N	O	P	Q	R	S
1						
2	Sum of Revenue		Date			
3	Category	Region	2009	2010	2011	Grand Total
4	⊞ Bar Equipment	Midwest		22,113	41,508	63,621
5		North		5,950	14,195	20,145
6		Northeast		30,683	37,622	68,305
7		South		667,438	523,901	1,191,339
8		Southeast		165,241	118,655	283,896
9		Southwest		18,652	54,819	73,471
10		West		1,337	67,218	68,555
11	Bar Equipment Total			911,415	857,917	1,769,332
12	⊟ Commercial Appliances	Midwest	27,017	113,643	58,528	199,188

Eliminating Blank Cells

The blank cells in a pivot table are annoying. There are two kinds of blank cells that you will want to fix. Blank cells occur in the Values area when there were no records for a particular combination. For example, in Figure 12.11, the company did not sell bar equipment in 2009, so Cells P4:P11 are blank.

Most people would prefer to have zeroes instead of those blank cells. Blank cells also occur in the row labels area when you have multiple row fields. The words Bar Equipment appear in Cell N4, but then Cells N5:N10 are blank. Microsoft added a new property to fill these blank cells in Excel 2010.

To replace blanks in the values area with zeroes, use:

```
PT.NullString = "0"
```

> **NOTE**
> Although the proper code is to set this value to a text zero, Excel actually puts a real zero in the empty cells.

To fill in the blanks in the label area in Excel 2010, use:

```
PT.RepeatAllLabels xlRepeatLabels
```

The .RepeatAllLabels code fails in Excel 2007 and earlier. The only solution in legacy versions of Excel is to convert the pivot table to values, then set the blank cells to a formula that grabs the value from the row above:

```
Dim FillRange As Range
Set PT = ActiveSheet.PivotTables("PivotTable1")
' Locate outer row column
Set FillRange = PT.TableRange1.Resize(, 1)
' Convert entire table to values
PT.TableRange2.Copy
PT.TableRange2.PasteSpecial xlPasteValues
' Fill Special Cells Blanks with the value from above
FillRange.SpecialCells(xlCellTypeBlanks).FormulaR1C1 = _
    "=R[-1]C"
' Convert those formulas to values
FillRange.Value = FillRange.Value
```

Controlling the Sort Order with AutoSort

The Excel user interface offers a Sort option that enables you to sort a field in descending order based on revenue. The equivalent code in VBA to sort the region and category fields by descending revenue uses the AutoSort method:

```
PT.PivotFields("Region").AutoSort Order:=xlDescending, _
    Field:="Sum of Revenue"
PT.PivotFields("Category").AutoSort Order:=xlDescending, _
    Field:="Sum of Revenue"
```

Changing Default Number Format

Numbers in the values area of a pivot table need to have a suitable number format applied. You cannot count on the numeric format of the underlying field to carry over to the pivot table.

To show the Revenue values with zero decimal places and a comma, use:

```
PT.PivotFields("Sum of Revenue").NumberFormat = "#,##0"
```

Some companies have customers who typically buy thousands or millions of dollars' worth of goods. You can display numbers in thousands by using a single comma after the number format. To do this, you need to include a K abbreviation to indicate that the numbers are in thousands:

```
PT.PivotFields("Sum of Revenue").NumberFormat = "#,##0,K"
```

Local custom dictates the thousands abbreviation. If you are working for a relatively young computer company where everyone uses K for the thousands separator, you are in luck because Microsoft makes it easy to use this abbreviation. However, if you work at a more than 100 year-old soap company where you use M for thousands and MM for millions, you have a few more hurdles to jump. You are required to prefix the M character with a backslash to have it work:

```
PT.PivotFields("Sum of Revenue").NumberFormat = "#,##0,\M"
```

12

Alternatively, you can surround the M character with double quotation marks. To put double quotation marks inside a quoted string in VBA, you must put two sequential quotation marks. To set up a format in tenths of millions that uses the #,##0.0,,"MM" format, you would use this line of code:

```
PT.PivotFields("Sum of Revenue").NumberFormat = "#,##0.0,, ""MM"""
```

Here, the format is quotation mark, pound, comma, pound, pound, zero, period, zero, comma, comma, space, quotation mark, quotation mark, M,M, quotation mark, quotation mark, quotation mark. The three quotation marks at the end are correct. You use two quotation marks to simulate typing one quotation mark in the custom number format box and a final quotation mark to close the string in VBA.

Figure 12.12 shows the pivot table blanks filled in, numbers shown in thousands, and category and region sorted descending.

Figure 12.12
After filling in blanks and sorting, you only have a few extraneous totals and labels to remove.

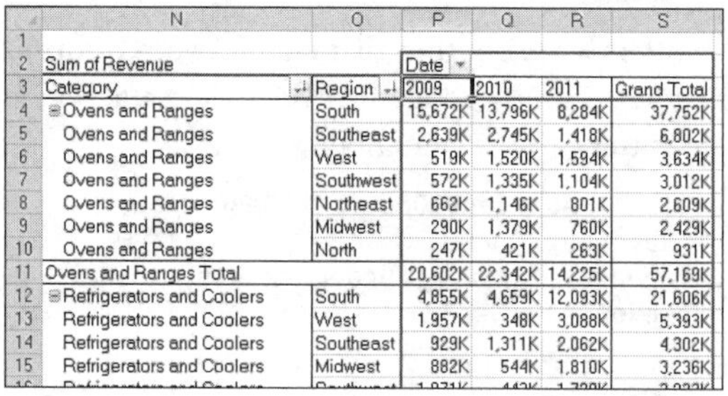

	N	O	P	Q	R	S
1						
2	Sum of Revenue		Date			
3	Category	Region	2009	2010	2011	Grand Total
4	Ovens and Ranges	South	15,672K	13,796K	8,284K	37,752K
5	Ovens and Ranges	Southeast	2,639K	2,745K	1,418K	6,802K
6	Ovens and Ranges	West	519K	1,520K	1,594K	3,634K
7	Ovens and Ranges	Southwest	572K	1,335K	1,104K	3,012K
8	Ovens and Ranges	Northeast	662K	1,146K	801K	2,609K
9	Ovens and Ranges	Midwest	290K	1,379K	760K	2,429K
10	Ovens and Ranges	North	247K	421K	263K	931K
11	Ovens and Ranges Total		20,602K	22,342K	14,225K	57,169K
12	Refrigerators and Coolers	South	4,855K	4,659K	12,093K	21,606K
13	Refrigerators and Coolers	West	1,957K	348K	3,088K	5,393K
14	Refrigerators and Coolers	Southeast	929K	1,311K	2,062K	4,302K
15	Refrigerators and Coolers	Midwest	882K	544K	1,810K	3,236K

Suppressing Subtotals for Multiple Row Fields

As soon as you have more than one row field, Excel automatically adds subtotals for all but the innermost row field. That extra row field can get in the way if you plan on reusing the results of the pivot table as a new data set for some other purpose. In the current example, you have taken 87,000 rows of data and produced a tight 50-row summary of yearly sales by category and region. That new data set would be interesting for sorting, filtering, and charting, if you could remove the total row and the category subtotals. Although accomplishing this task manually might be relatively simple, the VBA code to suppress subtotals is surprisingly complex.

Most people do not realize that it is possible to show multiple types of subtotals. For example, you can choose to show Sum, Average, Min, and Max, as shown in Figure 12.13.

To suppress subtotals for a field, you must set the `Subtotals` property equal to an array of 12 `False` values. The first `False` turns off automatic subtotals, the second `False` turns off the `Sum` subtotal, the third `False` turns off the `Count` subtotal, and so on. This line of code suppresses the `Category` subtotal:

```
PT.PivotFields("Category").Subtotals = Array(False, False, False, False, _
    False, False, False, False, False, False, False, False)
```

Figure 12.13
Rarely used, the Custom Subtotals option enables many subtotals to be defined for one field.

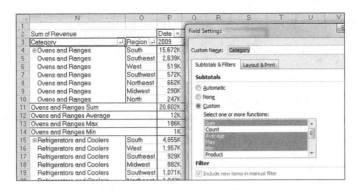

A different technique is to turn on the first subtotal. This method automatically turns off the other 11 subtotals. You can then turn off the first subtotal to make sure that all subtotals are suppressed:

```
PT.PivotFields("Category").Subtotals(1) = True
PT.PivotFields("Category").Subtotals(1) = False
```

To remove the grand total row, use

```
PT.ColumnGrand = False
```

Copying Finished Pivot Table as Values to a New Workbook

If you plan on repurposing the results of the pivot table, you need to convert the table to values. This section shows you how to copy the pivot table to a brand new workbook.

To make the code more portable, assign object variables to the original workbook, new workbook, and first worksheet in the new workbook. At the top of the procedure, add these statements:

```
Dim WSR As Worksheet
Dim WBO As Workbook
Dim WBN As Workbook
Set WBO = ActiveWorkbook
Set WSD = Worksheets("Data")
```

After the pivot table has been successfully created, build a blank Report workbook with this code:

```
' Create a New Blank Workbook with one Worksheet
Set WBN = Workbooks.Add(xlWorksheet)
Set WSR = WBN.Worksheets(1)
WSR.Name = "Report"
' Set up Title for Report
With WSR.Range("A1")
    .Value = "Revenue by Category, Region and Year"
    .Style = "Title"
End With
```

There are a few remaining annoyances in the pivot table. The borders are annoying. There are stray labels such as Sum of Revenue and Date in the first row of the pivot table. You can solve all three of these problems by excluding the first row(s) of PT.TableRange2 from the .Copy method and then using PasteSpecial(xlPasteValuesAndNumberFormats) to copy the data to the report sheet.

> **CAUTION**
>
> In legacy versions of Excel 2000, `xlPasteValuesAndNumberFormats` was not available. Instead, you had to use Paste Special twice: once as `xlPasteValues` and once as `XlPasteFormats`.

In the current example, the .TableRange2 property includes only one row to eliminate, Row 2, as shown in Figure 12.13. If you had a more complex pivot table with several column fields and/or one or more page fields, you would have to eliminate more than just the first row of the report. It helps to run your macro to this point, look at the result, and figure out how many rows you need to delete. You can effectively not copy these rows to the report by using the Offset property. Copy the TableRange2 property, offset by one row.

Purists will note that this code copies one extra blank row from below the pivot table, but this really does not matter because the row is blank. After copying, you can erase the original pivot table and destroy the pivot cache:

```
' Copy the Pivot Table data to row 3 of the Report sheet
' Use Offset to eliminate the title row of the pivot table
PT.TableRange2.Offset(1, 0).Copy
WSR. Range("A3").PasteSpecial Paste:=xlPasteValuesAndNumberFormats
PT.TableRange1.Clear
Set PTCache = Nothing
```

> **TIP**
>
> Note that you use the Paste Special option to paste just values and number formats. This gets rid of both borders and the pivot nature of the table. You might be tempted to use the All Except Borders option under Paste, but this keeps the data in a pivot table, and you will not be able to insert new rows in the middle of the data.

Handling Final Formatting

The last steps for the report involve some basic formatting tasks and then adding the subtotals. You can bold and right-justify the headings in Row 3. Set up rows 1–3 so that the top three rows print on each page:

```
' Do some basic formatting
' Autofit columns, format the headings, right-align
Range("A3").EntireRow.Style = "Heading 4"
Range("A3").CurrentRegion.Columns.AutoFit
Range("A3").EntireRow.HorizontalAlignment = xlRight
Range("A3:B3").HorizontalAlignment = xlLeft
   ' Repeat rows 1-3 at the top of each page
WSR.PageSetup.PrintTitleRows = "$1:$3"
```

Adding Subtotals to Get Page Breaks

Automatic subtotals are a powerful feature found on the Data tab. Figure 12.14 shows the Subtotal dialog box. Note the option Page Break Between Groups.

Figure 12.14
Use automatic subtotals because doing so enables you to add a page break after each category. Using this feature ensures that each category manager has a clean report with only her data on it.

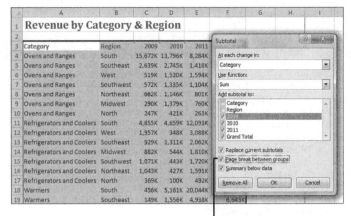

Page break between groups

If you were sure that you would always have three years and a total, the code to add subtotals for each Line of Business group would be the following:

```
' Add Subtotals by Category.
' Be sure to add a page break at each change in category
Selection.Subtotal GroupBy:=1, Function:=xlSum, TotalList:=Array(3, 4, _
    5, 6), PageBreaks:=True
```

However, this code fails if you have more or less than three years. The solution is to use the following convoluted code to dynamically build a list of the columns to total, based on the number of columns in the report:

```
Dim TotColumns()
Dim I as Integer
FinalCol = Cells(3, Columns.Count).End(xlToLeft).Column
ReDim Preserve TotColumns(1 To FinalCol - 2)
For i = 3 To FinalCol
    TotColumns(i - 2) = i
Next i
Selection.Subtotal GroupBy:=1, Function:=xlSum, TotalList:=TotColumns,_
    Replace:=True, PageBreaks:=True, SummaryBelowData:=True
```

Finally, with the new totals added to the report, you need to autofit the numeric columns again with this code:

```
Dim GrandRow as Long
' Make sure the columns are wide enough for totals
GrandRow = Cells(Rows.Count, 1).End(xlUp).Row
Cells(3, 3).Resize(GrandRow - 2, FinalCol - 2).Columns.AutoFit
Cells(GrandRow, 3).Resize(1, FinalCol - 2).NumberFormat = "#,##0,K"
```

12

```
' Add a page break before the Grand Total row, otherwise
' the  manager for the final category will have two totals
WSR.HPageBreaks.Add Before:=Cells(GrandRow, 1)
```

Putting It All Together

Listing 12.3 produces the product line manager reports in a few seconds.

Listing 12.3   Code That Produces the Category Report in Figure 12.15

```
Sub CategoryRegionReport()
    ' Category and Region as Row
    ' Years as Column
    Dim WSD As Worksheet
    Dim PTCache As PivotCache
    Dim PT As PivotTable
    Dim PRange As Range
    Dim FinalRow As Long
    Dim TotColumns()

    Set WSD = Worksheets("Data")
    Dim WSR As Worksheet
    Dim WBO As Workbook
    Dim WBN As Workbook
    Set WBO = ActiveWorkbook

    ' Delete any prior pivot tables
    For Each PT In WSD.PivotTables
        PT.TableRange2.Clear
    Next PT
    WSD.Range("N1:XFD1").EntireColumn.Clear

    ' Define input area and set up a Pivot Cache
    FinalRow = WSD.Cells(Application.Rows.Count, 1).End(xlUp).Row
    FinalCol = WSD.Cells(1, Application.Columns.Count). _
        End(xlToLeft).Column
    Set PRange = WSD.Cells(1, 1).Resize(FinalRow, FinalCol)
    Set PTCache = ActiveWorkbook.PivotCaches.Add(SourceType:= _
        xlDatabase, SourceData:=PRange.Address)

    ' Create the Pivot Table from the Pivot Cache
    Set PT = PTCache.CreatePivotTable(TableDestination:=WSD. _
        Cells(2, FinalCol + 2), TableName:="PivotTable1")

    ' Turn off updating while building the table
    PT.ManualUpdate = True

    ' Set up the row fields
    PT.AddFields RowFields:=Array("Category", _
        "Region"), ColumnFields:="Date"

    ' Set up the data fields
    With PT.PivotFields("Revenue")
        .Orientation = xlDataField
        .Function = xlSum
        .Position = 1
```

```
        .NumberFormat = "#,##0"
End With


' Ensure tabular layout is used
PT.RowAxisLayout xlTabularRow

' Calc the pivot table before grouping dates
PT.ManualUpdate = False
PT.ManualUpdate = True
Stop
PT.PivotFields("Date").LabelRange.Group _
    Periods:=Array(False, False, False, False, False, False, True)

' Change number format of Revenue
PT.PivotFields("Sum of Revenue").NumberFormat = "#,##0,K"

' Fill in blank cells
PT.NullString = "0"
PT.RepeatAllLabels xlRepeatLabels

' Sort both label fields by descending revenue
PT.PivotFields("Category").AutoSort Order:=xlDescending, _
    field:="Sum of Revenue"
PT.PivotFields("Region").AutoSort Order:=xlDescending, _
    field:="Sum of Revenue"


' Suppress Category totals
PT.PivotFields("Category").Subtotals(1) = True
PT.PivotFields("Category").Subtotals(1) = False
PT.ColumnGrand = False

' Calc the pivot table
PT.ManualUpdate = False
PT.ManualUpdate = True

' Create a New Blank Workbook with one Worksheet
Set WBN = Workbooks.Add(xlWBATWorksheet)
Set WSR = WBN.Worksheets(1)
WSR.Name = "Report"
' Set up Title for Report
With WSR.[A1]
    .Value = "Revenue by Category & Region"
    .Style = "Title"
End With

' Copy the Pivot Table data to row 3 of the Report sheet
' Use Offset to eliminate the title row of the pivot table
PT.TableRange1.Offset(1, 0).Copy
WSR.[A3].PasteSpecial Paste:=xlPasteValuesAndNumberFormats
PT.TableRange2.Clear
Set PTCache = Nothing

' Do some basic formatting
' Autofit columns, bold the headings, right-align
Range("A3").EntireRow.Style = "Heading 4"
Range("A3").CurrentRegion.Columns.AutoFit
Range("A3").EntireRow.HorizontalAlignment = xlRight
```

12

```
Range("A3:B3").HorizontalAlignment = xlLeft

' Repeat rows 1-3 at the top of each page
WSR.PageSetup.PrintTitleRows = "$1:$3"

' Add subtotals
FinalCol = Cells(3, 255).End(xlToLeft).Column
ReDim Preserve TotColumns(1 To FinalCol - 2)
For i = 3 To FinalCol
    TotColumns(i - 2) = i
Next i
Range("A3").CurrentRegion.Subtotal GroupBy:=1, Function:=xlSum, _
    TotalList:=TotColumns, Replace:=True, _
    PageBreaks:=True, SummaryBelowData:=True

' Make sure the columns are wide enough for totals
GrandRow = Cells(Rows.Count, 1).End(xlUp).Row
Cells(3, 3).Resize(GrandRow - 2, FinalCol - 2).Columns.AutoFit
Cells(GrandRow, 3).Resize(1, FinalCol - 2).NumberFormat = "#,##0,K"
' Add a page break before the Grand Total row, otherwise
' the product manager for the final Line will have two totals
WSR.HPageBreaks.Add Before:=Cells(GrandRow, 1)

End Sub
```

Figure 12.15 shows the report produced by this code.

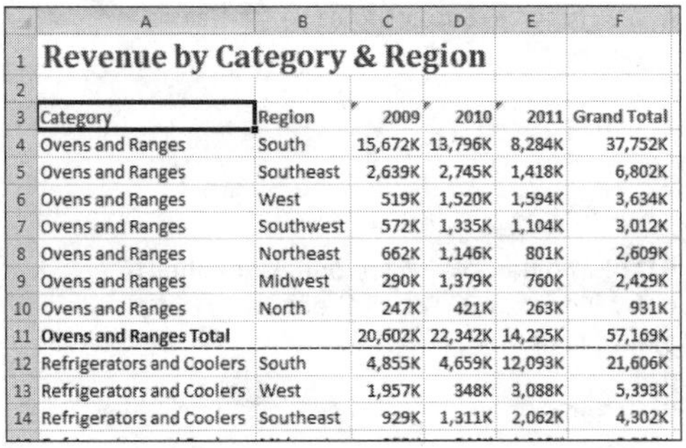

Figure 12.15

Converting 80,000 rows of transactional data to this useful report takes less than two seconds if you use the code that produced this example. Without pivot tables, the code would be far more complex.

	A	B	C	D	E	F
1	**Revenue by Category & Region**					
2						
3	Category	Region	2009	2010	2011	Grand Total
4	Ovens and Ranges	South	15,672K	13,796K	8,284K	37,752K
5	Ovens and Ranges	Southeast	2,639K	2,745K	1,418K	6,802K
6	Ovens and Ranges	West	519K	1,520K	1,594K	3,634K
7	Ovens and Ranges	Southwest	572K	1,335K	1,104K	3,012K
8	Ovens and Ranges	Northeast	662K	1,146K	801K	2,609K
9	Ovens and Ranges	Midwest	290K	1,379K	760K	2,429K
10	Ovens and Ranges	North	247K	421K	263K	931K
11	**Ovens and Ranges Total**		20,602K	22,342K	14,225K	57,169K
12	Refrigerators and Coolers	South	4,855K	4,659K	12,093K	21,606K
13	Refrigerators and Coolers	West	1,957K	348K	3,088K	5,393K
14	Refrigerators and Coolers	Southeast	929K	1,311K	2,062K	4,302K

You have now seen the VBA code to produce useful summary reports from transactional data. The next section will deal with additional features in pivot tables.

Calculating with a Pivot Table

So far, the pivot tables have presented a single field in the values area of the pivot table and that field was always shown as a sum calculation. You can add more fields to the values area. You can change from Sum to any of eleven functions or alter the sum to display running totals, percentage of total, and more. You can also add new calculated fields or calculated items to the pivot table.

Addressing Issues with Two or More Data Fields

It is possible to have multiple fields in the Values section of a pivot report. For example, you might have Quantity, Revenue, and Cost in the same pivot table.

When you have two or more data fields in an Excel 2010 pivot table that you built in the Excel interface, the value fields will go across the columns. However, VBA will build the pivot table with the values fields going down the innermost row field. This creates the bizarre-looking table shown in Figure 12.16.

Figure 12.16
This ugly view was banished in the Excel interface after Excel 2003. VBA still produces it by default.

State	▼	Data	Total
AL		Sum of Revenue	752,789.55
		Sum of Cost	1,428,976.74
		Sum of Quantity	1,890
AR		Sum of Revenue	134,244.75
		Sum of Cost	77,682.78
		Sum of Quantity	130
AZ		Sum of Revenue	3,687,831.25
		Sum of Cost	3,715,843.89
		Sum of Quantity	6,950
CA		Sum of Revenue	11,322,124.25
		Sum of Cost	11,775,024.06
		Sum of Quantity	14,585
CO		Sum of Revenue	1,000,417.15

To correct this problem, you should specify that a virtual field called "Data" is one of the column fields.

> **NOTE**
> In this instance, note that "Data" is not a column in your original data; it is a special name used to indicate the orientation of the multiple values fields.

To have multiple values fields go across the report, use this code:

```
PT.AddFields RowFields:="State", ColumnFields:="Data"
```

After adding a column field called Data, you would then go on to define multiple data fields:

```
' Set up the data fields
With PT.PivotFields("Revenue")
    .Orientation = xlDataField
    .Function = xlSum
    .Position = 1
    .NumberFormat = "#,##0.00"
End With

With PT.PivotFields("Cost")
    .Orientation = xlDataField
    .Function = xlSum
    .Position = 2
    .NumberFormat = "#,##0.00"
```

```
    End With

    With PT.PivotFields("Quantity")
        .Orientation = xlDataField
        .Function = xlSum
        .Position = 3
        .NumberFormat = "#,##0"
    End With
```

This code will produce a pivot table, as shown in Figure 12.17.

Figure 12.17

By specifying the virtual field "Data" as a column field, multiple values go across the report.

State	Data Sum of Revenue	Sum of Cost	Sum of Quantity
AL	752,789.55	1,428,976.74	1,890
AR	134,244.75	77,682.78	130
AZ	3,687,831.25	3,715,843.89	6,950
CA	11,322,124.25	11,775,024.06	14,585
CO	1,280,417.15	892,116.17	1,730
FL	65,272,493.30	122,148,378.05	103,763
GA	27,955,642.10	50,758,752.59	48,897
IA	816,462.00	542,146.20	950
ID	229,274.00	132,473.73	276

Using Calculations Other Than Sum

So far, all of the pivot tables in this chapter have used the Sum function to calculate. There are eleven functions available including Sum. To specify a different calculation, specify one of these values as the .Function property:

- xlAverage—Average.
- xlCount—Count.
- xlCountNums—Count numerical values only.
- xlMax—Maximum.
- xlMin—Minimum.
- xlProduct—Multiply.
- xlStDev—Standard deviation, based on a sample.
- xlStDevP—Standard deviation, based on the whole population.
- xlSum—Sum.
- xlVar—Variation, based on a sample.
- xlVarP—Variation, based on the whole population.

Note that when you add a field to the Values area of the pivot table, Excel modifies the field name with the function name and the word "of". For example, "Revenue" becomes "Sum of Revenue". "Cost" might become "StdDev of Cost". If you later need to refer to those fields in your code, you need to refer to them using the new name such as "Average of Quantity".

You can improve the look of your pivot table by changing the .Name of the field. If you do not want the words "Sum of Revenue" appearing in the pivot table, change the .Caption to "Total Revenue". This sounds less awkward than "Sum of Revenue". Remember that you cannot have a name that exactly matches an existing field name in the pivot table. "Revenue" is not suitable as a name. " Revenue" (with a leading space) is fine to use as a name.

For text fields, the only function that makes sense is a count. You will frequently count the number of records by adding a text field to the pivot table and using the count function.

The following code fragment will calculate total revenue, a count of records by counting a text field, and average quantity:

```
With PT.PivotFields("Revenue")
    .Orientation = xlDataField
    .Function = xlSum
    .Position = 1
    .NumberFormat = "$#,##0.00"
    .Name = " Revenue"
End With

With PT.PivotFields("Customer")
    .Orientation = xlDataField
    .Function = xlCount
    .Position = 2
    .NumberFormat = "#,##0"
    .Name = "# of Records"
End With

With PT.PivotFields("Revenue")
    .Orientation = xlDataField
    .Function = xlAverage
    .Position = 3
    .NumberFormat = "#,##0.00"
    .Name = "Average Revenue"
End With
```

Figure 12.18 shows the pivot table that would result from this code.

Figure 12.18

You can change the function used to summarize columns in the value area of the pivot table.

Rep	Revenue	# of Records	Average Revenue
Alda Carden	$2,225,244	799	2,785.0
Annabel Locklear	$48,013	61	787.1
Ashleigh Friedman	$5,582,120	2,910	1,918.3
Austen Cope	$282,422	159	1,776.2
Carma Gough	$848,890	466	1,821.7
Donte Drummond	$3,820	4	955.0
Dustin Gamboa	$1,308,212	1,059	1,235.3
Edward Cooley	$65,016	58	1,121.0
Jasper Witcher	$381,836	348	1,097.2
Kirstie Paulson	$36,442	48	759.2
Maleah Menard	$292,028	262	1,114.6
Marlin Stubblefield	$331,932	396	838.2
Martin Stamps	$575,548	385	1,494.9
Megan Winston	$206,988	191	1,083.7
Norman Stackhouse	$177,349	185	958.6
Pauline Mccollum	$13	1	13.0
Tory Hanlon	$3,045,306	1,192	2,554.8
Truman Dubois	$173,245	182	951.9
Grand Total	**$15,584,422**	**8,706**	**1,790.1**

12

Generating a Count Distinct

Note that the Count function is not a Count Distinct. If you have seven line items per invoice and ask for a Count of Invoice Number, the function will return the total number of line items, not the number of unique invoice numbers.

There is a clever workaround to find the count distinct. Say that you want to figure out how many unique customers were handled by each sales rep. Add a new formula to the original data set that will figure out how many other records in the data set match both the customer name and sales rep name for the current row's records. Once you know this number, divide it into the number 1. You will then sum this field in the pivot table to produce a count of the distinct number of customers per sales rep.

If this sounds confusing, it is. Follow this logic: say that a particular customer placed 17 orders with their sales rep this year. The COUNTIFS portion of this formula will calculate that a total of 17 records have this customer name and sales rep name. When you divide 1/17, you will get 0.058824 for each of those records. When the pivot table sums that field, those 17 records will appear as a 1 in the result!

The formula to code below will add this formula as a new Column M of the original data set:

```
1/COUNTIFS($D$2:$D$87061,D2, $E$2:$E$87061,E2)
```

The following code fragment will produce a pivot table that contrasts the count of customer with the sum of this calculated field:

```
' Add a calculated column in M to count how many other records
' match the Customer in D and the Rep in E.
FinalRow = WSD.Cells(Application.Rows.Count, 1).End(xlUp).Row
Range("M1").Value = "CustPerRep"
Range("M2").Resize(FinalRow - 1, 1).Formula = "_
    =1/COUNTIFS(D$2:D$" & FinalRow & _
    ",D2,E$2:E$" & FinalRow & ",E2)"
' This calculation takes long to recalc. Change to values
Range("M2").Resize(FinalRow - 1, 1).Value = _
    Range("M2").Resize(FinalRow - 1, 1).Value

' Define input area and set up a Pivot Cache
FinalRow = WSD.Cells(Application.Rows.Count, 1).End(xlUp).Row
FinalCol = WSD.Cells(1, Application.Columns.Count). _
    End(xlToLeft).Column
Set PRange = WSD.Cells(1, 1).Resize(FinalRow, FinalCol)
Set PTCache = ActiveWorkbook.PivotCaches.Add(SourceType:= _
    xlDatabase, SourceData:=PRange.Address)

' Create the Pivot Table from the Pivot Cache
Set PT = PTCache.CreatePivotTable(TableDestination:=WSD. _
    Cells(2, FinalCol + 2), TableName:="PivotTable1")

' Turn off updating while building the table
PT.ManualUpdate = True

' Set up the row fields
PT.AddFields RowFields:=Array("Rep", "State"), ColumnFields:="Data"
```

```
' Set up the data fields
With PT.PivotFields("Revenue")
    .Orientation = xlDataField
    .Function = xlSum
    .Position = 1
    .NumberFormat = "$#,##0"
    .Name = " Revenue"
End With

With PT.PivotFields("Customer")
    .Orientation = xlDataField
    .Function = xlCount
    .Position = 2
    .NumberFormat = "#,##0"
    .Name = "# of Records"
End With

With PT.PivotFields("CustPerRep")
    .Orientation = xlDataField
    .Function = xlSum
    .Position = 3
    .NumberFormat = "#,##0"
    .Name = "# of Customers"
End With
```

The results of the pivot table are shown in Figure 12.19. Although Column R is a "count of customer," it really shows the total number of records for the customers. The results in Column S make use of the CustPerRep field and show a true Count Distinct calculation.

Figure 12.19
Calculating a distinct number of customers requires a new formula in the original data set.

	CustPerRep	Rep	Revenue	# of Records	# of Customers
1			Data		
2	1				
3	1	Rep	Revenue	# of Records	# of Customers
4	1	Alda Carden	$2,225,244	799	135
5	1	Annabel Locklear	$48,013	61	20
6	1	Ashleigh Friedman	$5,582,120	2,910	653
7	1	Austen Cope	$282,422	159	88
8	0.125	Carma Gough	$848,690	466	158
9	0.125	Donte Drummond	$3,820	4	4
10	0.125	Dustin Gamboa	$1,308,212	1,059	567
11	0.125	Edward Cooley	$65,016	58	47
12	0.125	Jasper Witcher	$381,836	348	128
13	0.125	Kirstie Paulson	$36,442	48	16
14	0.125	Maleah Menard	$292,028	262	144
15	0.125	Merlin Stubblefield	$331,932	396	233
16	1	Merlin Stamps	$575,548	385	210
17	0.5	Megan Winston	$206,988	191	106
18	0.5	Norman Stackhouse	$177,349	185	95
19	1	Pauline Mccollum	$13	1	1
20	1	Tory Hanlon	$3,045,306	1,192	264
21	1	Truman Dubois	$173,245	182	104
22	0.166667	**Grand Total**	**$15,584,422**	**8,706**	**2,973**
23	0.166667				

CAUTION

The Count Distinct formula in Column M is hard-coded to assume that you will have sales reps in the row area of the pivot table. Later, if you want to find out the number of customers per state, you need to rewrite the formula in Column M.

Calculated Data Fields

Pivot tables offer two types of formulas. The most useful type defines a formula for a calculated field. This adds a new field to the pivot table. Calculations for calculated fields are always done at the summary level. If you define a calculated field for average price as Revenue divided by Units Sold, Excel first adds the total revenue and total quantity, and then it does the division of these totals to get the result. In many cases, this is exactly what you need. If your calculation does not follow the associative law of mathematics, it might not work as you expect.

To set up a calculated field, use the Add method with the CalculatedFields object. You have to specify a field name and a formula.

```
PT.CalculatedFields.Add "ACS", Formula:="=Revenue /CustPerRep"
```

Once you define the field, add it as a data field:

```
With PT.PivotFields("ACS")
    .Orientation = xlDataField
    .Function = xlSum
    .Position = 3
    .NumberFormat = "$#,##0.00"
    .Caption = "Avg Cust Size"
End With
```

Note that the field is calculating an average, but the function is a sum. This forces Excel to use a label such as "Sum of ACS". Use the .Caption property to insert a different label in the actual pivot table.

Figure 12.20 shows a report with the calculated field.

Figure 12.20

A calculation in the original data set and a calculated field in the pivot table produce average customer size per sales rep.

Rep	Revenue	# of Customers	Avg Cust Size
Alda Carden	$2,225,244	135	$16,483.29
Annabel Locklear	$48,013	20	$2,400.66
Ashleigh Friedman	$5,582,120	653	$8,548.42
Austen Cope	$282,422	88	$3,209.34
Carma Gough	$848,890	158	$5,372.72
Donte Drummond	$3,820	4	$955.00
Dustin Gamboa	$1,308,212	567	$2,307.25
Edward Cooley	$65,016	47	$1,383.32
Jasper Witcher	$381,836	128	$2,983.09
Kirstie Paulson	$36,442	16	$2,277.63
Maleah Menard	$292,028	144	$2,027.97
Marlin Stubblefield	$331,932	233	$1,424.60
Martin Stamps	$575,548	210	$2,740.70
Megan Winston	$206,988	106	$1,952.72
Norman Stackhouse	$177,349	95	$1,866.83
Pauline Mccollum	$13	1	$13.00
Tory Hanlon	$3,045,306	264	$11,535.25
Truman Dubois	$173,245	104	$1,665.82
Grand Total	**$15,584,422**	**2,973**	**$5,241.99**

Calculated Items

Calculated items have the potential to produce incorrect results in your pivot table. Say that you have a report of sales by eight states. You want to show a subtotal of four of the states. A calculated item would add a ninth item to the state column. While the pivot table would gladly calculate this new item, it will cause the grand total to appear overstated.

Figure 12.21 shows a pivot table with these eight states. The total revenue is $10 million. When a calculated item provides a subtotal of four states (see Figure 12.22), the grand total increases to $15 million. This means that the items that make up the calculated item are included in the total twice. If you like restating numbers to the Securities and Exchange Commission, feel free to use calculated items.

Figure 12.21
This pivot table adds up to $10 Million.

Revenue	
State	Total
Arizona	$550,550
California	$3,165,104
Colorado	$616,097
Louisiana	$814,431
Nevada	$1,170,320
New Mexico	$322,168
Oklahoma	$186,715
Texas	$2,559,021
Utah	$632,897
Grand Total	$10,017,303

Figure 12.22
Add a calculated item and the total is overstated.

Revenue	
State	Total
California	$3,165,104
Nevada	$1,170,320
Arizona	$550,550
New Mexico	$322,168
DesertStates	$5,208,142
Colorado	$616,097
Louisiana	$814,431
Oklahoma	$186,715
Texas	$2,559,021
Utah	$632,897
Grand Total	$15,225,445

Calculated item

Overstated by $5.2 million

The code to produce the calculated item is shown here. Calculated items are added as the final position along the field, so this code changes the .Position property to move the Desert States item to the proper position:

```
PT.PivotFields("State").CalculatedItems.Add _
    Name:="DesertStates", _
    Formula:="=California +Nevada +Arizona +'New Mexico'"
PT.PivotFields("State").PivotItems("California").Position = 1
PT.PivotFields("State").PivotItems("Nevada").Position = 2
```

```
PT.PivotFields("State").PivotItems("Arizona").Position = 3
PT.PivotFields("State").PivotItems("New Mexico").Position = 4
PT.PivotFields("State").PivotItems("DesertStates").Position = 5
```

If you hope to use a calculated item, you should either remove the grand total row or remove the four states that go into the calculated item. This code hides the four states. The resulting pivot table returns to the correct total, as shown in Figure 12.23:

```
PT.PivotFields("State").CalculatedItems.Add _
    Name:="DesertStates", _
    Formula:="=California +Nevada +Arizona +'New Mexico'"
' Hide the items included in the new subtotal
With PT.PivotFields("State")
    .PivotItems("California").Visible = False
    .PivotItems("Nevada").Visible = False
    .PivotItems("Arizona").Visible = False
    .PivotItems("New Mexico").Visible = False
End With
```

Figure 12.23

One way to use calculated items is to remove any elements that went into the calculated item.

Revenue	
State ⬛	Total
DesertStates	$5,208,142
Colorado	$616,097
Louisiana	$814,431
Oklahoma	$186,715
Texas	$2,559,021
Utah	$632,897
Grand Total	**$10,017,303**

A better solution, which is discussed in the next section, is to skip Calculated Items and to use text grouping.

Calculating Groups

If you need to calculate subtotals for certain regions, a better solution is to use text grouping to define the groups. If you group the four states, Excel will add a new field to the row area of the pivot table.

Although this process requires some special handling, it is worthwhile and creates a nice-looking report.

To group four states in the Excel interface, you would select the cells that contain those four states and select Group Selection from the PivotTable Tools Options tab. This immediately does several things:

- The items in the group are moved together in the row area.
- A new field is added to the left of the state field. If the original field was called "State", the new field will be called "State2".
- Annoyingly, the subtotals property for the new State2 field is set to None instead of Automatic.

- A subtotal for the selected items is added with the name of "Group1".
- Any items not in a group have a new subtotal added to State2 with the state name repeated.

In VBA, it is somewhat tricky to select the cells that contain the proper states. The following code uses the LabelRange property to point to the cells and then uses the UNION method to refer to the four non-contiguous cells:

```
Set R1 = PT.PivotFields("State").PivotItems("California").LabelRange
Set R2 = PT.PivotFields("State").PivotItems("Arizona").LabelRange
Set R3 = PT.PivotFields("State").PivotItems("New Mexico").LabelRange
Set R4 = PT.PivotFields("State").PivotItems("Nevada").LabelRange
Union(R1, R2, R3, R4).Group
```

After setting up the first group, rename the newly created States2 field to have a suitable name:

```
PT.PivotFields("State2").Caption = "State Group"
```

Then, change the name of this region from Group1 to the desired group name:

```
PT.PivotFields("State Group").PivotItems("Group1").Caption = "Desert States"
```

Change the subtotals property to Automatic from None:

```
PT.PivotFields("State Group").Subtotals(1) = True
```

Once you have set up the first group, you can define the remaining groups with this code:

```
Set R1 = PT.PivotFields("State").PivotItems("Utah").LabelRange
Set R2 = PT.PivotFields("State").PivotItems("Colorado").LabelRange
Union(R1, R2).Group
PT.PivotFields("State Group").PivotItems("Group2").Caption = "Rockies"

Set R1 = PT.PivotFields("State").PivotItems("Texas").LabelRange
Set R2 = PT.PivotFields("State").PivotItems("Louisiana").LabelRange
Set R3 = PT.PivotFields("State").PivotItems("Oklahoma").LabelRange
Union(R1, R2, R3).Group
PT.PivotFields("State Group").PivotItems("Group3").Caption = "Oil States"
```

The result is a pivot table with new virtual groups as shown in Figure 12.24.

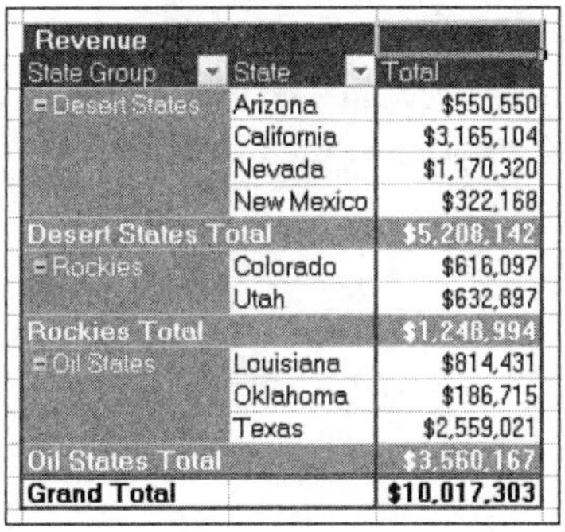

Figure 12.24
Grouping text fields allows for reporting by territories that are not in the original data.

State Group	State	Total
Desert States	Arizona	$550,550
	California	$3,165,104
	Nevada	$1,170,320
	New Mexico	$322,168
Desert States Total		$5,208,142
Rockies	Colorado	$616,097
	Utah	$632,897
Rockies Total		$1,248,994
Oil States	Louisiana	$814,431
	Oklahoma	$186,715
	Texas	$2,559,021
Oil States Total		$3,560,167
Grand Total		$10,017,303

Using Show Values As to Perform Other Calculations

The Show Values As drop-down on the Options tab offers 15 different calculations available. These calculations allow you to change from numbers to percentage of total, running totals, ranks, and more.

Change the calculation by using the .Calculation option for the pivot field.

> **NOTE** Note that the .Calculation property works in conjunction with the .BaseField and .BaseItem properties. Depending on the selected calculation, you might be required to specify a BaseField and BaseItem, or sometimes only a BaseField, or sometimes neither of them.

Some calculations such as % of Column or % of Row need no further definition; you do not have to specify a base field. Here is code to show revenue as a percentage of total revenue:

```
With PT.PivotFields("Revenue")
    .Orientation = xlDataField
    .Function = xlSum
    .Calculation = xlPercentOfTotal
    .Position = 2
    .NumberFormat = "0.0%"
    .Name = "% of Total"
End With
```

Other calculations need a base field. If you are showing revenue and ask for the descending rank, you could specify that the base field is the state field. In this case, you are asking for this state's rank based on revenue:

```
With PT.PivotFields("Revenue")
    .Orientation = xlDataField
    .Calculation = xlRankDecending
    .BaseField = "State"
    .Position = 4
    .NumberFormat = "0%"
    .Name = "RankD"
End With
```

A few calculations require both a base field and a base item. If you wanted to show every state's revenue as a percentage of California revenue, you would have to specify % Of as the calculation, state as the base field and California as the base item:

```
With PT.PivotFields("Revenue")
    .Orientation = xlDataField
    .Calculation = xlPercentOf
    .BaseField = "State"
    .BaseItem = "California"
    .Position = 5
    .NumberFormat = "0%"
    .Name = "% of CA"
End With
```

Some of the calculations fields are new in Excel 2010. In Figure 12.25, Column I uses the new % of Parent calculation and Column H uses the old % of Total calculation. In both columns, Desert States is 52% of the Grand Total (Cells H8 and I8). However, Cell I5 shows that California is 60.8% of Desert States, while Cell H5 shows that California is 31.6% of the grand total.

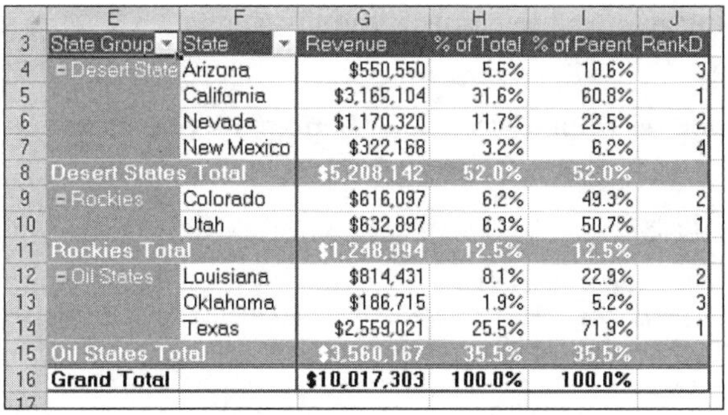

	E	F	G	H	I	J
3	State Group	State	Revenue	% of Total	% of Parent	RankD
4	Desert State	Arizona	$550,550	5.5%	10.6%	3
5		California	$3,165,104	31.6%	60.8%	1
6		Nevada	$1,170,320	11.7%	22.5%	2
7		New Mexico	$322,168	3.2%	6.2%	4
8	Desert States Total		$5,208,142	52.0%	52.0%	
9	Rockies	Colorado	$616,097	6.2%	49.3%	2
10		Utah	$632,897	6.3%	50.7%	1
11	Rockies Total		$1,248,994	12.5%	12.5%	
12	Oil States	Louisiana	$814,431	8.1%	22.9%	2
13		Oklahoma	$186,715	1.9%	5.2%	3
14		Texas	$2,559,021	25.5%	71.9%	1
15	Oil States Total		$3,560,167	35.5%	35.5%	
16	Grand Total		$10,017,303	100.0%	100.0%	
17						

Figure 12.25
% of Parent in Column I is new in Excel 2010.

Table 12.4 shows the complete list of .Calculation options. The second column indicates if the calculation is compatible with previous versions of Excel. The third column indicates if you need a base field and base item.

Table 12.4 Calculation Options Available in Excel 2010 VBA

Calculation	Version	BaseField/BaseItem
xlDifferenceFrom	All	Both required
xlIndex	All	Neither
xlNoAdditionalCalculation	All	Neither
xlPercentDifferenceFrom	All	Both required
xlPercentOf	All	Both required
xlPercentOfColumn	All	Neither
xlPercentOfParent	2010 Only	BaseField only
xlPercentOfParentColumn	2010 Only	Both required
xlPercentOfParentRow	2010 Only	Both required
xlPercentOfRow	All	Neither
xlPercentOfTotal	All	Neither
xlPercentRunningTotal	2010 Only	BaseField only
xlRankAscending	2010 Only	BaseField only
xlRankDescending	2010 Only	BaseField only
xlRunningTotal	All	BaseField only

Using Advanced Pivot Table Techniques

Even if you are a pivot table pro, you may never have run into some of the really advanced techniques available with pivot tables. The following sections discuss such techniques.

Using AutoShow to Produce Executive Overviews

If you are designing an executive dashboard utility, you might want to spotlight the top five markets.

This setting lets you select either the top or bottom n records based on any data field in the report.

The code to use AutoShow in VBA uses the `.AutoShow` method:

```
' Show only the top 5 Markets
PT.PivotFields("Market").AutoShow Top:=xlAutomatic, Range:=xlTop, _
    Count:=5, Field:= "Sum of Revenue"
```

When you create a report using the `.AutoShow` method, it is often helpful to copy the data and then go back to the original pivot report to get the totals for all markets. In the following code, this is achieved by removing the Market field from the pivot table and copying the grand total to the report. Listing 12.4 produces the report shown in Figure 12.26.

Figure 12.26
The Top 5 Markets report contains two pivot tables.

	A	B	C	D	E
1	Top 5 Markets				
2					
3	Market	Bar Equipment	Commercial Appliances	Concession Equipment	Fryers
4	Florida	1,131,779	5,667,799	6,665,865	2,266,932
5	Charlotte	283,676	1,525,742	1,569,949	450,661
6	California	66,233	294,080	415,598	260,156
7	Dallas	59,560	255,146	306,037	150,839
8	Buffalo	37,366	237,298	187,711	127,128
9	Top 5 Total	1,578,614	7,980,064	9,145,160	3,255,716
10					
11	Total Company	1,769,332	8,562,837	9,876,342	3,835,963

Listing 12.4   Code Used to Create the Top 5 Markets Report

```
Sub Top5Markets()
    ' Produce a report of the top 5 markets
    Dim WSD As Worksheet
    Dim WSR As Worksheet
    Dim WBN As Workbook
    Dim PTCache As PivotCache
    Dim PT As PivotTable
    Dim PRange As Range
    Dim FinalRow As Long
    Set WSD = Worksheets("Data")

    ' Delete any prior pivot tables
    For Each PT In WSD.PivotTables
        PT.TableRange2.Clear
    Next PT
    WSD.Range("M1:Z1").EntireColumn.Clear
```

```
' Define input area and set up a Pivot Cache
FinalRow = WSD.Cells(Application.Rows.Count, 1).End(xlUp).Row
FinalCol = WSD.Cells(1, Application.Columns.Count). _
    End(xlToLeft).Column
Set PRange = WSD.Cells(1, 1).Resize(FinalRow, FinalCol)
Set PTCache = ActiveWorkbook.PivotCaches.Add(SourceType:= _
    xlDatabase, SourceData:=PRange.Address)

' Create the Pivot Table from the Pivot Cache
Set PT = PTCache.CreatePivotTable(TableDestination:=WSD. _
    Cells(2, FinalCol + 2), TableName:="PivotTable1")

' Turn off updating while building the table
PT.ManualUpdate = True

' Set up the row fields
PT.AddFields RowFields:="Market", ColumnFields:="Category"

' Set up the data fields
With PT.PivotFields("Revenue")
    .Orientation = xlDataField
    .Function = xlSum
    .Position = 1
    .NumberFormat = "#,##0"
    .Name = "Total Revenue"
End With

' Ensure that we get zeroes instead of blanks in the data area
PT.NullString = "0"

' Sort markets descending by sum of revenue
PT.PivotFields("Market").AutoSort Order:=xlDescending, _
    field:="Total Revenue"

' Show only the top 5 markets
PT.PivotFields("Market").AutoShow Type:=xlAutomatic, Range:=xlTop, _
    Count:=5, field:="Total Revenue"

' Calc the pivot table to allow the date label to be drawn
PT.ManualUpdate = False
PT.ManualUpdate = True

' Create a new blank workbook with one worksheet
Set WBN = Workbooks.Add(xlWBATWorksheet)
Set WSR = WBN.Worksheets(1)
WSR.Name = "Report"
' Set up ritle for report
With WSR.[A1]
    .Value = "Top 5 Markets"
    .Font.Size = 14
End With

' Copy the pivot table data to row 3 of the report sheet
' Use offset to eliminate the title row of the pivot table
PT.TableRange2.Offset(1, 0).Copy
WSR.[A3].PasteSpecial Paste:=xlPasteValuesAndNumberFormats
LastRow = WSR.Cells(Rows.Count, 1).End(xlUp).Row
```

12

```
        WSR.Cells(LastRow, 1).Value = "Top 5 Total"

        ' Go back to the pivot table to get totals without the AutoShow
        PT.PivotFields("Market").Orientation = xlHidden
        PT.ManualUpdate = False
        PT.ManualUpdate = True
        PT.TableRange2.Offset(2, 0).Copy
        WSR.Cells(LastRow + 2, 1).PasteSpecial Paste:=xlPasteValuesAndNumberForma
ts
        WSR.Cells(LastRow + 2, 1).Value = "Total Company"

        ' Clear the pivot table
        PT.TableRange2.Clear
        Set PTCache = Nothing

        ' Do some basic formatting
        ' Autofit columns, bold the headings, right-align
        WSR.Range(WSR.Range("A3"), WSR.Cells(LastRow + 2, 9)).Columns.AutoFit
        Range("A3").EntireRow.Font.Bold = True
        Range("A3").EntireRow.HorizontalAlignment = xlRight
        Range("A3").HorizontalAlignment = xlLeft

        Range("A2").Select
        MsgBox "CEO Report has been Created"

    End Sub
```

The Top 5 Markets report actually contains two snapshots of a pivot table. After using the AutoShow feature to grab the top five markets with their totals, the macro went back to the pivot table, removed the AutoShow option, and grabbed the total of all markets to produce the Total Company row.

Using `ShowDetail` to Filter a Recordset

Take any pivot table in the Excel user interface. Double-click any number in the table. Excel inserts a new sheet in the workbook and copies all the source records that represent that number. In the Excel user interface, this is a great way to perform a drill-down query into a data set.

The equivalent VBA property is `ShowDetail`. By setting this property to `True` for any cell in the pivot table, you generate a new worksheet with all the records that make up that cell:

```
    PT.TableRange1.Offset(2, 1).Resize(1, 1).ShowDetail = True
```

Listing 12.5 produces a pivot table with the total revenue for the top three stores and `ShowDetail` for each of those stores. This is an alternative method to using the Advanced Filter report. The results of this macro are three new sheets. Figure 12.27 shows the first sheet created.

Listing 12.5   **Code Used to Create a Report for Each of the Top Three Customers**

```
    Sub RetrieveTop3CustomerDetail()
        ' Retrieve Details from Top 3 Customers
        Dim WSD As Worksheet
```

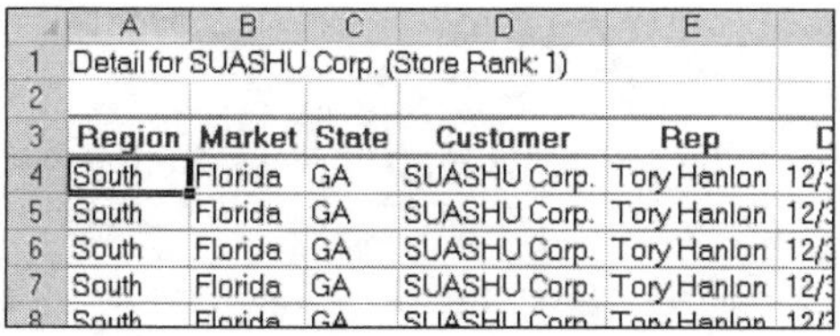

	A	B	C	D	E	D
1	Detail for SUASHU Corp. (Store Rank: 1)					
2						
3	Region	Market	State	Customer	Rep	D
4	South	Florida	GA	SUASHU Corp.	Tory Hanlon	12/3
5	South	Florida	GA	SUASHU Corp.	Tory Hanlon	12/3
6	South	Florida	GA	SUASHU Corp.	Tory Hanlon	12/3
7	South	Florida	GA	SUASHU Corp.	Tory Hanlon	12/3
8	South	Florida	GA	SUASHU Corp.	Tory Hanlon	12/3

Figure 12.27
Pivot table applications are incredibly diverse. This macro created a pivot table of the top three stores and then used the ShowDetail property to retrieve the records for each of those stores.

```
Dim WSR As Worksheet
Dim WBN As Workbook
Dim PTCache As PivotCache
Dim PT As PivotTable
Dim PRange As Range
Dim FinalRow As Long
Set WSD = Worksheets("Data")

' Delete any prior pivot tables
For Each PT In WSD.PivotTables
    PT.TableRange2.Clear
Next PT
WSD.Range("M1:Z1").EntireColumn.Clear

' Define input area and set up a Pivot Cache
FinalRow = WSD.Cells(Application.Rows.Count, 1).End(xlUp).Row
FinalCol = WSD.Cells(1, Application.Columns.Count). _
    End(xlToLeft).Column
Set PRange = WSD.Cells(1, 1).Resize(FinalRow, FinalCol)
Set PTCache = ActiveWorkbook.PivotCaches.Add(SourceType:= _
    xlDatabase, SourceData:=PRange.Address)

' Create the Pivot Table from the Pivot Cache
Set PT = PTCache.CreatePivotTable(TableDestination:=WSD. _
    Cells(2, FinalCol + 2), TableName:="PivotTable1")

' Turn off updating while building the table
PT.ManualUpdate = True

' Set up the row fields
PT.AddFields RowFields:="Customer", ColumnFields:="Data"

' Set up the data fields
With PT.PivotFields("Revenue")
    .Orientation = xlDataField
    .Function = xlSum
    .Position = 1
    .NumberFormat = "#,##0"
    .Name = "Total Revenue"
End With

' Sort Stores descending by sum of revenue
PT.PivotFields("Customer").AutoSort Order:=xlDescending, _
    field:="Total Revenue"

' Show only the top 3 stores
```

```
PT.PivotFields("Customer").AutoShow Type:=xlAutomatic, Range:=xlTop, _
    Count:=3, field:="Total Revenue"

' Ensure that we get zeroes instead of blanks in the data area
PT.NullString = "0"

' Calc the pivot table to allow the date label to be drawn
PT.ManualUpdate = False
PT.ManualUpdate = True

' Produce summary reports for each customer
For i = 1 To 3
    PT.TableRange2.Offset(i + 1, 1).Resize(1, 1).ShowDetail = True
    ' The active sheet has changed to the new detail report
    ' Add a title
    Range("A1:A2").EntireRow.Insert
    Range("A1").Value = "Detail for " & _
        PT.TableRange2.Offset(i + 1, 0).Resize(1, 1).Value & _
        " (Store Rank: " & i & ")"
Next i

MsgBox "Detail reports for top 3 stores have been created."

End Sub
```

Creating Reports for Each Region or Model

A pivot table can have one or more Report Filter fields. A Report Filter field goes in a separate set of rows above the pivot report. It can serve to filter the report to a certain region, certain model, or certain combination of region and model. In VBA, Report Filter fields are called *page fields*.

You might create a pivot table with several filter fields in order to allow someone to do ad-hoc analyses. However, it is more likely that you will use the filter fields in order to produce reports for each region.

To set up a report filter in VBA, add the `PageFields` parameter to the `AddFields` method. The following line of code creates a pivot table with Region in the Report Filter:

```
PT.AddFields RowFields:= "Product", _
    ColumnFields:= "Data", PageFields:= "Region"
```

The preceding line of code sets up the Region report filter with the value (All), which returns all regions. To limit the report to just the North region, use the `CurrentPage` property:

```
PT.PivotFields("Region").CurrentPage = "North"
```

One use of a report filter is to build a user form in which someone can select a particular region or particular product. You then use this information to set the `CurrentPage` property and display the results of the user form.

One amazing trick is to use the Show Pages feature to replicate a pivot table for every item in one filter field drop-down. After creating and formatting a pivot table, you can run this single line of code. If you have eight regions in the data set, eight new worksheets will be inserted in the workbook, one for each region. The pivot table will appear on each worksheet, with the appropriate region chosen from the drop-down:

```
PT.ShowPages PageField:=Region
```

To determine how many regions are available in the data, use `PT.PivotFields("Region")`. `PivotItems.Count`. Either of these loops would work:

```
For i = 1 To PT.PivotFields("Region").PivotItems.Count
    PT.PivotFields("Region").CurrentPage = _
            PT.PivotFields("Region").PivotItems(i).Name
    PT.ManualUpdate = False
    PT.ManualUpdate = True
Next i

For Each PivItem In PT.PivotFields("Region").PivotItems
    PT.PivotFields("Region").CurrentPage = PivItem.Name
    PT.ManualUpdate = False
    PT.ManualUpdate = True
Next PivItem
```

Of course, in both of these loops, the three region reports fly by too quickly to see. In practice, you would want to save each report while it is displayed.

So far in this chapter, you have been using `PT.TableRange2` when copying the data from the pivot table. The `TableRange2` property includes all rows of the pivot table, including the page fields. There is also a `.TableRange1` property, which excludes the page fields. You can use either statement to get the detail rows:

```
PT.TableRange2.Offset(3, 0)
PT.TableRange1.Offset(1, 0)
```

Which you use is your preference, but if you use `TableRange2`, you will not have problems when you try to delete the pivot table with `PT.TableRange2.Clear`. If you were to accidentally attempt to clear `TableRange1` when there are page fields, you would end up with the dreaded `"Cannot move or change part of a pivot table"` error.

Listing 12.6 produces a new workbook for each region, as shown in Figure 12.28.

Listing 12.6   Code That Creates a New Workbook Per Region

```
Sub Top5ByRegionReport()
    ' Produce a report of top 5 customers for each region
    Dim WSD As Worksheet
    Dim WSR As Worksheet
    Dim WBN As Workbook
    Dim PTCache As PivotCache
    Dim PT As PivotTable
    Dim PRange As Range
    Dim FinalRow As Long

    Set WSD = Worksheets("Data")

    ' Delete any prior pivot tables
```

12

Figure 12.28
By looping through all
items found in the Region
page field, the macro produced one workbook for
each regional manager.

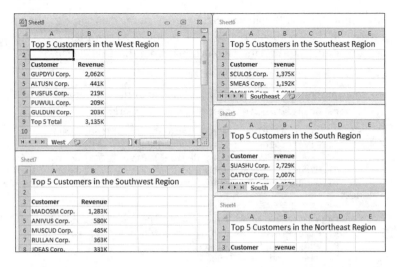

```
For Each PT In WSD.PivotTables
    PT.TableRange2.Clear
Next PT
WSD.Range("M1:Z1").EntireColumn.Clear

' Define input area and set up a Pivot Cache
FinalRow = WSD.Cells(Application.Rows.Count, 1).End(xlUp).Row
FinalCol = WSD.Cells(1, Application.Columns.Count). _
    End(xlToLeft).Column
Set PRange = WSD.Cells(1, 1).Resize(FinalRow, FinalCol)
Set PTCache = ActiveWorkbook.PivotCaches.Add(SourceType:= _
    xlDatabase, SourceData:=PRange.Address)

' Create the Pivot Table from the Pivot Cache
Set PT = PTCache.CreatePivotTable(TableDestination:=WSD. _
    Cells(2, FinalCol + 2), TableName:="PivotTable1")

' Turn off updating while building the table
PT.ManualUpdate = True

' Set up the row fields
PT.AddFields RowFields:="Customer", ColumnFields:="Data", _
    PageFields:="Region"

' Set up the data fields
With PT.PivotFields("Revenue")
    .Orientation = xlDataField
    .Function = xlSum
    .Position = 1
    .NumberFormat = "#,##0,K"
    .Name = "Total Revenue"
End With
Stop

' Sort stores descending by sum of revenue
PT.PivotFields("Customer").AutoSort Order:=xlDescending, _
    field:="Total Revenue"
```

```
' Show only the top 5 stores
PT.PivotFields("Customer").AutoShow Type:=xlAutomatic, Range:=xlTop, _
    Count:=5, field:="Total Revenue"

' Ensure that we get zeroes instead of blanks in the data area
PT.NullString = "0"

' Calc the pivot table
PT.ManualUpdate = False
PT.ManualUpdate = True
Stop
Ctr = 0

' Loop through each region
For Each PivItem In PT.PivotFields("Region").PivotItems
    Ctr = Ctr + 1
    PT.PivotFields("Region").CurrentPage = PivItem.Name
    PT.ManualUpdate = False
    PT.ManualUpdate = True
    Stop

    ' Create a new blank workbook with one worksheet
    Set WBN = Workbooks.Add(xlWBATWorksheet)
    Set WSR = WBN.Worksheets(1)
    WSR.Name = PivItem.Name
    ' Set up Title for Report
    With WSR.[A1]
        .Value = "Top 5 Customers in the " & PivItem.Name & " Region"
        .Font.Size = 14
    End With

    ' Copy the pivot table data to row 3 of the report sheet
    ' Use offset to eliminate the page & title rows of the pivot table
    PT.TableRange2.Offset(3, 0).Copy
    WSR.[A3].PasteSpecial Paste:=xlPasteValuesAndNumberFormats
    LastRow = WSR.Cells(65536, 1).End(xlUp).Row
    WSR.Cells(LastRow, 1).Value = "Top 5 Total"

    ' Do some basic formatting
    ' Autofit columns, bold the headings, right-align
    WSR.Range(WSR.Range("A2"), WSR.Cells(LastRow, 3)).Columns.AutoFit
    Range("A3").EntireRow.Font.Bold = True
    Range("A3").EntireRow.HorizontalAlignment = xlRight
    Range("A3").HorizontalAlignment = xlLeft
    Range("B3").Value = "Revenue"

    Range("A2").Select

Next PivItem

' Clear the pivot table
PT.TableRange2.Clear
Set PTCache = Nothing

MsgBox Ctr & " Region reports have been created"

End Sub
```

12

Manually Filtering Two or More Items in a PivotField

In addition to setting up a calculated pivot item to display the total of a couple of products that make up a dimension, you can manually filter a particular PivotField.

For example, you have one client who sells shoes. In the report showing sales of sandals, he wants to see just the stores that are in warm-weather states. The code to hide a particular store is:

```
PT.PivotFields("Store").PivotItems("Minneapolis").Visible = False
```

You need to be very careful never to set all items to False; otherwise, the macro ends with an error. This tends to happen more than you would expect. An application may first show products A and B and then on the next loop show products C and D. If you attempt to make A and B not visible before making C and D visible, no products will be visible along the PivotField, which causes an error. To correct this, always loop through all PivotItems, making sure to turn them back to visible before the second pass through the loop.

This process is easy in VBA. After building the table with Product in the page field, loop through to change the Visible property to show only the total of certain products:

```
' Make sure all PivotItems along line are visible
For Each PivItem In _
    PT.PivotFields("Product").PivotItems
    PivItem.Visible = True
Next PivItem

' Now - loop through and keep only certain items visible
For Each PivItem In _
    PT.PivotFields("Product").PivotItems
    Select Case PivItem.Name
        Case "Landscaping/Grounds Care", _
            "Green Plants and Foliage Care"
            PivItem.Visible = True
        Case Else
            PivItem.Visible = False
    End Select
Next PivItem
```

Using the Conceptual Filters

Beginning with Excel 2007, conceptual filters for date fields, numeric fields, and text fields are provided. In the PivotTable Field List, hover the mouse cursor over any active field in the field list portion of the dialog box. In the drop-down that appears, you can choose Label Filters, Date Filters, or Value Filters.

To apply a label filter in VBA, use the PivotFilters.Add method. The following code filters to the Customers that start with 1:

```
PT.PivotFields("Customer").PivotFilters.Add _
    Type:=xlCaptionBeginsWith, Value1:="1"
```

To clear the filter from the Customer field, use the ClearAllFilters method:

```
PT.PivotFields("Customer").ClearAllFilters
```

To apply a date filter to the date field to find records from this week, use this code:

```
PT.PivotFields("Date").PivotFilters.Add Type:=xlThisWeek
```

The value filters allow you to filter one field based on the value of another field. For example, to find all the markets where the total revenue is over $100,000, you would use this code:

```
PT.PivotFields("Market").PivotFilters.Add _
    Type:=xlValueIsGreaterThan, _
    DataField:=PT.PivotFields("Sum of Revenue"), _
    Value1:=100000
```

Other value filters might allow you to specify that you want branches where the revenue is between $50,000 and $100,000. In this case, you would specify one limit as Value1 and the second limit as Value2:

```
PT.PivotFields("Market").PivotFilters.Add _
    Type:=xlValueIsBetween, _
    DataField:=PT.PivotFields("Sum of Revenue"), _
    Value1:=50000, Value2:=100000
```

Table 12.5 lists all the possible filter types.

Table 12.5 Filter Types

Filter Type	Description
xlBefore	Filters for all dates before a specified date
xlBeforeOrEqualTo	Filters for all dates on or before a specified date
xlAfter	Filters for all dates after a specified date
xlAfterOrEqualTo	Filters for all dates on or after a specified date
xlAllDatesInPeriodJanuary	Filters for all dates in January
xlAllDatesInPeriodFebruary	Filters for all dates in February
xlAllDatesInPeriodMarch	Filters for all dates in March
xlAllDatesInPeriodApril	Filters for all dates in April
xlAllDatesInPeriodMay	Filters for all dates in May
xlAllDatesInPeriodJune	Filters for all dates in June
xlAllDatesInPeriodJuly	Filters for all dates in July
xlAllDatesInPeriodAugust	Filters for all dates in August
xlAllDatesInPeriodSeptember	Filters for all dates in September
xlAllDatesInPeriodOctober	Filters for all dates in October
xlAllDatesInPeriodNovember	Filters for all dates in November
xlAllDatesInPeriodDecember	Filters for all dates in December
xlAllDatesInPeriodQuarter1	Filters for all dates in Quarter 1

12

Filter Type	Description
xlAllDatesInPeriodQuarter2	Filters for all dates in Quarter 2
xlAllDatesInPeriodQuarter3	Filters for all dates in Quarter 3
xlAllDatesInPeriodQuarter4	Filters for all dates in Quarter 4
xlBottomCount	Filters for the specified number of values from the bottom of a list
xlBottomPercent	Filters for the specified percentage of values from the bottom of a list
xlBottomSum	Sums the values from the bottom of the list
xlCaptionBeginsWith	Filters for all captions beginning with the specified string
xlCaptionContains	Filters for all captions that contain the specified string
xlCaptionDoesNotBeginWith	Filters for all captions that do not begin with the specified string
xlCaptionDoesNotContain	Filters for all captions that do not contain the specified string
xlCaptionDoesNotEndWith	Filters for all captions that do not end with the specified string
xlCaptionDoesNotEqual	Filters for all captions that do not match the specified string
xlCaptionEndsWith	Filters for all captions that end with the specified string
xlCaptionEquals	Filters for all captions that match the specified string
xlCaptionIsBetween	Filters for all captions that are between a specified range of values
xlCaptionIsGreaterThan	Filters for all captions that are greater than the specified value
xlCaptionIsGreaterThanOrEqualTo	Filters for all captions that are greater than or match the specified value
xlCaptionIsLessThan	Filters for all captions that are less than the specified value
xlCaptionIsLessThanOrEqualTo	Filters for all captions that are less than or match the specified value
xlCaptionIsNotBetween	Filters for all captions that are not between a specified range of values
xlDateBetween	Filters for all dates that are between a specified range of dates
xlDateLastMonth	Filters for all dates that apply to the previous month
xlDateLastQuarter	Filters for all dates that apply to the previous quarter
xlDateLastWeek	Filters for all dates that apply to the previous week
xlDateLastYear	Filters for all dates that apply to the previous year

12

Filter Type	Description
`xlDateNextMonth`	Filters for all dates that apply to the next month
`xlDateNextQuarter`	Filters for all dates that apply to the next quarter
`xlDateNextWeek`	Filters for all dates that apply to the next week
`xlDateNextYear`	Filters for all dates that apply to the next year
`xlDateThisMonth`	Filters for all dates that apply to the current month
`xlDateThisQuarter`	Filters for all dates that apply to the current quarter
`xlDateThisWeek`	Filters for all dates that apply to the current week
`xlDateThisYear`	Filters for all dates that apply to the current year
`xlDateToday`	Filters for all dates that apply to the current date
`xlDateTomorrow`	Filters for all dates that apply to the next day
`xlDateYesterday`	Filters for all dates that apply to the previous day
`xlNotSpecificDate`	Filters for all dates that do not match a specified date
`xlSpecificDate`	Filters for all dates that match a specified date
`xlTopCount`	Filters for the specified number of values from the top of a list
`xlTopPercent`	Filters for the specified percentage of values from a list
`xlTopSum`	Sums the values from the top of the list
`xlValueDoesNotEqual`	Filters for all values that do not match the specified value
`xlValueEquals`	Filters for all values that match the specified value
`xlValueIsBetween`	Filters for all values that are between a specified range of values
`xlValueIsGreaterThan`	Filters for all values that are greater than the specified value
`xlValueIsGreaterThanOrEqualTo`	Filters for all values that are greater than or match the specified value
`xlValueIsLessThan`	Filters for all values that are less than the specified value
`xlValueIsLessThanOrEqualTo`	Filters for all values that are less than or match the specified value
`xlValueIsNotBetween`	Filters for all values that are not between a specified range of values
`xlYearToDate`	Filters for all values that are within one year of a specified date

Using the Search Filter

Excel 2010 added a Search box to the filter drop-down. While this is a slick feature in the Excel interface, there is no equivalent magic in VBA. While Figure 12.29 shows the "Select

All Search Results" check box, the equivalent VBA simply lists all of the items that match the selection.

Figure 12.29
The Excel 2010 interface offers a search box. In VBA, you can emulate using the old xlCaption-Contains filter.

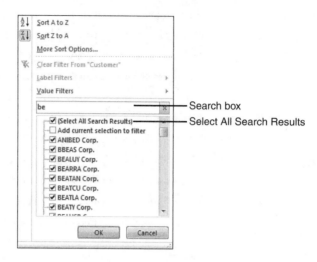

Search box — Select All Search Results

There is nothing new in Excel 2010 VBA to emulate the search box. To achieve the same results in VBA, use the xlCaptionContains filter described in the previous section.

Setting Up Slicers to Filter a Pivot Table

Excel 2010 introduced the concept of slicers to filter a pivot table. A slicer is a visual filter. Slicers can be resized and repositioned. You can control the color of the slicer and control the number of columns in a slicer. You can also select or clear items from a slicer using VBA.

Figure 12.30 shows a pivot table with two slicers. The State slicer has been modified to have five columns. The slicer with a caption of "Territory" is actually based on the Region field. You can give the slicers a friendlier caption which might be helpful when the underlying field is called IDKTxtReg or some other bizarre name invented by the I.T. department.

Figure 12.30
Slicers provide a visual filter for State and Region.

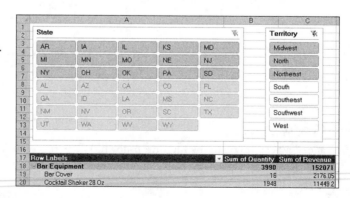

A slicer is comprised of a SlicerCache and a Slicer. To define a slicer cache, you need to specify a pivot table as the source and a field name as the SourceField. The SlicerCache is defined at the workbook level. This allows you to have the Slicer on a different worksheet than the actual pivot table:

```
Dim SCS as SlicerCache
Dim SCR as SlicerCache
Set SCS = ActiveWorkbook.SlicerCaches.Add(Source:=PT, SourceField:="State")
Set SCR = ActiveWorkbook.SlicerCaches.Add(Source:=PT, SourceField:="Region")
```

Once you have defined the slicer cache, you can add the slicer. The slicer is defined as an object of the slicer cache. Specify a worksheet as the destination. The name argument controls the internal name for the slicer. The Caption argument is the heading that will be visible in the slicer. Specify the size of the slicer using height and width in points. Specify the location using top and left in point. In the code below, the values for top, left, height, and width are assigned to be equal to the location or size of certain cell ranges:

```
Dim SLS as Slicer
Set SLS = SCS.Slicers.Add(SlicerDestination:=WSD, Name:="State", _
    Caption:="State", _
    Top:=WSD.Range("O2").Top, _
    Left:=WSD.Range("O2").Left, _
    Width:=WSR.Range("O2:U2").Width, _
    Height:=WSD.Range("O2:O17").Height)
' Format the color and number of columns
```

All slicers start out as one column. You can change the style and number of columns with this code:

```
With SLS
    .Style = "SlicerStyleLight6"
    .NumberOfColumns = 5
End With
```

> **NOTE** I find that when I create slicers in the Excel interface, I spend many mouse clicks making adjustments to the slicers. After adding two or three slicers, they are arranged in an overlapping tile arrangement. I always tweak the location, size, number of columns, and so on. In my seminars, I always brag that I can create a complex pivot table in six mouse clicks. Slicers are admittedly powerful, but seem to take 20 mouse clicks before they look right. Having a macro make all of these adjustments at once is a time-saver.

Once the slicer is defined, you can actually use VBA to choose which items are activated in the slicer. It seems counter-intuitive, but to choose items in the slicer, you have to change the SlicerItem, which is a member of the SlicerCache, not a member of the slicer:

```
With SCR
    .SlicerItems("Midwest").Selected = True
    .SlicerItems("North").Selected = True
    .SlicerItems("Northeast").Selected = True
    .SlicerItems("South").Selected = False
    .SlicerItems("Southeast").Selected = False
```

12

```
            .SlicerItems("Southwest").Selected = False
            .SlicerItems("West").Selected = False
        End With
```

You might need to deal with slicers that already exist. If a slicer is created for the state field, the name of the SlicerCache will be "Slicer_State". The following code was used to format the slicers in Figure 12.30:

```
Sub MoveAndFormatSlicer()
    Dim SCS As SlicerCache
    Dim SLS As Slicer
    Dim SCR As SlicerCache
    Dim SLR As Slicer
    Dim WSD As Worksheet
    Set WSD = ActiveSheet

    Set SCS = ActiveWorkbook.SlicerCaches("Slicer_State")
    Set SLS = SCS.Slicers("State")
    With SLS
        .Style = "SlicerStyleLight6"
        .NumberOfColumns = 5
        .Top = WSD.Range("A1").Top + 5
        .Left = WSD.Range("A1").Left + 5
        .Width = WSD.Range("A1:B14").Width - 60
        .Height = WSD.Range("A1:B14").Height
    End With

    Set SCR = ActiveWorkbook.SlicerCaches("Slicer_Region")
    Set SLR = SCR.Slicers("Region")
    With SLR
        .Style = "SlicerStyleLight3"
        .NumberOfColumns = 1
        .Top = WSD.Range("C1").Top + 5
        .Left = WSD.Range("C1").Left - 20
        .Width = WSD.Range("C1").Width
        .Height = WSD.Range("C1:C14").Height
        .Caption = "Territory"
    End With

    ' Choose three regions
    With SCR
        .SlicerItems("Midwest").Selected = True
        .SlicerItems("North").Selected = True
        .SlicerItems("Northeast").Selected = True
        .SlicerItems("South").Selected = False
        .SlicerItems("Southeast").Selected = False
        .SlicerItems("Southwest").Selected = False
        .SlicerItems("West").Selected = False
    End With

End Sub
```

Filtering an OLAP Pivot Table Using Named Sets

Ready for some Good News, Bad News, and Sneaky News?

Good News

Microsoft added an amazing feature to Excel 2010 pivot tables called Named Sets. This feature allows you to create filters that were never possible before. For example, in Figure 12.31, the pivot table shows Actuals and Budget for FY2009 and FY2010. It would have been impossible to show an asymmetric report with only FY2009 Actuals and FY 2010 Budget: when you turned off Budget for 2009, it would have been turned off for all years. Named Sets allow you to overcome this.

Figure 12.31
You want to show 2009 Actuals and 2010 Budget.

2009 Actuals   2010 Budget

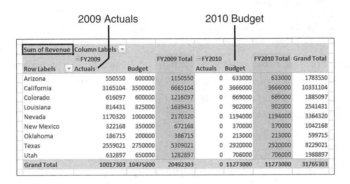

Bad News

Named sets only work for data coming from OLAP pivot tables. If you are dealing with pivot tables based on regular Excel data, you will have to wait until a future release of Excel to tap into the power of Named Sets.

Sneaky News

A pivot table produced using the PowerPivot add-in is actually an OLAP pivot table. To create the pivot table shown in Figure 12.31, you can copy the Excel data, paste as a new table in the PowerPivot Add-in, and then return to Excel to create the pivot table.

This is a minor use for a powerful tool. The PowerPivot add-in is designed to mash-up multi-million row record sets from various sources. To take a single flat table and paste it into the powerful tool is admittedly underutilizing the tool. However, it is one great way to get an unbalanced pivot table report.

One common use for named sets is to show only a subset of items. For example, you might only be responsible for the states of Louisiana, Oklahoma and Texas. If this grouping is not defined in the data, you will find yourself constantly re-filtering the report to include only your states. Defining a named sets creates a virtual column that contains only your states. This virtual column can be re-used across many reports.

Another common use is to show an asymmetric selection from two column fields. In Figure 12.31, you would like to show last year's actual and this year's budget.

12

To define a named set, you will have to build a formula that uses the MDX language. MDX stands for Multidimensional Expressions Language. There are many MDX tutorials on the Internet. Luckily, you can turn on the macro recorder while you define a named set using the Excel 2010 interface and have the macro recorder write the MDX formula for you.

When you are defining a named set, you will define both a CalculatedMember and then add a CubeField Set. These declarations at the top of the macro initialize two calculated members:

```
Dim PT As PivotTable
Dim CM1 As CalculatedMember
Dim CM2 As CalculatedMember
Set PT = ActiveSheet.PivotTables(1)
```

The MDX Formula is the key to the named set. In this code, the formula contains three specific states plus the grand total of all the states. The formula starts and ends with curly braces indicating that the formula contains an array of values. Each line of code is adding another specific state to the array:

```
' Define a named set to grab three states
FText = "{([Financials].[State].&[Louisiana]),"
FText = FText & "([Financials].[State].&[Oklahoma]),"
FText = FText & "([Financials].[State].&[Texas]),"
FText = FText & "([Financials].[State].[All])}"
```

Once you have defined the formula, use the following code to add the calculated member to the data set:

```
Set CM2 = ActiveWorkbook.Connections("PowerPivot Data"). _
    OLEDBConnection.CalculatedMembers.Add( _
    Name:="[OilStates]", _
    Formula:=FText, _
    Type:=xlCalculatedSet, _
    Dynamic:=False, _
    HierarchizeDistinct:=False)
CM2.FlattenHierarchies = False
PT.CubeFields.AddSet Name:="[OilStates]", Caption:="OilStates"
```

This code will add a new folder to the pivot table field list called Sets. In that folder, an item called OilStates is available as field just like the field called States. In your code, you need to replace the States field in the pivot table with the OilStates field:

```
' Remove the State field, replace with OilStates
PT.CubeFields("[Financials].[State]").Orientation = xlHidden
PT.CubeFields("[OilStates]").Orientation = xlRowField
```

Figure 12.32 shows the asymmetric report.

CAUTION

Selecting All as a member of the set causes the true Grand Total of all states to appear in the pivot table. In the current example, this is probably not what you want. The $10 million in Cell C9 of Figure 12.32 is not the total of Cells C6:C8. It includes the states not in the set.

Figure 12.32
Named sets enable asymmetric reporting.

Named Sets in Field List

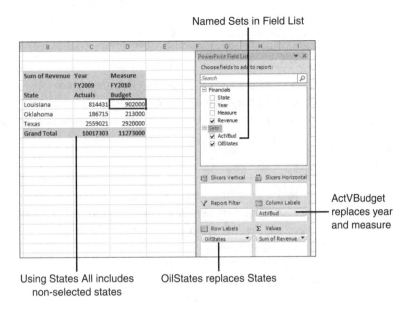

Using States All includes non-selected states

OilStates replaces States

ActVBudget replaces year and measure

Formatting a Pivot Table

There are a number of options available when formatting a pivot table. This section will cover the layout options, style options from the Design tab, and applying a data visualization to a pivot table.

Applying a Table Style

The Design tab offers two groups dedicated to formatting the pivot table, as shown in Figure 12.33. The PivotTable Style Options group has four check boxes that modify the styles in the PivotTable Styles Gallery.

Figure 12.33
The four check boxes and gallery of styles offer many variations for formatting the pivot table.

The following four lines of code are equivalent to selecting all four settings in the PivotTable Style Options group:

```
PT.ShowTableStyleRowHeaders = True
PT.ShowTableStyleColumnHeaders = True
PT.ShowTableStyleRowStripes = True
PT.ShowTableStyleColumnStripes = True
```

To apply a table style from the gallery, use the TableStyle2 property. If you want to get the correct name, it might be best to record a macro:

```
' Format the pivot table
PT.ShowTableStyleRowStripes = True
PT.TableStyle2 = "PivotStyleMedium3"
```

> **NOTE**
>
> Legacy versions of Excel offered an AutoFormat feature for pivot tables. This feature was annoy-
> ing because it actually changed the layout of your pivot table. That obsolete command used the
> TableStyle property. Therefore, Excel 2007 had to use TableStyle2 as the property name for
> the new style tables.

> **CAUTION**
>
> It is possible to create custom table styles. If you have a custom table style named MyStyle44 and
> use this name in a macro, the macro will run fine on your computer but may not run on anyone else's
> computer. To alleviate the chance of a runtime error, you use On Error Resume Next before
> applying TableStyle2.

Changing the Layout

The Layout group of the Design tab contains four drop-downs. These drop-downs control the location of subtotals (top or bottom), the presence of grand totals, the report layout, and the presence of blank rows.

Subtotals can appear either at the top or bottom of a group of pivot items. The SubtotalLocation property applies to the entire pivot table; valid values are xlAtBottom or xlAtTop:

```
PT.SubtotalLocation:=xlAtTop
```

Grand totals can be turned on or off for rows or columns. The following code turns them off for both:

```
PT.ColumnGrand = False
PT.RowGrand = False
```

There are three settings for the report layout. The Tabular layout is similar to the default layout in Excel 2003. The Outline layout was optionally available in Excel 2003. The Compact layout was introduced in Excel 2007.

Excel can remember the last layout used and will apply it to additional pivot tables created in the same Excel session. For this reason, you should always explicitly choose the layout that you want. Use the RowAxisLayout method; valid values are xlTabularRow, xlOutlineRow, or xlCompactRow:

```
PT.RowAxisLayout xlTabularRow
PT.RowAxisLayout xlOutlineRow
PT.RowAxisLayout xlCompactRow
```

Starting in Excel 2007, you can add a blank line to the layout after each group of pivot items. Although the Design tab offers a single setting to affect the entire pivot table, the setting is actually applied to each individual pivot field individually. The macro recorder responds by recording a dozen lines of code for a pivot table with 12 fields. You can intelligently add a single line of code for the outer row field(s):

```
PT.PivotFields("Region").LayoutBlankLine = True
```

Applying a Data Visualization

Excel 2007 introduced fantastic data visualizations such as icon sets, color gradients, and in-cell data bars. When you apply a visualization to a pivot table, you should exclude the total rows from the visualization.

If you have 30 branches that average $50,000 in revenue each, the total for the 30 branches is $1.5 million. If you include the total in the data visualization, the total gets the largest bar, and all the branch records have tiny bars.

Figure 12.34 shows a solution; apply the visualization to the category records but not to the grand total row.

Figure 12.34
Data bars in a pivot table should exclude the Grand Total cell.

Revenue	
Category ▾	Total
Bar Equipment	1,769,332
Commercial Appliances	8,562,837
Concession Equipment	9,876,342
Fryers	3,835,963
Ovens and Ranges	57,168,593
Refrigerators and Coolers	41,793,565
Warmers	37,482,133
Grand Total	160,488,764

In the Excel user interface, you always want to use the Add Rule or Edit Rule choice to select the option All Cells Showing "Sum of Revenue" for "Category".

In VBA, you can limit the data bar to only the detail rows by using this code:

```
Selection.FormatConditions(1).ScopeType = xlFieldsScope
```

The code in Listing 12.7 adds a pivot table and applies a data bar to the revenue field.

Listing 12.7 Code That Creates a Pivot Table with Data Bars

```
Sub CreatePivotDataBar()
    Dim WSD As Worksheet
    Dim PTCache As PivotCache
    Dim PT As PivotTable
    Dim PRange As Range
    Dim FinalRow As Long

    Set WSD = Worksheets("Data")
    Dim WSR As Worksheet

    ' Delete any prior pivot tables
    For Each PT In WSD.PivotTables
        PT.TableRange2.Clear
    Next PT
    WSD.Range("M1:Z1").EntireColumn.Clear
```

12

```vba
' Define input area and set up a Pivot Cache
FinalRow = WSD.Cells(Application.Rows.Count, 1).End(xlUp).Row
FinalCol = WSD.Cells(1, Application.Columns.Count). _
    End(xlToLeft).Column
Set PRange = WSD.Cells(1, 1).Resize(FinalRow, FinalCol)
Set PTCache = ActiveWorkbook.PivotCaches.Add(SourceType:= _
    xlDatabase, SourceData:=PRange.Address)

' Create the Pivot Table from the Pivot Cache
Set PT = PTCache.CreatePivotTable(TableDestination:=WSD. _
    Cells(2, FinalCol + 2), TableName:="PivotTable1")

' Turn off updating while building the table
PT.ManualUpdate = True

' Set up the row & column fields
PT.AddFields RowFields:="Category"

' Set up the data fields
With PT.PivotFields("Revenue")
    .Orientation = xlDataField
    .Function = xlSum
    .Position = 1
    .NumberFormat = "#,##0"
    .Name = " Revenue"
End With

' Calc the pivot table
PT.ManualUpdate = False
PT.ManualUpdate = True

' Apply a Databar
PT.TableRange2.Cells(3, 2).Select
Selection.FormatConditions.AddDatabar
Selection.FormatConditions(1).ShowValue = True
Selection.FormatConditions(1).SetFirstPriority
With Selection.FormatConditions(1)
    .MinPoint.Modify newtype:=xlConditionValueLowestValue
    .MaxPoint.Modify newtype:=xlConditionValueHighestValue
End With
With Selection.FormatConditions(1).BarColor
    .ThemeColor = xlThemeColorAccent2
    .TintAndShade = 0.6
End With
Selection.FormatConditions(1).ScopeType = xlFieldsScope

WSD.Activate
Range("N1").Select

End Sub
```

Next Steps

In the next chapter, you will learn a myriad of techniques for handling common questions and issues with pivot tables.

Advanced Pivot Table Tips and Techniques

Unique Solutions to Common Pivot Table Problems

In this chapter, you discover techniques that provide unique solutions to some of the more common pivot table problems. Take time to glance at the topics covered here. Who knows? You might find a few unique tips that can help you tackle some of your pivot table conundrums!

Tip 1: Force Pivot Tables to Refresh Automatically

In some situations, you might need to have your pivot tables refresh themselves automatically. For instance, suppose you created a pivot table report for your manager. You might not be able to trust that he will refresh the pivot table when needed.

You can force each pivot table to automatically refresh when the workbook opens by following these steps:

1. Right-click your pivot table and select PivotTable Options.
2. In the activated dialog box, select the Data tab.
3. Select the Refresh Data When Opening the File property check box.

When this property is activated, the pivot table refreshes itself each time the workbook in which it's located is opened.

> **NOTE**
> The Refresh Data When Opening the File property must be set for each pivot table individually.

Tip 2: Refresh All Pivot Tables in a Workbook at the Same Time

When you have multiple pivot tables in a workbook, refreshing all of them can be bothersome. There are several ways to avoid the hassle of manually refreshing multiple pivot tables. Here are a couple options:

Option 1: You can configure each pivot table in your workbook to automatically refresh when the workbook opens. To do so, right-click your pivot table and select PivotTable Options. This activates the PivotTable Options dialog box. Then, select the Data tab and select the Refresh Data When Opening the File property check box. After you have configured all pivot tables in the workbook, they automatically refresh when the workbook is opened.

Option 2: You can create a macro to refresh each pivot table in the workbook. This option is ideal when you need to refresh your pivot tables on demand, rather than only when the workbook opens. The idea is to start recording a macro. While the macro is recording, simply go to each pivot table in your workbook and refresh. After all pivot tables are refreshed, stop recording. The result is a macro that can be fired any time you need to refresh all pivot tables.

> → Revisit Chapter 11,"Enhancing Pivot Table Reports with Macros," to get more detail on using macros with pivot tables.

Option 3: You can use VBA to refresh all pivot tables in the workbook on demand. This option can be used when it is impractical to record and maintain macros that refresh all pivot tables. This approach entails the use of the `RefreshAll` method of the `Workbook` object. To employ this technique, start a new module and enter the following code:

```
Sub Refresh_All()
ThisWorkbook.RefreshAll
End Sub
```

You can now call this procedure any time you want to refresh all pivot tables within your workbook.

> **NOTE**
> Keep in mind that the `RefreshAll` method refreshes all external data ranges along with pivot tables. This means that if your workbook contains data from external sources, such as databases and external files, that data is refreshed along with your pivot tables.

Tip 3: Sort Data Items in a Unique Order (Not Ascending or Descending)

Figure 13.1 shows the default sequence of regions in a pivot table report. Alphabetically, the regions are shown in sequence of Midwest, North, South, and West. If your company is based in California, company traditions might dictate that the West region should be shown first, followed by Midwest, North, and South. Unfortunately, neither an ascending sort order nor a descending sort order can help you.

You can rearrange data items in your pivot table manually by simply typing the exact name of the data item where you would like to see its data. You can also drag the data item where you want it.

	A	B	C	D	E	F
1						
2						
3	Sum of Sales_Amount	Column Labels				
4	Row Labels	MIDWEST	NORTH	SOUTH	WEST	Grand Total
5	Cleaning & Housekeeping Services	$174,518	$534,282	$283,170	$146,623	$1,138,593
6	Facility Maintenance and Repair	$463,077	$606,747	$846,515	$444,820	$2,361,158
7	Fleet Maintenance	$448,800	$610,791	$1,046,231	$521,976	$2,627,798
8	Green Plants and Foliage Care	$93,562	$155,021	$157,821	$870,379	$1,276,783
9	Landscaping/Grounds Care	$190,003	$299,309	$335,676	$365,928	$1,190,915
10	Predictive Maintenance/Preventative Maintenance	$478,928	$572,860	$472,045	$655,092	$2,178,925
11	Grand Total	$1,848,887	$2,779,009	$3,141,458	$3,004,818	$10,774,172
12						
13						

Figure 13.1
Although company traditions dictate that the Region field should be in West, Midwest, North, and South sequence, they appear in alphabetical order.

To solve the problem in this example, you simply type the word **West** in cell B4, and then press Enter. The pivot table responds by resequencing the regions. The $3 million in sales for the West region automatically moves from column E to column B. The remaining regions move over to the next two columns.

Tip 4: Turn Pivot Tables into Hard Data

You created your pivot table only to summarize and shape your data. You do not want to keep the source data or the pivot table with all its overhead.

Turning your pivot table into hard data enables you to utilize the results of the pivot table without having to deal with the source data or a pivot cache. How you turn your pivot table into hard data depends on how much of your pivot table you are going to copy.

If you are copying just a portion of your pivot table, do the following:

1. Select the data you want to copy from the pivot table, and then right-click and select Copy.
2. Right-click anywhere on a spreadsheet and select Paste.

If you are copying your entire pivot table, follow these steps:

1. Select the entire pivot table, right-click, and select Copy.
2. Right-click anywhere on a spreadsheet and select Paste Special.
3. Select Values, and then click OK.

TIP

You might want to consider removing any subtotals before turning your pivot table into hard data. Subtotals typically aren't very useful when you are creating a standalone data set.

To remove the subtotals from your pivot table, first identify the field for which subtotals are being calculated. Then, right-click the field's header (either in the pivot table itself or in the PivotTable Field List) and select Field Settings. Selecting this option opens the Field Settings dialog box. Here, you change the Subtotals option to None. After you click OK, your subtotals are removed.

Tip 5: Fill the Empty Cells Left by Row Fields

When you turn a pivot table into hard data, you are left not only with the values created by the pivot table, but also the pivot table's data structure. For example, the data in Figure 13.2 came from a pivot table that had a tabular layout.

Notice that the Market field kept the same row structure it had when this data was in the row area of the pivot table. It would be unwise to use this table anywhere else without filling in the empty cells left by the row field, but how do you easily fill these empty cells?

Figure 13.2
It would be impractical to use this data anywhere else without filling in the empty cells left by the row field.

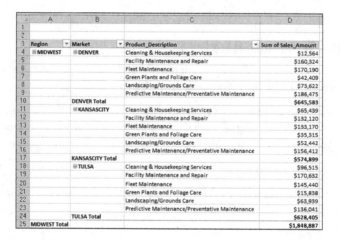

Excel 2010 actually provides you two effective ways of fixing this problem.

Option 1: Implement the New Repeat All Data Items Feature

The first option is to apply Excel 2010's new Repeat Item Labels functionality. This new feature ensures that all item labels are repeated to create a solid block of contiguous cells. To implement this feature, place your cursor anywhere in your pivot table. Then, go up to the Ribbon and select Design, Report Layout, Repeat All Item labels (see Figure 13.3).

Figure 13.4 shows what a pivot table with this feature applied looks like.

Figure 13.3
The Repeat All Item Labels option enables you to show your pivot data in one contiguous block of data.

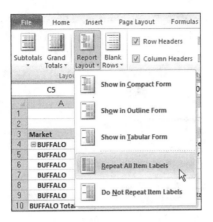

Figure 13.4
The Repeat All Item Labels option fills all cells with data items.

Region	Market	Product_Description	Sum of Sales_Amount
⊟MIDWEST	⊟DENVER	Cleaning & Housekeeping Services	$12,564
MIDWEST	DENVER	Facility Maintenance and Repair	$160,324
MIDWEST	DENVER	Fleet Maintenance	$170,190
MIDWEST	DENVER	Green Plants and Foliage Care	$42,409
MIDWEST	DENVER	Landscaping/Grounds Care	$73,622
MIDWEST	DENVER	Predictive Maintenance/Preventative Maintenance	$186,475
MIDWEST	DENVER Total		$645,583
MIDWEST	⊟KANSASCITY	Cleaning & Housekeeping Services	$65,439
MIDWEST	KANSASCITY	Facility Maintenance and Repair	$132,120
MIDWEST	KANSASCITY	Fleet Maintenance	$133,170
MIDWEST	KANSASCITY	Green Plants and Foliage Care	$35,315
MIDWEST	KANSASCITY	Landscaping/Grounds Care	$52,442
MIDWEST	KANSASCITY	Predictive Maintenance/Preventative Maintenance	$156,412
MIDWEST	KANSASCITY Total		$574,899
MIDWEST	⊟TULSA	Cleaning & Housekeeping Services	$96,515
MIDWEST	TULSA	Facility Maintenance and Repair	$170,632
MIDWEST	TULSA	Fleet Maintenance	$145,440
MIDWEST	TULSA	Green Plants and Foliage Care	$15,838
MIDWEST	TULSA	Landscaping/Grounds Care	$63,939
MIDWEST	TULSA	Predictive Maintenance/Preventative Maintenance	$136,041
MIDWEST	TULSA Total		$628,405
MIDWEST Total			$1,848,887

Now you can turn this pivot table into hard values, ending up with a contiguous table of data without gaps.

Option 2: Use Excel's GOTO Special Functionality

The other solution to this problem involves using Excel's GOTO Special functionality.

In order to implement this method, you will need to first convert your pivot table to hard data. You can do this by following these steps:

1. Select the entire pivot table, right-click, and select Copy.

2. Right-click anywhere on a spreadsheet and select Paste Special.

3. Select Values, and then click OK.

Now, you can select a range in columns A and B that extends from the first row with blanks to the row just above the grand total. In the present example, this includes cells A4:B100. Press F5 to activate the Go To dialog box. The Go To Special dialog box is a powerful feature that enables you to modify your selection based on various conditions. In the lower-left

13

corner of the Go To dialog box, select the Special button. This activates the Go To Special dialog you see in Figure 13.5. From here, you select the option for Blanks.

Figure 13.5
Using the Go To Special dialog box enables you to select all the blank cells to be filled.

The result is that only the blank cells within your selection are selected.

Enter a formula to copy the pivot item values from the cell above to the blank cells. You can do this with four keystrokes, but it helps if you don't look at the screen while you perform them. Type = (equal sign). Press the up-arrow key. Hold down the Ctrl key while pressing Enter.

> NOTE
> The equal sign tells Excel that you are entering a formula in the active cell. Pressing the up-arrow key points to the cell above the active cell. Pressing Ctrl+Enter tells Excel to enter a similar formula in all the selected cells instead of just the active cell. As Figure 13.6 illustrates, with these few keystrokes, you enter a formula to fill in all the blank cells at once.

You still should convert those formulas to values. However, if you attempt to copy the current selection, Excel presents an error; you cannot copy a selection that contains multiple selections. By selecting Blanks from the Go To Special dialog box, you actually selected many areas of the spreadsheet.

You have to reselect the original range of cells A4:B100. You can then press Ctrl+C to copy, and then select Edit, Paste Special, Values to convert the formulas to values.

This method provides a quick way to fill in the outline view provided by the pivot table.

Tip 6: Add a Rank Number Field to Your Pivot Table

When you are sorting and ranking a field with a large number of data items, it can be difficult to determine the number ranking of the current data item you are analyzing.

Figure 13.6
Pressing Ctrl+Enter
enters the formula in all
selected cells.

	A	B	C	D
1				
2				
3	Region	Market	Product_Description	Sum of Sales_Amount
4	MIDWEST	DENVER	Cleaning & Housekeeping Services	$12,564
5	MIDWEST	DENVER	Facility Maintenance and Repair	$160,324
6	MIDWEST	DENVER	Fleet Maintenance	$170,190
7	MIDWEST	DENVER	Green Plants and Foliage Care	$42,409
8	MIDWEST	DENVER	Landscaping/Grounds Care	$73,622
9	MIDWEST	DENVER	Predictive Maintenance/Preventative Maintenance	$186,475
10	MIDWEST	DENVER Total		$645,583
11	MIDWEST	KANSASCITY	Cleaning & Housekeeping Services	$65,439
12	MIDWEST	KANSASCITY	Facility Maintenance and Repair	$132,120
13	MIDWEST	KANSASCITY	Fleet Maintenance	$133,170
14	MIDWEST	KANSASCITY	Green Plants and Foliage Care	$35,315
15	MIDWEST	KANSASCITY	Landscaping/Grounds Care	$52,442
16	MIDWEST	KANSASCITY	Predictive Maintenance/Preventative Maintenance	$156,412
17	MIDWEST	KANSASCITY Total		$574,899
18	MIDWEST	TULSA	Cleaning & Housekeeping Services	$96,515
19	MIDWEST	TULSA	Facility Maintenance and Repair	$170,632
20	MIDWEST	TULSA	Fleet Maintenance	$145,440
21	MIDWEST	TULSA	Green Plants and Foliage Care	$15,838
22	MIDWEST	TULSA	Landscaping/Grounds Care	$63,939
23	MIDWEST	TULSA	Predictive Maintenance/Preventative Maintenance	$136,041

Furthermore, you might want to turn your pivot table into hard values for further analysis. An integer field that contains the actual rank number of each data item could prove to be helpful in analysis outside the pivot table.

Start with a pivot table similar to the one shown in Figure 13.7. Notice that the same data measure is shown twice; in this case, it is SumOfSalesAmount.

Figure 13.7
Start with a pivot table
where the data value is
listed twice.

	A	B	C
1			
2			
3	Market	Sum of Sales_Amount	Sum of Sales_Amount2
4	BUFFALO	450478.27	450478.27
5	CALIFORNIA	2254735.38	2254735.38
6	CANADA	776245.27	776245.27
7	CHARLOTTE	890522.49	890522.49
8	DALLAS	467089.47	467089.47
9	DENVER	645583.29	645583.29
10	FLORIDA	1450392	1450392
11	KANSASCITY	574898.97	574898.97
12	MICHIGAN	678704.95	678704.95
13	NEWORLEANS	333453.65	333453.65
14	NEWYORK	873580.91	873580.91
15	PHOENIX	570255.09	570255.09
16	SEATTLE	179827.21	179827.21
17	TULSA	628404.83	628404.83
18	Grand Total	10774171.78	10774171.78

Right-click the second instance of data measure. Select Show Values As, and then Rank Largest to Small Smallest (see Figure 13.8).

After your ranking is applied, you can adjust the labels and formatting, as demonstrated in Figure 13.9. This leaves you with a clean-looking ranking report.

13

Figure 13.8
Adding a Rank field is simple with Excel 2010's new Show Values As option.

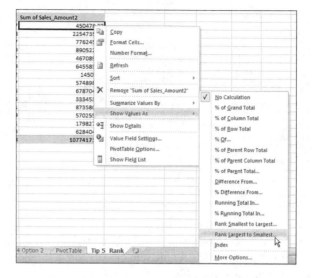

Figure 13.9
Your final pivot table with ranking applied.

	Market	Revenue	Rank
3	**Market** ▼	**Revenue**	**Rank**
4	BUFFALO	$ 450,478.27	12
5	CALIFORNIA	$ 2,254,735.38	1
6	CANADA	$ 776,245.27	5
7	CHARLOTTE	$ 890,522.49	3
8	DALLAS	$ 467,089.47	11
9	DENVER	$ 645,583.29	7
10	FLORIDA	$ 1,450,392.00	2
11	KANSASCITY	$ 574,898.97	9
12	MICHIGAN	$ 678,704.95	6
13	NEWORLEANS	$ 333,453.65	13
14	NEWYORK	$ 873,580.91	4
15	PHOENIX	$ 570,255.09	10
16	SEATTLE	$ 179,827.21	14
17	TULSA	$ 628,404.83	8
18	**Grand Total**	$ 10,774,171.78	1

Tip 7: Reduce the Size of Your Pivot Table Reports

When you initiate the creation of a pivot table report, Excel takes a snapshot of your data set and stores it in a pivot cache. A pivot cache is nothing more than a special memory subsystem in which your data source is duplicated for quick access. That is to say, Excel literally makes a copy of your data, and then stores it in a cache that is attached to your workbook.

Each pivot table report you create from a separate data source creates its own pivot cache that increases your file size. The increase in file size depends on the size of the original data source that is being duplicated to create the pivot cache.

Of course, the benefit you get from a pivot cache is optimization. Any changes you make to the pivot table report, such as rearranging fields, adding new fields, or hiding items, are made rapidly and with minimal overhead.

The down side of the pivot cache is that it basically doubles the size of your workbook. So every time you make a new pivot table from scratch, you essentially add to the file size of your workbook.

The following sections discuss a few ways you can avoid pivot table-induced file bloat.

Copy and Paste Instead of Creating From Scratch

Sometimes you need to make multiple pivot tables from the same data source. Instead of making each pivot table from scratch, which adds to the file's size, copy and paste the pivot table. When you copy an existing pivot table and paste it, you essentially create a pivot table that reads from the same pivot cache. That is, you create a new pivot table without creating another memory container to add to the file size.

Delete Your Source Data Tab

If your workbooks have both your pivot table and your source data tab, you are wasting space. That is, you are essentially distributing two copies of the same data. You can delete your source data, and your pivot table functions just fine. After deleting the source data, saving shrinks the file.

> **NOTE** Note that pivot tables that share the same pivot cache also share calculated fields, calculated items, and groupings.

Your clients can use the pivot table as normal, and your workbook is half as big. The only functionality you lose is the ability to refresh the pivot data because the source data is not there.

> **NOTE** So what happens if your clients need to see the source data? They can simply double-click the intersection of the row and column grand totals. This tells Excel to output the contents of the pivot table's cache into a new worksheet. With one double-click, your clients can re-create the source data that makes up the pivot table!

Use a Duplicate Cache Finder

If you already have a workbook filled with pivot tables, you can use a Duplicate Cache Finder to find and fix all duplicate caches. That is to say, a Cache Finder helps you point all your pivot tables to the same pivot cache. In this way, shrink your file size by eliminating duplicate caches.

NOTE Debra Dalgleish, purveyor of www.contextures.com, has a nifty workbook that does just that. Her Cache Finder can be found at http://www.contextures.com/PivotCacheFix.zip.

Tip 8: Create an Automatically Expanding Data Range

You will undoubtedly encounter situations in which you have pivot table reports that are updated daily. That is, records are constantly added to the source data. When records are added to a pivot table's source data set, you must redefine the range that is captured before the new records are brought into the pivot table. Redefining the source range for a pivot table once in a while is no sweat, but when the source data is changed on a daily or weekly basis, it can start to get bothersome.

The solution is to turn your source data table into a table before creating your pivot table. Again, Excel tables enable you to create a defined range that automatically shrinks or expands with the data. This enables any component, chart, pivot table, or formula tied to that range to keep up with changes in your data.

To implement this trick, simply highlight your source data, and then click the table icon on the Insert tab (see Figure 13.10). Confirm the range to be included in your table, and then click OK.

Figure 13.10
Convert your source data into a table.

After your source data has been converted to a table, any pivot table you build on top of it automatically keeps when your source data expands or shrinks.

> **NOTE** Keep in mind that although you don't have to redefine the source range anymore, you still need to trigger a Refresh to have your pivot table show the current data.

Tip 9: Comparing Tables with a PivotTable

If you've been an analyst for more than a week, you've been asked to compare two separate tables to come up with some brilliant analysis about the differences between them. This is a common scenario where leveraging a pivot table can save some time.

In this scenario, imagine you have two tables that show customers in 2009 and in 2010. Figure 13.11 illustrates two separate tables. For this example, the tables were made small for instructional purposes. Imagine you're working with something bigger here.

Figure 13.11
You need to compare these two tables.

	A	B	C	D	E	F	G
1	2009 Customers				2010 Customers		
2	Customer_Name	Fiscal Year	Revenue		Customer_Name	Fiscal Year	Revenue
3	PHALCO Corp.	2009	$456.27		PHALSM Corp.	2010	$1,902.25
4	PHALLA Corp.	2009	$3,974.07		PHALTA Corp.	2010	$2,095.01
5	PHALSE Corp.	2009	$565.34		PHALWH Corp.	2010	$1,740.27
6	PHALSM Corp.	2009	$1,902.25		PHMAN Corp.	2010	$3,228.33
7	POMTRA Corp.	2009	$2,201.90		POPPIT Corp.	2010	$604.18
8	POPAUS Corp.	2009	$1,891.73		POPUSL Corp.	2010	$870.28
9	POPCOA Corp.	2009	$1,284.61		POPUSP Corp.	2010	$2,421.01
10	PORADA Corp.	2009	$10,131.22		PORADA Corp.	2010	$10,131.22
11	PORCFA Corp.	2009	$1,187.71		PORADY Corp.	2010	$1,012.94
12					PORCFA Corp.	2010	$1,187.71

The idea is to create one table you can use to pivot. Be sure you have a way to tag which data comes from which table. As you see in Figure 13.12, you have a column called Fiscal Year that serves this purpose.

Figure 13.12
Combine your tables into one table.

	A	B	C
1	Customer_Name	Fiscal Year	Revenue
2	PHALCO Corp.	2009	$456.27
3	PHALLA Corp.	2009	$3,974.07
4	PHALSE Corp.	2009	$565.34
5	PHALSM Corp.	2009	$1,902.25
6	POMTRA Corp.	2009	$2,201.90
7	POPAUS Corp.	2009	$1,891.73
8	POPCOA Corp.	2009	$1,284.61
9	PORADA Corp.	2009	$10,131.22
10	PORCFA Corp.	2009	$1,187.71
11	PHALSM Corp.	2010	$1,902.25
12	PHALTA Corp.	2010	$2,095.01
13	PHALWH Corp.	2010	$1,740.27
14	PHMAN Corp.	2010	$3,228.33
15	POPPIT Corp.	2010	$604.18
16	POPUSL Corp.	2010	$870.28
17	POPUSP Corp.	2010	$2,421.01
18	PORADA Corp.	2010	$10,131.22
19	PORADY Corp.	2010	$1,012.94
20	PORCFA Corp.	2010	$1,187.71

After your tables have been combined, use the combined data set to create a new pivot table. Format the pivot table so that the table *tag* (the identifier telling you which table the data came from) is in the column area of the pivot table. In Figure 13.13, years are in the column area, and customers are in the row area. The data area contains the count records for each customer name.

As you see in Figure 13.13, you instantly get a visual indication of which customers are only in the 2009 table, which are in the 2010 table, and which are in both tables.

Figure 13.13
Create a pivot table to see an easy-to-read visual comparison of the two data sets.

	A	B	C
1			
2			
3	**Count of Customer_Name**	**Fiscal Yea**	
4	**Customer_Name**	**2009**	**2010**
5	PHALCO Corp.	1	
6	PHALLA Corp.	1	
7	PHALSE Corp.	1	
8	PHALSM Corp.	1	1
9	PHALTA Corp.		1
10	PHALWH Corp.		1
11	PHMAN Corp.		1
12	POMTRA Corp.	1	
13	POPAUS Corp.	1	
14	POPCOA Corp.	1	
15	POPPIT Corp.		1
16	POPUSL Corp.		1
17	POPUSP Corp.		1
18	PORADA Corp.	1	1
19	PORADY Corp.		1
20	PORCFA Corp.	1	1

Tip 10: AutoFilter a PivotTable

The conventional wisdom is that you can't apply an Autofilter to a PivotTable. Technically, that's true, but there is a way to trick Excel into making it happen.

The trick is to place your cursor directly adjacent to the last title in the PivotTable, as demonstrated in Figure 13.14. After you have it there, you can go to the application menu, select Data, and then select AutoFilter.

13

Figure 13.14
Place your cursor just outside your pivot table.

	A	B	C	D
1	Market	(All)		
2				
3	Customer_Name	Revenue	Transaction Count	
4	ACASCO Corp.	$675	4	
5	ACECUL Corp.	$593	6	
6	ACEHUA Corp.	$580	4	
7	ACOPUL Corp.	$675	4	
8	ACORAR Corp.	$2,232	13	
9	ACSBUR Corp.	$720	4	
10	ADACEC Corp.	$345	4	
11	ADADUL Corp.	$690	8	
12	ADANAS Corp.	$345	4	
13	ADCOMP Corp.	$553	4	
14	ADDATI Corp.	$379	4	

At this point, you have AutoFilters on your PivotTable! With this, you can do something cool like apply a Custom AutoFilter to find all customers with an above average transaction count (see Figure 13.15).

Figure 13.15
With AutoFilters implemented, you can take advantage of custom filtering not normally available to pivot tables.

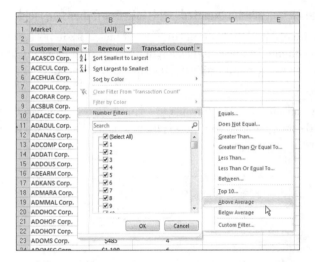

This is a fantastic way to add an extra layer of analytical capabilities to your pivot table reports.

Tip 11: Transposing a Data Set with a PivotTable

In Chapter 2, "Creating a Basic Pivot Table," you learned that the perfect layout for the source data in a pivot table is a tabular layout. A tabular layout is a particular table structure where the following attributes exist: no blank rows or columns, every column has a heading, every field has a value in every row, and columns do not contain repeating groups of data.

Unfortunately, you often encounter data sets like the one shown in Figure 13.16. The problem is that the month headings are spread across the top of the table, pulling double duty as column labels and actual data values. In a pivot table, this format would force you to manage and maintain 12 fields, each representing a different month.

Figure 13.16
You need to convert this matrix-style table to a tabular data set.

	A	B	C	D	E	F	G
1	Market	Product_Description	Jan	Feb	Mar	Apr	May
2	BUFFALO	Cleaning & Housekeeping Services	$6,219.66	$4,263.92	$5,386.12	$6,443.99	$4,36
3	BUFFALO	Facility Maintenance and Repair	$3,255.82	$9,490.00	$4,409.23	$4,957.62	$8,85
4	BUFFALO	Fleet Maintenance	$5,350.03	$8,924.71	$6,394.43	$6,522.46	$9,46
5	BUFFALO	Green Plants and Foliage Care	$2,415.08	$2,579.61	$2,401.91	$2,981.01	$2,70
6	BUFFALO	Landscaping/Grounds Care	$5,474.22	$4,500.52	$5,324.36	$5,705.68	$5,26
7	BUFFALO	Predictive Maintenance/Preventative	$9,810.95	$10,180.23	$9,626.31	$11,700.73	$10,94
8	CALIFORNIA	Cleaning & Housekeeping Services	$2,840.76	$2,997.18	$2,096.78	$4,102.20	$47
9	CALIFORNIA	Facility Maintenance and Repair	$16,251.01	$35,878.99	$18,368.55	$21,843.53	$28,72
10	CALIFORNIA	Fleet Maintenance	$22,574.77	$36,894.89	$22,016.38	$27,871.10	$31,98
11	CALIFORNIA	Green Plants and Foliage Care	$48,250.90	$90,013.42	$51,130.17	$75,527.58	$69,41
12	CALIFORNIA	Landscaping/Grounds Care	$19,401.16	$21,190.57	$21,292.00	$20,918.35	$19,46
13	CALIFORNIA	Predictive Maintenance/Preventative	$38,712.24	$46,072.56	$43,949.95	$46,999.02	$41,09

13

Interestingly enough, you can fix this issue by using a Multiple Consolidated Pivot Table. Follow these basic steps to convert this matrix-style data set to one that is appropriate for use with a pivot table:

Step 1: Combine All Noncolumn Oriented Fields into One Dimension Field

Due to the nature of Multiple Consolidation PivotTables, it's important that you have only one dimension column. In this example, anything that isn't a month field is considered a dimension. So, the Market and Product_Description fields need to be pulled into one column.

To do this, you can simply type a formula that concatenates these two fields with a semicolon delimiter. Be sure you give your new column a name. You can see the exact formula to use in the formula bar in Figure 13.17.

Figure 13.17
Concatenate the Market and Product_Description fields with a semicolon delimiter.

After you create your concatenated column, be sure to convert the formulas into hard data. Select the newly created concatenated column, press Ctrl+C to copy, and then select Edit, Paste Special, Values to convert the formulas to values.

Now, you can remove the Market and Product_Description fields (see Figure 13.18).

Figure 13.18
Be sure to remove all but one dimension field.

	A	B	C	D	E	F
1	Key	Jan	Feb	Mar	Apr	May
2	BUFFALO;Cleaning & Housekeeping Services	$6,219.66	$4,263.92	$5,386.12	$6,443.99	$4,36
3	BUFFALO;Facility Maintenance and Repair	$3,255.82	$9,490.00	$4,409.23	$4,957.62	$8,85
4	BUFFALO;Fleet Maintenance	$5,350.03	$8,924.71	$6,394.43	$6,522.46	$9,46
5	BUFFALO;Green Plants and Foliage Care	$2,415.08	$2,579.61	$2,401.91	$2,981.01	$2,70
6	BUFFALO;Landscaping/Grounds Care	$5,474.22	$4,500.52	$5,324.36	$5,705.68	$5,26
7	BUFFALO;Predictive Maintenance/Preventative Maintenance	$9,810.95	$10,180.23	$9,626.31	$11,700.73	$10,94
8	CALIFORNIA;Cleaning & Housekeeping Services	$2,840.76	$2,997.18	$2,096.78	$4,102.20	$47
9	CALIFORNIA;Facility Maintenance and Repair	$16,251.01	$25,872.99	$19,368.55	$21,843.53	$28,72

Step 2: Create a Multiple Consolidation Ranges PivotTable

The next step is to start the old PivotTable and PivotChart Wizard. Press Alt+D+P to call up the old wizard. You need the old wizard because it's the only place you find the Multiple Consolidation Ranges option. Here are the steps to walk through the wizard:

1. Click the option for Multiple Consolidation Ranges, and then click Next.
2. Select the I Will Create the Page Fields option, and then click Next.
3. Define the range you are working with, and then click Finish.

Step 3: Double-Click Grand Total Intersection of Row and Column

At this point, you should have a multiple consolidation pivot table that looks practically useless. Go to the intersection of the row and column Grand Totals and double-click the number (see Figure 13.19).

Figure 13.19
Double-click the intersection of Row and Column Grand Totals.

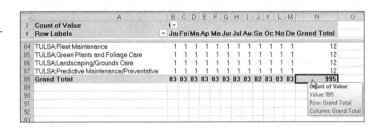

	A	B	C	D	E	F	G	H	I	J	K	L	M	N	O
3	Count of Value														
4	Row Labels	Jai	Fel	Ma	Ap	Ma	Jur	Jul	Au	Se	Oc	No	De	Grand Total	
84	TULSA;Fleet Maintenance	1	1	1	1	1	1	1	1	1	1	1		12	
85	TULSA;Green Plants and Foliage Care	1	1	1	1	1	1	1	1	1	1	1		12	
86	TULSA;Landscaping/Grounds Care	1	1	1	1	1	1	1	1	1	1	1		12	
87	TULSA;Predictive Maintenance/Preventative	1	1	1	1	1	1	1	1	1	1	1		12	
88	Grand Total	83	83	83	83	83	83	83	83	82	83	83	83	995	

Count of Value
Value: 995
Row: Grand Total
Column: Grand Total

You get a new sheet similar to the one shown in Figure 13.20. This is essentially a transposed version of your data.

Figure 13.20
Your data set has been transposed.

	A	B	C
1	Row	Column	Value
2	BUFFALO;Cleaning & Housekeeping Services	Jan	6219.66
3	BUFFALO;Cleaning & Housekeeping Services	Feb	4263.92
4	BUFFALO;Cleaning & Housekeeping Services	Mar	5386.12
5	BUFFALO;Cleaning & Housekeeping Services	Apr	6443.99
6	BUFFALO;Cleaning & Housekeeping Services	May	4360.14
7	BUFFALO;Cleaning & Housekeeping Services	Jun	5097.46
8	BUFFALO;Cleaning & Housekeeping Services	Jul	7566.19
9	BUFFALO;Cleaning & Housekeeping Services	Aug	4263.92
10	BUFFALO;Cleaning & Housekeeping Services	Sep	7245.64
11	BUFFALO;Cleaning & Housekeeping Services	Oct	3847.15
12	BUFFALO;Cleaning & Housekeeping Services	Nov	6540.21
13	BUFFALO;Cleaning & Housekeeping Services	Dec	5610.45
14	BUFFALO;Facility Maintenance and Repair	Jan	3255.82
15	BUFFALO;Facility Maintenance and Repair	Feb	9490
16	BUFFALO;Facility Maintenance and Repair	Mar	4409.23
17	BUFFALO;Facility Maintenance and Repair	Apr	4957.62

Step 4: Parse Your Dimension Column into Separate Fields

Now all there is left to do is parse out the Row column into separate fields again. The first step in that process is to ensure there are enough columns to parse into. Because the Row column has one semicolon, you need one extra empty column. So, as demonstrated in Figure 13.21, add a new empty column next to the Row column.

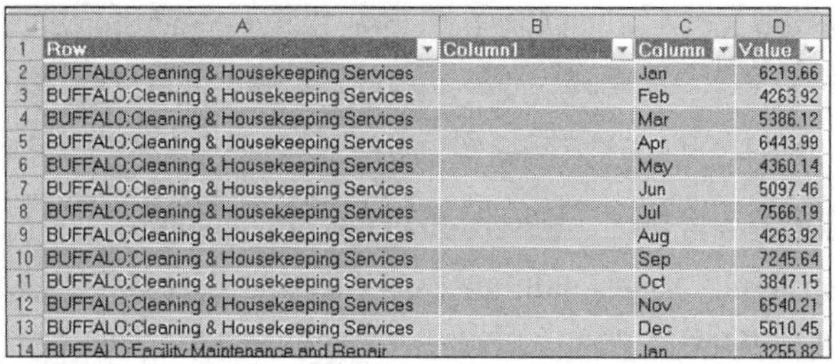

Figure 13.21
Add an empty column so there is room to parse the Row field.

Select the Row (column A) and call up the Text to Columns dialog box. Go to the Ribbon select Data, and then select Text to Columns. The idea here is to parse out the concatenated field using the semicolon delimiter.

In the Wizard, select the Delimited option, and then click Next.

On the next screen, select the Semicolon option, and then click Finish, as demonstrated in Figure 13.22.

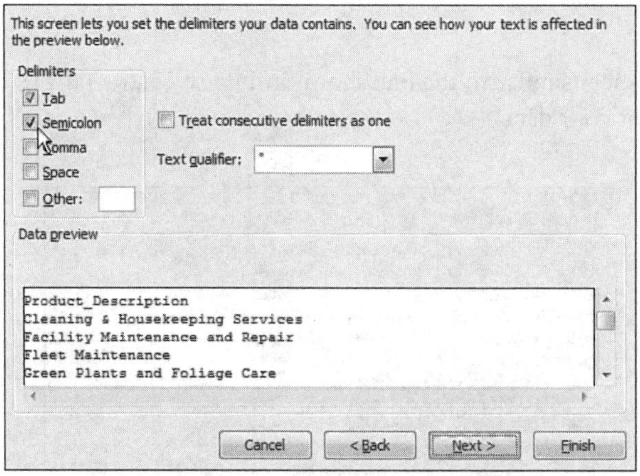

Figure 13.22
Select the Delimited option, and then click Finish.

After a few relabeling and formatting actions, your transposed data set should look similar to Figure 13.23.

Tip 12: Forcing Two Number Formats in a Pivot Table

Every now and then, you have to deal with a situation where a normalized data set makes it difficult to build an appropriate pivot table. For example, the data set shown in Figure 13.24 contains metrics information for each Market. Notice a column that identifies the Measure and a column that specifies the corresponding Value.

Figure 13.23
Your final transposed
data set.

	A	B	C	D
1	Market	Product Description	Month	Value
2	BUFFALO	Cleaning & Housekeeping Services	Jan	$6,220
3	BUFFALO	Cleaning & Housekeeping Services	Feb	$4,264
4	BUFFALO	Cleaning & Housekeeping Services	Mar	$5,386
5	BUFFALO	Cleaning & Housekeeping Services	Apr	$6,444
6	BUFFALO	Cleaning & Housekeeping Services	May	$4,360
7	BUFFALO	Cleaning & Housekeeping Services	Jun	$5,097
8	BUFFALO	Cleaning & Housekeeping Services	Jul	$7,566
9	BUFFALO	Cleaning & Housekeeping Services	Aug	$4,264
10	BUFFALO	Cleaning & Housekeeping Services	Sep	$7,246
11	BUFFALO	Cleaning & Housekeeping Services	Oct	$3,847
12	BUFFALO	Cleaning & Housekeeping Services	Nov	$6,540
13	BUFFALO	Cleaning & Housekeeping Services	Dec	$5,610
14	BUFFALO	Facility Maintenance and Repair	Jan	$3,256
15	BUFFALO	Facility Maintenance and Repair	Feb	$9,490
16	BUFFALO	Facility Maintenance and Repair	Mar	$4,499

Figure 13.24
This metric table has
many different data types
in one Value field.

	A	B	C	D	E
1	Region	Market	Category	Measure	Values
2	MIDWEST	KANSASCITY	Grow Revenue	Conversions	369727.5089
3	MIDWEST	KANSASCITY	Customer Service	Availability Percentage	0.682249714
4	MIDWEST	KANSASCITY	Profitability	Created Products	555.453714
5	MIDWEST	KANSASCITY	Grow Revenue	Transactions	589779.2402
6	MIDWEST	KANSASCITY	Grow Revenue	Triple Play %	0.529021053
7	MIDWEST	KANSASCITY	Grow Revenue	Videos	3674.041779
8	MIDWEST	KANSASCITY	Productivity	% Inactive	0.880656688
9	MIDWEST	KANSASCITY	Productivity	% Reconnected	0.043136054
10	MIDWEST	KANSASCITY	Grow Revenue	Freed Projects	47317.60578
11	MIDWEST	KANSASCITY	Customer Service	% Resolutoin	0.22085565
12	MIDWEST	KANSASCITY	Productivity	% Reuse	0.401537815
13	MIDWEST	KANSASCITY	Profitability	Tonnage Removed	8678.140595

Although this is generally a nicely formatted table, you notice that some of the measures are meant to be Number format while others are meant to be Percentage. In the database where this data set originated, the Values field is a Double data type, so this works.

The problem is that when you create a pivot table out of this data set, you can't assign two different number formats for the Values field. After all, one field is one number format.

As you see in Figure 13.25, trying to set the number format for the percentage measures also changes the format for the measure that are supposed to be straight numbers.

Figure 13.25
You can only have one
number format assigned
to each data measure.

	A	B
1	Region	(All)
2	Market	(All)
3		
4	Average of Values	
5	Measure	Total
6	% Inactive	57%
7	% Reconnected	53%
8	% Resolutoin	42%
9	% Reuse	44%
10	Availability Percentage	50%
11	Conversions	134874483%
12	Created Products	43418%
13	Freed Projects	5024551%
14	Tonnage Removed	989828%
15	Transactions	36746620%
16	Triple Play %	46%
17	Videos	550002%
18	Grand Total	14852433%
19		

13

The solution is to apply a custom number format that formats any value greater than 1.5 to a number. Any value less than 1.5 is formatted as a percent. In the Format Cells dialog box, click Custom, and then enter the following syntax in the Type input (see Figure 13.26):

```
[>=1.5]#,##0;[<1.5]0.0%
```

Figure 13.26
Apply a custom number format telling Excel to format any number less 1.5 to a percent.

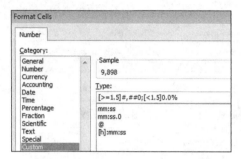

The result, as shown in Figure 13.27, is that each Measure is now formatted appropriately. Obviously, you have to get a little lucky with the parameters of the situation you're working in. Although this technique wouldn't work in all scenarios, it does open some interesting options.

Figure 13.27
Two formats in one Data field. Amazing!

	A	B
1	Region	(All)
2	Market	(All)
3		
4	Average of Values	
5	Measure	Total
6	% Inactive	57.3%
7	% Reconnected	52.5%
8	% Resolutoin	42.2%
9	% Reuse	44.0%
10	Availability Percentage	50.3%
11	Conversions	1,348,745
12	Created Products	434
13	Freed Projects	50,246
14	Tonnage Removed	9,898
15	Transactions	367,466
16	Triple Play %	45.7%
17	Videos	5,500
18	Grand Total	148,524
19		

Tip 13: Creating a Frequency Distribution with a Pivot Table

If you've created a frequency distribution with the Frequency function, you know it can quickly devolve into a confusing mess. The fact that it's an array formula doesn't help matters, and then there's that Histogram functionality you find in the Analysis Tool Pack. That doesn't make life much better. Each time you have to change your Bin ranges, you have to restart the entire process again.

In this tip, you learn how you can use a pivot table to quickly implement a simple frequency distribution.

First, you need to create a pivot table where the data values are plotted in the Row area (not the Values area). Notice in Figure 13.28 the Sales_Amount field is placed in the Row Labels area.

Figure 13.28
Place your data measure into the Row area.

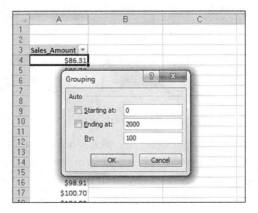

Next, right-click any value in the Row area and select Group. In the Grouping dialog box shown in Figure 13.29, set the start and end values, and then set the intervals. This essentially creates your frequency distribution.

Figure 13.29
Use the Grouping functionality to create your frequency intervals.

13

After you click OK, you can leverage the result to create a distribution view of your data.

In Figure 13.30, you can see that Customer_Name has been added to get a frequency distribution of the number of customer transactions by dollar amount.

Figure 13.30
You now have the distribution of customer transactions by dollar amount.

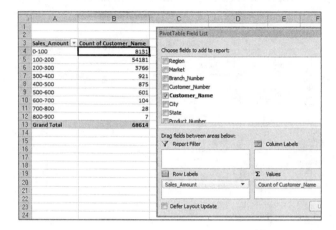

The benefit to this technique is you can use the pivot table's Report Filter to interactively filter the data based on other dimensions like Region and Market. Also, unlike the Analysis Tool Pack Histogram, you can quickly adjust your frequency intervals by simply right-clicking on any number in the Row area and selecting Group.

Tip 14: Use a Pivot Table to Explode a Data Set to Different Tabs

One of the most common requests an analyst gets is to create a separate pivot table report for each region, market, manager, and so on. These types of requests usually lead to a painful manual process in which you copy a pivot table onto a new worksheet, and then change the filter field to the appropriate region or manager. You then repeat this process as many times as you need to get through each selection.

Creating separate pivot table reports is one area where Excel really comes to the rescue. Excel has a function called Show Report Filter Pages that automatically creates a separate pivot table for each item in your filter fields.

To use this function, simply create a pivot table with a filter field, as shown in Figure 13.31.

Place your cursor anywhere on the pivot table, and then go up to the Ribbon to select the Options tab. On the Options tab, go to the PivotTable group and click the Options dropdown. Click the Show Report Filter Pages button, as demonstrated in Figure 13.32.

A dialog box opens, enabling you to choose the filter field for which you would like to create separate pivot tables. Select the appropriate filter field and click OK.

Figure 13.31
Start with a pivot table
that contains a filter field.

	A	B	C	D	E
1	Market	(All)			
2					
3	Sum of Sales_Amount	Sales_Period			
4	Product_Description	P01	P02	P03	P04
5	Cleaning & Housekeeping Services	$80,083	$89,750	$78,182	$8
6	Facility Maintenance and Repair	$121,304	$305,832	$115,232	$18
7	Fleet Maintenance	$148,565	$297,315	$145,821	$21
8	Green Plants and Foliage Care	$75,716	$135,529	$72,293	$9
9	Landscaping/Grounds Care	$92,353	$99,173	$87,138	$9
10	Predictive Maintenance/Preventative Maintenance	$163,844	$189,317	$158,946	$18
11	Grand Total	$681,865	$1,116,916	$657,611	$86
12					

Figure 13.32
Click the Show Report
Filter Pages button.

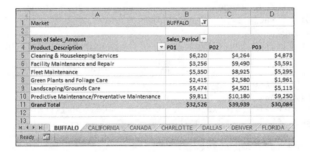

Your reward is a sheet for each item in your filter field containing its own pivot table.
Figure 13.33 illustrates the result. Note the newly created tabs are named to correspond
with the filter item shown in the pivot table.

Figure 13.33
With just a few clicks, you
can have a separate pivot
table for each market!

	A	B	C	D
1	Market	BUFFALO		
2				
3	Sum of Sales_Amount	Sales_Period		
4	Product_Description	P01	P02	P03
5	Cleaning & Housekeeping Services	$6,220	$4,264	$4,873
6	Facility Maintenance and Repair	$3,256	$9,490	$3,591
7	Fleet Maintenance	$5,350	$8,925	$5,295
8	Green Plants and Foliage Care	$2,415	$2,580	$1,961
9	Landscaping/Grounds Care	$5,474	$4,501	$5,113
10	Predictive Maintenance/Preventative Maintenance	$9,811	$10,180	$9,250
11	Grand Total	$32,526	$39,939	$30,084
12				
13				

BUFFALO / CALIFORNIA / CANADA / CHARLOTTE / DALLAS / DENVER / FLORIDA
Ready

NOTE Be aware that you can use Show Report Filter Pages on only one filter field at a time.

13

Tip 15: Use a Pivot Table to Explode a Data Set to Different Workbooks

Imagine you have a data set with more than 50,000 rows of data. You have been asked to
create a separate workbook for each market in this data set. In this tip, you discover how
you can accomplish this task by using a pivot table and a little Visual Basic for Applications
(VBA).

Place the field you need to use as the group dimension (in this case, Market) into the
ReportFilter field. Place the count of Market into the data field. Your pivot table should
look similar to the one shown in Figure 13.34.

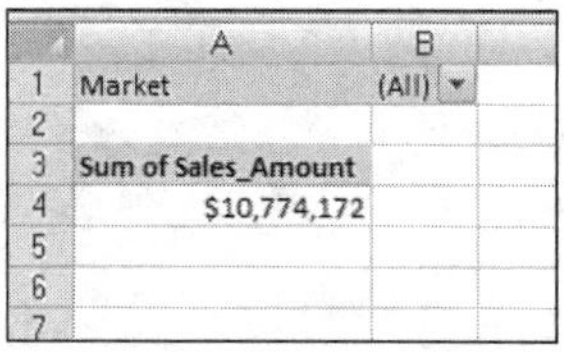

Figure 13.34
Create a simple pivot table with one data field and a Report Filter.

	A	B
1	Market	(All) ▼
2		
3	**Sum of Sales_Amount**	
4	$10,774,172	
5		
6		
7		

You can also manually select a Market in the Page/Filter field, and then double-click the Count of Market. This gives a new tab containing all the records that make up the number you double-clicked. You can imagine how you could do this for every market in the Market field and save the resulting tabs to their own workbook.

Using this same concept, you can implement the following VBA that goes through each item in your chosen page field and essentially calls the ShowDetails function for you, creating a raw data tab. The procedure then saves that raw data tab to a new workbook:

```
Sub ExplodeTable()
Dim PvtItem As PivotItem
Dim PvtTable As PivotTable
'Change variables to suit your scenario
    Const strFieldName = "Market"
'<-Change Field Name
    Const strTriggerRange = "B4"    '<-Change Trigger Range
'Set the pivot table name if needed
    Set PvtTable =
ActiveSheet.PivotTables("PivotTable1") '<-Change PivotTable Name
if Needed
'Start looping through each item in the selected field
    For Each PvtItem In
PvtTable.PivotFields(strFieldName).PivotItems
PvtTable.PivotFields(strFieldName).CurrentPage = PvtItem.Name
        Range(strTriggerRange).ShowDetail =
True
        'Name the temp sheet
for easy cleanup later
        ActiveSheet.Name =
"TempSheet"
        'copy data to new
workboook and delete the temp sheet
        ActiveSheet.Cells.Copy
        Workbooks.Add
        ActiveSheet.Paste
        Cells.EntireColumn.AutoFit
        Application.DisplayAlerts = False
        ActiveWorkbook.SaveAs Filename:=ThisWorkbook.Path & "\" & PvtItem.Name
& ".xls"
        ActiveWorkbook.Close
        Sheets("Tempsheet").Delete
        Application.DisplayAlerts = True
    Next PvtItem
End Sub
```

To implement this technique, enter this code into a new VBA Module.

Be sure to change these constants and variables if needed.

- **Const strFieldName:** The field name is the name of the field you want to separate the data. In other words, this is the field you put in the Page/Filter area of the pivot table.

- **Const strTriggerRange:** The trigger range is essentially the range that holds the one number in the pivot table's Data area. For example, if you look at Figure 13.34, you'll see the trigger cell in A4.

As you see in Figure 13.35, running this procedure outputs data for each Market into its own separate workbook.

Figure 13.35
After you run this VBA, you have a separate workbook for each filtered dimension.

Name	Date modified	Type	Size
TULSA.xls	2/1/2010 8:51 AM	Microsoft Office Ex...	406 KB
PHOENIX.xls	2/1/2010 8:51 AM	Microsoft Office Ex...	296 KB
SEATTLE.xls	2/1/2010 8:51 AM	Microsoft Office Ex...	101 KB
NEWORLEANS.xls	2/1/2010 8:51 AM	Microsoft Office Ex...	180 KB
NEWYORK.xls	2/1/2010 8:51 AM	Microsoft Office Ex...	439 KB
MICHIGAN.xls	2/1/2010 8:51 AM	Microsoft Office Ex...	334 KB
FLORIDA.xls	2/1/2010 8:51 AM	Microsoft Office Ex...	1,047 KB
KANSASCITY.xls	2/1/2010 8:51 AM	Microsoft Office Ex...	342 KB
DENVER.xls	2/1/2010 8:51 AM	Microsoft Office Ex...	386 KB
DALLAS.xls	2/1/2010 8:51 AM	Microsoft Office Ex...	309 KB
CANADA.xls	2/1/2010 8:51 AM	Microsoft Office Ex...	444 KB
CHARLOTTE.xls	2/1/2010 8:51 AM	Microsoft Office Ex...	493 KB
CALIFORNIA.xls	2/1/2010 8:51 AM	Microsoft Office Ex...	1,227 KB
BUFFALO.xls	2/1/2010 8:51 AM	Microsoft Office Ex...	243 KB

Next Steps

In Chapter 14, "Dr. Jekyll and Mr. GetPivotData," you learn about one of the most hated pivot table features—the GetPivotData function. However, you also learn how to use this function to create refreshable reports month after month.

13

Dr. Jekyll and
Mr. GetPivotData

This chapter shows you a technique that solves many annoying pivot table problems. If you have been using pivot tables for a while, you might have run into these problems:

- ■ Formatting tends to be destroyed when you refresh your pivot table. Numeric formats are lost. Column widths go away.
- ■ There is no way to build an asymmetric pivot table. Named Sets offer hope, but only for those using OLAP data or those who have the time to convert their Excel data to the PowerPivot window.
- ■ Excel cannot remember a template. If you frequently have to re-create a pivot table, you must redo the groupings, calculated fields, calculated items, and so on.

The techniques in this chapter solve all those problems. They are not new. In fact, they have been around since Excel 2002.

I have taught Power Excel seminars to thousands of accountants who use Excel 40–60 hours a week. Out of those thousands of people, I have only had three people say that they use this technique.

Ironically, far more than 0.3 percent of people know of this feature. One common question that I get at seminars is, "Why did this feature show up in Excel 2002, and how the heck can you turn it off?"

This same feature, which is reviled by most Excellers, is the key to creating reusable pivot table templates.

The credit for this chapter must go to Rob Collie, who spent years on the Excel project management team. He spent this last development cycle working on the PowerPivot product. Rob happened to relocate to Cleveland, Ohio. Because Cleveland is not a

14

hotbed of Microsoft developers, Dave Gainer gave me a heads-up that Rob was moving to my area, and we started having lunch.

Rob and I talked about Excel and had great conversations. During our second lunch, Rob said something that threw me for a loop. He said, "We find that our internal customers use GetPivotData all the time to build their reports, and we are not sure they will like the way PowerPivot interacts with GetPivotData."

I stopped Rob to ask if he was crazy. I told him that in my experience with about 5,000 accountants, only three of them had ever admitted to liking GetPivotData. What did he mean that he finds customers actually using GetPivotData?

Rob explained the key word in his statement. He was talking about *internal* customers, which are the people inside Microsoft who use Excel to do their jobs. Those people had become incredibly reliant on GetPivotData. He agreed that outside of Microsoft, hardly anyone ever uses GetPivotData. In fact, the only question he ever gets outside of Microsoft is how to turn off the stupid feature.

I had to know more, so I asked Rob to explain how the evil GetPivotData could ever be used for good purposes. Rob explained it to me, and I use this chapter to explain it to you.

However, I know that 99 percent of you are reading this chapter because:

- You ran into the evil GetPivotData.
- You turned to the index of this book to find information on GetPivotData.
- You are expecting me to tell you how to turn off GetPivotData.

So, let's start there.

Turning Off the Evil GetPivotData Problem

GetPivotData has been the cause of so many headaches. All of a sudden, around the time of Excel 2002, without any fanfare, pivot table behavior changed slightly. Any time you build formulas outside of a pivot table that point back inside the pivot table, you run into this evil problem.

Say you built a pivot table, as shown in Figure 14.1. Those years across the top are built by grouping daily dates up to years. You would like to compare this year versus last year. Unfortunately, you are not allowed to add calculated items to a grouped field.

Add a % Growth heading in Cell D4. Copy the formatting from C4 over to D4. In Cell D5, type an equal sign. Click Cell C5. Type a / (slash) for division. Click B5. Type **-1** and press Ctrl+Enter to stay in the same cell.

Format the result as a percentage. You see that the Midwest region grew by 35.3 percent. That is impressive growth. It is good to see that the economic woes of late 2009 and 2010 are now gone (see Figure 14.2).

Figure 14.1
You want to add a formula to show % Growth year after year.

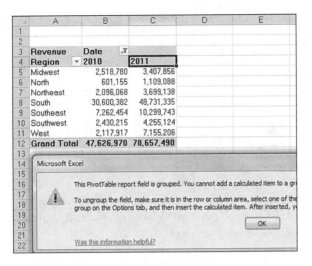

Figure 14.2
Build the formula in D5 using the mouse or the arrow keys.

NOTE

If you started using spreadsheets back in the days of Lotus 1-2-3, then you can use this alternative method to build the formula in D5: Type an = (equal sign) and press the left arrow once. Type the / (slash sign for division). Press the left arrow twice. Press Enter. As you see, the evil GetPivotData problem strikes no matter which method you use.

After entering your first formula, select Cell D5. Double-click the tiny square dot in the lower right corner of the cell. This is the Fill Handle, and it copies the formula down to the end of the report.

Immediately, you notice something is wrong because every region managed to grow by exactly 35.3 percent (see Figure 14.3).

There is no way that this happens in real life. The data must be fabricated. Look around. Are you working at Enron? If not, then there must be another solution.

Think about the formula you built: 2011 divided by 2010 minus 1. You probably could create that formula with your eyes closed. (Okay, people who used a mouse could not actually do it with their eyes closed, but the people who built the formula using arrow keys probably could without looking at the screen.)

14

Figure 14.3
When the formula is copied down, somehow the growth was 35.3 percent for every region.

Revenue	Date		
Region	2010	2011	% Growth
Midwest	2,518,780	3,407,856	35.3%
North	601,155	1,109,088	35.3%
Northeast	2,096,068	3,699,138	35.3%
South	30,600,382	48,731,335	35.3%
Southeast	7,262,454	10,299,743	35.3%
Southwest	2,430,215	4,255,124	35.3%
West	2,117,917	7,155,206	35.3%
Grand Total	47,626,970	78,657,490	35.3%

That is what allows you not to notice something completely evil when you built the formula. When you went through the steps to build the formula, any rational person would expect Excel to create a formula such as =C5/B5-1.

However, go back to Cell D5 and press the F2 to look at the formula (see Figure 14.4). Something evil has happened. The simple formula of =C5/B5-1 is no longer there. Instead, Excel generated some GetPivotData nonsense. Although the formula works in D5, it is not working when you copy the formula down.

Figure 14.4
What is GetPivotData?

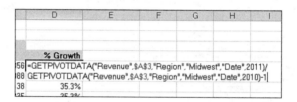

```
% Growth
=GETPIVOTDATA("Revenue",$A$3,"Region","Midwest","Date",2011)/
GETPIVOTDATA("Revenue",$A$3,"Region","Midwest","Date",2010)-1
35.3%
```

When this occurs, your reaction is something like, "What is GetPivotData, and why is it screwing up my report?" Your next reaction is, "How can I turn it off?" If it is not a pressure cooker of a day, you might even wonder, "Why would Microsoft put this evil thing in there?"

I am sure this never happened back in Excel 2000. After being stung by GetPivotData repeatedly, I hated GetPivotData. I was thrown for a loop in one of the Power Analyst Boot Camps when someone stopped to ask me how it could possibly be used. I had never considered that question. In my mind, and in most people's minds, GetPivotData was evil and no good.

Great news—there are two ways to turn it off, which are presented in the next sections.

Preventing GetPivotData by Typing the Formula

The simple method for avoiding GetPivotData is to create your formula without touching the mouse or the arrow keys. To do this, follow these steps:

1. Go to Cell D5; type = (equal sign).
2. Type **C5**.
3. Type the / (slash sign for division).
4. Type **B5**.
5. Type **-1**.
6. Press Enter.

You have now built a regular Excel formula that can be copied down to produce real results, as shown in Figure 14.5.

Figure 14.5
Type =C5/B5-1 and the formula works as expected.

	A	B	C	D
1				
2				
3	Revenue	Date		
4	Region	2010	2011	% Growth
5	Midwest	2,518,780	3,407,856	35.3%
6	North	601,155	1,109,088	84.5%
7	Northeast	2,096,068	3,699,138	76.5%
8	South	30,600,382	48,731,335	59.3%
9	Southeast	7,262,454	10,299,743	41.8%
10	Southwest	2,430,215	4,255,124	75.1%
11	West	2,117,917	7,155,206	237.8%
12	Grand Total	47,626,970	78,657,490	65.2%
13				
14				

D5 = =C5/B5-1

It is a relief to see you can still build formulas outside of pivot tables that point into a pivot tables. I have run into people who simply thought this could not be done.

You might be a bit annoyed that you have to abandon your normal way of entering formulas. If so, the next section offers an alternative.

GetPivotData Is Surely Evil—Turn It Off

If you do not plan to read the second half of this chapter, you can simply turn off GetPivotData forever. Who needs it? It is evil—just turn it off.

Back in Excel 2002 and Excel 2003, it was hard to turn off. You had to go to Tools, Customize, Commands. Select Data from the left listbox, then scroll 83 percent of the way through the right listbox to find an icon called Generate GetPivotData. Drag that icon onto the Excel 2003 toolbar. Close the dialog. Click the icon once to turn it off. Then, you could Alt+Drag the icon off the toolbar because you would never need to turn on this evil feature again.

In Excel 2010, follow these steps:

1. Move the cell pointer back inside a pivot table so that the PivotTable Tools tabs appear.
2. Click the Options tab.

14

3. Notice the Options icon on the left side of the Ribbon (see Figure 14.6). Do not click the icon. Next to the options icon there is a drop-down arrow. Click the drop-down arrow.

Figure 14.6
Don't click the large Options icon. Click the tiny dropdown arrow next to the icon.

Options icon

4. Inside the Options drop-down, there is a choice for Generate GetPivotData (see Figure 14.7). By default, this option is selected. Click that item to clear this check box.

Figure 14.7
Select Generate GetPivotData to turn the feature off.

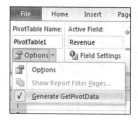

The previous steps assume that you have a pivot table in the workbook that you can select in order to access the PivotTable tabs. If you don't have a pivot table in the current workbook, you can use File, Options. In the Formulas category, uncheck Use GetPivotData functions for PivotTable References.

Why Did Microsoft Force GetPivotData on Us?

If GetPivotData is so evil, why did the fine people at Microsoft turn on that feature by default? Everyone simply turns it off. Why would they bother to leave it on? Are they trying to make sure that there is a market for my Power Excel seminars?

I have a theory about this that I came up with during the Excel 2007 launch. I had written many books about Excel 2007, somewhere around 1800 pages of content. When the Office 2007 launch events were happening around the country, I was given an opportunity to work at the event. I watched with interest when the presenter talked about the new features in Excel 2007.

There were at least 15 amazing features in Excel 2007. The presenter took three minutes and glossed over perhaps two and a half of the features.

I was perplexed. How could Microsoft marketing do such a horrible job of showing what was new in Excel?

Then, I realized that this must always happen. Marketing asks the development team what is new. The project manager gives them a list of 15 items. The marketing guy says something like, "There is not room for 15 items in the presentation. Can you cut 80 percent of those items out of the list and give me just the ones with glitz and sizzle?"

Whoever worked on GetPivotData certainly knew that GetPivotData would never have enough sizzle to make it into the marketing news about Excel 2002. So, by making it the default, they hoped someone would notice GetPivotData and try to figure out how it could be used. Instead, most people, including me, just turned it off and thought it was another step in the Microsoft plot to make our lives miserable by making it harder to work in Excel.

Using GetPivotData to Solve Pivot Table Annoyances

You would not be reading this book if you have not realized that pivot tables are the greatest invention ever. Six clicks can create a pivot table that obsoletes an arcane process of using Advanced Filter, =DSUM, and Data Tables. Pivot tables enable you to produce one-page summaries of massive data sets. So what if the formatting is ugly? And so what if you usually end up converting most pivot tables to values so you can delete the columns you do not need but cannot turn off?

Figure 14.8 illustrates a typical pivot table experience. In this case, you should start with raw data. Produce a pivot table and use all sorts of advanced pivot table tricks to get it close. Convert the pivot table to values and do the final formatting in regular Excel.

Figure 14.8
Typical pivot table process.

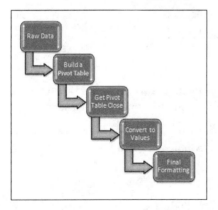

NOTE
I rarely get to refresh a pivot table because I never let pivot tables live long enough to have new data. The next time that I get data, I start creating the pivot table over again. If it is a long process, I write a macro that lets me fly through the five steps in Figure 14.8 in a couple of keystrokes.

The new method introduced by Rob Collie and described in the rest of this chapter puts a different spin on this. In this method, you build an ugly pivot table. You do not care about the formatting of this pivot table. You then go through a one-time, relatively painful process of building a nicely formatted shell to hold your final report. You then use GetPivotData to populate the shell report quickly.

From then on, when you get new data, you simply put it on the data sheet, refresh the ugly pivot table, and print the shell report.

Figure 14.9 illustrates this process.

Figure 14.9
How people inside of
Microsoft use pivot tables.

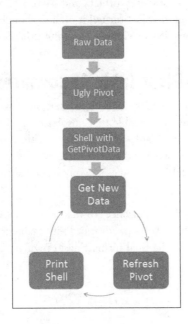

There are huge advantages to this method. For example, you do not have to worry about formatting the report after the first time. It comes much closer to an automated process.

The rest of this chapter walks you through the steps to build a dynamic report that shows actuals for months that have been completed and a forecast for future months.

Build an Ugly Pivot Table

You have transactional data showing budget and actuals for each region of a company. The budget data is at a monthly level. The actuals data is at a daily level. Budget data exists for the entire year. Actuals exist only for the months that have been completed. Figure 14.10 shows the original data set.

Because you will be updating this report every month, it makes the process easier if you have a pivot table data source that grows as you add new data to the bottom. While legacy

Figure 14.10
The original data includes budget and actuals.

	A	B	C	D
1	Region	Date	Measure	Revenue
2	Midwest	1/1/2011	Budget	248000
3	North	1/1/2011	Budget	90000
4	Northeast	1/1/2011	Budget	266000
5	South	1/1/2011	Budget	360000
6	Southeast	1/1/2011	Budget	675000
7	Southwest	1/1/2011	Budget	293000
8	West	1/1/2011	Budget	563000

versions of Excel would achieve this through a named dynamic range using the OFFSET function, you can do this in Excel 2010 by selecting one cell in your data and pressing Ctrl+T. Click OK to confirm that your data has headers.

You now have a formatted data set, as shown in Figure 14.11.

Figure 14.11
Format as a table to enable the pivot source data to expand in future months.

	A	B	C	D
1	Region	Date	Measure	Revenue
2	Midwest	1/1/2011	Budget	248000
3	North	1/1/2011	Budget	90000
4	Northeast	1/1/2011	Budget	266000
5	South	1/1/2011	Budget	360000
6	Southeast	1/1/2011	Budget	675000
7	Southwest	1/1/2011	Budget	293000
8	West	1/1/2011	Budget	563000
9	Midwest	2/1/2011	Budget	248000

Your next step is to create a pivot table that has every possible value needed in your final report. You learn that GetPivotData is powerful, but it can only return values that are visible in the actual pivot table. It cannot reach through to the pivot cache to calculate items that are not in the pivot table.

Create the pivot table by following these steps:

1. Select Insert, PivotTable, OK.
2. In the PivotTable Field List, select the Date field. Daily dates appear down the left side (see Figure 14.12).

Figure 14.12
Start with daily dates down the left.

	A
1	
2	
3	Row Labels
4	1/1/2011
5	2/1/2011
6	3/1/2011
7	4/1/2011
8	5/1/2011
9	6/1/2011
10	7/1/2011
11	8/1/2011
12	9/1/2011
13	10/1/2011
14	11/1/2011
15	12/1/2011
16	Grand Total
17	

3. Select the first date cell in A4. From the PivotTable Options tab, select Group Field. Select Months and Years, as shown in Figure 14.13. Click OK. You now have actual month names down the left side, as shown in Figure 14.14.

Figure 14.13
Group the daily dates up to months and years.

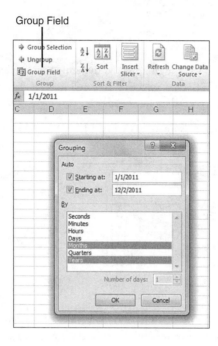

Figure 14.14
You have month names instead of dates.

4. Drag the Years and Date field to the Column Labels drop zone in the Pivot Table Field List.

5. Drag Measure to the Column Labels drop zone.

6. Select Region to have it appear along the left column of the pivot table.

7. Select Revenue to have it appear in the Values area of the pivot table.

As shown in Figure 14.15, you now have one ugly pivot table. You might hate the words "Row Labels" and "Column Labels." And having a total of January Actuals in Column B and January Budget in Column D is completely pointless. This is ugly. And for once, you do not care because no one other than you will ever see this pivot table.

Figure 14.15
The world's ugliest pivot table.

	A	B	C	D	E	F
3	Sum of Revenue	Column Labels				
4		=2011				
5		=Jan		Jan Total	=Feb	
6	Row Labels	Actuals	Budget		Actuals	Budget
7	Midwest	312387	248000	560387	266949	248000
8	North	100742	90000	190742	95197	90000
9	Northeast	277435	266000	543435	336005	266000
10	South	4182773	360000	4542773	4182773	360000
11	Southeast	926977	675000	1601977	789647	675000
12	Southwest	361686	293000	654686	329772	293000
13	West	578379	563000	1141379	596267	563000
14	Grand Total	6740379	2495000	9235379	6596610	2495000

At this point, the goal is to have a pivot table with every possible data point that you could ever need in your final report. It is fine if the pivot table has extra data that you will never need in your report.

Build the Shell Report

Insert a blank worksheet in your workbook. Put away your pivot table hat and take out your straight Excel hat. You are going to use basic Excel formulas and formatting to create a nicely formatted report suitable for giving to your manager.

Follow these steps:

1. Put a report title in Cell A1.

2. Use the Cell Styles drop-down on the Home tab to format cell A1 as a Title.

3. Put a date in Cell A2 by using the formula **=EOMONTH(TODAY(),0)**. This enters the serial number of the last day of the previous month in Cell B1. If you want to see how the formula is working, you can format the cell as a Date. If you are reading this on July 14, 2011, the date that appears in Cell B1 is June 30, 2011.

4. Select Cell A2. Press Ctrl+1 to go to Format Cells. On the Number tab, click Custom. Type a custom number format of **Actuals Through mmmm/yyyy**. This causes the calculated date to appear as text.

5. There is a chance that the text in Cell A2 is going to be wider than you want Column A to be. Select both Cells A2 and B2. Press Ctrl+1 to format cells. On the Alignment tab, select Merge Cells. This allows the formula in Cell A2 to spill over into B2 if necessary.

6. Type a Region heading in Cell A5.

7. Down the rest of Column A, type your region names. These names should match the names in the pivot table.

> **NOTE** If the names in the pivot table are region codes, you can hide the codes in a new hidden Column A and put friendly region names in Column B.

8. Where appropriate, add labels in Column A for Division totals.

9. Add a line for Total Company at the bottom of the report.

10. Month names stretch from Cells B4:M4. Enter this formula in Cell B4: **=DATE(YEAR($A$2),COLUMN(A1),1)**.

11. Select Cell B4. Press Ctrl+1 to Format Cells. On the Number tab, select Custom and type a custom number format of **MMM**.

12. Right-justify Cell B4. Use the Cell Styles drop-down to select Heading 4.

13. Copy Cell B4 to Cells C4:M4. You now have true dates across the top that appear as month labels.

14. Enter this formula in Cell B5: **=IF(MONTH(B4)<=MONTH($A$2),"Actuals","Budget")**. Right-justify Cell B5. Copy across to Cells C5:M5. This should provide the word Actuals for past months, but the word Budget for future months.

15. Add a Total column heading in Cell N5. Add a Total Budget column in Cell O5. Enter Var % in Cell P5.

16. Fill in the regular Excel formulas necessary to provide division totals, the total company row, the grand total column, and the variance % column. For example:

   - =SUM(B6:B7) in Cell B8 and copy across
   - =SUM(B6:M6) in Cell N6 and copy down
   - =IFERROR((N6/O6)-1,0) in Cell P6 and copy down
   - =SUM(B10:B12) in Cell B13 and copy across
   - =SUM(B15:B16) in Cell B17 and copy across
   - =SUM(B6:B18)/2 in Cell B19 and copy across

17. Apply Heading 4 cell style to the labels in Column A and the headings in Rows 4:5.

18. Apply #,##0 number format to Cells B6:O19.

19. Apply 0.0% number format to Column P.

You now have a completed shell report, as shown in Figure 14.16 and Figure 14.17. This report has all the necessary formatting as desired by your manager. It has totals that add up the numbers that eventually come from the pivot table.

In the next section, you use GetPivotData to complete the report.

Figure 14.16
The left side of the shell report.

Figure 14.17
The right side of the shell report. Any place with a zero is a regular Excel formula.

Using GetPivotData to Populate the Shell Report

At this point, you are ready to take advantage of the thing that has been driving you crazy for years—that crazy Generate GetPivotData setting.

If you have ever cleared the setting back in Figure 14.7, go in and select this again. When it is selected, you see a checkmark next to Generate GetPivotData.

Go to Cell B6 on the shell report. This is the cell for Northeast region, January, Actuals.

1. Type = (equal sign) to start a formula (see Figure 14.18).
2. Move to the pivot table worksheet and click the cell for Northeast, January, Actuals. In Figure 14.19, this is Cell B9.
3. Press Enter to return to the shell report and complete the formula. Excel adds a GetPivotData function in Cell B6.

The formula says that the Northeast region actuals are $277,435.

14

Figure 14.18
Start a formula on the shell report.

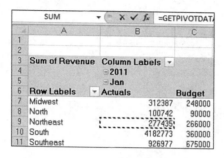

Figure 14.19
Using the mouse, click the correct cell in the pivot table.

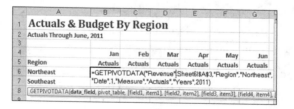

> **TIP**
> Jot down this number because you will want to compare it to the result of the formula that you later edit.

The initial formula is =GETPIVOTDATA("Revenue",Sheet6!$A$3,"Region","Northeast"," Date",1,"Measure","Actuals","Years",2011).

After years of ignoring the GetPivotData formula, you need to look at this monster formula closely to understand what it is doing. Figure 14.20 shows the formula in edit mode, along with the formula tool tip.

Figure 14.20
The GetPivotData formula generated by Microsoft.

	A	B	C	D	E	F	G
1	**Actuals & Budget By Region**						
2	Actuals Through June, 2011						
3							
4		Jan	Feb	Mar	Apr	May	Jun
5	Region	Actuals	Actuals	Actuals	Actuals	Actuals	Actuals
6	Northeast	=GETPIVOTDATA("Revenue","Sheet6!$A$3,"Region","Northeast",					
7	Southeast	"Date",1,"Measure","Actuals","Years",2011)					
8		GETPIVOTDATA(data_field, pivot_table, [field1, item1], [field2, item2], [field3, item3], [field4, item4],					

Here are the arguments in the formula:

- **Data Field**—This is the field in the Value area of the pivot table. Note that you use Revenue, not Sum of Revenue.

- **Pivot Table**—This is Microsoft's way of asking, "Which pivot table do you mean?" All you have to do here is point to one single cell within the pivot table. The entry of Sheet6!$A$3 is the first populated cell in the pivot table. You are free to choose any cell in the pivot table that you want. However, because it does not matter which cell you choose, don't worry about getting clever here. Leave the formula pointing to $A$3, and you will be fine.

- **Field 1, Item 1**—The formula generated by Microsoft shows Region as the field name and Northeast as the item value. Aha! So this is why the GetPivotData formulas that Microsoft generates cannot be copied. They are essentially hard-coded to point to one specific value. You want your formula to change as you copy it through your report. Edit the formula to change Northeast to $A6. By using only a single dollar sign before the A, you are enabling the row portion of the reference to vary as you copy the formula down.

- **Field 2, Item 2**—The next two pairs of arguments specify the Date field should be a 1. When the original pivot table was grouped by month and year, the month field retains the original field name of Date. The value for month is 1, which means January. You probably thought I was insane to build that outrageous formula and custom number format in Cell B4. That formula becomes useful now. Instead of hard coding a 1, use MONTH(B$4). Again, the single dollar sign before Row 4 indicates that the formula can get data from other months as it is copied across, but it should always reach back up to Row 4 as it is copied down.

- **Field 3, Item 3**—The field name is Measure and the item is Actuals. This happens to be correct for January, but when you get to future months, you want the measure to switch to Budget. Change the hard-coded Actuals to point to B$5.

- **Field 4, Item 4**—This is Years and 2011. I was almost ready to leave this one alone because it would be months before we have a new year. However, why not change the 2011 to YEAR($A$2)?

The new formula is shown in Figure 14.21. Rather than a formula that is hard-coded to work with only one value, you have created a formula that can be copied throughout the data set.

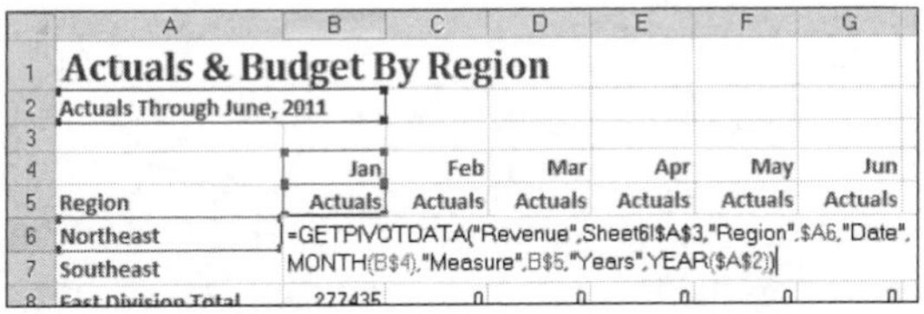

Figure 14.21
After editing, the GetPivotData formula is suitable for copying.

When you press Enter, you have the exact same answer that you had before editing the formula (see Figure 14.22). Compare this with the number you jotted down earlier to make sure.

The edited formula is =GETPIVOTDATA("Revenue",Sheet6!$A$3,"Region",$A6,"Date", MONTH(B$4),"Measure",B$5,"Years",YEAR($A$2)).

Figure 14.22
The result of the edited formula should match the result before editing.

	A	B	C
1	**Actuals & Budget By Regio**		
2	Actuals Through June, 2011		
3			
4		Jan	Feb
5	Region	Actuals	Actuals
6	Northeast	277,435	
7	Southeast		
8	East Division Total	277,435	0
9			

Copy this formula to all the blank calculation cells in Columns B:M. Do not copy the formula to Column O yet.

Now that you have real numbers in the report, you might have to adjust some column widths.

The GetPivotData formula for the months can be tweaked to get the total budget. If you copy one formula to Cell O6, you get a #REF! error because the word Total in Cell O4 does not evaluate to a month.

Edit the formula to the pairs of arguments for Month and Years. You still have an error.

For GetPivotData to work, the number you are looking for must be in the pivot table. Because the original pivot table had Measure as the third column field, there is no actual column for Budget total.

Move the Measure field to be the first Column field, as shown in Figure 14.23.

Figure 14.23
Tweak the layout of the Column Labels fields so you have a Budget Total column.

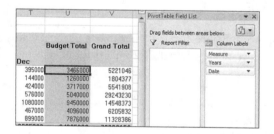

When you return to the shell report, you find that the Total Budget formula in Cell O6 is now working fine (see Figure 14.24). Copy that formula down to the other blank data cells in Column O (see Figure 14.25).

The formula in O6 is =GETPIVOTDATA("Revenue",Sheet6!$A$3,"Region",$A6, "Measure",O$5).

You now have a nicely formatted shell report that grabs values from a live pivot table. It certainly took more time to set up this report for the first month that you have to produce it, but it will be a breeze to update the report in future months.

Figure 14.24
After rearranging the pivot table, you have a working formula for Total Budget.

Nov Budget	Dec Budget	Total	Total Budget	Var. %
319,000	424,000	3,771,908	3,717,000	1.5%
810,000	1,080,000	10,048,373		0.0%
1,129,000	1,504,000	13,820,281	3,717,000	271.8%

Figure 14.25
Copy the formula down to other cells in the Budget column to finish the report.

Dec Budget	Total	Total Budget	Var. %
424,000	3,832,665	3,717,000	3.1%
1,080,000	10,266,017	9,450,000	8.6%
1,504,000	14,098,682	13,167,000	7.1%
395,000	3,604,194	3,466,000	4.0%
144,000	1,203,104	1,260,000	-4.5%
576,000	30,503,565	5,040,000	505.2%
1,115,000	35,310,863	9,766,000	261.6%
899,000	7,552,026	7,876,000	-4.1%
467,000	4,331,609	4,096,000	5.8%
1,366,000	11,883,635	11,972,000	-0.7%
3,985,000	61,293,180	34,905,000	75.6%

 To see the shell report in action, search for Pivot Table Data Crunching 14 at YouTube.

Updating the Report in Future Months

In future months, you can update your report by following these steps:

1. Paste actuals for the new month just below the original data set. Because the original data set is a Table, the table formatting automatically extends to the new rows. The pivot table source definition also extends (see Figure 14.26).

Figure 14.26
Copy new data below the old data.

127	West	6/1/2011	Actuals	566454
128	Midwest	7/1/2011	Actuals	281148
129	North	7/1/2011	Actuals	88727
130	Northeast	7/1/2011	Actuals	326757
131	South	7/1/2011	Actuals	4020335

Sheet2 / Data / Outline / Diagram / Sheet7

2. Go to the pivot table. Click the Refresh button on the Options tab (see Figure 14.27). The shape of the pivot table changes, but you do not care.

3. Go to the shell report. In real life, you are done, but to test it, enter a date in Cell B2 such as 8/30/2011.

14

> **NOTE**
> Every month, these three steps are the payoff to this chapter. As shown in Figure 14.28, the data for July changed from Budget to Actuals. Formulas throughout recalculated. You do not have to worry about re-creating formats, formulas, and so on.

Figure 14.27
Refresh the pivot table.

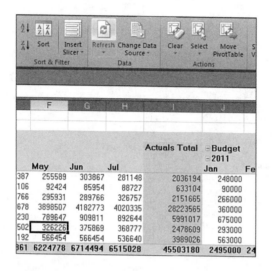

Figure 14.28
Even if the pivot table changed shape, the shell report grabs data from the correct place.

This process is so simple, that you will probably forget about the pain that you used to endure to create these monthly reports. The one risk is that a company reorg will add new regions to the pivot table. To be sure that your formulas are still working, add a small check section outside of the print range of the report. This formula in Cell A22 checks to see if the budget total calculated in Cell O19 matches the budget total back in the pivot table. Here is the formula:

=IF(GETPIVOTDATA("Revenue",Sheet6!$A$3,"Measure","Budget")=$O$19,"","Ca ution!!! It appears that new regions have been added to the pivot table. You might have to add new rows to this report for those regions."

In case the new region comes from a misspelling in the actuals, this formula checks the YTD actuals against the pivot table. Enter the following formula in Cell A23:

=IF(SUMIF(B5:M5,"Actuals",B19:M19)=GETPIVOTDATA("Revenue",Sheet6!$A$3, "Measure","Actuals"),"","Caution!!! It appears that new regions have been added to the pivot table. You might have to add new rows to this report for those regions.")

Figure 14.29

Formulas in a check section monitor the calculated totals and the pivot totals to see if a new region appeared.

	A22	▾	f_x =IF(GETPIVOTDATA("Revenue",Sheet6!$A$3,"Measure","Budget")=$O$19,"","Caution!!! It appea									
	A	B	C	D	E	F	G	H	I	J	K	
1	**Actuals & Budget By Region**											
2	Actuals Through July, 2011											
3												
4		Jan	Feb	Mar	Apr	May	Jun	Jul	Aug	Sep	Oct	
5	Region	Actuals	Actuals	Actuals	Actuals	Actuals	Actuals	Actuals	Budget	Budget	Budget	Bu
6	Northeast	277,435	336,005	336,005	289,766	295,931	289,766	326,757	266,000	353,000	319,000	31
7	Southeast	926,977	789,647	884,061	798,230	789,647	909,811	892,644	675,000	900,000	810,000	81
8	East Division Total	1,204,412	1,125,652	1,220,066	1,087,996	1,085,578	1,199,577	1,219,401	941,000	1,253,000	1,129,000	1,12
9												
10	Midwest	312,387	266,949	303,867	312,387	255,589	303,867	281,148	248,000	329,000	298,000	29
11	North	100,742	95,197	85,954	84,106	92,424	85,954	88,727	90,000	120,000	108,000	10
12	South	4,182,773	4,182,773	3,979,726	3,776,678	3,898,507	4,182,773	4,020,335	360,000	480,000	432,000	43
13	Central Division Total	4,595,902	4,544,919	4,369,547	4,173,171	4,246,520	4,572,594	4,390,210	698,000	929,000	838,000	83
14												
15	West	578,379	596,267	536,640	608,192	566,454	566,454	0	563,000	749,000	676,000	67
16	Southwest	361,686	329,772	368,777	347,502	326,226	375,869	368,777	293,000	389,000	352,000	35
17	West Division Total	940,065	926,039	905,417	955,694	892,680	942,323	368,777	856,000	1,138,000	1,028,000	1,02
18												
19	Total Company	6,740,379	6,596,610	6,495,030	6,216,861	6,224,778	6,714,494	5,978,388	2,495,000	3,320,000	2,995,000	2,99
20												
21												
22												
23	Caution!!! It appears that new regions have been added to the pivot table. You might have to add new rows to this report for those regions.											

Change the font color of both of those cells to be red. You do not even notice them down there until something goes wrong, as shown in Figure 14.29.

I thought that I would never write these words: GetPivotData is the greatest thing ever. How could we ever live without it?

Next Steps

The appendix is for those of you who have upgraded directly from Excel 2003 (or earlier) to Excel 2010. By the way, kudos for skipping Excel 2007! The appendix assists you in finding old pivot table commands on the Excel 2010 ribbon.

14

Finding Pivot Table Commands on the Ribbon

If you were accustomed to the PivotTable toolbar in Excel 97 through Excel 2003, you might be frustrated initially by the new Ribbon interface.

This appendix provides a map. If you know where a command was located in a legacy version Excel interface, the tables in this chapter help you find the command in the new interface.

Inserting a Pivot Table

In legacy versions of Excel, the entry point for creating a pivot table was always on the Data menu. After you selected PivotTable and PivotChart Report, you chose either a pivot table or pivot chart in the first step of the wizard.

Excel 2010 includes three entry points for creating a pivot table:

- There is an icon and a drop-down at the start of the Insert tab. Click the top half of the icon to create a pivot table. Use the drop-down at the bottom of the icon to create either a pivot table or pivot chart (see Figure A.1).

Figure A.1
Use the Insert tab to create a pivot table or pivot chart.

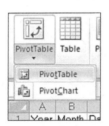

- If you converted your data set to a table using Ctrl+T, you can create a pivot table using the Table Tools Design tab. Select Summarize with Pivot from the Tools group.

- If you miss the old PivotTable and PivotChart Wizard, press Alt+D+P to bring back the old wizard, as shown in Figure A.2. This is the only way to build one of the obscure pivot tables, such as the Multiple Consolidation Range pivot table.

Figure A.2
The PivotTable Wizard still exists.

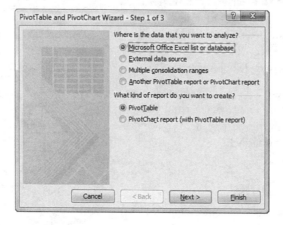

Finding Commands from the Legacy PivotTable Toolbar

Legacy versions of Excel offered a PivotTable toolbar, as shown in Figure A.3. Most of the commands were in the PivotTable drop-down on the left of the toolbar.

Figure A.3
The legacy PivotTable toolbar, showing the PivotTable drop-down.

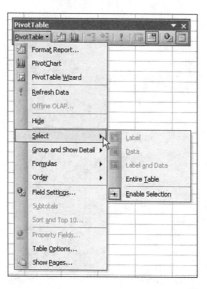

Table A.1 shows every command on the PivotTable toolbar and the location of the equivalent command in Excel 2010.

Table A.1   Commands on the PivotTable Toolbar

Excel 2003 Command	Excel 2010 Command
PivotTable, Format Report	Pivot Table Tools Design, PivotTable Styles
PivotTable, PivotChart	PivotTable Tools Options, Tools, PivotChart
PivotTable, PivotTable Wizard	Alt+D+P
PivotTable, Refresh Data	PivotTable Tools Options, Data, Refresh, Refresh
PivotTable, Refresh Data	Table Tools Design, External Table Data, Refresh
PivotTable, Refresh Data	PivotChart Tools Analyze, Data, Refresh
PivotTable, Refresh Data	Data, Refresh All
PivotTable, Offline OLAP	PivotTable Tools Options, Tools, OLAP, Tools, Offline OLAP
PivotTable, Delete	Row/Column shortcut menu, Delete
PivotTable, Select	PivotTable Tools Options, Actions, Select
PivotTable, Select, Label	PivotTable Tools Options, Actions, Select, Label
PivotTable, Select, Data	PivotTable Tools Options, Actions, Select, Data
PivotTable, Select, Label and Data	PivotTable Tools Options, Actions, Select, Label and Data
PivotTable, Select, Entire Table	PivotTable Tools Options, Actions, Select, Entire Table
PivotTable, Select, Enable Selection	PivotTable Tools Options, Actions, Select, Enable Selection
PivotTable, Group and Show Detail, Hide Detail	PivotTable Tools Options, Active Field, Collapse Entire Field
PivotTable, Group and Show Detail, Show Detail	PivotTable Tools Options, Active Field, Expand Entire Field
PivotTable, Group and Show Detail, Group	PivotTable Tools Options, Group, Group Field
PivotTable, Group and Show Detail, Ungroup	PivotTable Tools Options, Group, Ungroup Field Ungroup
PivotTable, Formulas, Calculated Field	PivotTable Tools Options, Calculation, Fields, Items & Sets, Calculated Field
PivotTable, Formulas, Calculated Item	PivotTable Tools Options, Calculation, Fields, Items & Sets, Calculated Item
PivotTable, Formulas, Solve Order	PivotTable Tools Options, Calculation, Fields, Items & Sets, Solve Order
PivotTable, Formulas, List Formulas	PivotTable Tools Options, Calculation, Fields, Items & Sets, List Formulas
PivotTable, Order, Move to Beginning	Right-click shortcut menu, Move
PivotTable, Order, Move Up	Right-click shortcut menu, Move

A

A

Excel 2003 Command	Excel 2010 Command
PivotTable, Order, Move Down	Right-click shortcut menu, Move
PivotTable, Order, Move to End	Right-click shortcut menu, Move
PivotTable, Order, Move to Column	Right-click shortcut menu, Move
PivotTable, Field Settings	PivotTable Tools Options, Active Field, Field Settings
PivotTable, Subtotals	PivotTable Tools Design, Layout, Subtotals
PivotTable, Sort and Top 10	PivotTable Tools Options, Sort & Filter
PivotTable, Property Fields	PivotTable Tools Options, Tools, OLAP Tools, Property Fields
PivotTable, Table Options	PivotTable Tools Options, PivotTable, Options, Options
PivotTable, Show Pages	PivotTable Tools Options, PivotTable Options dropdown, Show Report Filter Pages
Format Report	PivotTable Tools Design, PivotTable Styles gallery
Chart Wizard	PivotTable Tools Options, Tools, PivotChart
Hidden Items in Totals	PivotTable Tools, Options, Options, Totals & Filters, Include Filtered Items in Set Totals
Always Display Items	PivotTable Tools Options, Active Field, Field Settings, Layout & Print, Show Items With No Data
Field Settings	PivotTable Tools Options, Active Field, Field Settings
Show Field List	PivotTable Tools Options, Show/Hide, Field List

Excel 2003 offered a single tab in the PivotTable Options dialog, as shown in Figure A.4. Excel 2010's Options dialog offers six tabs, as shown in Figure A.5

Table A.2 shows the settings in the Excel 2003 dialog and where they can be found in Excel 2010.

Table A.2   Commands on the PivotTable Options Dialog

2003 Setting	Location in 2010
Pivot Table Name	Options tab, Pivot Table Group
Grand Total for Columns	Options dialog, Totals & Filters tab
Grand Total for Rows	Options dialog, Totals & Filters tab
AutoFormat Table	Deprecated
Subtotal Hidden Page Items	Options dialog, Totals & Filters tab

Figure A.4
Options dialog in Excel 2003.

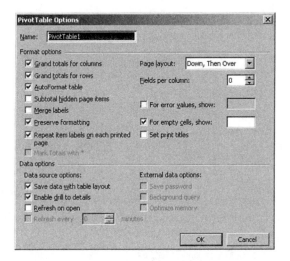

Figure A.5
Options dialog in Excel 2010.

2003 Setting	Location in 2010
Merge Labels	Options dialog, Layout & Format
Preserve Formatting	Options dialog, Layout & Format
Repeat Item Labels on Each Printed Page	Options dialog, Printing tab
Mark Totals with *	Deprecated
Page Layout...Down, then Over	Options dialog, Layout & Format
Fields Per Column	Options dialog, Layout & Format
For Error values, show:	Options dialog, Layout & Format
For empty cells, show:	Options dialog, Layout & Format
Set Print Titles	Options dialog, Printing tab
Save Data with Table Layout	Options dialog, Data tab

A

2003 Setting	Location in 2010
Enable Drill to Details	Options dialog, Data tab
Refresh On Open	Options dialog, Data tab
Refresh Every *n* Minutes	Data tab
Save Password	Options tab, OLAP Tools
Background Query	Options tab, OLAP Tools
Optimize Memory	Options tab, OLAP Tools

When a pivot chart was displayed in legacy versions of Excel, a PivotChart drop-down replaced the PivotTable drop-down in the PivotTable toolbar, as shown in Figure A.6.

Figure A.6
The legacy PivotTable toolbar, showing the PivotChart drop-down.

Table A.3 shows the commands on the PivotChart drop-down and their equivalent commands in Excel 2010.

Table A.3   Commands on the PivotChart Drop-Down

Excel 2003 Command	Excel 2010 Command
PivotChart, Field Settings	PivotTable Tools Options, Active Field, Field Settings
PivotChart, Options	PivotTable Tools Options, PivotTable, Options, Options
PivotChart, Refresh Data	PivotTable Tools Options, Data, Refresh
PivotChart, Refresh Data	PivotTable Tools Options, Data, Refresh, Refresh
PivotChart, Hide PivotChart Field Buttons	PivotChart Tools, Analyze, Show/Hide, Field Buttons
PivotChart, Formulas, Calculated Field	PivotTable Tools Options, Calculations, Fields, Items & Sets, Calculated Field

Excel 2003 Command	Excel 2010 Command
PivotChart, Formulas, Calculated Item	PivotTable Tools Options, Calculations, Fields, Items & Sets, Calculated Item
PivotChart, Formulas, Solve Order	PivotTable Tools Options, Calculations, Fields, Items & Sets, Solve Order
PivotChart, Formulas, List Formulas	PivotTable Tools Options, Calculations, Fields, Items & Sets, List Formulas
PivotChart, Remove Field	PivotTable Field List, Uncheck Item

A

INDEX

Symbols

% of option, 74

% Running Total In option, 70-71

A

activating
PivotChart wizard, 155
PivotTable wizard, 155

ActiveX controls versus form controls, 237

adding
calculated fields
with formulas, 108-109
manual method, 108
fields to pivot table, 29-32
grand total row, 60
layers to pivot table, 32
macro functionality with VBA, 238-242

add-ins, PowerPivot
combination layouts, 228-229
free cost of, 198-199
installing, 200
limitations of, 200
report formatting, 228-231
slicers, 211-212
usage guidelines, 212-213

alternatives to pivot charts, 138-142

analyzing
data sources, 25
multiple consolidation ranges

Column field, 160
Pages field, 161
Row field, 160
Value field, 160

analyzing activity by market, case study, 38-39

applying
Autofilter, 322-323
conditional formatting, 147
data visualizations with VBA, 309-310
multiple number formats, 326-328
numeric format, 48-49
table styles, 47
table styles with VBA, 307-308
themes, 62

areas section
drop-down arrows, 88-89
Report Filter area, 101-105

asymmetric reporting, 228

Autofilter, applying, 322-323

automatically refreshing pivot tables, 310-312

AutoShow method (VBA), 290-292

Autosort, 93

Average function, 64

B

benefits of PowerPivot, 1 95-198

blank cells
filling in, 25
filling in data area with VBA, 261
incorrect count calculations, troubleshooting, 63-64
replacing with zeros, 49-50

browsers, viewing pivot tables with, 181-183

building
pivot tables with external data sources, 161-168
Microsoft Access data, 162-165
SQL Server data, 165-168
PowerPivot reports, 201-212
calculated columns, adding with DAX, 208-209
copying and pasting data, 205-206
defining relationships, 207-208
linking data, 206
text file, importing, 201-204

buttons, pivot field buttons, 132

C

calculated columns, DAX, 214-218

calculated fields, 107-108
adding, manual method, 108
creating, 109-112

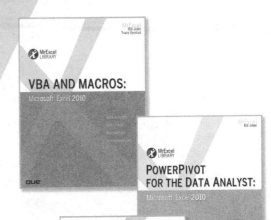

FREE Online Edition

Your purchase of **Pivot Table Data Crunching: Microsoft Excel 2010** includes access to a free online edition for 45 days through the Safari Books Online subscription service. Nearly every Que book is available online through Safari Books Online, along with more than 5,000 other technical books and videos from publishers such as Addison-Wesley Professional, Cisco Press, Exam Cram, IBM Press, O'Reilly, Prentice Hall, and Sams.

SAFARI BOOKS ONLINE allows you to search for a specific answer, cut and paste code, download chapters, and stay current with emerging technologies.

Activate your FREE Online Edition at
www.informit.com/safarifree

> **STEP 1:** Enter the coupon code: DQGFGDB.

> **STEP 2:** New Safari users, complete the brief registration form.
> Safari subscribers, just log in.

Addison Wesley · Adobe Press · ALPHA · Cisco Press · FT Press · IBM Press · lynda.com · Microsoft Press · New Riders · O'REILLY · Peachpit Press · PRENTICE HALL · Que · Redbooks · SAMS · SAS Publishing · Sun Microsystems · WILEY